An Introduction to Econometric Theory

An Introduction to Econometric Theory

James Davidson
University of Exeter
UK

WILEY

This edition first published 2018

Registered Offices
John Wiley & Sons, Inc., 111 River Street, Hoboken, NJ 07030, USA
John Wiley & Sons Ltd, The Atrium, Southern Gate, Chichester, West Sussex, PO19 8SQ, UK

Editorial Office
9600 Garsington Road, Oxford, OX4 2DQ, UK

For details of our global editorial offices, customer services, and more information about Wiley products visit us at www.wiley.com.

Wiley also publishes its books in a variety of electronic formats and by print-on-demand. Some content that appears in standard print versions of this book may not be available in other formats.

Library of Congress Cataloging-in-Publication Data

Names: Davidson, James, 1944- author.
Title: An introduction to econometric theory / by Prof. James Davidson, University of Exeter.
Description: Hoboken, NJ : John Wiley & Sons, Inc., [2018] | Includes bibliographical references and index. |
Identifiers: LCCN 2018009800 (print) | LCCN 2018011202 (ebook) | ISBN 9781119484936 (pdf) |
ISBN 9781119484929 (epub) | ISBN 9781119484882 (cloth)
Subjects: LCSH: Econometrics.
Classification: LCC HB139 (ebook) | LCC HB139 .D3664 2018 (print) | DDC 330.01/5195–dc23
LC record available at https://lccn.loc.gov/2018009800

Cover Design: Wiley
Cover Image: © maciek905/iStockphoto

Set in 10/12pt WarnockPro by SPi Global, Chennai, India

10 9 8 7 6 5 4 3 2 1

Contents

List of Figures

Preface

This book has its origin in a course of lectures offered to second year economics undergraduates who are simultaneously taking a core module in applied econometrics. Courses of the latter type, typically based on excellent texts such as Wooldridge's *Introductory Econometrics* or Stock and Watson's *Introduction to Econometrics*, teach modern techniques of model building and inference, but necessarily a good deal of technical material has to be taken on trust. This is like following a cake recipe that dictates ingredients in given proportions and then the baking time and oven temperature but does not tell you *why* these instructions give a good result. One can drive a car without knowing anything about spark plugs and transmissions, but one cannot so easily fix it. For students with the requisite motivation, these lectures have aimed to provide a look under the bonnet (being British; their American counterparts would of course be wanting to look under the hood).

A problem has been that no very suitable textbook has existed to accompany the lectures. The reading list has had to cite chapters from various large and indigestible texts, often with special reference to the technical appendices. To master the mathematics underlying econometric methods requires a detailed study of matrix algebra and a sound grasp of distribution theory, and to find readings with the right focus and at the right level is not easy. Sometimes, books written a generation ago and now out of print appear to do a better job than modern texts. Hence, this book.

Jargon, obscure conventions, and austere expository style all conspire to make this kind of material hard for beginners to access. This book may or may not succeed in its aim, but its aim is clear, which is to be successfully read by students who do not have too many techniques at their fingertips. As little as possible is done without a full explanation and careful cross-referencing to relevant results. This may make the discussion long-winded and repetitive at times, but hopefully it is helpful if at every stage the reader is told why things are being done, and what previous material is informing the argument. The style is deliberately informal, with numbered theorems and lemmas avoided. However, there is no dumbing down! Very few technical results are quoted without some form of explanation, demonstration, or proof.

It is expected that readers will have taken the standard mathematics and statistics courses for economics undergraduates, but the prior knowledge required is actually quite small. The treatment is as far as possible self-contained, with almost all the mathematical concepts needed being explained either *in situ* or in the appendices.

The chapters are grouped into four parts distinguishing the type of analysis undertaken in each.

Part I, "Fitting", is about summarizing and fitting data sets. Matrices are the main tools, and regression is the unifying principle for explaining and predicting data. The main topics are the solution of systems of equations and fitting by least squares. These are essential tools in econometrics proper, but at this stage there is no statistical modelling. The role of the calculations is purely descriptive.

Part II, "Modelling", invokes the methods of Part I to study the connections between a sample of data and the environment in which those data were generated, via econometric models. The probability distribution is the essential theoretical tool. The key idea of the sampling distribution of an estimator is introduced and allows attributes of estimators such as unbiasedness and efficiency to be defined and studied.

Part III "Testing", shows how to use the modelling framework of Part II to pose and answer questions. The central, beautiful idea of statistical inference is that noise and randomness can be domesticated and analyzed scientifically, so that when decisions to accept or reject a hypothesis have to be made, the chance of making the wrong decision can be quantified. These methods are used both to test simplifying restrictions on econometric models and to check out the adequacy and stability of the models themselves.

Up to this point in the story, the focus is wholly on the classical regression model. Elegant and powerful, while relying only on elementary statistical concepts, the classical model nonetheless suffers major limitations in the analysis of economic data. Part IV, "Extensions", is about breaking out of these limitations. These chapters provide a gentle introduction to some of the more advanced techniques of analysis that are the staple of current econometric research.

Finally, Part V contains four brief appendices reviewing some important bits of mathematics, including essential calculus.

Each of the chapters is supplied with a collection of exercises, some of which are straightforward and others more challenging. The first exercise in each case is a collection of statements with the question "true or false?" Some of these are true, some are subtly misstated, and some are nonsensical. After completing each chapter, readers are strongly encouraged to check their understanding before going further, by working through and making their choices. The correct answers are always to be found by a careful reading of the chapter material.

It may be helpful to mention some stylistic conventions adopted here to give hints to the reader. Formal definitions are generally avoided, but a technical term being used for the first time and receiving a definition is generally put in italics. Single quotation marks around words or phrases are used quite extensively, to provide emphasis and alert readers to the fact that common words are being used in a specialized or unusual way. Double quotes also get used to enclose words that we might imagine being articulated, although not actual quotations.

As the title emphasizes, this is no more than a primer, and there is no attempt to cover the whole field of econometric theory. The treatment of large sample theory is brief, and nothing is said about the analysis of time series and panel data, to name but two important topics. Some of the many excellent texts available that deal with these and other questions are listed in the "Recommended Reading" section at the end. Among others, my own earlier textbook *Econometric Theory* (Oxford: Blackwell Publishers, 2000) may be found useful. There is some overlap of material, and I have even taken the liberty of recycling one of the fancier illustrations from that volume. However, a different audience is addressed here. The earlier book was intended, as is the way with graduate texts, to report on the cutting edge of econometric research, with much emphasis on time series problems and the most advanced asymptotic theory. By contrast the present book might appear somewhat old fashioned, but with a purpose. The hope is that it can provide beginners with some of the basic intellectual equipment, as well as the confidence, to go further with the fascinating discipline of econometrics.

Exeter, December 2017 *James Davidson*

About the Companion Website

The companion website for this book is at

www.wiley.com/go/davidson/introecmettheory

This contains the full set of solutions to the exercises. There is also a set of lecture slides designed for instructors' use in conjunction with the text.

Scan this QR code to visit the companion website.

Part I

Fitting

1

Elementary Data Analysis

1.1 Variables and Observations

Where to begin? Data analysis is the business of summarizing a large volume of information into a smaller compass, in a form that a human investigator can appreciate, assess, and draw conclusions from. The idea is to smooth out incidental variations so as to bring the 'big picture' into focus, and the fundamental concept is *averaging*, extracting a representative value or central tendency from a collection of cases. The correct interpretation of these averages, and functions of them, on the basis of a model of the environment in which the observed data are generated,[1] is the main concern of statistical theory. However, before tackling these often difficult questions, gaining familiarity with the methods of summarizing sample information and doing the associated calculations is an essential preliminary.

Information must be recorded in some numerical form. Data may consist of measured magnitudes, which in econometrics are typically monetary values, prices, indices, or rates of exchange. However, another important data type is the binary indicator of membership of some class or category, expressed numerically by ones and zeros. A thing or entity of which different instances are observed at different times or places is commonly called a *variable*. The instances themselves, of which collections are to be made and then analyzed, are the *observations*. The basic activity to be studied in this first part of the book is the application of mathematical formulae to the observations on one or more variables.

These formulae are, to a large extent, human-friendly versions of coded computer routines. In practice, econometric calculations are always done on computers, sometimes with spreadsheet programs such as Microsoft Excel but more often using specialized econometric software packages. Simple cases are traditionally given to students to carry out by hand, not because they ever need to be done this way but hopefully to cultivate insight into what it is that computers do. Making the connection between formulae on the page and the results of running estimation programs on a laptop is a fundamental step on the path to econometric expertise.

1 "Data" is the plural of the word "datum", which denotes a piece of information. "The data is ..." is a usage to be avoided at all costs.

An Introduction to Econometric Theory, First Edition. James Davidson.

Companion website: www.wiley.com/go/davidson/introecmettheory

The most basic manipulation is to add up a column of numbers, where the word "column" is chosen deliberately to evoke the layout of a spreadsheet but could equally refer to the page of an accounting ledger in the ink-and-paper technology of a now-vanished age. Nearly all of the important concepts can be explained in the context of a *pair* of variables. To give them names, call them x and y. Going from two variables up to three and more introduces no fundamental new ideas. In linear regression analysis, variables are always treated in pairs, no matter how many are involved in the calculation as a whole.

Thus, let (x, y) denote the pair of variables chosen for analysis. The enclosure of the symbols in parentheses, separated by a comma, is a simple way of indicating that these items are to be taken together, but note that (y, x) is not to be regarded as just another way of writing (x, y). The order in which the variables appear is often significant.

Let T, a positive whole number, denote the number of observations or in other words the number of rows in the spreadsheet. Such a collection of observations, whose order may or may not be significant, is often called a *series*. The convention for denoting which row the observation belongs to is to append a subscript. Sometimes the letters i, j, or k are used as row labels, but there are typically other uses for these, and in this book we generally adopt the symbol t for this purpose. Thus, the contents of a pair of spreadsheet columns may be denoted symbolically as

$$(x_t, y_t), \ t = 1, \dots, T.$$

We variously refer to the x_t and y_t as the *elements* or the *coordinates* of their respective series.

This brings us inevitably to the question of the context in which observations are made. Very frequently, macroeconomic or financial variables (prices, interest rates, demand flows, asset stocks) are recorded at successive dates, at intervals of days, months, quarters, or years, and then t is simply a date, standardized with respect to the time interval and the first observation. Such data sets are called *time series*. Economic data may also be observations of individual economic units. These can be workers or consumers, households, firms, industries, and sometimes regions, states, and countries. The observations can represent quantities such as incomes, rates of expenditure on consumption or investment, and also individual characteristics, such as family size, numbers of employees, population, and so forth. If these observations relate to a common date, the data set is called a *cross-section*. The ordering of the rows typically has no special significance in this case.

Increasingly commonly studied in economics are data sets with both a time and a cross-sectional dimension, known as *panel data*, representing a succession of observations on the same cross section of entities. In this case two subscripts are called for, say i and t. However, the analysis of panel data is an advanced topic not covered in this book, and for observations we can stick to single subscripts henceforth.

1.2 Summary Statistics

As remarked at the beginning, the basic statistical operation of averaging is a way of measuring the central tendency of a set of data. Take a column of T numbers, add them up, and divide by T. This operation defines the *sample mean* of the series, usually written as the symbol for the designated variable with a bar over the top. Thus,

$$\bar{x} = \frac{x_1 + x_2 + \cdots + x_T}{T}$$
$$= \frac{1}{T}\sum_{t=1}^{T} x_t \quad (1.1)$$

where the second equality defines the 'sigma' representation of the sum. The Greek letter Σ, decorated with upper and lower limits, is a neat way to express the adding-up operation, noting the vital role of the subscript in showing which items are to be added together. The formula for $\bar{y}$ is constructed in just the same way.

The idea of the series mean extends from raw observations to various constructed series. The *mean deviations* are the series

$$x_t - \bar{x}, \quad t = 1, \ldots, T.$$

Naturally enough this 'centred' series has zero mean, identically:

$$\frac{1}{T}\sum_{t=1}^{T}(x_t - \bar{x}) = \bar{x} - \bar{x}$$
$$= 0. \quad (1.2)$$

Not such an interesting fact, perhaps, but the statistic obtained as the mean of the *squared* mean deviations is very interesting indeed. This is the sample *variance*,

$$s^2 = \frac{1}{T-1}\sum_{t=1}^{T}(x_t - \bar{x})^2, \quad (1.3)$$

which contains information about how the series varies about its central tendency. The same information, but with units of measurement matching the original data, is conveyed by the square root $s = \sqrt{s^2}$, called the *standard deviation* of the series. If $\bar{x}$ is a measure of *location*, then s is a measure of *dispersion*.

One of the mysteries of the variance formula is the division by $T - 1$, not T as for the mean itself. There are important technical reasons for this,[2] but to convey the intuition involved here, it may be helpful to think about the case where $T = 1$, a single observation. Clearly, the mean formula still makes sense, because it gives $\bar{x} = x_1$. This is the best that can be done to measure location. There is clearly no possibility of computing a measure of dispersion, and the fact that the formula would involve dividing by zero gives warning that it is not meaningful to try. In other words, to measure the dispersion as $(x_1 - x_1)^2 = 0$, which is what (1.3) would produce with division by T instead of $T - 1$, would be misleading. Rather, it is correct to say that no measure of dispersion exists.

Another property of the variance formula worth remarking is found by multiplying out the squared terms and summing them separately, thus:

$$\sum_{t=1}^{T}(x_t - \bar{x})^2 = \sum_{t=1}^{T} x_t^2 - 2\bar{x}\sum_{t=1}^{T} x_t + T\bar{x}^2$$
$$= \sum_{t=1}^{T} x_t^2 - T\bar{x}^2. \quad (1.4)$$

2 Sections 7.5 and 10.3 give the details.

In the first equality, note that "adding up" T instances of $\bar{x}$ (which does not depend on t) is the same thing as just multiplying by T. The second equality then follows by cancellation, given the definition (1.1). This result shows that to compute the variance, there is no need to perform T subtractions. Simply add up the squares of the coordinates, and subtract T times the squared mean. Clearly, this second formula is more convenient for hand calculations than the first one.

The information contained in the standard deviation is nicely captured by a famous result in statistics called *Chebyshev's rule*, after the noted Russian mathematician who discovered it.[3] Consider, for some chosen positive number ε, whether a series coordinate x_t falls 'far from' the central tendency of the data set in the sense that either $x_t < \bar{x} - \varepsilon$ or $x_t > \bar{x} + \varepsilon$. In other words, does x_t lie beyond a distance ε from the mean, either above or below? This condition can be expressed as

$$(x_t - \bar{x})^2 > \varepsilon^2. \tag{1.5}$$

Letting n_ε denote the number of cases x_t that satisfy inequality (1.5), the inequality

$$\sum_{(x_t-\bar{x})^2>\varepsilon^2} (x_t - \bar{x})^2 > n_\varepsilon \varepsilon^2 \tag{1.6}$$

is true by definition, where the 'sigma' notation variant expresses compactly the sum of the terms satisfying the stated condition. However, it is also the case that

$$\sum_{(x_t-\bar{x})^2>\varepsilon^2} (x_t - \bar{x})^2 < Ts^2 \tag{1.7}$$

since, remembering the definition of s^2 from (1.3), the sum cannot exceed $(T-1)s^2$, even with $\varepsilon = 0$. Putting together the inequalities in (1.6) and (1.7) and also dividing through by T and by ε^2 yields the result

$$\frac{n_\varepsilon}{T} < \frac{s^2}{\varepsilon^2}. \tag{1.8}$$

In words, the *proportion* of series coordinates x_t falling beyond a distance ε from the mean is *at most* s^2/ε^2.

To put this another way, let $m = \varepsilon/s$ denote the distance expressed in units of standard deviations. The upper bound on the proportion of coordinates lying more than m standard deviations from the mean is $1/m^2$. This rule gives a clear idea of what s conveys about the scatter of the data points – whether they are spread out or concentrated closely about the mean. However, the constraint applies in one direction only. It gives no information about the actual number of data points lying outside the specified interval, which could be none. There is simply a bound on the maximum number. *Any* number of data points can lie beyond one standard deviation of the mean, so the rule says nothing about this case. However, at most a quarter of the coordinates can lie more than two standard deviations from the mean, and at most a ninth beyond three standard deviations from the mean.

1.3 Correlation

Measuring the characteristics of a single series, location and dispersion, is as a rule just a preliminary to considering series in pairs. Relationships are what really matter.

3 Pafnuty Chebyshev, 1821–1894

Given T pairs of observations on variables x and y, with means $\bar{x}$ and $\bar{y}$ and standard deviations s_x^2 and s_y^2, define their *covariance* as the average of the products of the mean deviations:

$$s_{xy} = \frac{1}{T-1}\sum_{t=1}^{T}(x_t - \bar{x})(y_t - \bar{y}). \tag{1.9}$$

Note right away the alternative version of this formula, by analogy with (1.4),

$$\sum_{t=1}^{T}(x_t - \bar{x})(y_t - \bar{y}) = \sum_{t=1}^{T} x_t y_t - T\bar{x}\bar{y}. \tag{1.10}$$

The interpretation of (1.9) is best conveyed by an illustration. Figure 1.1 shows quarterly series for short and long interest rates for the UK, covering the period 1963 quarter 1 to 1984 quarter 2 (86 observations). The horizontal axis in this figure shows the date, so the observations appear in time order, and for visual convenience the points are joined by line segments to make a continuous path. RS is the 3-months local authorities' lending rate, and RL is the rate on $2\frac{1}{2}\%$ Consols, undated British Government securities similar to 10-year bonds. These rates moved in a similar manner through time, both responding to the rate of price inflation in the UK, which over the period in question was high and volatile. The mean and standard deviation of RS are respectively 9.48 and 3.48, while the mean and standard deviation of RL are 10.47 and 3.16. Their covariance, calculated by (1.9), is 9.13.

The same data are represented in a different way in Figure 1.2, as a scatter plot, where the axes of the diagram are respectively the values of RL (vertical) and RS (horizontal). Here, each plotted point represents a pair of values. To convey exactly the same information as Figure 1.1 would require labelling each plotted point with the date in question, but for clarity this is not done here. The crosshairs in the scatter plot denote the point of sample means, so that the diagram shows the disposition of the terms contributing to the sum in formula (1.9). The positions of the means divide the plot into four quadrants. In the top-right and bottom-left quadrants, the mean deviations have the same signs, positive in the first case, negative in the second. In either case $(x_t - \bar{x})(y_t - \bar{y}) > 0$, so these data points make positive contributions to the sum in (1.9). On the other hand, the top-left and bottom-right quadrants contain points where the mean deviations have

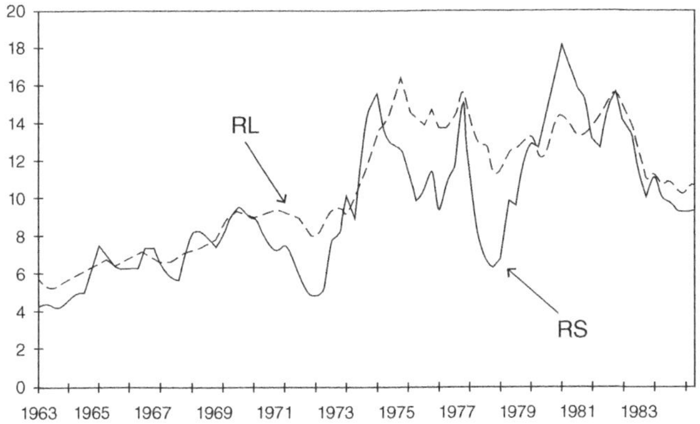

Figure 1.1 Long and short UK interest rates.

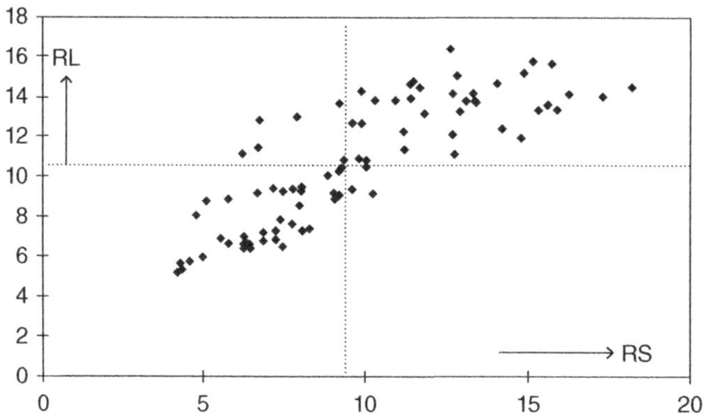

Figure 1.2 Scatter plot of the interest rate series.

different signs. In these cases, $(x_t - \bar{x})(y_t - \bar{y}) < 0$, so these points make a negative contribution to the sum. The overall positive association that is evident from the scatter plot is captured by the covariance having a positive value, since the positive contributions to the sum of products outweigh the negative contributions, as is clearly the case from the plot. As well as counting positive and negative contributions, the contributions are larger absolutely (of whichever sign) as the pairs of data points in question are further away from the point of the means. If either point happened to be equal to its mean, the contribution to the sum would of course be zero.

The problem with the covariance is that like the means and standard deviations, its value depends on the units of measurement of the data. While the sign indicates a direction of association, it is difficult to answer the question "How big is big?" The solution is to normalize by dividing by the product of the standard deviations, to yield the *correlation coefficient*,

$$r_{xy} = \frac{s_{xy}}{s_x s_y}.$$

The divisor $T - 1$ cancels in this ratio, so an equivalent formula is

$$r_{xy} = \frac{\sum_{t=1}^{T}(x_t - \bar{x})(y_t - \bar{y})}{\sqrt{\sum_{t=1}^{T}(x_t - \bar{x})^2 \sum_{t=1}^{T}(y_t - \bar{y})^2}}. \tag{1.11}$$

The correlation coefficient of the interest rates is 0.837.

The remarkable fact about the correlation coefficient is that it cannot exceed 1 in absolute value. This makes sense, if a series cannot be more closely correlated with any other series than it is with itself. Putting $y_t = x_t$ for every t in (1.11) gives $r_{xx} = 1$. Putting $y_t = -x_t$ for every t gives $r_{x,-x} = -1$. However, this is not quite the same thing as saying that r_{xy} can never fall outside the interval $[-1, 1]$ whatever pair of series is chosen. This is in fact a rather deep result, an instance of what is called by mathematicians the *Cauchy-Schwarz inequality*.

The demonstration is a bit magical and not too technical to follow, so it is worth setting it out in simple steps. Here's how. Using an abbreviated notation to keep the equations as simple as possible, write

$$r_{xy} = \frac{\Sigma x_t y_t}{\sqrt{\Sigma x_t^2 \Sigma y_t^2}} \tag{1.12}$$

so that the sum limits and the mean deviations are taken as implicit. In this setup, note first that for any pair of numbers a and b, and any pair of series x and y,

$$\Sigma(ax_t - by_t)^2 \geq 0. \tag{1.13}$$

This is a sum of squares and the smallest it can get is zero, if $ax_t = by_t$ for every t. Except in this case, it must be positive.

Multiplying out the square and adding up the components individually, an equivalent way to write the relation in (1.13) (check this!) is

$$a^2\Sigma x_t^2 + b^2\Sigma y_t^2 \geq 2ab\Sigma x_t y_t. \tag{1.14}$$

Now (the clever bit!) choose $a = \Sigma x_t y_t$ and $b = \Sigma x_t^2$. Substituting in (1.14) gives

$$(\Sigma x_t y_t)^2 \Sigma x_t^2 + (\Sigma x_t^2)^2 \Sigma y_t^2 \geq 2\Sigma x_t^2 (\Sigma x_t y_t)^2. \tag{1.15}$$

Noting that Σx_t^2 appears in each term and is necessarily positive, it can be cancelled, so inequality (1.15) implies

$$(\Sigma x_t y_t)^2 + \Sigma x_t^2 \Sigma y_t^2 \geq 2\,(\Sigma x_t y_t)^2.$$

Finally, subtract $(\Sigma x_t y_t)^2$ from both sides to get

$$\Sigma x_t^2 \Sigma y_t^2 \geq (\Sigma x_t y_t)^2.$$

In words, "the product of the sums of squares is never smaller than the square of the sum of products." Comparing with (1.12), the argument shows that $r_{xy}^2 \leq 1$, and this must hold for any pair of series whatever. The claim that

$$-1 \leq r_{xy} \leq 1$$

is established directly.

Given this result, a correlation coefficient of 0.837 represents quite a strong positive relationship, nearer to 1 than to 0 at least. However, there is another aspect to correlation not to be overlooked. It is clear that scatter patterns yielding a large positive value must have the characteristic "big with big, small with small". In other words, the pairs of points must tend to be on the same side of their means, above or below. In the case of negative correlation we should find "big with small, small with big", with most points in the top left or bottom right quadrants. In other words, the scatter of points has to be clustered around a straight line, either with positive slope, or negative slope.

However, it is not difficult to imagine a case where "big goes with either big or small, but small goes with intermediate". For example, the points might be clustered around a quadratic curve. A close relationship is perfectly compatible with similar numbers of points in all four quadrants and a correspondingly small value for r_{xy}. The implication is that correlation measures specifically the strength of *linear* relationships.

1.4 Regression

Correlation is a way of describing relationships between pairs of variables, but in a neutral and context-free way, simply posing the question "Is there a connection?" But most commonly in economics, such questions *do* have a context. One of these might be "Is there a causal connection? Does y change *because* x changes?" Another might be "In a situation where I observe x but I don't observe y, could I exploit their correlation to predict y?" Note that in the latter case there need be no implication about a direction of causation; it's just a question of what is and is not observed. However, in either situation there is an asymmetry in the relationship. Consider y to be the object of interest and x as the means to explain it. *Regression* is the tool for using correlation to try to answer such questions.

Since correlation is a feature of linear relationships, it is a natural step to write down the equation for a straight line to embody the relationship of interest. Such an equation has the form

$$y = \alpha + \beta x$$

and is illustrated in Figure 1.3. The coefficients α and β are known respectively as the *intercept* and the *slope*, and the illustration shows the roles that they play.

Given the series of pairs (y_t, x_t) for $t = 1, \ldots, T$, consider how to express the idea of an *approximate* linear relationship between observed variables. Figure 1.4 shows what

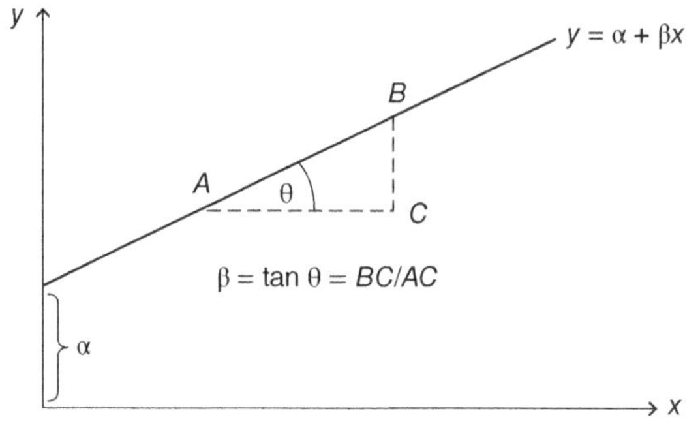

Figure 1.3 The regression line

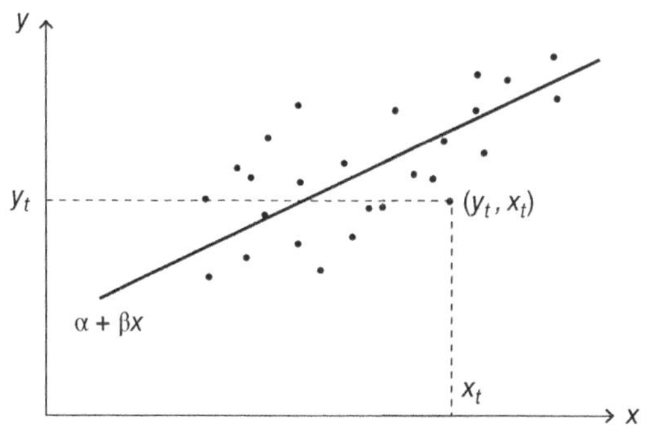

Figure 1.4 The regression line and the data

the teaming up of a scatter of observed pairs with a regression line might look like. To express the same idea algebraically requires an equation of the form

$$y_t = \alpha + \beta x_t + u_t \tag{1.16}$$

in which a new series, u_t for $t = 1, \dots, T$, has to be introduced to close the equation. This is not a part of the data set, although given fixed values for α and β, equation (1.16) is nothing but an identity defining u_t as a function of the observed series, and if those values were known, it could be calculated from the formula. Think of u_t, commonly referred to as the *residual*, as the component of y_t left unexplained by x_t in this equation.

Figure 1.5 shows a single data point in close-up, with u_t identified as the *vertical* distance between the line and point. This is an important consequence of placing y_t on the left-hand side of the equation with coefficient normalized to unity. If x and y were to change places in the equation, the implicit residual would then be the horizontal distance between line and point.

Be careful to appreciate that equation (1.16) by itself has no content, because α and β can be anything, and therefore u_t can be anything. However, it introduces a framework within which a very important new idea can be introduced. This is the notion of an econometric *model*, a theoretical statement about the environment generating the data. The key idea here is that there exist α and β such that u_t possesses certain specific properties. Thus, if y_t and x_t show a common pattern of variation but u_t consists of nothing but noise, reflecting none of this pattern, this suggests the existence of a relationship of which (1.16) is the model – a simplified version of the reality represented by the scatter in Figure 1.4, hopefully capturing the important features.

The content of the model must hinge on the precise understanding of what is meant by 'noise'. The key feature of the regression model, in particular, is that *u_t is not correlated with x_t*. Given its role in the equation of closing an identity, u_t must share some common patterns with either x_t or y_t, or indeed both, but the regression model imposes the condition that it is correlated exclusively with y_t. This embodies the assumption of a causal model. It says that y_t is driven by x_t and by 'other things', and here u_t fulfils the role of the other things, in general unobserved. However, if u_t were to be correlated with x_t, this would necessarily imply some reverse causation. Requiring the model to be causal imposes the uncorrelatedness. In this scheme x_t must be determined outside, and prior to, the mechanism determining y_t. In the forecasting context, on the other hand, u_t is nothing but the forecast error. If x_t and u_t were correlated, this would imply the presence of some neglected information that could be used to improve the forecast, so

Figure 1.5 The regression residual

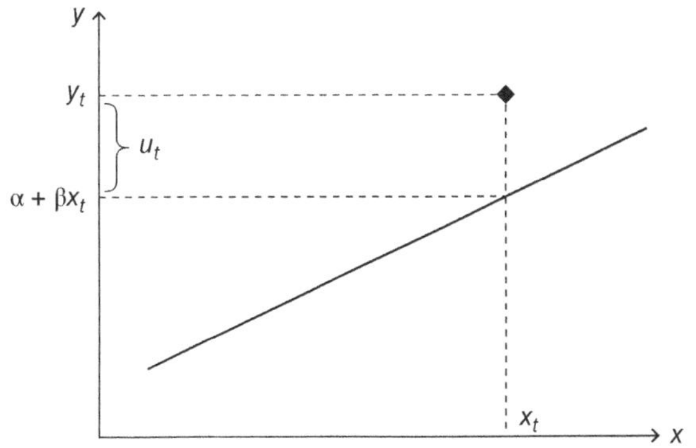

the idea of equation (1.16) with u_t omitted as representing the 'best linear forecast' must also imply uncorrelatedness of x_t and u_t.

When they have the required properties, α and β are called the *regression coefficients*. There is some standard terminology for referring to the variables in this setup; x_t is called the *regressor*, or alternatively, the explanatory variable. Technically, y_t is known as the *regressand*, although this usage is less common, and it is more usual to refer to y_t simply as the dependent variable.

Something to emphasize here is that in econometrics, a useful model must invoke some significantly stronger assumptions before useful inferences can be made from the data analysis. The key linkage between the sample data and circumstances in which it arose to be measured is going to be provided by the concept of a *probability distribution*. Distribution theory allows the sample to be placed in a wider context and the properties and predictions of the model to be evaluated scientifically. These questions are pursued in detail in Parts II and III of this book. In this and the next three chapters, the focus is chiefly on computational matters, and the mathematics of data fitting.

1.5 Computing the Regression Line

If the regression line is to describe the sample of data points adequately, the residuals should be collectively 'small'. Looking at Figure 1.4, there are many ways that a line might be drawn in relation to the set of data points, but for most of them, it appears the vertical distances between line and points would be collectively larger than in the case shown. However, to make this idea precise requires a notion of what is meant by 'collectively', since moving the line must increase the magnitudes of some residuals at the same time as reducing others.

Consider a framework for reviewing this question. Let a and b denote 'trial' values of the coefficients α and β, and using these, write a trial version of the regression relation as

$$y_t - a - bx_t = e_t(a, b), \quad t = 1, \dots, T.$$

The symbol e_t represents the trial residuals and in particular, $u_t = e_t(\alpha, \beta)$ in (1.16). While α and β are unknown, for any choices of a and b, the e_t can be calculated as functions of these values and the data.

'Collectively small' now has several possible interpretations. It is the absolute magnitudes of the e_t that matter here, so the signs must be discarded in the comparisons. Taking absolute values $|e_t(a, b)|$ and squares $e_t(a, b)^2$ are two different ways of discarding the signs, suggesting two possible ways to choose a and b:

1. *Least Absolute Values*: minimize $\sum_{t=1}^T |e_t(a, b)|$ with respect to a and b.
2. *Least Squares*: minimize $\sum_{t=1}^T e_t(a, b)^2$ with respect to a and b.

There is a lot to be said for least absolute values (LAV), and this method has its advocates for use in certain specific situations. However, these are quite rare, and in practice the overwhelming favourite is least squares. The reasons for this are not the ones you would hope for. Least squares has two decisive advantages. There is a simple formula to compute the solutions to the minimization problem, and working out the properties of the resulting formulae on the basis of statistical theory is fairly straightforward. Neither of these nice attributes holds for the LAV method.

There are reasons for wishing that the facts were different, since the least squares solution has some undesirable properties. Because the residuals are squared, large ones play an excessively large role in determining the value of the sum of squares function, and small ones are correspondingly less important. This means that outlying observations are very influential in fixing the position of the regression line, while it might be preferred that the 'typical' observations in the body of the scatter are the most influential, which is how LAV works. However, ease of use and ease of interpretation prove in practice to trump such advantages.

By convention, the solution to the least squares problem is denoted by the decorated symbols $\hat{\alpha}$ and $\hat{\beta}$ (say "alpha-hat" and "beta-hat"). The object is to find formulae for these quantities as computable functions of the data. The corresponding least squares residual is defined as

$$\hat{u}_t = y_t - \hat{\alpha} - \hat{\beta}x_t. \tag{1.17}$$

Rearranging this equation as

$$y_t = \hat{u}_t + \hat{\alpha} + \hat{\beta}x_t, \tag{1.18}$$

consider the residual at trial values a and b. Substituting for y_t from (1.18), this may be written as

$$\begin{aligned} e_t &= y_t - a - bx_t \\ &= \hat{u}_t + (\hat{\alpha} - a) + (\hat{\beta} - b)x_t. \end{aligned}$$

Use this formula to construct the trial sum of squares by multiplying out the squares and summing the terms individually.

$$\begin{aligned} \sum_{t=1}^{T} e_t(a,b)^2 &= \sum_{t=1}^{T} (\hat{u}_t + (\hat{\alpha} - a) + (\hat{\beta} - b)x_t)^2 \\ &= \sum_{t=1}^{T} \hat{u}_t^2 + \sum_{t=1}^{T} ((\hat{\alpha} - a) + (\hat{\beta} - b)x_t)^2 \\ &\quad + 2(\hat{\alpha} - a)\sum_{t=1}^{T} \hat{u}_t + 2(\hat{\beta} - b)\sum_{t=1}^{T} x_t\hat{u}_t. \end{aligned} \tag{1.19}$$

Then pose the question: what values of a and b will make this sum of sums as small as possible? There are four sums to consider. The first one does not depend on a and b. The second one is a sum of squares and becomes as small as possible (which means, becomes zero) by setting $a = \hat{\alpha}$ and $b = \hat{\beta}$. However, the third and fourth terms are problematic, because in general values of a and b could be chosen that will make them negative. In other words, there is no guarantee without some further conditions that $\sum_{t=1}^{T} e_t(a,b)^2$ cannot be smaller than $\sum_{t=1}^{T} \hat{u}_t^2$, with $a \neq \hat{\alpha}$ and $b \neq \hat{\beta}$. The second term must then be larger than zero, but that does not prevent the net contribution of the terms depending on a and b being negative. Because squaring a small number makes it smaller, there are certainly cases of (a, b) close enough to $(\hat{\alpha}, \hat{\beta})$ to make this happen. The only way to avoid this outcome is to choose $\hat{\alpha}$ and $\hat{\beta}$ so as to make the last two terms vanish. Recalling that equation (1.17) defines $\hat{u}_t$, the conditions under which $(\hat{\alpha}, \hat{\beta})$ are the minimizing values are

$$\sum_{t=1}^{T} \hat{u}_t = 0 \tag{1.20}$$

and

$$\sum_{t=1}^{T} x_t \hat{u}_t = 0. \tag{1.21}$$

To have $\hat{\alpha}$ and $\hat{\beta}$ solve these equations is necessary *and* sufficient for a unique solution to the minimization problem.

Before proceeding to the solutions, take some time to review the notable implications of (1.20) and (1.21). First, consider (1.20). This says that the least squares residuals should sum to zero, which of course is the same as the condition that their mean is zero. This makes sense; intuitively the best-fitting line must pass through the centre of gravity of the scatter and have as many data points above it as below it, on average.

However, (1.21) is even more interesting. The first thing to notice is that

$$\sum_{t=1}^{T} x_t \hat{u}_t - \bar{x} \sum_{t=1}^{T} \hat{u}_t = \sum_{t=1}^{T} (x_t - \bar{x}) \hat{u}_t. \tag{1.22}$$

Since both terms on the left-hand side are required to vanish, (1.21) holds equivalently if x_t is put into mean deviation form. Since u_t is in mean deviation form by construction according to (1.20), dividing (1.22) by $T - 1$ gives an expression of exactly the same form as (1.9). In other words, the least squares residual is required to be uncorrelated with the regressor. This is exactly the condition required to interpret the regression model as a causal model. This property jumps right out of the least squares solution.

These facts show that the least squares solution does more than give the best fit of the line to the points, in a particular sense. It also enforces a particular form of relationship between regressor and dependent variable, specifically a causal mechanism. Never forget that least squares imposes this view of the economic interaction. If the relationship is not believed to be really causal and that influences may pass in both directions to determine how these variables interact, then $\hat{\alpha}$ and $\hat{\beta}$ are not the coefficients needed. The LAV coefficients do not satisfy (1.20) and (1.21) and so cannot embody the causality condition in the same way, although correlation is not the only way for variables to be related, so caution is needed in drawing conclusions from this. On the other hand, if the motivation in fitting a regression is to forecast y_t from x_t, condition (1.22) says that the least squares forecast error $\hat{u}_t$ is linearly unpredictable by x_t and hence cannot be reduced without additional information. This motivation for least squares appeals to observability rather than causality, but these are really two sides of the same coin.

To solve the pair (1.20) + (1.21), substitute into these equations from (1.17) and rearrange the terms of the sums to get

$$\sum_{t=1}^{T} y_t - T\hat{\alpha} - \hat{\beta} \sum_{t=1}^{T} x_t = 0 \tag{1.23}$$

$$\sum_{t=1}^{T} x_t y_t - \hat{\alpha} \sum_{t=1}^{T} x_t - \hat{\beta} \sum_{t=1}^{T} x_t^2 = 0. \tag{1.24}$$

These are the *least squares normal equations*, two equations in the two unknowns $\hat{\alpha}$ and $\hat{\beta}$. The usual solution procedure involves three steps.

1. Solve (1.23) for $\hat{\alpha}$ as a function of $\hat{\beta}$, using $\bar{x} = T^{-1} \sum_{t=1}^{T} x_t$, etc. This rearrangement yields

$$\hat{\alpha} = \bar{y} - \hat{\beta}\bar{x}. \tag{1.25}$$

2. Substitute the solution from (1.25) into (1.24) to get

$$\sum_{t=1}^{T} x_t y_t - T\bar{x}\,\bar{y} + \hat{\beta} T \bar{x}^2 - \hat{\beta} \sum_{t=1}^{T} x_t^2 = 0 \tag{1.26}$$

which is a function of $\hat{\beta}$ alone.
3. Solve (1.26) for $\hat{\beta}$.

$$\begin{aligned}\hat{\beta} &= \frac{\sum_{t=1}^{T} x_t y_t - T\bar{x}\bar{y}}{\sum_{t=1}^{T} x_t^2 - T\bar{x}^2} \\ &= \frac{\sum_{t=1}^{T}(x_t - \bar{x})(y_t - \bar{y})}{\sum_{t=1}^{T}(x_t - \bar{x})^2} \\ &= \frac{s_{xy}}{s_x^2}\end{aligned} \tag{1.27}$$

where in the last equality the insertion of $1/(T-1)$ into both numerator and denominator changes nothing and is optional.

A fourth step would be to substitute $\hat{\beta}$ into the formula for $\hat{\alpha}$, but for ordinary calculations there is no need for this. The second equality in (1.27) applies (1.10) and (1.4), but note that putting the dependent variable in mean deviations is also optional. The numerator can equally be written as

$$\sum_{t=1}^{T}(x_t - \bar{x})y_t$$

in view of (1.2).

It turns out that the regression coefficients have familiar components. The intercept is a combination of the sample means, while the slope coefficient is the ratio of the covariance of x and y to the variance of x. As such it bears some resemblance to the correlation coefficient, but of course there is the crucial difference that r_{xy} is symmetric in the two variables, while the regression coefficient assigns them different roles. The regression model can be viewed as a device for exploiting a correlation between two variables to predict one from the other. If the variables are interchanged and x regressed on y, it is easily verified that the product of this slope coefficient with $\hat{\beta}$ is none other than r_{xy}^2.

In some expositions of least squares theory, the formulae (1.25) and (1.27) are obtained using calculus. Equations (1.23) and (1.24) can be obtained as the first-order conditions for the minimum of a quadratic function, equating the first partial derivatives to zero. With this approach it is necessary to show that these are conditions for a minimum, not a maximum, by evaluating the second-order conditions. By contrast, our approach does not invoke calculus and derives the minimum by a pleasingly direct argument.

To conclude this section, it is useful for future developments to consider the special case of the regression equation with no regressor. This is simply

$$y_t = \alpha + u_t, \quad t = 1, \dots, T \tag{1.28}$$

To find the minimizer of $\sum_{t=1}^{T} (y_t - \alpha)^2$, consider the argument based on (1.19) where x_t is set to zero for each t so that there is no dependence on b. It is clear that the single normal equation (1.20) needs to be solved, and

$$\sum_{t=1}^{T} \hat{u}_t = \sum_{t=1}^{T} y_t - T\hat{\alpha} = 0$$

has the solution

$$\hat{\alpha} = \bar{y}. \tag{1.29}$$

In other words, the sample mean is the coefficient that minimizes the sum of squares in equation (1.28). This proves to be a useful characterization of the mean, allowing its statistical properties to be studied. See Section 8.1 for the details.

1.6 Multiple Regression

While correlation is rather naturally a story about pairs of variables, ideas such as causal relations and prediction are typically going to involve two or more explanatory variables. The simple regression setup is nothing more than a springboard to launch into the treatment of regression theory proper. This must accommodate an arbitrary number of regressors, even if the number should normally be small in comparison with the number of observations.

Consider the equation with two regressors,

$$y_t = \alpha + \beta_1 x_{1t} + \beta_2 x_{2t} + u_t, \quad t = 1, \dots, T. \tag{1.30}$$

Here the data set consists of the collection of triples (y_t, x_{1t}, x_{2t}). Instead of a two-dimensional scatter, their geometrical representation is as points in three-dimensional space. The image of a swarm of gnats hanging in the air on a summer evening is an appealing one, except of course that these gnats are frozen in fixed positions in space.

The regression line now generalizes to a *plane* – a two-dimensional subset of three-dimensional space. Already drawing pictures is getting awkward, but this can just about be visualized as in Figure 1.6. Imagination must supply the swarm of gnats clustered about the surface. The sum of squares function is constructed exactly as one would expect, as $\sum_{t=1}^{T} e_t(a, b_1, b_2)^2$ where

$$e_t(a, b_1, b_2) = y_t - a - b_1 x_{1t} - b_2 x_{2t}. \tag{1.31}$$

Denoting the least squares coefficients by $\hat{\alpha}$, $\hat{\beta}_1$, and $\hat{\beta}_2$, the argument based on (1.19) goes through here in virtually the same way. Substituting

$$\hat{u}_t = y_t - \hat{\alpha} - \hat{\beta}_1 x_{1t} - \hat{\beta}_2 x_{2t} \tag{1.32}$$

into (1.31) to obtain

$$e_t = \hat{u}_t + (\hat{\alpha} - a) + (\hat{\beta}_1 - b_1)x_{1t} + (\hat{\beta}_2 - b_2)x_{2t},$$

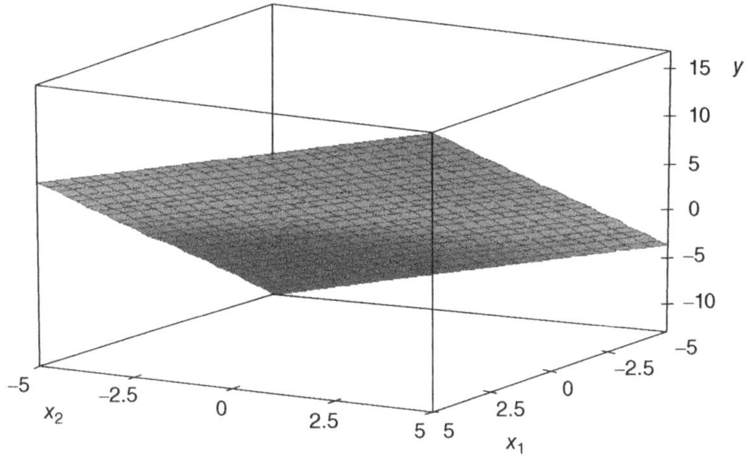

Figure 1.6 Plot of $y = 2 + 2x_1 + x_2$

the expression

$$\sum_{t=1}^{T} e_t^2 = \sum_{t=1}^{T} \hat{u}_t^2 + \sum_{t=1}^{T} ((\hat{\alpha} - a) + (\hat{\beta}_1 - b_1)x_{1t} + (\hat{\beta}_2 - b_2)x_{2t})^2 + \\ 2(\hat{\alpha} - a)\sum_{t=1}^{T} \hat{u}_t + 2(\hat{\beta}_1 - b_1)\sum_{t=1}^{T} x_{1t}\hat{u}_t + 2(\hat{\beta}_2 - b_2)\sum_{t=1}^{T} x_{2t}\hat{u}_t$$

must be shown to be minimized at the points $a = \hat{\alpha}$, $b_1 = \hat{\beta}_1$, and $b_2 = \hat{\beta}_2$. Similarly to before, this holds under the conditions:

$$\sum_{t=1}^{T} \hat{u}_t = 0$$

$$\sum_{t=1}^{T} x_{1t}\hat{u}_t = 0$$

$$\sum_{t=1}^{T} x_{2t}\hat{u}_t = 0.$$

These normal equations are conveniently expanded by substituting from (1.32) as

$$T\hat{\alpha} + \hat{\beta}_1 \sum_{t=1}^{T} x_{1t} + \hat{\beta}_2 \sum_{t=1}^{T} x_{2t} = \sum_{t=1}^{T} y_t \tag{1.33}$$

$$\hat{\alpha} \sum_{t=1}^{T} x_{1t} + \hat{\beta}_1 \sum_{t=1}^{T} x_{1t}^2 + \hat{\beta}_2 \sum_{t=1}^{T} x_{1t}x_{2t} = \sum_{t=1}^{T} x_{1t}y_t \tag{1.34}$$

$$\hat{\alpha} \sum_{t=1}^{T} x_{2t} + \hat{\beta}_1 \sum_{t=1}^{T} x_{2t}x_{1t} + \hat{\beta}_2 \sum_{t=1}^{T} x_{2t}^2 = \sum_{t=1}^{T} x_{2t}y_t \tag{1.35}$$

to be solved for unknowns $\hat{\alpha}$, $\hat{\beta}_1$, and $\hat{\beta}_2$.

However, this is the point to pause and take stock. It appears feasible to solve these equations stepwise, as was done for the simple regression, but this is tedious and results in bulky expressions. How then to extend to three regressors, and so to arbitrary numbers not specified in advance? These calculations are not a job for pencil and paper. A computer algorithm is required, and matrix algebra provides the fundamental framework on which such solution algorithms are based.

There are also more subtle issues to worry about. It is not self-evident that (1.33)–(1.35) have a unique solution. Could there be more than one set of values $(\hat{\alpha}, \hat{\beta}_1, \hat{\beta}_2)$ that satisfy these equations? It is not hard to see that this is possible, because on choosing $x_{1t} = x_{2t}$ for every t, equations (1.34) and (1.35) become identical, and there would only be two equations from which to solve three unknowns. No unique solution could exist. The point is not that this would be a foolish choice. If something so simple could cause trouble, what difficulties might lie in wait when going to larger numbers of regressors? The next task is to set up the fundamental ideas required to solve this computational problem, and also to gain insight into the form of the solution.

1.7 Exercises

1 Are the following statements true or false?
 (a) The correlation of a variable with itself is always 1.
 (b) Chebyshev's rule says that at least a proportion $1/m^2$ of any sample lies beyond m standard deviations from the mean.
 (c) The least absolute values fitting method is more influenced by outlying observations than least squares.
 (d) The sample mean is the least squares measure of location.
 (e) The slope coefficient in the simple regression is the tangent of the angle of the regression line with the horizontal axis.
 (f) The least squares estimator of the slope coefficient (y on x) is the sum of the products of y with the mean deviations of x, divided by the sum of squares of the mean deviations of x.
 (g) Run a regression in both directions (y on x and x on y), and the product of the two slope coefficients is equal to the squared correlation coefficient.

A *spreadsheet, a regression package, and a calculator with pencil and paper are all valid ways to answer Questions 2, 3, and 4.*

2 Here are 12 observations on a variable x:

$$86, 109, 81, 53, 86, -14, 65, -39, 65, 34, 79, -27$$

 (a) Compute the mean.
 (b) Compute the sequence of mean deviations.
 (c) Compute the standard deviation.
 (d) How many of these data points lie more than (i) one, (ii) two, or (iii) three standard deviations from the mean?

(e) Include the following observations in the set, and obtain the mean and standard deviation for this case.

$$209, 475, -114, 46$$

(f) Repeat exercise (d) for the enlarged data set.

3 Here are 12 observations on a variable y.

$$43, 62, 26, 46, 48, 3, 52, -10, 37, 5, 42, 4$$

(a) Compute the mean.
(b) Compute the standard deviation.
(c) Compute the correlation coefficient of y with x in Question 2.
(d) Include the following data points in the set and compute the correlation coefficient with the enlarged data set of Question 2.

$$110, 42, -50, 44$$

(e) Draw scatter plots of the data in the two cases.

4 Compute the regression of y on x (original sample).
(a) Report the fitted slope and intercept coefficients, and the residuals $\hat{u}$.
(b) Verify that $\hat{u}$ has zero correlation with x. Draw the scatter plot of the two variables.
(c) Consider the prediction equation

$$\check{y} = 5 + 0.6x.$$

Show that the prediction errors are correlated with x. Compare the mean of the squared prediction errors in this case with the mean of the squared regression residuals.
(d) Compute the regression of y on x (extended sample). Report the fitted coefficients and comment.

5 (a) Solve the following equation system for $\hat{\beta}_1$.

$$\hat{\beta}_1 \sum_{t=1}^{T} x_{1t}^2 + \hat{\beta}_2 \sum_{t=1}^{T} x_{1t}x_{2t} = \sum_{t=1}^{T} x_{1t}y_t \qquad (1)$$

$$\hat{\beta}_1 \sum_{t=1}^{T} x_{2t}x_{1t} + \hat{\beta}_2 \sum_{t=1}^{T} x_{2t}^2 = \sum_{t=1}^{T} x_{2t}y_t \qquad (2)$$

(b) Define $\hat{\alpha} = \bar{y} - \hat{\beta}_1\bar{x}_1 - \hat{\beta}_1\bar{x}_2$. Show that if $T\hat{\alpha}\bar{x}_1$ is subtracted from the right-hand side of equation (1), and $T\hat{\alpha}\bar{x}_2$ is subtracted from the right-hand side of equation (2), the resulting equations are modified by having the variables expressed in mean deviation form.
(c) What is $\hat{\alpha}$?

6 Show that the α that minimizes $\sum_{t=1}^{T}(y_t - \alpha)^2$ is the sample mean of $y_1, \ldots, y_T$.

2

Matrix Representation

2.1 Systems of Equations

A *matrix* is a rectangular array whose cells contain numbers, represented in mathematical manipulations by a single symbol. A computer spreadsheet, with rows and columns, is a natural image to have in mind here. The key component of the notation is one already seen in (1.30), the double subscript, where typically, but *not* invariably, the first subscript indicates the row of the entry and the second indicates the column. The elements x_{1t} and x_{2t} are natural instances, but note that these reverse the usual ordering, if t is the row subscript and 1 or 2 the column subscript. In econometrics, this happens!

Consider the case of three rows and three columns:

$$\boldsymbol{A} = \begin{bmatrix} a_{11} & a_{12} & a_{13} \\ a_{21} & a_{22} & a_{23} \\ a_{31} & a_{32} & a_{33} \end{bmatrix}$$

A convention used in some (but not all) texts is to use a boldface font for the symbol representing a matrix, and also typically a capital letter. Boldface is always used in this book. The *elements* of a matrix, written as a_{ij} with generic subscripts, are numbers of the usual kind.[1] Sometimes it is convenient to represent a matrix in terms of its generic element, as in $\boldsymbol{A} = \{a_{ij}\}$. A matrix whose elements are all zeros is an important special case, and is represented in this book by the boldface digit, $\boldsymbol{0}$.

A matrix having a single column, or a single row, is known as a *vector*. It is usual to have just one subscript in these cases, and the convention used in this book is to have boldface lowercase letters represent vectors. A column vector with three elements is

$$\boldsymbol{b} = \begin{bmatrix} b_1 \\ b_2 \\ b_3 \end{bmatrix}.$$

The terminology is inherited from the physical sciences and reflects the common geometrical interpretation of such objects as points in a multidimensional space. In econometrics, most applications are remote from geometry, and the best image to keep in mind for a vector is of a column of data in a spreadsheet.

1 In mathematics textbooks, it would be customary to call these elements *real* numbers, because the possibility that they might be complex, having imaginary parts, would not be ruled out. Here such cases won't arise and real is understood, but curious readers can find out about complex numbers in Section 9.2.

An Introduction to Econometric Theory, First Edition. James Davidson.

Companion website: www.wiley.com/go/davidson/introecmettheory

Vectors and matrices provide the notation needed to compactly represent systems of linear equations. For example, defining $\boldsymbol{x}$ to be a vector of unknown coefficients to be calculated and letting $\boldsymbol{A}$ and $\boldsymbol{b}$ be a matrix and a vector containing known constants, consider the equation

$$\boldsymbol{Ax} = \boldsymbol{b}. \tag{2.1}$$

This simple expression can represent the normal equations (1.33)–(1.35). To see this, let

$$\boldsymbol{A} = \begin{bmatrix} T & \sum_{t=1}^{T} x_{1t} & \sum_{t=1}^{T} x_{2t} \\ \sum_{t=1}^{T} x_{1t} & \sum_{t=1}^{T} x_{1t}^2 & \sum_{t=1}^{T} x_{1t}x_{2t} \\ \sum_{t=1}^{T} x_{2t} & \sum_{t=1}^{T} x_{2t}x_{1t} & \sum_{t=1}^{T} x_{2t}^2 \end{bmatrix},$$

$$\boldsymbol{b} = \begin{bmatrix} \sum_{t=1}^{T} y_t \\ \sum_{t=1}^{T} x_{1t}y_t \\ \sum_{t=1}^{T} x_{2t}y_t \end{bmatrix},$$

and

$$\boldsymbol{x} = \begin{bmatrix} \hat{\alpha} \\ \hat{\beta}_1 \\ \hat{\beta}_2 \end{bmatrix}.$$

With these definitions, (2.1) is an equivalent representation of (1.33)–(1.35). To check out the resemblances, note first that this is an equation with a 3-vector on the right-hand side, and these elements match the three right-hand sides of (1.33)–(1.35). Clearly, a matrix equation represents a column of scalar equations. The only mystery is how the 'product' $\boldsymbol{Ax}$ is equated with the vector of left-hand sides.

Comparing the two expressions term by term, it is clear that the multiplication rule has the form

$$\boldsymbol{Ax} = \begin{bmatrix} a_{11}x_1 + a_{12}x_2 + a_{13}x_3 \\ a_{21}x_1 + a_{22}x_2 + a_{23}x_3 \\ a_{31}x_1 + a_{32}x_2 + a_{33}x_3 \end{bmatrix} = \begin{bmatrix} b_1 \\ b_2 \\ b_3 \end{bmatrix} = \boldsymbol{b}.$$

In words, the rule can be expressed as follows:

> For $i = 1, 2$ and 3: to get b_i, the ith element of $\boldsymbol{b}$, multiply together the elements a_{ij} and x_j, for $j = 1, 2$ and 3, and add up the products.

To remember the multiplication rule, it may provide a useful mental image to think of the following sequence of operations:

1. Pick up $\boldsymbol{x}$ and turn it on its side (make it a row).
2. Drop it on top of a row of $\boldsymbol{A}$.
3. Multiply each of the paired elements together.
4. Add up the products to get the corresponding element of $\boldsymbol{Ax}$.
5. Do this for each row of $\boldsymbol{A}$ in turn.

What is done here, in effect, is to define an expression in matrix algebra. It is now time to introduce some formalities and learn some technical terms and definitions. The rest of this chapter is inevitably somewhat dry, and it will be a very attentive reader who remembers everything in it by the time they reach the end. Therefore, keep in mind that its main role is for reference. The best approach is to skim it now but be prepared to return frequently while working through the subsequent chapters.

2.2 Matrix Algebra Basics

Let m and n be given integers. A *matrix* with m rows and n columns is

$$A = \begin{bmatrix} a_{11} & a_{12} & \cdots & a_{1n} \\ a_{21} & a_{22} & \cdots & a_{2n} \\ \vdots & \vdots & \ddots & \vdots \\ a_{m1} & a_{m2} & \cdots & a_{mn} \end{bmatrix} (m \times n).$$

Note the convention for denoting the dimensions of a matrix. $m \times n$ is shorthand for "number of rows times number of columns" and symbolically indicates the number of elements. If $m = n$, then $\boldsymbol{A}$ is said to be a *square* matrix.A *column vector* with m elements is

$$\boldsymbol{a} = \begin{bmatrix} a_1 \\ a_2 \\ \vdots \\ a_m \end{bmatrix} (m \times 1).$$

In the context of matrix algebra, ordinary numbers are known as *scalars* since they possess scale but no dimension. If a_{11} is a scalar one may also define $[a_{11}]$ as a 1×1 matrix. These are strictly speaking different objects, but 1×1 matrices and scalars behave equivalently under the rules of matrix algebra, and equating them is sometimes a convenient trick.

These are the basic classes of object that appear in matrix expressions. They are teamed with a set of operations that allow new matrices to be created from existing matrices.

Transposition is the interchanging of rows and columns. The notation

$$\boldsymbol{B} = \boldsymbol{A}'$$

defines a $n \times m$ matrix called the *transpose* of $\boldsymbol{A}$, with the property $b_{ij} = a_{ji}$ for $i = 1, \dots, n$ and $j = 1, \dots, m$. Science and engineering textbooks often use the notation $\boldsymbol{A}^{\mathrm{T}}$ to denote the transpose, but the 'prime' notation is usual in econometrics and is a lot tidier, especially in complicated expressions. If $\boldsymbol{A}$ is a square $(m \times m)$ matrix and $\boldsymbol{A} = \boldsymbol{A}'$, then $\boldsymbol{A}$ is said to be *symmetric*.

A row vector can be thought of as a transposed column:

$$\boldsymbol{a}' = [a_1 \quad a_2 \quad \cdots \quad a_m] \quad (1 \times m).$$

When a vector is defined in this book, it will always be a column vector. A row vector is always specified as the transpose of a previously defined column vector. In this spirit, a column vector of zeros is denoted $\mathbf{0}$, and a row vector of zeros as $\mathbf{0}'$.

Matrices can be added and subtracted, subject to satisfying appropriate conditions. Matrices $\boldsymbol{A}$ and $\boldsymbol{B}$ are said to be *conformable for addition* if they have the same dimensions; say, both are $m \times n$. Then,

$$\boldsymbol{C} = \boldsymbol{A} + \boldsymbol{B}$$

is the *sum* of $\boldsymbol{A}$ and $\boldsymbol{B}$ having elements

$$c_{ij} = a_{ij} + b_{ij}, \; i = 1, \dots, m, \; j = 1, \dots, n.$$

If $\boldsymbol{B}$ is $m \times n$ and a is a scalar, the *scalar product*

$$\boldsymbol{C} = a\boldsymbol{B} \; (m \times n)$$

is the matrix with elements

$$c_{ij} = ab_{ij}, \quad i = 1, \dots, m, \; j = 1, \dots, n.$$

In particular, putting $a = -1$ defines subtraction of one matrix from another

$$\boldsymbol{A} - \boldsymbol{B} = \boldsymbol{A} + (-1)\boldsymbol{B}.$$

Rather naturally, the transpose of the sum of two conformable matrices is the sum of their transposes:

$$(\boldsymbol{A} + \boldsymbol{B})' = \boldsymbol{A}' + \boldsymbol{B}'.$$

The next definition is familiar from the preceding discussion of the least squares normal equations. Given a matrix $\boldsymbol{A}$ $(m \times n)$ and a vector $\boldsymbol{x}$ $(n \times 1)$, the *linear equation*

$$\boldsymbol{y} = \boldsymbol{A}\boldsymbol{x} \tag{2.2}$$

defines a vector $\boldsymbol{y}$ $(m \times 1)$ by the relations

$$y_i = a_{i1}x_1 + \cdots + a_{in}x_n \text{ for } i = 1, \dots m.$$

In linear algebra, $\boldsymbol{A}$ represents a *linear operator*, defining a mapping that takes a point $\boldsymbol{x}$ in n-dimensional space to a point $\boldsymbol{y}$ in m-dimensional space.

Matrix multiplication is a fundamental operation defined for pairs of matrices satisfying certain conformability conditions, although these are different from the conditions for a sum. If $\boldsymbol{A}$ is $m \times n$ and $\boldsymbol{B}$ is $n \times p$, the *matrix product*

$$\boldsymbol{C} = \boldsymbol{A}\boldsymbol{B} \; (m \times p)$$

is the matrix with elements

$$c_{ij} = \sum_{k=1}^{n} a_{ik}b_{kj}, \quad i = 1, \dots, m, \; j = 1, \dots, p \tag{2.3}$$

Notice the pattern in this expression, of summation over the matching inner pair of subscripts to define an element whose position in the product matrix is defined by the left-most subscript (the row) and right-most subscript (the column). If $p = 1$ so that $\boldsymbol{B}$ is a column vector, this formula simply reproduces (2.2).

The condition of conformability for multiplication is: "The number of rows in $\boldsymbol{B}$ matches the number of columns in $\boldsymbol{A}$." There is no restriction on the number of rows of $\boldsymbol{A}$ or columns of $\boldsymbol{B}$, and these define the dimensions of the product matrix. Note that $\boldsymbol{BA}$ is something entirely different from $\boldsymbol{AB}$ and may not even exist if the conformability rule is violated. To clarify this distinction, it is usual to say that $\boldsymbol{A}$ *premultiplies* $\boldsymbol{B}$ and equivalently that $\boldsymbol{B}$ *postmultiplies* $\boldsymbol{A}$.

A natural way to understand matrix multiplication is in terms of the effect of two successive linear operations. If $\boldsymbol{y} = \boldsymbol{Ax}$ represents the linear operation of taking point $\boldsymbol{x}$ to point $\boldsymbol{y}$ using operator $\boldsymbol{A}$, then $\boldsymbol{C} = \boldsymbol{AB}$ is the matrix that represents the double operation "first $\boldsymbol{B}$, then $\boldsymbol{A}$." The multiplication formula can be verified by comparing $\boldsymbol{y} = \boldsymbol{Cx}$ with $\boldsymbol{y} = \boldsymbol{Az}$ where $\boldsymbol{z} = \boldsymbol{Bx}$.

The rule for product transposition is at first sight a little counter-intuitive. The transpose of the product of conformable matrices is the product of the transposes *in reverse order*:

$$(\boldsymbol{AB})' = \boldsymbol{B}'\boldsymbol{A}'. \tag{2.4}$$

A little thought will show that no other rule is possible, because the transposes are not surely conformable for multiplication without this inversion. However, the best way to convince oneself, as with any such matrix operation, is to carry it out with pencil and paper for a simple case (2×2) and see it work.

The special case of the product of conformable vectors is important. Let $\boldsymbol{a}$ $(m \times 1)$ and $\boldsymbol{b}$ $(m \times 1)$ be a pair of columns. Transposing $\boldsymbol{a}$ defines a row vector $\boldsymbol{a}'$, which is conformable for postmultiplication by $\boldsymbol{b}$, and their product is a one-dimensional matrix, or in effect a scalar:

$$\boldsymbol{a}'\boldsymbol{b} = \sum_{j=1}^{m} a_j b_j.$$

This is known as the *inner product* of the vectors. The transpose $\boldsymbol{b}'\boldsymbol{a}$ has the same value as $\boldsymbol{a}'\boldsymbol{b}$. The transpose of a scalar is the same scalar, confirming the rule for transposed products in this case. The inner product of a vector with itself is the sum of the squared elements, and the scalar quantity

$$\|\boldsymbol{a}\| = \sqrt{\boldsymbol{a}'\boldsymbol{a}} \tag{2.5}$$

is called the *length* of $\boldsymbol{a}$, also known as the *Euclidean norm* of the vector. As a measure of magnitude, the length is most easily appreciated by considering the case $m = 2$. If elements a_1 and a_2 denote the sides of a right-angled triangle in the plane, $\sqrt{a_1^2 + a_2^2}$ is the length of the hypotenuse of the triangle, by Pythagoras's theorem. This is the distance of the vector, represented as a point in the plane, from the origin. The same logic, although harder to represent graphically, applies to vectors of any order n viewed as points in n-dimensional space.

By contrast, given an m-vector $\boldsymbol{a}$ and n-vector $\boldsymbol{b}$ for any m and n, the product $\boldsymbol{ab}'$ is called the *outer product* of the vectors. This is a $m \times n$ matrix, which can be written out in terms of its generic elements as

$$\boldsymbol{ab}' = \begin{bmatrix} a_1 b_1 & \cdots & a_1 b_n \\ \vdots & \ddots & \vdots \\ a_m b_1 & \cdots & a_m b_n \end{bmatrix}. \tag{2.6}$$

The outer product of an n-vector with itself, defining a square symmetric $n \times n$ matrix containing the products of each vector element with each other element, the squared elements appearing on the so-called *main diagonal*, is a construction that often arises in regression theory.

2.3 Rules of Matrix Algebra

Recall the rules obeyed by ordinary (scalar) algebra. If a, b, and c are scalars, the result of multiplying them together is the same whichever order the operations are carried out. Specifically, $(ab)c = a(bc)$. This is called the *associative* rule. The *distributive* rule is that the sum of products is the same as the product of sums, so that $ab + ac = a(b + c)$. The third rule of scalar algebra is the *commutative* rule, which says that $ab = ba$. The value of the product is invariant to the order in which the factors appear.

Matrix algebra also satisfies the associative rule. If $\boldsymbol{A}$ and $\boldsymbol{B}$ are conformable for multiplication and $\boldsymbol{B}$ and $\boldsymbol{C}$ are likewise conformable, then

$$\boldsymbol{ABC} = \boldsymbol{A}(\boldsymbol{BC}) = (\boldsymbol{AB})\boldsymbol{C}.$$

The distributive rule holds likewise. If $\boldsymbol{A}$ is conformable for multiplication with $\boldsymbol{B}$ and also with $\boldsymbol{C}$, and $\boldsymbol{B}$ and $\boldsymbol{C}$ are conformable for addition, then

$$\boldsymbol{A}(\boldsymbol{B} + \boldsymbol{C}) = \boldsymbol{AB} + \boldsymbol{AC}.$$

In these respects, doing matrix algebra is very similar to doing scalar algebra provided the conformability rules are observed.

However, as already noted, there is no commutative rule. If $\boldsymbol{A}$ and $\boldsymbol{B}$ are conformable for multiplication, there is no implication that $\boldsymbol{B}$ and $\boldsymbol{A}$ are conformable, and even if they are,

$$\boldsymbol{AB} \neq \boldsymbol{BA} \tag{2.7}$$

except in special cases. In the product $\boldsymbol{AB}$, $\boldsymbol{A}$ *pre*multiplies $\boldsymbol{B}$ and equivalently $\boldsymbol{B}$ *post*multiplies $\boldsymbol{A}$, and pre- and postmultiplication are distinct operations that may or may not be defined for a given pair of matrices.

The one exception to the no-commutation rule is the scalar product. One can easily see, just by reflecting on (2.3), that if c is a scalar and $\boldsymbol{A}$ and $\boldsymbol{B}$ are conformable matrices, then

$$\boldsymbol{A}(c\boldsymbol{B}) = c\boldsymbol{AB}.$$

This is convenient, because it means that scale factors can always be located at the left-hand end of any matrix expression, without any loss of generality.

It is undoubtedly the case that by far the commonest error made by beginners in matrix algebra is the neglect of conformability rules. In ordinary (scalar) algebra one proceeds happy in the knowledge that any number can be added to, or multiplied by, any other number. In matrix algebra, every object encountered has row and column dimensions, and these must conform in the right way. Forgetting this and proceeding as if under the rules of scalar algebra, it is extremely easy to write down nonsense expressions. To avoid such nonsenses, a good visual imagination is very helpful. Try to keep a picture in mind of the matrices being added or multiplied – square, or long and thin, as the case may be – so that observing conformability becomes instinctive.

The absence of the commutation property turns out to be a considerable convenience when manipulating matrix formulae. This is because the order that matrices appear in a product is immutable, unlike the case of scalar products where the terms can be written in any order. The product of three or more matrices (a construction that will arise rather commonly in the sequel) can always be evaluated by starting at one end and computing the pairwise products in sequence. The author always finds the most natural way to do this is to start at the right-hand end and work from right to left, but obviously this is going to be a matter of individual preference.

2.4 Partitioned Matrices

It is often convenient to break a matrix into blocks of rows, or blocks of columns, to distinguish different components of an expression or to ease certain calculations. Thus, given a matrix A $(m \times n)$, let the matrix composed of the first m_1 rows of A be denoted A_1, and let the remaining rows, m_2 in number where $m = m_1 + m_2$, form a matrix A_2. The partition can then be written as

$$\underset{m\times n}{A} = \begin{bmatrix} A_1 \\ A_2 \end{bmatrix} \begin{matrix} m_1 \\ m_2 \end{matrix} \tag{2.8}$$

Note the various styles for indicating dimensions in this expression.

Now suppose that there is also a partition of the columns into sets of dimension n_1 and n_2, where $n_1 + n_2 = n$, so that $A_1 = [A_{11} \quad A_{12}]$ and $A_2 = [A_{21} \quad A_{22}]$. The complete partition, by rows and by columns, now appears as

$$\underset{m\times n}{A} = \begin{bmatrix} A_{11} & A_{12} \\ A_{21} & A_{22} \end{bmatrix}$$

One may write the generic case of the blocks as A_{ij} of dimension $m_i \times n_j$ for $i, j = 1, 2$. This is not the only case possible, since the row blocks might be partitioned at different points in different column blocks, but the case where the partitioning dimensions match is certainly the most useful one.

The most important aspect of partitioning is its treatment in algebraic manipulations. There is a basic, very simple rule. When adding or multiplying partitioned matrices, the rules can be applied almost as if the blocks were just scalar elements. The one difference is that conformability rules must be respected, which places constraints on the partition dimensions of the terms or factors. Consider a matrix

$$A = [A_1 \ A_2] \quad (m \times n)$$

partitioned into n_1 and n_2 columns. Also, consider a matrix

$$B = \begin{bmatrix} B_1 \\ B_2 \end{bmatrix} \quad (n \times p)$$

partitioned into n_1 and n_2 rows. Note that the product AB $(m \times p)$ is well defined, in view of the matching dimension n, but more important is that the blocks are individually conformable. It can now be verified that

$$\begin{aligned} AB &= [A_1 \ A_2] \begin{bmatrix} B_1 \\ B_2 \end{bmatrix} \\ &= A_1 B_1 + A_2 B_2. \end{aligned} \tag{2.9}$$

The multiplication rule (2.3) works perfectly well for this case, with blocks substituting for matrix elements, only remembering that the conformability rules must be obeyed.

Something this formula highlights is that $\boldsymbol{AB}$ is invariant to permutations of the columns of $\boldsymbol{A}$ and rows of $\boldsymbol{B}$ when these match. The premultiplication of a matrix by its own transpose is a common construction in econometrics, and it can be useful to remember that $\boldsymbol{A}'\boldsymbol{A}$ takes the same value however the rows of $\boldsymbol{A}$ are ordered.

Now consider the case when $\boldsymbol{A}$ is partitioned by rows as in (2.8), with row dimensions m_1 and m_2 and column dimension n. Let $\boldsymbol{B}$ be partitioned by columns, with row dimension n and column dimensions p_1 and p_2. This product has the partitioned representation

$$\begin{aligned}\boldsymbol{AB} &= \begin{bmatrix}\boldsymbol{A}_1\\ \boldsymbol{A}_2\end{bmatrix}[\boldsymbol{B}_1\ \boldsymbol{B}_2]\\ &= \begin{bmatrix}\boldsymbol{A}_1\boldsymbol{B}_1 & \boldsymbol{A}_1\boldsymbol{B}_2\\ \boldsymbol{A}_2\boldsymbol{B}_1 & \boldsymbol{A}_2\boldsymbol{B}_2\end{bmatrix}\end{aligned} \tag{2.10}$$

noting that the blocks $\boldsymbol{A}_i$ and $\boldsymbol{B}_j$ are each conformable for multiplication with common dimension n, and the dimensions of the products $\boldsymbol{A}_i\boldsymbol{B}_j$ are $m_i \times p_j$. This is the block generalization of the outer product for vectors, defined in (2.6).

2.5 Exercises

1 Are the following statements true or false?
   (a) If for matrices $\boldsymbol{A}$ and $\boldsymbol{B}$ both of the products $\boldsymbol{AB}$ and $\boldsymbol{BA}$ exist, then $\boldsymbol{A}$ and $\boldsymbol{B}$ must be square.
   (b) Symmetric matrices must be square.
   (c) If $\boldsymbol{A}$ and $\boldsymbol{B}$ are square matrices conformable for multiplication, then

$$\boldsymbol{AB} = \boldsymbol{BA}$$

   (d) If $\boldsymbol{A}$, $\boldsymbol{B}$, and $\boldsymbol{C}$ are matrices having the same dimensions $m \times n$, then

$$(\boldsymbol{A}'(\boldsymbol{B}+\boldsymbol{C}))' = \boldsymbol{B}'\boldsymbol{A} + \boldsymbol{C}'\boldsymbol{A}$$

   (e) The inner product is defined for pairs of conformable vectors, while the outer product is defined for any pair of vectors.
   (f) The scalar product obeys the commutative rule.
   (g) If $\boldsymbol{A}$ and $\boldsymbol{B}$ are matrices conformable for multiplication such that $\boldsymbol{AB}$ exists and are also partitioned conformably, then

$$[\boldsymbol{A}_1\ \ \boldsymbol{A}_2]\begin{bmatrix}\boldsymbol{B}_1\\ \boldsymbol{B}_2\end{bmatrix} = \begin{bmatrix}\boldsymbol{A}_1\boldsymbol{B}_1 & \boldsymbol{A}_2\boldsymbol{B}_1\\ \boldsymbol{A}_1\boldsymbol{B}_2 & \boldsymbol{A}_2\boldsymbol{B}_2\end{bmatrix}$$

2 Let

$$\boldsymbol{A} = \begin{bmatrix}1 & 4\\ 2 & 5\\ 3 & 6\end{bmatrix}, \quad \boldsymbol{B} = \begin{bmatrix}1 & 2 & 3\\ 1 & 2 & 3\end{bmatrix}.$$

Compute

(a) $\boldsymbol{A} + \boldsymbol{B}'$
(b) $5\boldsymbol{B}$
(c) $\boldsymbol{AB}$
(d) $\boldsymbol{BA}$
(e) $\boldsymbol{A}'\boldsymbol{A}$
(f) $\boldsymbol{BB}'$

3 Let $\boldsymbol{A}$ and $\boldsymbol{B}$ be as in Question 2 and

$$\boldsymbol{c} = \begin{bmatrix} 1 \\ 0 \\ 1 \end{bmatrix}, \quad \boldsymbol{d} = \begin{bmatrix} 1 \\ 1 \end{bmatrix}.$$

Compute

(a) $\boldsymbol{Bc}$
(b) $\boldsymbol{B}'\boldsymbol{d}$
(c) $\boldsymbol{A} + \boldsymbol{cd}'$
(d) $\boldsymbol{c}'\boldsymbol{c}$
(e) $\boldsymbol{cc}'$
(f) $\|\boldsymbol{c}\|$
(g) $\boldsymbol{d}'\boldsymbol{Bc}$
(h) $\boldsymbol{c}'\boldsymbol{AA}'\boldsymbol{c}$

4 If $\boldsymbol{A}$, $\boldsymbol{B}$, $\boldsymbol{c}$, and $\boldsymbol{d}$ are defined as in Questions 2 and 3, write down *ten* matrix expressions involving one or more of these components that *do not exist* (violate conformability).

3

Solving the Matrix Equation

3.1 Matrix Inversion

The last chapter discussed how the interpret the matrix equation

$$\boldsymbol{Ax} = \boldsymbol{b} \tag{3.1}$$

and established that the least squares normal equations have this form. The next question to address is, knowing $\boldsymbol{A}$ and $\boldsymbol{b}$, how to discover $\boldsymbol{x}$? And indeed, to determine whether an $\boldsymbol{x}$ exists to satisfy (3.1) and, if so, whether it is unique? All these questions can now be answered.

The first requirement is to define a special class of matrices. The *identity matrix* of dimension $n \times n$ is the square matrix having 1s in the diagonal positions and zeros elsewhere. In generic form, this is written

$$\boldsymbol{I}_n = \begin{bmatrix} 1 & 0 & \cdots & 0 \\ 0 & 1 & \cdots & 0 \\ \vdots & \vdots & \ddots & \vdots \\ 0 & 0 & \dots & 1 \end{bmatrix} \quad (n \times n)$$

The subscript indicating the dimension is often omitted when the context is clear.

The special feature of the identity matrix is that when it pre- or postmultiplies a conformable matrix or vector, it leaves it unchanged. In other words

$$\boldsymbol{AI} = \boldsymbol{A}$$

and also

$$\boldsymbol{IA} = \boldsymbol{A}.$$

$\boldsymbol{A}$ is not required to be square here. If $\boldsymbol{A}$ is $m \times n$, one may write

$$\boldsymbol{I}_m\boldsymbol{A} = \boldsymbol{AI}_n = \boldsymbol{A}.$$

Given system (3.1), where $\boldsymbol{A}$ is $n \times n$, suppose that a unique matrix $\boldsymbol{B}$ $(n \times n)$ exists such that

$$\boldsymbol{BA} = \boldsymbol{I}_n.$$

Premultiplying both sides of the equation by $\boldsymbol{B}$, it is evident that the solution must take the form

$$\boldsymbol{x} = \boldsymbol{Bb}.$$

An Introduction to Econometric Theory, First Edition. James Davidson.

Companion website: www.wiley.com/go/davidson/introecmettheory

If such a matrix as $\boldsymbol{B}$ exists, it is called the *inverse* of $\boldsymbol{A}$ and written $\boldsymbol{A}^{-1}$. This generalizes the operation of division to matrices. Formally define $\boldsymbol{A}^{-1}$, where it exists, to be the unique square matrix having the properties

$$\begin{aligned} \boldsymbol{A}^{-1}\boldsymbol{A} &= \boldsymbol{A}\boldsymbol{A}^{-1} \\ &= \boldsymbol{I}. \end{aligned} \tag{3.2}$$

The inverse is defined only for square matrices, noting in particular that only square conformable matrices can possess the property in (3.2).[1]

It is natural to interpret the inverse using the language of linear transformations (or operations). If

$$\boldsymbol{y} = \boldsymbol{A}\boldsymbol{x}$$

represents the linear operation taking a vector $\boldsymbol{x}$ $(n \times 1)$, a point in n-dimensional space, to another point $\boldsymbol{y}$ in the same space, then the *inverse transformation* is

$$\begin{aligned} \boldsymbol{A}^{-1}\boldsymbol{y} &= \boldsymbol{A}^{-1}\boldsymbol{A}\boldsymbol{x} \\ &= \boldsymbol{I}\boldsymbol{x} \\ &= \boldsymbol{x} \end{aligned}$$

recovering the original point $\boldsymbol{x}$ from the transformed point $\boldsymbol{y}$.

An important cautionary point before proceeding. The inverse of $\boldsymbol{A}$ is *never* written as $\frac{1}{\boldsymbol{A}}$. This is because, as already pointed out in (2.7), $\boldsymbol{A}^{-1}\boldsymbol{C} \neq \boldsymbol{C}\boldsymbol{A}^{-1}$ in general. The notation $\frac{\boldsymbol{C}}{\boldsymbol{A}}$ would be ambiguous, because there is no indication whether premultiplication or postmultiplication is intended.

The next task is to compute the inverse, the important first step being to determine whether it exists. Sometimes it does not, meaning that there is no unique solution to system (3.1). Noninvertible square matrices are said to be *singular*, the usual terminology for the invertible case being *nonsingular*. In scalar algebra, $x = 0$ is the unique case of a real number such that $1/x$ is not defined, and a singular matrix might be thought of as the matrix generalization of the number zero. However, there are many singular matrices.

Start with the simplest cases. If the matrix is 1×1 taking the form $\boldsymbol{A} = [a_{11}]$, it clearly fulfils the definition to set $\boldsymbol{A}^{-1} = [1/a_{11}]$. This inverse is undefined in the unique case $a_{11} = 0$. By contrast, one might stare at the 2×2 matrix

$$\boldsymbol{A} = \begin{bmatrix} a_{11} & a_{12} \\ a_{21} & a_{22} \end{bmatrix}$$

for any amount of time without a solution suggesting itself, although once the trick is revealed it is astoundingly neat and simple to remember. Construct a 2×2 matrix from the elements of $\boldsymbol{A}$ by interchanging the *positions* of the elements 'on the diagonal', that is, a_{11} and a_{22}, and the *signs* of the off-diagonal elements, a_{12} and a_{21}. Multiplying $\boldsymbol{A}$ by

1 There exists a generalized inversion concept for nonsquare matrices. See Appendix D for details.

this matrix using the rule in (2.3) has the result

$$\begin{bmatrix} a_{11} & a_{12} \\ a_{21} & a_{22} \end{bmatrix} \begin{bmatrix} a_{22} & -a_{12} \\ -a_{21} & a_{11} \end{bmatrix} = \begin{bmatrix} a_{11}a_{22} - a_{12}a_{21} & 0 \\ 0 & a_{11}a_{22} - a_{12}a_{21} \end{bmatrix}$$
$$= (a_{11}a_{22} - a_{12}a_{21}) \begin{bmatrix} 1 & 0 \\ 0 & 1 \end{bmatrix}. \tag{3.3}$$

Now interchange the factors, and see if the same result holds. Sure enough,

$$\begin{bmatrix} a_{22} & -a_{12} \\ -a_{21} & a_{11} \end{bmatrix} \begin{bmatrix} a_{11} & a_{12} \\ a_{21} & a_{22} \end{bmatrix} = (a_{11}a_{22} - a_{12}a_{21}) \begin{bmatrix} 1 & 0 \\ 0 & 1 \end{bmatrix}.$$

Thus, the solution of the inversion problem is immediate.

$$A^{-1} = \frac{1}{a_{11}a_{22} - a_{12}a_{21}} \begin{bmatrix} a_{22} & -a_{12} \\ -a_{21} & a_{11} \end{bmatrix}, \tag{3.4}$$

although this only works for the case where $a_{11}a_{22} - a_{12}a_{21} \neq 0$. This is the condition for the matrix to be nonsingular. As in the scalar case, there is a quantity that must act as a divisor, and so must be different from zero.

The operation of this solution can be checked with reference to the normal equations for the simple, single regressor case. Rearrange equations (1.23)+(1.24) as

$$\hat{\alpha}T + \hat{\beta}\sum_{t=1}^{T} x_t = \sum_{t=1}^{T} y_t$$
$$\hat{\alpha}\sum_{t=1}^{T} x_t + \hat{\beta}\sum_{t=1}^{T} x_t^2 = \sum_{t=1}^{T} x_t y_t$$

and thence in matrix form as

$$\begin{bmatrix} T & \sum_{t=1}^{T} x_t \\ \sum_{t=1}^{T} x_t & \sum_{t=1}^{T} x_t^2 \end{bmatrix} \begin{bmatrix} \hat{\alpha} \\ \hat{\beta} \end{bmatrix} = \begin{bmatrix} \sum_{t=1}^{T} y_t \\ \sum_{t=1}^{T} x_t y_t \end{bmatrix}.$$

Applying (3.4), the solution is

$$\begin{bmatrix} \hat{\alpha} \\ \hat{\beta} \end{bmatrix} = \frac{1}{T\sum_{t=1}^{T} x_t^2 - \left(\sum_{t=1}^{T} x_t\right)^2} \begin{bmatrix} \sum_{t=1}^{T} x_t^2 & -\sum_{t=1}^{T} x_t \\ -\sum_{t=1}^{T} x_t & T \end{bmatrix} \begin{bmatrix} \sum_{t=1}^{T} y_t \\ \sum_{t=1}^{T} x_t y_t \end{bmatrix}.$$

$$= \frac{1}{T\sum_{t=1}^{T} x_t^2 - \left(\sum_{t=1}^{T} x_t\right)^2} \begin{bmatrix} \sum_{t=1}^{T} y_t \sum_{t=1}^{T} x_t^2 - \sum_{t=1}^{T} x_t \sum_{t=1}^{T} x_t y_t \\ T\sum_{t=1}^{T} x_t y_t - \sum_{t=1}^{T} x_t \sum_{t=1}^{T} y_t \end{bmatrix}$$

These expressions are easily verified to simplify to the solutions obtained previously. In particular, observe that

$$T\sum_{t=1}^{T} x_t^2 - \left(\sum_{t=1}^{T} x_t\right)^2 = T\sum_{t=1}^{T} (x_t - \bar{x})^2$$

which shows that the least squares solution fails to exist only when, not unreasonably, the variance of the regressor is zero. This can only happen if x_t is the same, and hence equal to $\bar{x}$, for every t. If there is no variation in the explanatory variable there can be no least squares fit. The sum of squares function has no unique minimum and the calculation fails.

3.2 Determinant and Adjoint

The number

$$|A| = a_{11}a_{22} - a_{12}a_{21} \tag{3.5}$$

from (3.3) is called the *determinant* of A. This long-standing terminology describes a property of a system of linear equations that was known even before the development of matrix algebra, 'determining' the existence or otherwise of a unique solution. There is no solution if the determinant is zero. Be careful to note that the conventional notation $|A|$ in (3.5) represents a scalar, not a matrix. Sometimes the determinant is written as 'det A', although the 'bars' notation is very well established.

The matrix

$$\begin{bmatrix} a_{22} & -a_{12} \\ -a_{21} & a_{11} \end{bmatrix} \tag{3.6}$$

is called the *adjoint matrix* of A, written as 'adj A'.[2] Hence, the formula in (3.4) is compactly written as

$$A^{-1} = \frac{1}{|A|}\text{adj } A. \tag{3.7}$$

In fact, this formulation is perfectly general. Every square matrix, of any order, has a determinant and adjoint defined for it. Moreover, when the determinant is nonzero the inverse always has this form of a scalar product, with the reciprocal of the determinant appearing as the scalar.

The determinant of a matrix of higher dimension is a complicated object, and the best way to visualize it is in terms of a recursive rule. A *submatrix* of A is a matrix of smaller dimension constructed by deleting one or more rows and columns from A. The *minors* (or minor determinants) of A are the determinants of the square submatrices obtained by deletion of rows and columns.[3] In particular, let m_{ij} denote the determinant of the $(n-1)\times(n-1)$ submatrix obtained by deleting row i and column j from A. Taking $i, j = 1, \dots, n$, there are n^2 of these minors. The *cofactors* of A are then defined as the numbers

$$c_{ij} = (-1)^{i+j}m_{ij}$$

where $(-1)^{i+j}$ equals 1 if $i+j$ is an even number and equals -1 otherwise. If $i+j$ is odd, the sign of the minor is switched, while if $i+j$ is even it is left unchanged. This is called the *checkerboard rule*, noting that the pattern of pluses and minuses at row i and column j is like the white and black squares of the checkerboard or chessboard. With these definitions, the general formula for the determinant of A $(n \times n)$ can be given as follows: For *any* i, $1 \leq i \leq n$,

$$|A| = \sum_{j=1}^{n} a_{ij}c_{ij}. \tag{3.8}$$

2 The terms *adjugate* and *adjunct* are also used for this matrix.

3 The term *principal minor* is used for the cases where the retained row and column indices match.

This is, in many ways, a remarkable formula. The first interesting fact is that it holds true for any value of n. This can be used to evaluate any determinant. The second remarkable fact is that the choice of i is immaterial. Thinking of the formula as 'expanding along the ith row' of the matrix, with elements $(a_{i1}, a_{i2}, \dots, a_{in})$ appearing in the sum, formula (3.8) yields the same value for any choice of row i. Indeed, expansion by column is also equivalent, and the formula

$$|\boldsymbol{A}| = \sum_{i=1}^{n} c_{ij} a_{ij} \tag{3.9}$$

works for any j.

Formula (3.8) is recursive in the sense that it depends on the n minors m_{ij}, which are also determinants but in this case of dimension $n - 1$. To implement the formula, these also have to be computed, and the same formula may be applied where now the minors are of order $n - 2$. The recursion proceeds, applied to matrices of diminishing dimension, until there is just a single term in the sum, and then the cofactor is set to 1.

The formula covers the cases already described. For $n = 1$ the single cofactor is 1, while for $n = 2$, the two cofactors are the suitably signed (by the checkerboard rule) elements from the 'other' row. Expanding on the first row, these are a_{22} and $-a_{21}$ as in (3.5), although note how the formula also works for expansion on the second row, as well as on either column.

In the 3×3 case, write the matrix as

$$\boldsymbol{A} = \begin{bmatrix} a_{11} & a_{12} & a_{13} \\ a_{21} & a_{22} & a_{23} \\ a_{31} & a_{32} & a_{33} \end{bmatrix}.$$

Expanding on row 1, (3.8) gives

$$\begin{aligned} |\boldsymbol{A}| &= a_{11}(a_{22}a_{33} - a_{32}a_{23}) - a_{12}(a_{21}a_{33} - a_{31}a_{23}) + a_{13}(a_{21}a_{32} - a_{31}a_{22}) \\ &= a_{11}a_{22}a_{33} + a_{12}a_{23}a_{31} + a_{13}a_{21}a_{32} \\ &\qquad - a_{11}a_{23}a_{32} - a_{12}a_{21}a_{33} - a_{13}a_{22}a_{31} \end{aligned} \tag{3.10}$$

This is a sum of six terms, and each term is the product of three matrix elements, one drawn from each row of the matrix and also one from each column. The sign pattern is the consequence of the checkerboard rule operating at two levels. Apply formula (3.8) for the cases $i = 2$ and $i = 3$, and also for the three cases of (3.9), to verify that the identical formula (3.10) is obtained in each case.

The general rule for a $n \times n$ matrix is that the determinant is the sum of $n!$ terms,[4] each the product of n matrix elements, one from each row and one from each column, and half of them with changed sign. With choices of row or column for expansion at each recursive step, there are many ways to do the calculation, but reflection may convince the reader that the same formula must emerge in all cases. If the factors of each term are placed in order of the row subscripts, the sets of column subscripts include all the $n!$ possible permutations of $1, 2, \dots, n$. The acute reader may even observe the fact that the sign changes if the permutation of the column subscripts is obtained by an odd number

4 See Appendix A on n-factorial.

of position swaps and is unchanged in the case of an even number of position swaps. Just how the checkerboard rule achieves this pattern is something to ponder.

One useful fact that emerges from (3.8) is the rule for determinants of scalar products. Since a scalar product multiplies every element of the matrix by the scalar, it must be the case that for scalar c,

$$|c\boldsymbol{A}| = c^n|\boldsymbol{A}|. \tag{3.11}$$

Another very useful fact is that the determinant of a *triangular* matrix is the product of the diagonal elements. A lower triangular matrix has only zeros above the main diagonal (column subscripts exceeding row subscripts), and the result is easily shown by expanding along the top row in (3.8), so that the sums have a single nonzero term at each recursive step. An upper triangular matrix is just the transpose of the lower triangular case, and in this case expanding on the bottom rows at each stage yields the same result. The same logic extends to *diagonal* matrices, which have all nondiagonal elements zero and hence are both upper and lower triangular.

Formula (3.8) has in effect been plucked out of the air, and its only claim on our attention thus far is that (3.7) does yield the correct inverse matrix in the 1×1 and 2×2 cases. The task is now to show that the generalization is valid and that the formula is intimately connected with the construction of matrix inverses of any dimension.

The argument has three steps. First, consider the effect on the determinant of interchanging two rows of the matrix. With $n = 2$, it is easy to verify that thanks to the checkerboard rule, the effect is to change the sign of the determinant. But now visualize what happens if $n > 2$. At each recursion of (3.8) to evaluate minors of smaller dimension, there is a choice of row to expand on. Provided the chosen row is not one of those that has been interchanged, the 'a_{ij}' elements are the same as before. Let this be done each time, until the minors to be computed are of order 2 and the rows in question must be the switched ones. At this point, the factor of -1 enters the product. Each of the terms in (3.8) gets the sign change. The conclusion that swapping the positions of two rows changes the sign of the determinant holds for any size of matrix. As another way to visualize this effect, consider the 3×3 case and see how the switch results in the terms in (3.10) changing places and also signs.

Next, suppose that two rows of $\boldsymbol{A}$ are the same. Swapping them clearly cannot change the determinant, but it must at the same time change its sign, by the preceding argument. These two facts can only mean that the determinant of this matrix is zero.

Finally, consider a modified version of formula (3.8) in which the cofactors relate not to row i but to a different row, say, row k. Note that these cofactors are computed from elements of row i, as if it had not been deleted. The formula is identical to one that would be obtained with a matrix in which row i occurred twice. Hence, by the preceding paragraph, this formula must have the value zero. For each i and $k \neq i$, we have

$$\sum_{j=1}^{n} a_{ij}c_{kj} = 0. \tag{3.12}$$

Now for the clincher. Let $\boldsymbol{C}$ denote the matrix having cofactor c_{ij} for its $(i,j)^{\text{th}}$ element. Putting together (3.8) and (3.12) and applying the matrix product formula (2.3), the conclusion is that

$$\boldsymbol{A}\boldsymbol{C}' = |\boldsymbol{A}|\boldsymbol{I}_n.$$

In other words, if (3.7) does define the inverse matrix, it must be the case that

$$\text{adj } \boldsymbol{A} = \boldsymbol{C}'. \tag{3.13}$$

The adjoint matrix for the general $n \times n$ matrix is none other than the transpose of the matrix of cofactors. To satisfy both parts of (3.2) to define the inverse, reprise the argument using (3.9) to obtain

$$\boldsymbol{C}'\boldsymbol{A} = |\boldsymbol{A}|\boldsymbol{I}_n.$$

The problem of inverting a matrix is now solved! Given that the cofactors are just appropriately signed determinants, it turns out that, in principle, a sequence of determinant evaluations are all that is needed to invert a matrix.

3.3 Transposes and Products

The operations of inversion and transposition are interchangeable, as can be seen by considering the transposed form of (3.1),

$$\boldsymbol{x}'\boldsymbol{A}' = \boldsymbol{b}'.$$

This system can be solved by postmultiplying both sides by $(\boldsymbol{A}')^{-1}$ to get

$$\boldsymbol{x}' = \boldsymbol{b}'(\boldsymbol{A}')^{-1}. \tag{3.14}$$

However, applying rule (2.4) for transposition of a product to the solution of (3.1) gives

$$\begin{aligned}\boldsymbol{x}' &= (\boldsymbol{A}^{-1}\boldsymbol{b})' \\ &= \boldsymbol{b}'(\boldsymbol{A}^{-1})'.\end{aligned} \tag{3.15}$$

It follows that

$$(\boldsymbol{A}^{-1})' = (\boldsymbol{A}')^{-1}. \tag{3.16}$$

This equality amounts to

$$\frac{1}{|\boldsymbol{A}|}(\text{adj } \boldsymbol{A})' = \frac{1}{|\boldsymbol{A}'|}\text{adj } (\boldsymbol{A}').$$

Given the equivalence of (3.8) and (3.9), it follows in particular that

$$|\boldsymbol{A}'| = |\boldsymbol{A}|.$$

If $\boldsymbol{A}$ and $\boldsymbol{B}$ are $n \times n$ nonsingular matrices, what can be said about the product $\boldsymbol{AB}$? To answer this question, consider the system of equations

$$\boldsymbol{ABx} = \boldsymbol{c}$$

where $\boldsymbol{c}$ and $\boldsymbol{x}$ are n-vectors. Clearly, this system can be solved stepwise with first

$$\boldsymbol{Bx} = \boldsymbol{A}^{-1}\boldsymbol{c}$$

and then

$$\boldsymbol{x} = \boldsymbol{B}^{-1}\boldsymbol{A}^{-1}\boldsymbol{c}$$

This confirms the identity

$$(\boldsymbol{AB})^{-1} = \boldsymbol{B}^{-1}\boldsymbol{A}^{-1}. \tag{3.17}$$

Letting the matrix of cofactors of $\boldsymbol{A}$ be $\boldsymbol{C}_A$ and the matrix of cofactors of $\boldsymbol{B}$ be $\boldsymbol{C}_B$ and using rule (2.4) for transposition of a product,

$$\begin{aligned}(\boldsymbol{AB})^{-1} &= \boldsymbol{B}^{-1}\boldsymbol{A}^{-1} \\ &= \left(\frac{1}{|\boldsymbol{B}|}\boldsymbol{C}'_B\right)\left(\frac{1}{|\boldsymbol{A}|}\boldsymbol{C}'_A\right) \\ &= \frac{1}{|\boldsymbol{A}||\boldsymbol{B}|}(\boldsymbol{C}_A\boldsymbol{C}_B)'. \end{aligned} \tag{3.18}$$

The last member of (3.18) shows that the adjoint matrix of $\boldsymbol{AB}$ is the transposed product of the cofactor matrices and also that the determinant of the product is the product of the determinants:

$$|\boldsymbol{AB}| = |\boldsymbol{A}||\boldsymbol{B}|. \tag{3.19}$$

Further, consider the case $\boldsymbol{B} = \boldsymbol{A}^{-1}$ such that $\boldsymbol{AB} = \boldsymbol{I}$. The identity matrix, as a case of the rule for diagonal matrices, has a determinant of unity. Then, (3.19) shows that the determinant of the inverse is the reciprocal of the determinant:

$$|\boldsymbol{A}^{-1}| = \frac{1}{|\boldsymbol{A}|}. \tag{3.20}$$

3.4 Cramer's Rule

While the full-dress matrix inversion delivers the complete solution of a linear equation system, all that is strictly needed to solve

$$\boldsymbol{Ax} = \boldsymbol{b}$$

for $\boldsymbol{x}$ is to compute the product $\boldsymbol{A}^{-1}\boldsymbol{b}$. For this purpose alone, it is not necessary to compute the complete inverse. In fact, just two determinants suffice to evaluate each element of $\boldsymbol{x}$, one of which is $|\boldsymbol{A}|$ itself, so a total of just $n+1$ determinants does the whole job.

Consider x_j, the jth element of $\boldsymbol{x}$. Let $\boldsymbol{A}_j$ denote the matrix constructed by replacing column j of $\boldsymbol{A}$ by $\boldsymbol{b}$, and consider formula (3.8) applied to the transpose of this matrix, $\boldsymbol{A}'_j$, of which the vector $\boldsymbol{b}'$ is the jth row. Expanding on row j, the determinant in question has the form

$$|\boldsymbol{A}'_j| = \sum_{i=1}^{n} c_{ji}b_i \tag{3.21}$$

where c_{ji} is the $(i,j)^{\text{th}}$ element of the transposed cofactor matrix $\boldsymbol{C}'$. Since adj $\boldsymbol{A} = \boldsymbol{C}'$, the sum in (3.21), using the product formula (2.3), is the jth element of the n-vector

$$\begin{aligned}\boldsymbol{C}'\boldsymbol{b} &= (\text{adj } \boldsymbol{A})\boldsymbol{b} \\ &= |\boldsymbol{A}|\boldsymbol{A}^{-1}\boldsymbol{b} \\ &= |\boldsymbol{A}|\boldsymbol{x}.\end{aligned}$$

Since the determinant is invariant to transposition, $|A_j'| = |A_j|$, and it follows that

$$x_j = \frac{|A_j|}{|A|}.$$

3.5 Partitioning and Inversion

This section considers the inversion of matrices in partitioned form. The formulae may appear discouragingly complicated, but these results prove extremely useful in practice. By all means skip the derivations at first reading, but a little time and patience devoted to these arguments will sooner or later be amply rewarded.

Consider the partitioned equation system

$$\begin{bmatrix} A & B \\ C & D \end{bmatrix} \begin{bmatrix} x \\ y \end{bmatrix} = \begin{bmatrix} f \\ g \end{bmatrix} \tag{3.22}$$

where the partitioning of the $n \times n$ matrix is into n_1 and n_2 rows and also n_1 and n_2 columns, so $\boldsymbol{A}$ and $\boldsymbol{D}$ are both square. Assume that $\boldsymbol{D}$ is nonsingular, although there is no requirement for $\boldsymbol{A}$ to be nonsingular. $\boldsymbol{x}$ and $\boldsymbol{f}$ are both n_1-vectors, and $\boldsymbol{y}$ and $\boldsymbol{g}$ are both n_2-vectors. Write these equations in the form

$$\boldsymbol{Ax} + \boldsymbol{By} = \boldsymbol{f} \tag{3.23}$$

$$\boldsymbol{Cx} + \boldsymbol{Dy} = \boldsymbol{g}. \tag{3.24}$$

Solve this pair of equations stepwise. First solve (3.24) as

$$\boldsymbol{y} = \boldsymbol{D}^{-1}(\boldsymbol{g} - \boldsymbol{Cx}), \tag{3.25}$$

then substitute for $\boldsymbol{y}$ in (3.23) and rearrange to get

$$(\boldsymbol{A} - \boldsymbol{BD}^{-1}\boldsymbol{C})\boldsymbol{x} = \boldsymbol{f} - \boldsymbol{BD}^{-1}\boldsymbol{g}. \tag{3.26}$$

If the matrix in (3.22) is nonsingular, the $n_1 \times n_1$ matrix on the left-hand side of (3.26) is also nonsingular.[5] Therefore, without loss of generality define

$$\boldsymbol{E} = (\boldsymbol{A} - \boldsymbol{BD}^{-1}\boldsymbol{C})^{-1}$$

and solve (3.26) as

$$\boldsymbol{x} = \boldsymbol{Ef} - \boldsymbol{EBD}^{-1}\boldsymbol{g}. \tag{3.27}$$

The last step is to substitute (3.27) into (3.25) and rearrange, to give

$$\boldsymbol{y} = -\boldsymbol{D}^{-1}\boldsymbol{CEf} + (\boldsymbol{D}^{-1} + \boldsymbol{D}^{-1}\boldsymbol{CEBD}^{-1})\boldsymbol{g}. \tag{3.28}$$

Equations (3.27) and (3.28) are the complete solution to the partitioned system (3.22), and they show that the partitioned form of the inverse is

$$\begin{bmatrix} A & B \\ C & D \end{bmatrix}^{-1} = \begin{bmatrix} E & -EBD^{-1} \\ -D^{-1}CE & D^{-1} + D^{-1}CEBD^{-1} \end{bmatrix} \tag{3.29}$$

5 See equation (3.31), and also Problem 8 of Exercises 4.6.

At any rate, (3.29) is one version of the partitioned inverse formula. If $\boldsymbol{A}$ is nonsingular (though $\boldsymbol{D}$ could be singular), a complementary version of the formula can be found by solving (3.23) and (3.24) in reverse order (an exercise for the reader). This is

$$\begin{bmatrix} A & B \\ C & D \end{bmatrix}^{-1} = \begin{bmatrix} A^{-1} + A^{-1}BFCA^{-1} & -A^{-1}BF \\ -FCA^{-1} & F \end{bmatrix} \tag{3.30}$$

where $\boldsymbol{F} = (\boldsymbol{D} - \boldsymbol{C}\boldsymbol{A}^{-1}\boldsymbol{B})^{-1}$. Believe it or not, these two representations are identical in value.[6]

Partitioned determinant formulae can be found similarly. Assuming $\boldsymbol{D}$ nonsingular, consider the following easily verified decomposition of (3.29):

$$\begin{bmatrix} E & -EBD^{-1} \\ -D^{-1}CE & D^{-1} + D^{-1}CEBD^{-1} \end{bmatrix}$$

$$= \begin{bmatrix} E & \mathbf{0} \\ \mathbf{0} & I_{n_2} \end{bmatrix} \begin{bmatrix} I_{n_1} & \mathbf{0} \\ \mathbf{0} & D^{-1} \end{bmatrix} \begin{bmatrix} I_{n_1} & \mathbf{0} \\ -CE & I_{n_2} \end{bmatrix} \begin{bmatrix} I_{n_1} & -BD^{-1} \\ \mathbf{0} & I_{n_2} \end{bmatrix}$$

$$= P_1 P_2 P_3 P_4$$

say, where the second equality is just to assign symbols to the four matrix factors. Recall that the boldface $\mathbf{0}$ stands for a zero matrix of the appropriate dimension. It's a good exercise for the reader to perform these partitioned multiplications in sequence, to establish that the left-hand side really does match the right-hand side. The object here to calculate the determinant of each factor, recalling from (3.19) that the determinant of the product is the product of the determinants.

Applying formula (3.8) to $\boldsymbol{P}_1$, expand along the bottom rows at each of the first n_2 recursions, leading to the result $|\boldsymbol{P}_1| = |\boldsymbol{E}|$. The same reasoning gives $|\boldsymbol{P}_2| = |\boldsymbol{D}^{-1}|$. $\boldsymbol{P}_3$ and $\boldsymbol{P}_4$ are both triangular matrices, with ones on the diagonals, so $|\boldsymbol{P}_3| = |\boldsymbol{P}_4| = 1$. The conclusion is that the determinant of the matrix (3.29) has the form $|\boldsymbol{E}|\,|\boldsymbol{D}^{-1}|$. Finally, using (3.20), it follows immediately that

$$\begin{vmatrix} A & B \\ C & D \end{vmatrix} = |A - BD^{-1}C||D|. \tag{3.31}$$

Using the same lines of argument on the form (3.30), this time assuming $\boldsymbol{A}$ nonsingular yields the equivalent expression

$$\begin{vmatrix} A & B \\ C & D \end{vmatrix} = |D - CA^{-1}B||A|. \tag{3.32}$$

These formulae can be applied to most cases of interest, but it should be noted that matrices exist that are nonsingular in spite of both $\boldsymbol{A}$ and $\boldsymbol{D}$ being singular matrices in the partition. A simple example is

$$\begin{bmatrix} \mathbf{0} & I_n \\ I_n & \mathbf{0} \end{bmatrix} \tag{3.33}$$

---

6 Equating the top-left blocks in each formula and defining $\boldsymbol{G}$ by $\boldsymbol{D} = -\boldsymbol{G}^{-1}$ yields what is known as the *Woodbury identity*

$$(A + BGC)^{-1} = A^{-1} - A^{-1}B(G^{-1} + CA^{-1}B)^{-1}CA^{-1}.$$

where in this case $\mathbf{0}$ is a square $n \times n$ matrix of zeros. This particular case is easily verified to be its own inverse and hence to have a determinant of 1, but the square partitions of every order have both the diagonal blocks singular, with at least one zero column.

3.6 A Note on Computation

Econometric computation, except of the very simplest type, is always done using dedicated computer software. The way calculations are done in practice, with a view to speed and numerical precision, is often quite remote from the formal definition of the function in question. Take the determinant formula in (3.8). While this is a good formula for understanding how determinants behave, it is a bad one for actually computing a determinant unless the matrix is small, since for large matrices it is *extremely* slow. The number of 'floating point operations' (additions and multiplications) required to evaluate all the minors is of the order $n!$ where n is the dimension of the matrix. This is a number that rapidly becomes very large; for example, $10! = 3,628,800$.

There are various tricks that can vastly reduce this burden. The *elementary row operations* are transformations of a matrix that have known effects on its determinant, and the result of a sequence of such operations can make the determinant trivial to calculate. In particular, we have noted that the determinant of an upper triangular matrix is just the product of the diagonal elements.

The row operations are as follows:

1. *Interchange two rows.* As noted on page 36, this changes the sign of the determinant.
2. *Multiply a row by a scalar.* This multiplies the determinant by the same scalar, as is clear from (3.8).
3. *Add a scalar multiple of a row to another row.* This leaves the determinant unchanged. Expanding on row i, to which row k is added with scalar weight $b \neq 0$, it has the form

$$\sum_{j=1}^{n} a_{ij}c_{ij} + b\sum_{j=1}^{n} a_{kj}c_{ij} = \sum_{j=1}^{n} a_{ij}c_{ij}.$$

   As also pointed out on page 36, the second term is the determinant of a matrix with a repeated row, and vanishes.

Let the matrix in question, written out by rows, be

$$A = \begin{bmatrix} \boldsymbol{a}_1' \\ \boldsymbol{a}_2' \\ \vdots \\ \boldsymbol{a}_n' \end{bmatrix}.$$

Assuming $a_{11} \neq 0$, row operation 3 can be applied $n-1$ times to get

$$A^{(1)} = \begin{bmatrix} \boldsymbol{a}_1' \\ \boldsymbol{a}_2' - \dfrac{a_{21}}{a_{11}}\boldsymbol{a}_1' \\ \vdots \\ \boldsymbol{a}_n' - \dfrac{a_{n1}}{a_{11}}\boldsymbol{a}_1' \end{bmatrix}.$$

The first column of $\boldsymbol{A}^{(1)}$ has elements 2, ..., n equal to zero by construction. Now repeat this operation on matrix $\boldsymbol{A}^{(1)}$ starting from row 2, with the scale factors now set to $a_{j2}^{(1)}/a_{22}^{(1)}$. This has the effect of setting elements $3, \dots, n$ of column 2 of the transformed matrix, say $\boldsymbol{A}^{(2)}$, to zero. Repeating these steps for columns $1, 2, \dots, n-1$ in turn results in a upper triangular matrix $\boldsymbol{A}^{(n-1)}$, whose determinant matches that of the original and is easily computed as the product of the diagonal elements.

The one evident problem with this scheme is that one of the divisors, a_{11}, $a_{22}^{(1)}$, etc., might be zero. In this event, the workaround is to perform a row swap of the row in question for one of those below it. If on working through the rows in sequence all the elements in question are found to be zero, then the matrix must be singular. The algorithm can then return 0. Otherwise, all that is needed is to count the number of swaps, say m, and switch the sign of the determinant if m is odd. Multiplying it by $(-1)^m$ is the easiest way. The number of floating-point operations involved in these calculations is of the order n^3, a mere 1000 for the case $n = 10$.

Inverting a matrix can use the same tricks. The so-called *Gauss-Jordan elimination* technique works with the $n \times 2n$ matrix $[A\ I_n]$. Row operations are performed with the aim of reducing the first n columns of this matrix to $\boldsymbol{I}_n$, because these same operations convert the right-hand block to $\boldsymbol{A}^{-1}$. To appreciate this fact, note that

$$\boldsymbol{A}^{-1}[\boldsymbol{A}\ \boldsymbol{I}_n] = [\boldsymbol{I}_n\ \boldsymbol{A}^{-1}]. \tag{3.34}$$

Product formula (2.3) shows that each row of $\boldsymbol{I}_n = \boldsymbol{A}^{-1}\boldsymbol{A}$ is a linear combination of the rows of $\boldsymbol{A}$, with weights given by the rows of $\boldsymbol{A}^{-1}$. The same operations applied to the rows of $\boldsymbol{I}_n$ in the second block of (3.34) yield the weights themselves. These linear combinations can be effected by a sequence of elementary row operations that the elimination procedure must reproduce. This can be illustrated rather simply by the 2×2 case, so that

$$[\boldsymbol{A}\ \boldsymbol{I}_n] = \begin{bmatrix} a_{11} & a_{12} & 1 & 0 \\ a_{21} & a_{22} & 0 & 1 \end{bmatrix}.$$

Here are the four row operations required, where $D = a_{11}a_{22} - a_{12}a_{21}$.

$$\textbf{Step 1}: \quad \begin{bmatrix} 1 & \dfrac{a_{12}}{a_{11}} & \dfrac{1}{a_{11}} & 0 \\ a_{21} & a_{22} & 0 & 1 \end{bmatrix}$$

$$\textbf{Step 2}: \quad \begin{bmatrix} 1 & \dfrac{a_{12}}{a_{11}} & \dfrac{1}{a_{11}} & 0 \\ 0 & \dfrac{D}{a_{11}} & -\dfrac{a_{21}}{a_{11}} & 1 \end{bmatrix}$$

$$\textbf{Step 3}: \quad \begin{bmatrix} 1 & \dfrac{a_{12}}{a_{11}} & \dfrac{1}{a_{11}} & 0 \\ 0 & 1 & -\dfrac{a_{21}}{D} & \dfrac{a_{11}}{D} \end{bmatrix}$$

$$\textbf{Step 4}: \quad \begin{bmatrix} 1 & 0 & \dfrac{a_{22}}{D} & -\dfrac{a_{12}}{D} \\ 0 & 1 & -\dfrac{a_{21}}{D} & \dfrac{a_{11}}{D} \end{bmatrix}$$

At Step 1, the first row has been divided by a_{11}. At Step 2 the second row has had the first row times a_{21} subtracted from it, and notice that this produces 0 in the (2, 1) position and

$$a_{22} - \frac{a_{12}}{a_{11}} a_{21} = \frac{D}{a_{11}}$$

in the (2, 2) position. At Step 3, the second row has been divided by the second diagonal element D/a_{11}. Finally, at Step 4, the first row has the second row times the (1, 2) element a_{12}/a_{11} subtracted from it. This sequence of operations, division of row j by its diagonal element and then the augmentation of each of the other rows, for $j = 1, \ldots, n$, is easily coded for software implementation. In the case where the diagonal element is zero, an extra operation is needed, swapping with the next row below having the corresponding element nonzero. If no such row exists, then the matrix is singular.

Notwithstanding that students are often taught to perform the kind of exercise illustrated, these are really mindless jobs for machines to do. For matrices of order greater than three at most, matrix inversion by hand is only worth attempting if the matrix is *sparse*, meaning that it has a good number of zero elements. In such cases the partitioned inverse formula is often the most convenient computational aid.

3.7 Exercises

1 Are the following statements true or false?

(a) The adjoint of a square matrix is the matrix having the principal minors as its elements.

(b) If $\boldsymbol{A}$ and $\boldsymbol{D}$ are square matrices of the same dimension, $\boldsymbol{D}$ is nonsingular, and $\boldsymbol{B} = \boldsymbol{D}\boldsymbol{A}\boldsymbol{D}^{-1}$, the determinant of $\boldsymbol{B}$ is equal to the determinant of $\boldsymbol{A}$.

(c) The determinant of a matrix $\boldsymbol{A}$ $(n \times n)$ may be calculated as

$$|\mathbf{A}| = \sum_{j=1}^{n} (-1)^{n+j} a_{nj} m_{nj}$$

where m_{nj} denotes the determinant of the matrix obtained by deleting the nth row and j^{th} column from $\boldsymbol{A}$.

(d) If $\boldsymbol{A}$, $\boldsymbol{B}$, and $\boldsymbol{C}$ are all $n \times n$ symmetric nonsingular matrices,

$$(\boldsymbol{ABC})^{-1} = \boldsymbol{A}^{-1}\boldsymbol{B}^{-1}\boldsymbol{C}^{-1}.$$

(e) The determinant of a square matrix is equal to the determinant of its transpose if and only if the matrix is symmetric.

(f) The determinant of a lower triangular matrix is the product of the diagonal elements.

(g) The calculation of two determinants is sufficient to evaluate an unknown in a system of linear equations.

2 Do the following systems have (i) a unique solution, (ii) no solution, or (iii) many solutions? Draw graphs to illustrate your answers.

(a) $$\begin{aligned} 2x_1 + 3x_2 &= 1 \\ x_1 + 3x_2 &= 2 \end{aligned}$$

(b) $$\begin{aligned} 2x_1 + 3x_2 &= 1 \\ 2x_1 + 3x_2 &= 2 \end{aligned}$$

(c) $$\begin{aligned} 2x_1 + 3x_2 &= 1 \\ 4x_1 + 6x_2 &= 2 \end{aligned}$$

3 Calculate the inverses of these matrices.

(a) $$\begin{bmatrix} 1 & 0 & 0 \\ 0 & 2 & 4 \\ 0 & 0 & 1 \end{bmatrix}$$

(b) $$\begin{bmatrix} 3 & 0 & 0 & 0 \\ 0 & 2 & 0 & 0 \\ 0 & 0 & 1 & 1 \\ 1 & 0 & 1 & 2 \end{bmatrix}$$

(c) $$\begin{bmatrix} 1 & 0 & 0 & 0 & 1 \\ 0 & 2 & 0 & 0 & 0 \\ 0 & 0 & 3 & 0 & 0 \\ 0 & 0 & 0 & 3 & 1 \\ 0 & 0 & 1 & 0 & 1 \end{bmatrix}$$

4 What is the determinant of this matrix?

$$\begin{bmatrix} 3 & 0 & 0 & 0 & 0 & 0 & 0 \\ 0 & 2 & 0 & 0 & 0 & 0 & 0 \\ 0 & 0 & 1 & 0 & 0 & 0 & 0 \\ 1 & 0 & 1 & 2 & 0 & 0 & 0 \\ 5 & 2 & 33 & 29 & 2 & 0 & 0 \\ 5 & 2 & 0 & 5 & 3 & 1 & 0 \\ 5 & 0 & 4 & 4 & 0 & 0 & 2 \end{bmatrix}$$

5 Use Cramer's rule to solve the following systems of equations.

(a) $$\begin{bmatrix} 1 & 0 & 1 \\ 1 & 1 & 0 \\ 0 & 1 & 1 \end{bmatrix} \begin{bmatrix} x_1 \\ x_2 \\ x_3 \end{bmatrix} = \begin{bmatrix} 1 \\ 0 \\ 0 \end{bmatrix}$$

(b) $$\begin{bmatrix} 1 & 0 & 1 \\ 1 & 1 & 1 \\ 0 & 1 & 1 \end{bmatrix} \begin{bmatrix} x_1 \\ x_2 \\ x_3 \end{bmatrix} = \begin{bmatrix} 1 \\ 0 \\ 1 \end{bmatrix}$$

6 For the matrices

$$\boldsymbol{A} = \begin{bmatrix} 1 & 2 \\ 3 & 4 \end{bmatrix}, \quad \boldsymbol{B} = \begin{bmatrix} 2 & 1 \\ 1 & 2 \end{bmatrix}$$

calculate

(a) $(\boldsymbol{AB})^{-1}$
(b) $\boldsymbol{B}^{-1}\boldsymbol{A}^{-1}$
(c) $(\boldsymbol{BA})^{-1}$
(d) $\boldsymbol{A}^{-1}\boldsymbol{B}^{-1}$

7 Let $\boldsymbol{A}$ $(n \times n)$ and $\boldsymbol{D}$ $(m \times m)$ be nonsingular, and $\boldsymbol{B}$ $(n \times m)$ and $\boldsymbol{C}$ $(m \times n)$ be any matrices such that $\begin{bmatrix} A & B \\ C & D \end{bmatrix}$ is nonsingular.

(a) Show by direct calculation that

$$\begin{bmatrix} A & B \\ C & D \end{bmatrix}^{-1} = \begin{bmatrix} E & -EBD^{-1} \\ -D^{-1}CE & D^{-1} + D^{-1}CEBD^{-1} \end{bmatrix}$$

where $\boldsymbol{E} = (\boldsymbol{A} - \boldsymbol{BD}^{-1}\boldsymbol{C})^{-1}$.

(b) Show by direct calculation that

$$\boldsymbol{EBD}^{-1} = \boldsymbol{A}^{-1}\boldsymbol{BF}$$

where $\boldsymbol{E} = (\boldsymbol{A} - \boldsymbol{BD}^{-1}\boldsymbol{C})^{-1}$ and $\boldsymbol{F} = (\boldsymbol{D} - \boldsymbol{CA}^{-1}\boldsymbol{B})^{-1}$.

8 Obtain the partitioned inverse of the transposed matrix $\begin{bmatrix} A & B \\ C & D \end{bmatrix}'$, assumed to be nonsingular, and show that this is the transpose of the partitioned inverse of $\begin{bmatrix} A & B \\ C & D \end{bmatrix}$.

4

The Least Squares Solution

4.1 Linear Dependence and Rank

Think of a matrix $\boldsymbol{A}$ $(m \times n)$ as an ordered collection of columns. Write a partitioned representation in the form

$$\boldsymbol{A} = [\boldsymbol{a}_1 \;\; \boldsymbol{a}_2 \cdots \boldsymbol{a}_n]$$

where for $j = 1, \ldots, n$ the $\boldsymbol{a}_j$ are m-vectors. Also let

$$\boldsymbol{b} = \begin{bmatrix} b_1 \\ b_2 \\ \vdots \\ b_n \end{bmatrix}$$

and so consider the m-vector

$$\begin{aligned} \boldsymbol{c} &= \boldsymbol{Ab} \\ &= \boldsymbol{a}_1 b_1 + \boldsymbol{a}_2 b_2 + \cdots + \boldsymbol{a}_n b_n. \end{aligned} \tag{4.1}$$

The product $\boldsymbol{Ab}$ can be viewed as a weighted sum of the columns of $\boldsymbol{A}$, with scalar weights given by the elements $b_1, \ldots, b_n$.

Now collect some important definitions.

1. Consider the collection of all the possible m-vectors $\boldsymbol{c}$ that have representation (4.1) for different choices of n-vector $\boldsymbol{b}$. This infinite collection is called the *column space* of $\boldsymbol{A}$ or the *space spanned by the columns of* $\boldsymbol{A}$.
2. If there exists no $\boldsymbol{b} \neq \boldsymbol{0}$ (having at least one element different from zero) such that $\boldsymbol{Ab} = \boldsymbol{0}$, the columns of $\boldsymbol{A}$ are said to be *linearly independent*. If there does exist $\boldsymbol{b} \neq \boldsymbol{0}$ such that $\boldsymbol{Ab} = \boldsymbol{0}$, then the columns are said to be *linearly dependent*.
3. The *rank* of $\boldsymbol{A}$ is the maximum number of columns, n or fewer, that can be selected from $\boldsymbol{a}_1, \boldsymbol{a}_2, \cdots, \boldsymbol{a}_n$ to form a linearly independent set.
4. The collection of all vectors $\boldsymbol{b}$, if any, such that $\boldsymbol{Ab} = \boldsymbol{0}$ is the *kernel* or *null space* of $\boldsymbol{A}$.
5. The *nullity* of $\boldsymbol{A}$ is the dimension of the null space, that is, the maximum number of linearly independent $\boldsymbol{b}$ satisfying $\boldsymbol{Ab} = \boldsymbol{0}$.

The rank of a matrix is the dimension of its column space. In other words, every element of the column space can be formed as a linear combination of just this number of linearly independent columns. If the nullity is positive, there exist one or more additional

An Introduction to Econometric Theory, First Edition. James Davidson.

Companion website: www.wiley.com/go/davidson/introecmettheory

columns of $\boldsymbol{A}$ that can be constructed as linear combinations of the linearly independent set, and the nullity is the rank of the corresponding set of weight vectors. The column dimension of a matrix is the sum of the rank and the nullity. Note that $\boldsymbol{A} = \boldsymbol{0}$ $(m \times n)$ is the only case for which the rank is zero and the nullity equal to n.

A key fact about rank is

$$\text{rank } \boldsymbol{A}' = \text{rank } \boldsymbol{A}. \tag{4.2}$$

A matrix has r linearly independent columns if and only if it has r linearly independent rows, these being the columns of the transposed matrix. To see why this must be true, consider a simple construction. If $\boldsymbol{A}$ is $m \times n$ and $\boldsymbol{A} \neq \boldsymbol{0}$, define $r \leq \min\{m, n\}$ to be the smallest integer such that a decomposition $\boldsymbol{A} = \boldsymbol{B}\boldsymbol{C}'$ exists for full-rank matrices $\boldsymbol{B}$ $(m \times r)$ and $\boldsymbol{C}$ $(n \times r)$. Such a decomposition always exists, for if r is the dimension of the column space of $\boldsymbol{A}$, the columns of $\boldsymbol{B}$ can be chosen to span this space. The columns of $\boldsymbol{A}$ then lie in the column space of $\boldsymbol{B}$ by construction. But $\boldsymbol{A}' = \boldsymbol{C}\boldsymbol{B}'$, so that the columns of $\boldsymbol{A}'$ lie by construction in the column space of $\boldsymbol{C}$, which also has dimension r. However, while row rank equals column rank, don't overlook the fact that in nonsquare matrices, column nullity (nullity$\boldsymbol{A}$) and row nullity (nullity $\boldsymbol{A}'$) are different.

The concept of rank may appear somewhat obscure, but it plays a critical role in determining the nature of the solutions of equation systems. Consider a $n \times n$ matrix $\boldsymbol{A}$ having rank of $n - 1$ or less. Then, by definition there exists an n-vector $\boldsymbol{x} \neq \boldsymbol{0}$ such that

$$\boldsymbol{A}\boldsymbol{x} = \boldsymbol{0}. \tag{4.3}$$

Assuming $\boldsymbol{A}$ to be nonsingular leads to

$$\begin{aligned} \boldsymbol{x} &= \boldsymbol{A}^{-1}\boldsymbol{0} \\ &= \boldsymbol{0}, \end{aligned}$$

which is a contradiction. Hence $\boldsymbol{A}$ must be singular. Similarly, if $\boldsymbol{A}$ is nonsingular, then $\boldsymbol{A}\boldsymbol{x} = \boldsymbol{0}$ implies $\boldsymbol{x} = \boldsymbol{0}$. Hence, again by definition, $\boldsymbol{A}$ must have full rank. We conclude that $\boldsymbol{A}$ is nonsingular *if and only if* it has full rank. This also shows why the rank of a collection of n-vectors cannot exceed n. If $\boldsymbol{A}$ $(n \times n)$ is nonsingular, then for any $\boldsymbol{c}$ $(n \times 1)$ there must exist $\boldsymbol{x}$ such that

$$\boldsymbol{A}\boldsymbol{x} = \boldsymbol{c} \tag{4.4}$$

defined by $\boldsymbol{x} = \boldsymbol{A}^{-1}\boldsymbol{c}$. In this case, *every* n-vector lies in the column space of $\boldsymbol{A}$.

The correspondence between full rank and nonsingularity is important both because it connects the concept of rank with the problem of solving equations systems, and because it suggests an easily implemented method for testing rank. Suppose (with no loss of generality, since otherwise transpose it) that a matrix has more columns (n) than rows (m). Its rank cannot exceed m, so columns may be discarded to create a square $m \times m$ matrix whose rank may be tested by computing its determinant. There are $\binom{n}{m}$ different ways[1] to discard $n - m$ out of n columns, but there only needs to be one way to do this to produce a nonsingular matrix for the matrix to have rank m. It may be necessary to test several alternative deletions to find a full-rank case, and only if all of the $\binom{n}{m}$ choices yield a zero determinant does it follow that the matrix has rank smaller

---

1 See Appendix A for the explanation of $\binom{n}{m}$.

than m. At this point, both rows and columns need to be discarded. The rank of $\boldsymbol{A}$ is equated with the dimension of the largest nonsingular square submatrix of $\boldsymbol{A}$. In summary, to determine the rank of any matrix, not necessarily square, find the largest square submatrix having nonzero determinant.

If $\boldsymbol{A}$ is square and nonsingular, then setting $\boldsymbol{c} = \boldsymbol{0}$ in (4.4) necessarily gives the solution $\boldsymbol{x} = \boldsymbol{0}$. However, if $\boldsymbol{A}$ is singular, nonzero solutions exist to (4.3), and such equation systems are called *homogeneous*. The set of solutions of a homogeneous system spans the column null space of the matrix. Consider the partition of (4.3) into blocks of dimension r and $n - r$,

$$\begin{bmatrix} \boldsymbol{A}_{11} & \boldsymbol{A}_{12} \\ \boldsymbol{A}_{21} & \boldsymbol{A}_{22} \end{bmatrix} \begin{bmatrix} \boldsymbol{x}_1 \\ \boldsymbol{x}_2 \end{bmatrix} = \begin{bmatrix} \boldsymbol{0} \\ \boldsymbol{0} \end{bmatrix} \begin{matrix} r \\ n-r \end{matrix} \tag{4.5}$$

where $\boldsymbol{A}_{11}$ $(r \times r)$ is the largest nonsingular submatrix of $\boldsymbol{A}$, possibly after re-ordering of rows and columns. By construction, the second block of $n - r$ rows in (4.5) consists just of linear combinations of the first block, and there exists a matrix $\boldsymbol{B}$ $(n - r \times r)$ such that $\boldsymbol{A}_{21} = \boldsymbol{B}\boldsymbol{A}_{11}$ and $\boldsymbol{A}_{22} = \boldsymbol{B}\boldsymbol{A}_{12}$. The set of solutions can therefore be represented by

$$\boldsymbol{x} = \begin{bmatrix} \boldsymbol{x}_1 \\ \boldsymbol{x}_2 \end{bmatrix} = \begin{bmatrix} -\boldsymbol{A}_{11}^{-1}\boldsymbol{A}_{12} \\ \boldsymbol{I}_{n-r} \end{bmatrix} \boldsymbol{w} \tag{4.6}$$

for all vectors $\boldsymbol{w}$ of dimension $n - r$. In the case that arises most often with $r = n - 1$ (see in particular Section 9.3 in this connection), the solution is unique up to a scale factor. In (4.6), $\boldsymbol{w}$ is a scalar, and if $\boldsymbol{x}$ is a solution, so is $\lambda\boldsymbol{x}$ for any $\lambda \neq 0$.

It is of course possible to specify a system of equations where the number of unknowns is different from the number of equations. If $\boldsymbol{A}$ is $m \times n$, then (4.4) is a system of m equations in n unknowns. If $m < n$, there are many solutions, the system imposing restrictions on $\boldsymbol{x}$ but not determining it uniquely, similarly to the homogeneous case. Assuming the m equations are linearly independent, form the partition $\boldsymbol{A} = [\boldsymbol{A}_1\ \boldsymbol{A}_2]$ where $\boldsymbol{A}_1$ $(m \times m)$ has full rank, after rearrangement of the columns if necessary. The solutions can then be given the general form

$$\boldsymbol{x} = \begin{bmatrix} \boldsymbol{x}_1 \\ \boldsymbol{x}_2 \end{bmatrix} = \begin{bmatrix} \boldsymbol{A}_1^{-1}\boldsymbol{c} \\ \boldsymbol{0} \end{bmatrix} + \begin{bmatrix} -\boldsymbol{A}_1^{-1}\boldsymbol{A}_2 \\ \boldsymbol{I}_{n-m} \end{bmatrix} \boldsymbol{w}$$

for arbitrary choice of $\boldsymbol{w}$ $(n - m \times 1)$.[2] If $m > n$, with more equations than unknowns, the relevant partition of (4.4) has the form

$$\begin{bmatrix} \boldsymbol{A}_1 \\ \boldsymbol{A}_2 \end{bmatrix} \boldsymbol{x} = \begin{bmatrix} \boldsymbol{c}_1 \\ \boldsymbol{c}_2 \end{bmatrix}$$

assuming $\boldsymbol{A}_1$ $(n \times n)$ to be nonsingular. A solution exists only in the special case $\boldsymbol{c}_2 = \boldsymbol{A}_2\boldsymbol{A}_1^{-1}\boldsymbol{c}_1$.

There are some important rules concerning the ranks of matrix products. The general rule is that the rank of the product cannot exceed the smaller of the ranks of the individual matrices. Symbolically,

$$\text{rank}\,\boldsymbol{AB} \leq \min\{\text{rank}\,\boldsymbol{A}, \text{rank}\,\boldsymbol{B}\}. \tag{4.7}$$

This inequality must hold since the columns of $\boldsymbol{AB}$ lie in the column space of $\boldsymbol{A}$, by construction, while the columns of $\boldsymbol{B}'\boldsymbol{A}'$ lie in the column space of $\boldsymbol{B}'$, the rank of $\boldsymbol{B}'$

2 See Appendix D for an alternative treatment of multiple solutions using the generalized inverse concept.

equalling that of $\boldsymbol{B}$ by (4.2). However, if $\boldsymbol{B}$ is square and nonsingular, note that (4.7) implies

$$\begin{aligned}\text{rank } \boldsymbol{AB} &\geq \text{rank } \boldsymbol{ABB}^{-1} \\ &= \text{rank } \boldsymbol{A}.\end{aligned}$$

It follows that in this case,

$$\text{rank } \boldsymbol{AB} = \text{rank } \boldsymbol{A}. \tag{4.8}$$

Another important result required in the sequel is that

$$\text{rank } \boldsymbol{A}'\boldsymbol{A} = \text{rank } \boldsymbol{A}. \tag{4.9}$$

This is demonstrated by showing that the column nullities of $\boldsymbol{A}$ and $\boldsymbol{A}'\boldsymbol{A}$ are equal, for since they have the same column dimension, their ranks must then also match. For any $\boldsymbol{x} \neq \boldsymbol{0}$, if $\boldsymbol{Ax} = \boldsymbol{0}$ then $\boldsymbol{A}'\boldsymbol{Ax} = \boldsymbol{0}$, but also if $\boldsymbol{A}'\boldsymbol{Ax} = \boldsymbol{0}$, then it must be the case that

$$\begin{aligned}\boldsymbol{x}'\boldsymbol{A}'\boldsymbol{Ax} &= (\boldsymbol{Ax})'\boldsymbol{Ax} \\ &= 0.\end{aligned}$$

This object is a scalar, the sum of squares of the elements of the vector $\boldsymbol{Ax}$, and it can be zero *only* if $\boldsymbol{Ax} = \boldsymbol{0}$. Hence, the null spaces of the two matrices have to be the same. It follows in the same way, in view of (4.2), that

$$\text{rank } \boldsymbol{AA}' = \text{rank } \boldsymbol{A}. \tag{4.10}$$

4.2 The General Linear Regression

With the concepts of Section 4.1 in mind, it is time to return to the first major application of matrix theory, the solution of the least squares problem for arbitrary numbers of regressors. Let $x_{1t}, \dots, x_{kt}$ and y_t for $t = 1, \dots, T$ denote a sample of T observations on $k + 1$ variables, connected by the equation

$$y_t = \beta_1 x_{1t} + \beta_2 x_{2t} + \cdots + \beta_k x_{kt} + u_t \tag{4.11}$$

where $\beta_1, \dots, \beta_k$ are fixed but unknown parameters. In this general framework, the intercept is no longer given a special symbol, because it is easiest to treat it in the same way as the slope coefficients. It is henceforth assumed, unless specified otherwise, that $x_{kt} = 1$ for every t. In other words, one of the explanatory variables is specified to be a column of ones.

Geometrically, imagine the observations as specifying points in k-dimensional Euclidean space, which is not so easy to visualize as three-dimensional space. The regression plane of Figure 1.6 now becomes a $k - 1$-dimensional *hyperplane*. Visual analogies are of little use here, but the algebraic representation of the equation, once it becomes familiar, soon renders such analogies irrelevant.

The next step is to convert (4.11) into a matrix representation. Define the k-vectors

$$\boldsymbol{\beta} = \begin{bmatrix} \beta_1 \\ \vdots \\ \beta_k \end{bmatrix} \quad (k \times 1), \quad \boldsymbol{x}_t = \begin{bmatrix} x_{1t} \\ \vdots \\ x_{kt} \end{bmatrix} \quad (k \times 1).$$

With these definitions, it is possible to write (4.11) compactly as

$$y_t = \boldsymbol{x}_t'\boldsymbol{\beta} + u_t.$$

This representation is often found useful for writing the regression equation for a particular observation. However, the main object is to write the full sample of observations in a single expression, and to do this, define the objects

$$\boldsymbol{y} = \begin{bmatrix} y_1 \\ \vdots \\ y_T \end{bmatrix} \quad (T \times 1), \quad \boldsymbol{X} = \begin{bmatrix} \boldsymbol{x}_1' \\ \vdots \\ \boldsymbol{x}_T' \end{bmatrix} \quad (T \times k), \quad \boldsymbol{u} = \begin{bmatrix} u_1 \\ \vdots \\ u_T \end{bmatrix} \quad (T \times 1)$$

where the dimensions of each are shown following the definitions. These expressions are rather bulky, so it is a good idea to be aware of the transposed 'on the line' space-saving alternatives. One can write $\boldsymbol{\beta} = (\beta_1, \dots, \beta_k)'$, and $\boldsymbol{x}_t = (x_{1t}, \dots, x_{kt})'$, and also $\boldsymbol{y} = (y_1, \dots, y_T)'$, $\boldsymbol{X} = (\boldsymbol{x}_1, \dots, \boldsymbol{x}_T)'$ and $\boldsymbol{u} = (u_1, \dots, u_T)'$.

The well-known full-sample representation of the regression equation is

$$\boldsymbol{y} = \boldsymbol{X}\boldsymbol{\beta} + \boldsymbol{u}, \tag{4.12}$$

which is easily verified to represent the T equalities (4.11) in a single vector expression. The theory of the least squares fit can now be reprised for this fully general case. Let $\boldsymbol{b}$ be an arbitrary k-vector, and define the T-vector

$$\boldsymbol{e}(\boldsymbol{b}) = \boldsymbol{y} - \boldsymbol{X}\boldsymbol{b}.$$

The sum of squares function is

$$S(\boldsymbol{b}) = \boldsymbol{e}(\boldsymbol{b})'\boldsymbol{e}(\boldsymbol{b}). \tag{4.13}$$

Define the least squares coefficient vector to be the k-vector $\hat{\boldsymbol{\beta}}$ such that $S(\hat{\boldsymbol{\beta}}) \le S(\boldsymbol{b})$ for all $\boldsymbol{b}$. The least squares residuals are

$$\hat{\boldsymbol{u}} = \boldsymbol{y} - \boldsymbol{X}\hat{\boldsymbol{\beta}}. \tag{4.14}$$

The following is what, in this fully general form, might be called the *fundamental theorem of least squares.*

Theorem: $\hat{\boldsymbol{\beta}}$ is the unique minimizer of S if and only if the columns of $\boldsymbol{X}$ are linearly independent (rank $(\boldsymbol{X}) = k$) and

$$\boldsymbol{X}'\hat{\boldsymbol{u}} = \boldsymbol{0}. \tag{4.15}$$

Noting the form of $\hat{\boldsymbol{u}}$ in (4.14), the least squares normal equations may be written, after substitution into (4.15) and rearrangement, as

$$\boldsymbol{X}'\boldsymbol{y} = \boldsymbol{X}'\boldsymbol{X}\hat{\boldsymbol{\beta}}.$$

Then, if and only if $\boldsymbol{X}'\boldsymbol{X}$ is nonsingular, the unique solution of the normal equations is

$$\hat{\boldsymbol{\beta}} = (\boldsymbol{X}'\boldsymbol{X})^{-1}\boldsymbol{X}'\boldsymbol{y}. \tag{4.16}$$

Before going any further, it may be helpful to see how this formula is constructed from the fundamental ingredients of statistical analysis, sums of squares and sums of products of the observations. Write out the element-wise representations of the components, recalling the assumption that $x_{kt} = 1$ for every t, as

$$X'X = \begin{bmatrix} \sum_{t=1}^{T} x_{1t}^2 & \cdots & \sum_{t=1}^{T} x_{1t}x_{k-1,t} & \sum_{t=1}^{T} x_{1t} \\ \vdots & \ddots & \vdots & \vdots \\ \sum_{t=1}^{T} x_{1t}x_{k-1,t} & \cdots & \sum_{t=1}^{T} x_{k-1,t}^2 & \sum_{t=1}^{T} x_{k-1,t} \\ \sum_{t=1}^{T} x_{1t} & \cdots & \sum_{t=1}^{T} x_{k-1,t} & T \end{bmatrix}$$

and

$$X'y = \begin{bmatrix} \sum_{t=1}^{T} x_{1t}y_t \\ \vdots \\ \sum_{t=1}^{T} x_{k-1,t}y_t \\ \sum_{t=1}^{T} y_t \end{bmatrix}.$$

The formula includes all the simple sums, as well as the sums of products of everything with *almost* everything else. 'Almost', because $\sum_{t=1}^{T} y_t^2$ alone does not appear in this formula, although it will feature subsequently, in the formula for the residual sum of squares.

The significant feature to note, as was pointed out back in Section 1.1, is that a multiple regression is exclusively a function of pairwise averages. Whether one speaks of sums or averages here is immaterial, because the factors of $1/T$, if included in (4.16), would be immediately cancelled via the inverse. Teasing out relationships between multiple variables turns out to be a matter of analyzing their pairwise correlations, a very useful simplifying feature of the linear framework. Formulae often look complicated, but at heart they have a simple basic structure, one that matrix algebra is well adapted to exploit.

4.3 Definite Matrices

A new concept is needed before the truth of the fundamental theorem can be demonstrated. A $n \times n$ matrix A is called *positive definite* if it has the property

$$z'Az > 0 \text{ for all } n\text{-vectors } z \neq \mathbf{0}.$$

Also A is called *positive semidefinite* (and also, equivalently, non-negative definite) if it has the property

$$z'Az \geq 0 \text{ for all } n\text{-vectors } z \neq \mathbf{0}.$$

The difference is that the weak inequality (admitting equality as a case) replaces the strong inequality of the first definition. Negative definite and negative semidefinite matrices are defined likewise, with these inequalities reversed. Although technically any square matrix can have these properties, the cases that matter are always symmetric.

It may be helpful to think of a positive (semi-) definite matrix as the generalization of the concept of a positive (non-negative) number in scalar algebra. The quantity $z'Az$ is a scalar called a *quadratic form* in $\boldsymbol{A}$, since it is an expression involving the squares and products of the elements of $\boldsymbol{z}$. Consider the case $n = 2$ as a concrete example:

$$\begin{bmatrix} z_1 & z_2 \end{bmatrix} \begin{bmatrix} a_{11} & a_{12} \\ a_{21} & a_{22} \end{bmatrix} \begin{bmatrix} z_1 \\ z_2 \end{bmatrix} = a_{11}z_1^2 + (a_{12} + a_{21})z_1z_2 + a_{22}z_2^2.$$

Whether this sum of terms is positive for all choices of z_1 and z_2 is clearly dependent on the signs and relative magnitudes of the matrix elements, but it is neither necessary nor sufficient that all the elements be positive. There is a very evident difference between a positive matrix and a positive definite matrix.

Enumerated here for later reference are a number of important results concerning definite matrices.

1. If $\boldsymbol{B}$ is any $m \times n$ matrix, the symmetric $n \times n$ matrix $\boldsymbol{B}'\boldsymbol{B}$ is positive semidefinite, and positive definite if and only if $m \geq n$ and rank($\boldsymbol{B}$) $= n$. To see that there is no other possibility, define the m-vector

$$\boldsymbol{p} = \boldsymbol{Bz}$$

for n-vector $\boldsymbol{z} \neq \boldsymbol{0}$. Let $\boldsymbol{p} = (p_1, \dots, p_m)'$ (defining the elements of $\boldsymbol{p}$) and then

$$\begin{aligned} \boldsymbol{z}'\boldsymbol{B}'\boldsymbol{Bz} &= \boldsymbol{p}'\boldsymbol{p} \\ &= \sum_{i=1}^{m} p_i^2 \geq 0. \end{aligned}$$

According to (4.9), rank ($\boldsymbol{B}'\boldsymbol{B}$) $= n$ if and only if rank($\boldsymbol{B}$) $= n$. However, if and only if rank($\boldsymbol{B}$) $= n$, there can (by definition) exist no $\boldsymbol{z} \neq \boldsymbol{0}$ such that $\boldsymbol{p} = \boldsymbol{Bz} = \boldsymbol{0}$. For any choice of $\boldsymbol{z}$, at least one element of $\boldsymbol{p}$ must be nonzero, and

$$\sum_{i=1}^{m} p_i^2 > 0.$$

Thus, note that $\boldsymbol{B}'\boldsymbol{B}$ is positive definite if and only if it is nonsingular.

2. A symmetric positive definite $n \times n$ matrix $\boldsymbol{A}$ can always be decomposed as

$$\boldsymbol{A} = \boldsymbol{KK}', \tag{4.17}$$

where $\boldsymbol{K}$ is a nonsingular lower triangular $n \times n$ matrix. (4.17) is called the *Cholesky decomposition* of $\boldsymbol{A}$. A variant of this formula is

$$\boldsymbol{A} = \boldsymbol{LDL}' \tag{4.18}$$

where $\boldsymbol{L}$ is $n \times n$ lower triangular with ones on its diagonal and $\boldsymbol{D}$ is a diagonal $n \times n$ matrix with all the diagonal elements positive. Write $\boldsymbol{D}^{1/2}$ to denote the matrix whose diagonal elements are the square roots of those of $\boldsymbol{D}$, so that

$$\boldsymbol{D} = \boldsymbol{D}^{1/2}\boldsymbol{D}^{1/2}$$

and then

$$\boldsymbol{K} = \boldsymbol{LD}^{1/2}.$$

A Cholesky decomposition also exists in principle for positive semidefinite matrices, but is not computable in general.

3. The determinant of a positive definite matrix is positive. Noting that $|\boldsymbol{L}| = 1$ by construction, where $\boldsymbol{L}$ is defined in (4.18), it can be verified using (3.8) and other results from Section 3.2 that

$$\begin{aligned} |\boldsymbol{A}| &= |\boldsymbol{L}||\boldsymbol{D}||\boldsymbol{L}'| \\ &= |\boldsymbol{D}| \\ &= d_{11}d_{22}\cdots d_{nn} \\ &> 0. \end{aligned}$$

4. If a square matrix $\boldsymbol{A}$ $(m \times m)$ is symmetric and positive definite and $\boldsymbol{B}$ $(m \times n)$ is any conformable matrix, then $\boldsymbol{B}'\boldsymbol{A}\boldsymbol{B}$ is positive semidefinite, and positive definite if $\boldsymbol{B}$ has rank n, with $n \leq m$. Given the Cholesky decomposition of $\boldsymbol{A}$ and (4.8), this result follows by Property 1. Defining $\boldsymbol{y} = \boldsymbol{B}\boldsymbol{z}$, if $\boldsymbol{B}$ has full column rank then every choice of $\boldsymbol{z} \neq \boldsymbol{0}$ yields $\boldsymbol{y} \neq \boldsymbol{0}$ and

$$\begin{aligned} \boldsymbol{z}'\boldsymbol{B}'\boldsymbol{A}\boldsymbol{B}\boldsymbol{z} &= \boldsymbol{y}'\boldsymbol{A}\boldsymbol{y} \\ &> 0. \end{aligned}$$

Otherwise, $\boldsymbol{y} = \boldsymbol{0}$ is possible with $\boldsymbol{z} \neq \boldsymbol{0}$, but positive semidefiniteness still holds. A useful application is to show that if $\boldsymbol{A}$ is symmetric and positive definite, then so is its inverse, noting that

$$\boldsymbol{A}^{-1} = \boldsymbol{A}^{-1}\boldsymbol{A}\boldsymbol{A}^{-1}.$$

5. The *leading principal* submatrices of $\boldsymbol{A}$ are the square matrices obtained by deleting the last p rows and last p columns, for $p = 0, \ldots, n-1$. For all these matrices to have positive determinants (the leading principal minors) is both a necessary and a sufficient condition for $\boldsymbol{A}$ to be positive definite, and accordingly it provides a computable test for positive definiteness. This useful fact is demonstrated as follows, although the argument is somewhat fiddly and can be skipped to make progress on first reading. Let the leading principal submatrices of $\boldsymbol{A}$ be $\boldsymbol{A}_{(1)}, \ldots, \boldsymbol{A}_{(n)}$ where $\boldsymbol{A}_{(1)} = a_{11}$, the top-left element, and $\boldsymbol{A}_{(n)} = \boldsymbol{A}$. To show necessity, assume $\boldsymbol{A}$ is positive definite. For any $1 \leq k \leq n$, define

$$\boldsymbol{z} = \begin{bmatrix} \boldsymbol{z}_k \\ \boldsymbol{0} \end{bmatrix} \begin{matrix} k \\ n-k \end{matrix}$$

for any $\boldsymbol{z}_k \neq \boldsymbol{0}$, and note that

$$\begin{aligned} \boldsymbol{z}_k'\boldsymbol{A}_{(k)}\boldsymbol{z}_k &= \boldsymbol{z}'\boldsymbol{A}\boldsymbol{z} \\ &> \boldsymbol{0}. \end{aligned}$$

Therefore, $\boldsymbol{A}_{(k)}$ is positive definite and has a positive determinant by Property 3. An inductive argument is used to show sufficiency. Assume $|\boldsymbol{A}_{(k)}| > 0$ for each k. For any $k < n$, assume that $\boldsymbol{A}_{(k)}$ is positive definite and consider the partition

$$\begin{aligned} \boldsymbol{A}_{(k+1)} &= \begin{bmatrix} \boldsymbol{A}_{(k)} & \boldsymbol{b}_{(k)} \\ \boldsymbol{b}_{(k)}' & c_{(k)} \end{bmatrix} \\ &= \begin{bmatrix} \boldsymbol{I}_k & \boldsymbol{0} \\ \boldsymbol{b}_{(k)}'\boldsymbol{A}_{(k)}^{-1} & 1 \end{bmatrix} \begin{bmatrix} \boldsymbol{A}_{(k)} & \boldsymbol{0} \\ \boldsymbol{0}' & d_{(k)} \end{bmatrix} \begin{bmatrix} \boldsymbol{I}_k & \boldsymbol{A}_{(k)}^{-1}\boldsymbol{b}_{(k)} \\ \boldsymbol{0}' & 1 \end{bmatrix} \qquad (4.19) \end{aligned}$$

where $d_{(k)} = c_{(k)} - \boldsymbol{b}'_{(k)}\boldsymbol{A}^{-1}_{(k)}\boldsymbol{b}_{(k)}$. Observe that by (3.19) and (3.32),

$$|\boldsymbol{A}_{(k+1)}| = |\boldsymbol{A}_{(k)}|d_{(k)},$$

which is positive by assumption, so necessarily $d_{(k)} > 0$. It is easy to verify that the middle matrix in the product in (4.19) is positive definite, and hence $\boldsymbol{A}_{(k+1)}$ is positive definite by Property 4. For $k = 1$, a_{11} is necessarily a positive scalar, hence positive definite, and since what is true for k is true for $k+1$, as shown, it is true for $k = n$. This completes the argument.

6. Let $\boldsymbol{A}$ and $\boldsymbol{B}$ be positive definite matrices of the same dimension. If $\boldsymbol{A} - \boldsymbol{B}$ is positive definite (positive semidefinite), then $\boldsymbol{B}^{-1} - \boldsymbol{A}^{-1}$ is also positive definite (positive semidefinite). The demonstration of this result is not possible without additional theory, but it will be shown in Section 9.6.

The fundamental theorem of least squares can now be addressed as follows. Since $\boldsymbol{y} = \boldsymbol{X}\hat{\boldsymbol{\beta}} + \hat{\boldsymbol{u}}$ by definition of $\hat{\boldsymbol{u}}$,

$$\begin{aligned} S(\boldsymbol{b}) &= (\boldsymbol{y} - \boldsymbol{X}\boldsymbol{b})'(\boldsymbol{y} - \boldsymbol{X}\boldsymbol{b}) \\ &= (\hat{\boldsymbol{u}} + \boldsymbol{X}(\hat{\boldsymbol{\beta}} - \boldsymbol{b}))'(\hat{\boldsymbol{u}} + \boldsymbol{X}(\hat{\boldsymbol{\beta}} - \boldsymbol{b})) \\ &= S(\hat{\boldsymbol{\beta}}) + 2(\hat{\boldsymbol{\beta}} - \boldsymbol{b})'\boldsymbol{X}'\hat{\boldsymbol{u}} + (\hat{\boldsymbol{\beta}} - \boldsymbol{b})'\boldsymbol{X}'\boldsymbol{X}(\hat{\boldsymbol{\beta}} - \boldsymbol{b}). \end{aligned} \tag{4.20}$$

According to Property 1, if $\boldsymbol{X}$ has full rank then $\boldsymbol{X}'\boldsymbol{X}$ is positive definite. Hence, the last right-hand side term of (4.20) must be positive unless $\boldsymbol{b} = \hat{\boldsymbol{\beta}}$. However, if $\boldsymbol{X}'\hat{\boldsymbol{u}} \neq \boldsymbol{0}$ the cross-product term could be negative, and could dominate the last term, by the choice of $\boldsymbol{b}$. Consider the case $\boldsymbol{b} = \hat{\boldsymbol{\beta}} + d\boldsymbol{z}$ for a scalar d and k-vector $\boldsymbol{z}$. Choosing $\boldsymbol{z}$ so that $\boldsymbol{z}'\boldsymbol{X}'\hat{\boldsymbol{u}} > 0$, there must exist $d > 0$ small enough that

$$\begin{aligned} S(\boldsymbol{b}) - S(\hat{\boldsymbol{\beta}}) &= d(d\boldsymbol{z}'\boldsymbol{X}'\boldsymbol{X}\boldsymbol{z} - 2\boldsymbol{z}'\boldsymbol{X}'\hat{\boldsymbol{u}}) \\ &< 0. \end{aligned}$$

It follows that

$$S(\boldsymbol{b}) > S(\hat{\boldsymbol{\beta}})$$

for any $\boldsymbol{b} \neq \hat{\boldsymbol{\beta}}$ *if and only if* $\boldsymbol{X}'\hat{\boldsymbol{u}} = \boldsymbol{0}$.

This is nothing but the general case of the derivation already given for the cases of one and two regressors in Chapter 1. Two features of the solution are worth remarking. It is notable how clean and simple the algebra becomes once the basic concepts and notation have been set up. In (4.20), it may be helpful to point out that there are two cross-product terms, $(\hat{\boldsymbol{\beta}} - \boldsymbol{b})'\boldsymbol{X}'\hat{\boldsymbol{u}}$ and $\hat{\boldsymbol{u}}'\boldsymbol{X}(\hat{\boldsymbol{\beta}} - \boldsymbol{b})$, but these are scalars. A matrix expression that evaluates to a scalar is equal to its own transpose, so it suffices to include one of these multiplied by 2. Transposing a scalar is a trick that is exploited several times on the sequel.

The second point to remark is that the problem of the uniqueness of the solution, left unresolved at the end of Chapter 1, is now resolved. The key condition is on the rank of the matrix $\boldsymbol{X}$. If the columns of $\boldsymbol{X}$ are linearly dependent, then $\boldsymbol{X}'\boldsymbol{X}$ is not positive definite, and the last term in (4.20) is not guaranteed to be positive when $\boldsymbol{b} \neq \hat{\boldsymbol{\beta}}$. If $\boldsymbol{X}'\boldsymbol{X}$ is singular, then of course the solution (4.16) doesn't exist. Failure (or near-failure) of the rank condition is known as *multicollinearity*.

4.4 Matrix Calculus

The fundamental theorem of least squares has been proved by a direct examination of the sum of squares criterion. However, many textbooks appeal to differential calculus to find the minimum of the sum of squares, and this solution deserves to be reviewed for comparison.

Appendix C provides some basic facts about differential calculus. The minimum of a function is a stationary point at which small enough changes in the arguments do not change the function value. In the present case, S depends on k arguments, and this must be true for each of them. The necessary condition for a minimum, the *first-order condition*, is that each of the partial derivatives of S with respect to the b_i are zero at the minimum point for each $i = 1, \dots, k$.

To evaluate the partial derivatives, resort initially to 'sigma' notation, and write

$$S(b_1, \dots, b_k) = \sum_{t=1}^{T} (y_t - b_1 x_{1t} - \cdots - b_k x_{kt})^2.$$

Using the chain rule, the partial derivative with respect to b_i takes the form

$$\frac{\partial S}{\partial b_i} = -2 \sum_{t=1}^{T} (y_t - b_1 x_{1t} - \cdots - b_k x_{kt}) x_{it}.$$

In matrix terms, this sum is the inner product of the residual vector with the ith regressor. In matrix notation, these elements are stacked into a column to form the gradient of S, the k-vector

$$\frac{\partial S}{\partial \boldsymbol{b}} = -2\boldsymbol{X}'(\boldsymbol{y} - \boldsymbol{X}\boldsymbol{b}).$$

It is easy to verify that if $\boldsymbol{b}$ is chosen to equate the gradient to zero, the solution, $\hat{\boldsymbol{\beta}}$, is identical with (4.16).

This confirms $\hat{\boldsymbol{\beta}}$ as a stationary point of S, but it does not show that the point is a minimum. To confirm this, it is sufficient to verify that small changes in the arguments at the stationary point result in the function increasing. Given that the first-order condition is satisfied, the formula in (4.20) gives the answer. The matrix $\boldsymbol{X}'\boldsymbol{X}$ must be positive definite to ensure that any deviation of $\boldsymbol{b}$ from $\hat{\boldsymbol{\beta}}$ results in an increase in S. The second partial derivatives of S, defined for each $i, j = 1, \dots, k$ are

$$\begin{aligned}\frac{\partial^2 S}{\partial b_j \partial b_i} &= \frac{\partial}{\partial b_j}\left(\frac{\partial S}{\partial b_i}\right) \\ &= 2\sum_{t=1}^{T} x_{it} x_{jt}.\end{aligned}$$

These elements are assembled into a $k \times k$ matrix by thinking of the ith column as containing the partial derivatives with respect to $\boldsymbol{b}$ of $\partial S / \partial b_i$, an element of the row vector $\partial S / \partial \boldsymbol{b}'$. The matrix of second derivatives, known as the *Hessian matrix* of the function, is

$$\frac{\partial^2 S}{\partial \boldsymbol{b} \partial \boldsymbol{b}'} = 2\boldsymbol{X}'\boldsymbol{X}.$$

This demonstrates that the sufficient condition for a stationary point of a quadratic function in k variables to be a minimum is that the Hessian matrix is positive definite. This is the *second-order condition* for a minimum.

In the quadratic case, the Hessian does not depend on $\boldsymbol{b}$ and is constant, but the second-order condition is a general sufficient condition for the minimum of any twice-differentiable function of k variables. In the general case, the positive definiteness property must hold at the minimizing point, like the first-order condition. The rationale for this general requirement is the fact that in a sufficiently small neighbourhood of an extreme point, any twice-differentiable function is arbitrarily well approximated by a quadratic function. The calculus approach to finding the minimum of a function has the benefit that its rules generalize to any case where the first and second derivatives are well defined.

4.5 Goodness of Fit

To close this chapter, here is a miscellany of facts about regression that relate to the question of how much is explained. Define the T-vector of the *least squares predictions*,

$$\begin{aligned}\hat{\boldsymbol{y}} &= \boldsymbol{X}\hat{\boldsymbol{\beta}} \\ &= \boldsymbol{y} - \hat{\boldsymbol{u}}.\end{aligned}$$

Since it follows from the normal equations that

$$\begin{aligned}\hat{\boldsymbol{y}}'\hat{\boldsymbol{u}} &= \hat{\boldsymbol{\beta}}'\boldsymbol{X}'\hat{\boldsymbol{u}} \\ &= \boldsymbol{0}, \end{aligned} \tag{4.21}$$

the predictions and the residuals are identically uncorrelated in the sample. Using geometrical terminology, these series are said to be mutually *orthogonal*. A consequence of this fact is the *sum of squares decomposition*,

$$\begin{aligned}\boldsymbol{y}'\boldsymbol{y} &= (\hat{\boldsymbol{y}} + \hat{\boldsymbol{u}})'(\hat{\boldsymbol{y}} + \hat{\boldsymbol{u}}) \\ &= \hat{\boldsymbol{y}}'\hat{\boldsymbol{y}} + 2\hat{\boldsymbol{y}}'\hat{\boldsymbol{u}} + \hat{\boldsymbol{u}}'\hat{\boldsymbol{u}}. \\ &= \hat{\boldsymbol{y}}'\hat{\boldsymbol{y}} + \hat{\boldsymbol{u}}'\hat{\boldsymbol{u}}. \end{aligned} \tag{4.22}$$

Comparing the relative sizes of these two sums of squares, of the predictions and of the residuals, provides a measure of how much of the variations of $\boldsymbol{y}$ over the sample are explained by $\boldsymbol{X}$.

One way to perform this comparison is by computing the correlation coefficient $r_{y\hat{y}}$ of the actual $\boldsymbol{y}$ and predicted $\hat{\boldsymbol{y}}$. This is a convenient point to introduce an alternative to the sigma notation of Chapter 1 using matrix and vector notation, as in (4.22). A standard notation for a column vector of ones is $\boldsymbol{\iota}$ (Greek iota). Defining $\boldsymbol{\iota}$ as a T-vector allows the vector of the dependent variable to be written in mean deviation form as $\boldsymbol{y} - \bar{y}\boldsymbol{\iota}$. Noting that $\boldsymbol{\iota}'\boldsymbol{\iota} = T$ and $\boldsymbol{\iota}'\boldsymbol{y} = T\bar{y}$, the sum of squares of mean deviations can be given, in two equivalent forms, as

$$(\boldsymbol{y} - \bar{y}\boldsymbol{\iota})'(\boldsymbol{y} - \bar{y}\boldsymbol{\iota}) = \boldsymbol{y}'\boldsymbol{y} - T\bar{y}^2.$$

The squared correlation coefficient between the actual and predicted dependent variable, which contains all the relevant information since a negative correlation cannot arise here, has the form

$$r^2_{y\hat{y}} = \frac{(\mathbf{y}'\hat{\mathbf{y}} - T\bar{y}\bar{\hat{y}})^2}{(\mathbf{y}'\mathbf{y} - T\bar{y}^2)(\hat{\mathbf{y}}'\hat{\mathbf{y}} - T\bar{\hat{y}}^2)}. \tag{4.23}$$

Assume, as is the usual case, that the regression contains an intercept so that the kth column of $\boldsymbol{X}$ is $\boldsymbol{\iota}$. In this case, $\boldsymbol{\iota}'\hat{\boldsymbol{u}} = \mathbf{0}$, hence $\bar{\hat{y}} = \bar{y}$, and, in view of (4.21),

$$\begin{aligned}\hat{\mathbf{y}}'\mathbf{y} &= \hat{\mathbf{y}}'\hat{\mathbf{y}} + \hat{\mathbf{y}}'\hat{\boldsymbol{u}} \\ &= \hat{\mathbf{y}}'\hat{\mathbf{y}}.\end{aligned}$$

Therefore, (4.23) can be written equivalently as

$$\begin{aligned}r^2_{y\hat{y}} &= \frac{(\hat{\mathbf{y}}'\hat{\mathbf{y}} - T\bar{y}^2)^2}{(\mathbf{y}'\mathbf{y} - T\bar{y}^2)(\hat{\mathbf{y}}'\hat{\mathbf{y}} - T\bar{y}^2)} \\ &= \frac{\hat{\mathbf{y}}'\hat{\mathbf{y}} - T\bar{y}^2}{\mathbf{y}'\mathbf{y} - T\bar{y}^2}.\end{aligned}$$

The possibilities range from perfect fit where $\hat{\mathbf{y}} = \mathbf{y}$ and $r^2_{y\hat{y}} = 1$, to the worst case, in which all the slope coefficients are zero and $\hat{\mathbf{y}} = \bar{y}\boldsymbol{\iota}$, just the mean of $\mathbf{y}$ stacked up T times, and then $r^2_{y\hat{y}} = 0$.

This measure of fit is known as the *coefficient of determination* and is conventionally represented by the symbol R^2 or "R-squared". In view of the sum of squares decomposition, yet another way to write it is

$$R^2 = 1 - \frac{\hat{\boldsymbol{u}}'\hat{\boldsymbol{u}}}{\mathbf{y}'\mathbf{y} - T\bar{y}^2}. \tag{4.24}$$

This form clarifies the fact that it is the relative magnitude of the sum of squared residuals that determines where in the unit interval R^2 falls, and it is the one most frequently quoted in textbooks.

However, caution with this latter formula is necessary. It is derived on the assumption the regression contains an intercept, but it is by no means unknown to regress 'through the origin', suppressing the intercept. In such cases, R^2 is an incorrect measure and can even be negative, which results in embarrassment in view of the symbol adopted. By contrast, $r^2_{y\hat{y}}$ is always well defined, always falls in the interval $[0, 1]$, and in fact is a valid measure for any fitting method that results in the prediction of a variable, not necessarily least squares. As demonstrated, it also matches R^2 whenever R^2 is valid and is the recommended goodness of fit measure for all purposes.

It is often pointed out that, even if valid as described, R^2 is not a satisfactory measure of fit because adding a regressor to the set must necessarily increase it, whether or not the addition has any relevance. Adding a column to $\boldsymbol{X}$, provided it is linearly independent of the existing columns so that $\boldsymbol{X}$ retains full rank, must always reduce $\hat{\boldsymbol{u}}'\hat{\boldsymbol{u}}$. The easiest way to appreciate the problem is to imagine running the regression with the maximum possible dimension $k = T$. In this case, $\boldsymbol{X}$ is square $T \times T$, and if invertible the coefficient formula (4.16) becomes

$$\begin{aligned}\hat{\boldsymbol{\beta}} &= \boldsymbol{X}^{-1}(\boldsymbol{X}')^{-1}\boldsymbol{X}'\boldsymbol{y} \\ &= \boldsymbol{X}^{-1}\boldsymbol{y},\end{aligned} \tag{4.25}$$

and

$$\begin{aligned}\hat{\boldsymbol{u}} &= \boldsymbol{y} - \boldsymbol{X}\hat{\boldsymbol{\beta}} \\ &= \boldsymbol{y} - \boldsymbol{y} \\ &= \boldsymbol{0}.\end{aligned} \tag{4.26}$$

Thus, $R^2 = 1$, regardless of what 'explanation' is contained in $\boldsymbol{X}$. Clearly, R^2 can be meaningless as a measure of explanatory power.

For this reason, an alternative to R^2 is sometimes advocated, which includes a factor to account for the degree of parsimony in the specification and does not necessarily increase with k. This is

$$\bar{R}^2 = 1 - \frac{\hat{\boldsymbol{u}}'\hat{\boldsymbol{u}}/(T-k)}{(\boldsymbol{y}'\boldsymbol{y} - T\bar{y}^2)/(T-1)}$$

(say "R-bar-squared"). The idea is to compare the variances of the actual and residual series rather than the sums of squares, which makes a lot of sense, and it is clear that increasing k will increase $\bar{R}^2$ only if the reduction in $\hat{\boldsymbol{u}}'\hat{\boldsymbol{u}}$ outweighs the reduction in $T-k$. The full explanation of why the residual sum of squares is normalized by $T-k$, the so-called 'degrees of freedom of the regression' is given in Sections 7.5 and 10.3.

4.6 Exercises

1 Are the following statements true or false?
   (a) The row rank and column rank of a matrix are always equal.
   (b) The null space of a matrix is the collection of all the possible vectors of weights such that the weighted sum of the columns is the zero vector.
   (c) A homogeneous equation system has a solution equal to zero.
   (d) If the square matrix $\boldsymbol{A}$ is positive definite and $\boldsymbol{I}$ is the conformable identity matrix, then $\boldsymbol{I} - \boldsymbol{A}$ is also positive definite.
   (e) If $\boldsymbol{A} - \boldsymbol{B}$ is a positive definite matrix, then $\boldsymbol{A}^{-1} - \boldsymbol{B}^{-1}$ is also positive definite.
   (f) The gradient of the sum of squared residuals in a linear regression is a linear function of the arguments.
   (g) The coefficient of determination can be negative in a regression with intercept suppressed.

2 What is the rank of the following matrices?
   (a)
$$\begin{bmatrix} 1 & 2 & 3 \\ 1 & 2 & 3 \\ 1 & 2 & 3 \end{bmatrix}$$

(b) $$\begin{bmatrix} 5 & 5 & 5 \\ 3 & 0 & 1 \\ 6 & 0 & 2 \\ 9 & 0 & 3 \end{bmatrix}$$

(c) $$\begin{bmatrix} 1 & 0 & 1 \\ 1 & 1 & 0 \\ 1 & 0 & 1 \end{bmatrix}$$

(d) $$\begin{bmatrix} 0 & 2 & 0 & 0 \\ 1 & 0 & 1 & 0 \\ 0 & 0 & 0 & 1 \\ 0 & 0 & 2 & 0 \end{bmatrix}$$

(e) $$\begin{bmatrix} 3 & 6 & 9 & 1 \\ 6 & 12 & 18 & 1 \\ 9 & 18 & 27 & 1 \\ 0 & 0 & 0 & 0 \end{bmatrix}$$

3 Solve the following equation systems as far as possible.

(a) $$\begin{bmatrix} 0 & 2 & 2 \\ 1 & 1 & 0 \\ 0 & 0 & 1 \end{bmatrix} \begin{bmatrix} x \\ y \\ z \end{bmatrix} = \begin{bmatrix} 0 \\ 0 \\ 0 \end{bmatrix}$$

(b) $$\begin{bmatrix} 0 & 2 & 2 \\ 1 & 1 & 0 \\ -1 & 1 & 2 \end{bmatrix} \begin{bmatrix} x \\ y \\ z \end{bmatrix} = \begin{bmatrix} 0 \\ 0 \\ 0 \end{bmatrix}$$

(c) $$\begin{bmatrix} 0 & 2 & 2 \\ 1 & 1 & -1 \\ 1 & 3 & 1 \end{bmatrix} \begin{bmatrix} x \\ y \\ z \end{bmatrix} = \begin{bmatrix} 0 \\ 3 \\ 3 \end{bmatrix}$$

4 Are these matrices positive definite? positive semidefinite?

(a) $$\begin{bmatrix} 2 & 1 & 0 \\ 1 & 2 & 1 \\ 0 & 1 & 2 \end{bmatrix}$$

(b) $$\begin{bmatrix} 2 & -1 & -1 \\ -1 & 2 & 1 \\ -1 & 1 & 2 \end{bmatrix}$$

(c) $$\begin{bmatrix} 2 & -2 & -1 \\ -2 & 2 & 1 \\ -1 & 1 & -1 \end{bmatrix}$$

5 For *all* choices of $\boldsymbol{A}$ and $\boldsymbol{B}$ such that both matrices have full rank, are the following matrices (assumed to exist) (i) positive semidefinite? (ii) positive definite?

(a) $(\boldsymbol{A}'\boldsymbol{A})^{-1}$
(b) $\boldsymbol{B}'\boldsymbol{A}\boldsymbol{B}$
(c) $\boldsymbol{I} - \boldsymbol{A}(\boldsymbol{A}'\boldsymbol{A})^{-1}\boldsymbol{A}'$
(d) $\boldsymbol{A}'\boldsymbol{B}(\boldsymbol{B}'\boldsymbol{A}\boldsymbol{B})^{-1}\boldsymbol{B}'\boldsymbol{A}$
(e) $\boldsymbol{A}(\boldsymbol{A}'\boldsymbol{B}'\boldsymbol{B}\boldsymbol{A})^{-1}\boldsymbol{A}'$

6 Let

$$X = \begin{bmatrix} 3 & 0 & 1 \\ 0 & 2 & 1 \\ 0 & 3 & 1 \\ 1 & 0 & 1 \end{bmatrix}.$$

(a) Show that $\boldsymbol{X}'\boldsymbol{X}$ is positive definite.
(b) Calculate $(\boldsymbol{X}'\boldsymbol{X})^{-1}$. Is it also positive definite?
(c) If $\mathbf{y} = \begin{bmatrix} 3 \\ 2 \\ 3 \\ 1 \end{bmatrix}$, what is $\hat{\boldsymbol{\beta}} = (\boldsymbol{X}'\boldsymbol{X})^{-1}\boldsymbol{X}'\boldsymbol{y}$? What is $\hat{\boldsymbol{u}} = \boldsymbol{y} - \boldsymbol{X}\hat{\boldsymbol{\beta}}$?

7 In the equation $\boldsymbol{y} = \boldsymbol{X}\boldsymbol{\beta} + \boldsymbol{u}\ (T \times 1)$:

(a) Show that if $\boldsymbol{X}\ (T \times k)$ has full rank, setting $\boldsymbol{b} = (\boldsymbol{X}'\boldsymbol{X})^{-1}\boldsymbol{X}'\boldsymbol{y}$ minimizes

$$S(\boldsymbol{b}) = (\boldsymbol{y} - \boldsymbol{X}\boldsymbol{b})'(\boldsymbol{y} - \boldsymbol{X}\boldsymbol{b}).$$

(b) Explain the role of the rank condition in the result of part (a). What does a failure of the condition imply, and how might you proceed in such a case?
(c) What are the special features of this solution in the case $T = k$?

8 Suppose that $\boldsymbol{P} = \begin{bmatrix} \boldsymbol{A} & \boldsymbol{B} \\ \boldsymbol{C} & \boldsymbol{D} \end{bmatrix}$ $(n + m \times n + m)$ has full rank $n + m$, and $\boldsymbol{D}\ (m \times m)$ is non-singular.

(a) Find partitioned matrices $\boldsymbol{Q}$ and $\boldsymbol{R}$ such that

$$\boldsymbol{P}\boldsymbol{Q} = \boldsymbol{R}$$

and the partition of $\boldsymbol{R}$ has $\boldsymbol{A} - \boldsymbol{B}\boldsymbol{D}^{-1}\boldsymbol{C}\ (n \times n)$ as top-left block and $|\boldsymbol{R}| = |\boldsymbol{A} - \boldsymbol{B}\boldsymbol{D}^{-1}\boldsymbol{C}|$.
(b) Hence (or otherwise) show that $\boldsymbol{A} - \boldsymbol{B}\boldsymbol{D}^{-1}\boldsymbol{C}\ (n \times n)$ has full rank n.

Part II

Modelling

5

Probability Distributions

5.1 A Random Experiment

Imagine an archery contest. Figure 5.1 shows the scatter of hits on a target, as it might appear after 1000 arrows have been shot. We are all familiar with the fact that such patterns arise as a result of random events. It is not possible to predict with precision where the next shot will land, but one can predict with confidence that most hits will be in the neighbourhood of the aiming point (the bull's-eye with coordinates $(0, 0)$ in the figure), while a proportion of bad shots will be further away. The scatter shown in the figure (which was simulated on a computer, needless to say) is what might be obtained if the average magnitude of the aiming errors was the same in all directions – undershooting as likely to happen as overshooting, and so forth. It has also been assumed (reasonably?) that the vertical and horizontal deviations of the hits are not correlated – shooting too high/low is not systematically connected with a bias to left/right.

Randomness can be a difficult concept to make sense of. Archers fail to hit the mark they aim at for a variety of reasons, from wind variations to imperfect muscular control. One feels that such factors could in principle be understood and, with sufficient data, be predicted exactly, so that nothing is really 'random'. However, as a practical matter this cannot be done, and the best that can be done is to distinguish more and less probable outcomes, where here 'probable' is understood to refer to the accumulated experience of previous outcomes. Probability theory, and especially what is called distribution theory, uses mathematical formulae to describe such patterns of randomness and also to generate predictions of future outcomes.

As a first approach to understanding the pattern in Figure 5.1, try counting the incidence of hits in different regions of the target. Figure 5.2 shows a smoothed representation of the data, in which the regions of the plane with similar frequencies of hits have been connected by lines. The result is similar in appearance to a physical contour map, in which points of equal height above sea level are joined up with lines. A probability distribution is a mathematical model of a phenomenon such as target shooting, and the contour mapping idea is rather close to the way that frequencies of occurrence are handled mathematically. A formula called a *probability density function* (p.d.f. for short) quantifies, for each point of the target, the historical frequency of strikes in that region.

As has long been known, a mathematical formula that does jobs of this type with good accuracy is the *normal* curve, or normal 'surface' in the bivariate case, also called the *Gaussian* curve since an early proponent was the famous nineteenth century German

An Introduction to Econometric Theory, First Edition. James Davidson.

Companion website: www.wiley.com/go/davidson/introecmettheory

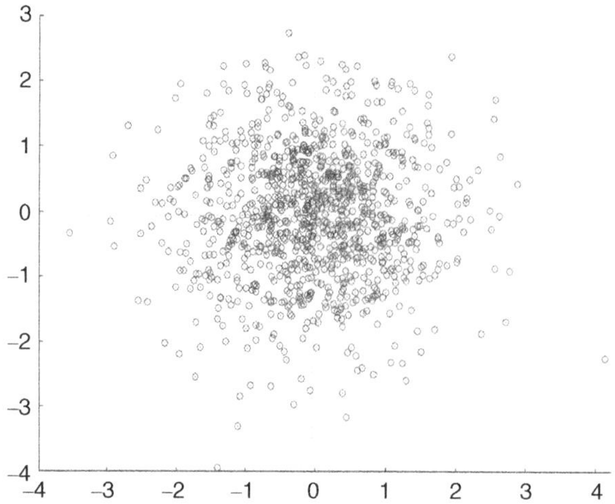

Figure 5.1 Archery target scatter.

mathematician C. F. Gauss.[1] The bivariate normal probability density function is shown as a three-dimensional image in Figure 5.3. The formula for this curve is

$$\phi(x, y) = \frac{1}{2\pi e^{(x^2+y^2)/2}} \tag{5.1}$$

where $\pi = 3.14159...$ is the ratio of the circumference of a circle to its diameter.[2] It may be apparent that the empirical contours sketched in Figure 5.2 would fit this surface rather well, with x denoting the horizontal deviation from the origin and y the vertical deviation.

The formula takes large values when x and y are close to zero with a maximum of $1/2\pi$ at $(0, 0)$, since $e^0 = 1$, but falls off rapidly to zero as either x or y increase in either direction. The squaring ensures the symmetry of the function, as is apparent from the figure. Its interpretation is as follows. Take a point (x, y) of the plane, and specify *small* increments dx and dy. The *relative* frequency of hits in the rectangular region of the target with corners at the points (x, y), $(x + dx, y)$, $(x, y + dy)$, $(x + dx, y + dy)$ is well approximated, after a large number of hits, by the quantity

$$\phi(x, y)dxdy.$$

This is just the approximate volume (height times length times breadth) of the small columnar region bounded by the rectangle and the surface. Ignoring the small piece at the top is permissible, provided dx and dy are small enough.

To determine the relatively frequency of hits in larger regions, the trick is to add a lot of these little volumes together. The aggregate volume is formally calculated by integration of the function. If the region in question is a rectangle with sides $[a_1, a_2]$ and $[b_1, b_2]$,

1 The terms 'normal' and 'Gaussian' are synonyms in this context. Both are used in the econometrics and statistics literature. In this book they are used almost interchangeably, but 'Gaussian' may be preferred to provide emphasis when contrasting this distribution with alternatives.
2 See Appendix B for information on the exponential function e^x.

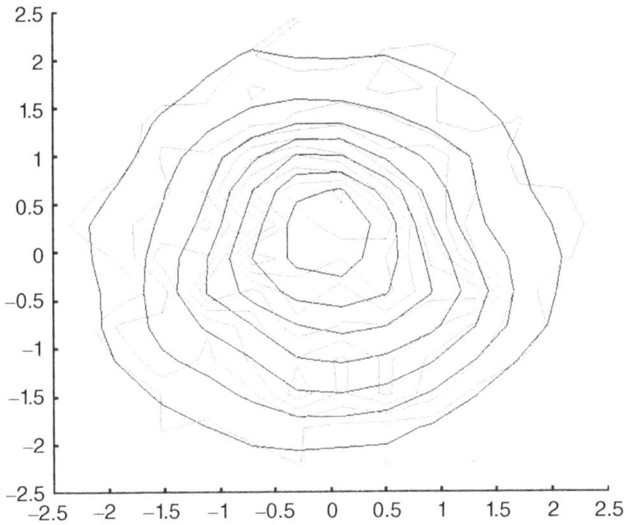

Figure 5.2 Archery target, frequency contours.

Figure 5.3 Bivariate normal probability density function.

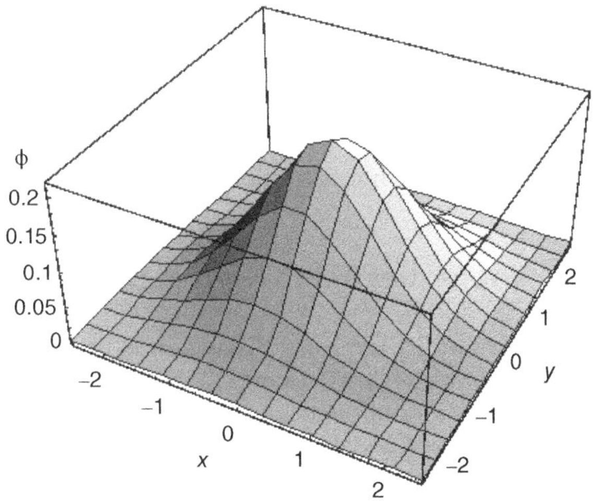

one can write

$$\Pr(a_1 < X < a_2, b_1 < Y < b_2) = \int_{b_1}^{b_2} \int_{a_1}^{a_2} \phi(x, y)\mathrm{d}x\mathrm{d}y. \tag{5.2}$$

This is a calculation for which there is no simple analytic formula. The integral represents an idealized calculation in which dx and dy approach zero, but in practice it would be approximated numerically on the computer by adding up the volumes for some finite set of small areas covering the desired region.

Please observe the use of the capital letters X and Y on the left-hand side here. These play a different role from the lowercase x and y. The latter denote actual values attained, and also function arguments, while X and Y can be thought of as standing for the as-yet-unobserved 'next shot'. Calculations such as (5.2) can be thought of as producing a prediction of this outcome. The notation $\Pr(\cdot)$ denotes the *probability* of the event specified in the parentheses. This is an idea clearly related to relative frequency, but is a statement about how often in many repeated shots an arrow may strike in this region and hence about how probable it is that the *next* shot will fall there.

Such calculations can be done for areas more general than rectangles. As a more practical example, consider the relative frequency of arrows striking inside a circle of radius 1, centred on the origin. This calculation can make use of the fact, which is just an application of Pythagoras's theorem, that for all the points (x, y) on or inside this circle, $x^2 + y^2 \leq 1$. The region of integration is more complicated in this instance than a rectangle, but it is no more difficult for a computer to carry out the calculation. It might be represented symbolically as

$$\Pr(X^2 + Y^2 \leq 1) = \int_{x^2+y^2\leq 1} \phi(x, y)\mathrm{d}x\mathrm{d}y. \tag{5.3}$$

This calculation actually yields (by a circuitous argument) the value 0.393. Just under 40% of these archers are predicted to achieve a shot within the inner circle and thereby maybe collect some points in the contest.

The role of the constant 2π in formula (5.1) is to ensure that the total volume encompassed by the surface is 1. It is possible to show (but there is no need to do so here!) that

$$\int_{-\infty}^{\infty}\int_{-\infty}^{\infty} \frac{1}{\mathrm{e}^{(x^2+y^2)/2}}\mathrm{d}x\mathrm{d}y = 2\pi.$$

The relative frequency (or probability) of the shot falling *somewhere* can only be 1, so this is the sensible normalization to adopt.

5.2 Properties of the Normal Distribution

A key idea in the foregoing discussion is that of the *random variable* (r.v. for short) denoted by X or Y in the example. The capital-letter convention is not always adhered to in applications but is helpful when discussing the theory. This is a subtle idea that is not always well understood. The Gaussian density function is a *model* of a real-world experiment producing a random outcome, such as shooting an arrow. X and Y represent 'place-holders' for the yet-to-be-observed next random hit. The Gaussian distribution allows predictions to be made about this outcome, with statements such as "The probability that $X \leq 0$ is 0.5." Probabilities are numbers on the interval $[0, 1]$ and are the theoretical counterpart of the relative frequencies observed after repeating a random experiment a large number of times. There is a long-running debate in statistics as to whether probabilities should be *defined* as the limiting cases of relative frequencies as the number of repetitions of an experiment increases to infinity. This is the so-called 'frequentist' view, contrasted with the 'Bayesian' view in which probability is regarded as subjective, the 'degree of belief' of an observer about the outcome. There are difficulties with both these approaches when taken too literally. The best course is to treat probabilities as nothing but numbers generated from a mathematical model, which may or may not prove useful in predicting real-world outcomes.

In practice, statistics does prove to be a useful discipline, for good reasons. The normal distribution is famous for its success in predicting a wide range of phenomena in the natural world and in social and economic contexts too. The heights and weights of (say) female students is another case of a random pair whose relative frequencies in the population are well predicted by a Gaussian p.d.f., although in this case there will be a positive correlation between the measurements, unlike the target shooting case. How to handle this extension is shown in the sequel. The reason for this success is widely attributed to the famous and remarkable result known as the central limit theorem, which says that the sum of a large number of independent random shocks must have a near-normal distribution, regardless of how the individual shocks are distributed. Section 13.3 discusses this phenomenon in detail.

The function $\phi(x, y)$ describes the probability associated with a region of the plane close to the point (x, y). This rather vague statement, like the use of the term 'probability density' rather than 'probability', draws our attention to the fact that positive probability cannot be assigned to a point. The Gaussian distribution is *continuous*, and as such it has the property $\Pr(X = x, Y = y) = 0$ for any choice of x and y. Only sets of points with positive extent, in this case areas of the plane, can have positive probabilities. The technical term for points with positive probability is *atoms*, and the normal distribution has no atoms. The story of Robin Hood, as told in numerous Hollywood movies, includes the most famous archery contest in popular legend. In the key scene, the Sheriff of Nottingham's champion puts his arrow into the bull's-eye. Robin Hood, in disguise, shoots next and strikes *exactly* the same spot, splitting the first arrow. (He's then discovered, there's a fight, he escapes, etc., etc., ... Check the movie.) The point is, sober statistical theory says that according to the normal distribution this feat should be assigned probability zero.

However, even though the normal is the best-known and most useful probability distribution, continuity is a slightly exotic property. That one cannot assign a positive probability to any point outcome is a counterintuitive feature that stems from the use of a smooth function to approximate a more complicated reality. In reality, arrow strikes cannot be arbitrarily close to one another, yet at the same time distinct, and measurements of distance are always in discrete units, such as millimeters. In this light, the Robin Hood story has more credibility than theory might allow. The fiction of continuity nonetheless proves a very effective simplifying device.

Suppose one is interested in only one dimension of variation, in left-right deviations, say, without caring about overshoots or undershoots. In this case the object of interest is the *marginal distribution* of X. The problem is simplified by the fact that the p.d.f. can be factorized as the product of marginal components. This is the property of *statistically independent* random variables. It is well known that the probability of two independent random events happening together is the product of the individual probabilities. For example, if A is the event that you win the National Lottery this week and B is the event that you win next week, the lottery organizers make the draw in such a way that $\Pr(A \text{ and } B) = \Pr(A)\Pr(B)$. This product rule reflects the fact that the next lottery outcome is not predictable from the last one – otherwise, how rich could we be?

This multiplicative property also applies to probability densities, which are nothing but rules for computing the probabilities of small regions. Inspection of formula (5.1) shows that the formula can be written in the form

$$\begin{aligned}\phi(x, y) &= \phi_X(x)\phi_Y(y)\\ &= \frac{1}{\sqrt{2\pi}e^{x^2/2}}\frac{1}{\sqrt{2\pi}e^{y^2/2}}\end{aligned} \tag{5.4}$$

and since it is a well-known result that

$$\int_{-\infty}^{+\infty} \frac{1}{e^{x^2/2}} dx = \sqrt{2\pi} \tag{5.5}$$

the marginal p.d.f. can be viewed as the result of integrating out the second variable. In other words, it answers the question "What is the probability density of X when Y can take any value?" The calculation takes the form

$$\begin{aligned} \phi_X(x) &= \int_{-\infty}^{+\infty} \phi(x, y) dy \\ &= \frac{1}{2\pi e^{x^2/2}} \int_{-\infty}^{+\infty} \frac{1}{e^{y^2/2}} dy \\ &= \frac{1}{\sqrt{2\pi} e^{x^2/2}}. \end{aligned} \tag{5.6}$$

This two-dimensional curve has the well-known bell shape, as illustrated in Figure 5.4, and the total area under it is 1. The shaded area shows the probability of X falling between 1 and 2. From the standard normal tabulation, to be found online or in the appendix of many statistics textbooks, this probability is about 0.136. Including the boundaries of the region is optional, since points have probability zero, as noted. In other words, $\Pr(1 < X < 2)$ and $\Pr(1 \leq X \leq 2)$ have the same value.

These calculations have assumed that the unit of measurement of the hits is such as to produce the pictures shown, with $(0, 0)$ representing the bull's-eye, and the scatter confined mainly to a circle of radius about 3. This is the standard normal distribution. If different units of measurement and a different origin are assumed, so that (say) x in the new units corresponds to $\dfrac{x - \mu_X}{\sigma_X}$ in the original units, the marginal density function formula becomes (writing the exponential function as $\exp\{\cdot\}$ when the argument is too elaborate to put conveniently in a superscript)

$$\phi_X(x) = \frac{1}{\sqrt{2\pi}\sigma_X} \exp\left\{-\frac{(x - \mu_X)^2}{2\sigma_X^2}\right\}. \tag{5.7}$$

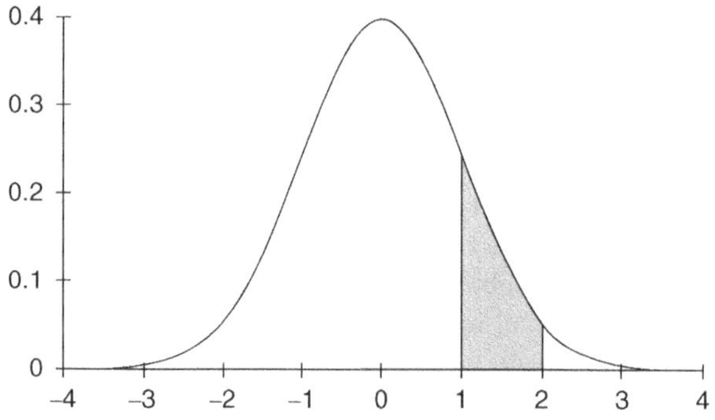

Figure 5.4 Normal p.d.f., shaded area shows $\Pr(1 < X < 2)$.

Take particular note of the new scale term. Because it changes the value of the exponential function at any point, the factor σ_X has to be included in the normalization to make sure the function integrates to unity. This is a basic rule of calculus.

It is customary to speak of the *family* of normal distributions, of which the standard normal with $\mu_X = 0$ and $\sigma_X^2 = 1$ is just the leading case. A commonly used shorthand is to write

$$X \sim \mathrm{N}(\mu_X,\ \sigma_X^2) \tag{5.8}$$

to denote a particular member of the family, where the tilde symbol $\sim$ stands for "is distributed like". This usage will be found for other distribution families in the sequel. Again, remember that X does *not* stand for an unknown value in (5.8). It represents a distribution from which values may be drawn, and this designation identifies the distribution in question.

μ_X is called the *mean* of the distribution, and σ_X^2 is called the *variance*. This is the same terminology as used in Section 1.2 to refer to the descriptive sample statistics, of which these are the theoretical counterparts, and if there is a need to make the distinction, the terms 'population mean' and 'population variance' might be substituted. A special property, implicit in this shorthand notation for the normal family, is that the marginal distribution of a Gaussian r.v. is completely described by just the two parameters, the mean and the variance. If the mean and variance are known, the standard density formula can be used to calculate probabilities. For example, the normal tabulation shows

$$\begin{aligned}\Pr(\mu_X - \sigma_X \leq X \leq \mu_X + \sigma_X) &= \Pr\left(-1 \leq \frac{X - \mu_X}{\sigma_X} \leq 1\right) \\ &= 0.683\end{aligned}$$

and

$$\begin{aligned}\Pr(\mu_X - 2\sigma_X \leq X \leq \mu_X + 2\sigma_X) &= \Pr\left(-2 \leq \frac{X - \mu_X}{\sigma_X} \leq 2\right) \\ &= 0.954.\end{aligned}$$

Among the nice properties of the normal distribution, convenient for doing calculations, the most important is *linearity*. A linear combination of jointly normal variates also has the normal distribution. For example, if $X \sim \mathrm{N}(\mu_X, \sigma_X^2)$ and $Y \sim \mathrm{N}(\mu_Y, \sigma_Y^2)$ *and* these variables are mutually independent, then

$$aX + bY \sim \mathrm{N}(a\mu_X + b\mu_Y,\ a^2\sigma_X^2 + b^2\sigma_Y^2). \tag{5.9}$$

This is merely a simple case of the general result to be given in Section 6.2. To derive the joint density of X and Y in this instance one multiplies their marginal densities together just as in (5.4). A particularly interesting case is where n identically and independently distributed normal variables with zero mean are added together, and the sum divided by $\sqrt{n}$. If $X_1, \ldots, X_n$ are independently distributed as $\mathrm{N}(0, \sigma^2)$, applying (5.9) gives

$$\frac{1}{\sqrt{n}} \sum_{i=1}^{n} X_i \sim \mathrm{N}(0, \sigma^2) \tag{5.10}$$

The distribution of the sum matches the distribution of the individual terms after the indicated normalization. This is neither the sum of the terms nor the average of the terms, but something in between; the 'square root rule' is critical. This reproductive property turns out to have wide ramifications, to be explored further in Section 13.3.

These properties help to explain why the normal distribution is loved by statisticians and invoked whenever possible. They are specific to the normal distribution, and it is important not to make the mistake of thinking of them as attributes of random variables generally. Other distributions, including those important cases to be studied in the sequel, behave differently.

5.3 Expected Values

Section 1.2 introduced the means, variances, and covariance of sample data, as measures of location, dispersion, and association. These were computed as the averages of certain specified series. In a *model* of the empirical distribution, of which the Gaussian distribution is our leading example, counterpart measures exist in which averages of finite samples are replaced by integrals over the range of variation, weighted by the probability density so that more frequently observed values receive a greater weight than rarer ones. These integrals are called *expected values* and are written as functions with the notation $\mathrm{E}(\cdot)$. It is natural to think of them as the limiting cases of averages as the sample becomes very large, replacing sigmas by integral signs and $1/T$ by $\mathrm{d}x$ or $\mathrm{d}y$.

The mean of a random variable is its expected value. In the case of the standard normal, for example, the mean is

$$\begin{aligned}\mathrm{E}(X) &= \int_{-\infty}^{+\infty} x\phi_X(x)\mathrm{d}x \\ &= 0.\end{aligned}$$

This result is easy to appreciate because ϕ_X is symmetric about zero, so the contributions of $x\phi_X(x)$ for positive and negative x are equal and opposite. This calculation should perhaps be expressed in terms of the joint distribution of X and Y, so note that the same result may also be obtained by making use of (5.6):

$$\begin{aligned}\mathrm{E}(X) &= \int_{-\infty}^{+\infty}\int_{-\infty}^{+\infty} x\phi(x,y)\mathrm{d}x\mathrm{d}y \\ &= \int_{-\infty}^{+\infty} x\left(\int_{-\infty}^{+\infty}\phi(x,y)\mathrm{d}y\right)\mathrm{d}x \\ &= \int_{-\infty}^{+\infty} x\phi_X(x)\mathrm{d}x.\end{aligned}$$

However, the fact that the expected value can be calculated from the marginal density is usually taken for granted and this step omitted.

An equally important calculation is the expected value of the square. For the standard normal distribution, this is

$$\begin{aligned}\mathrm{E}(X^2) &= \int_{-\infty}^{+\infty} x^2\phi_X(x)\mathrm{d}x \\ &= 1.\end{aligned}$$

This is a well-known property of ϕ_X, but for most people is not obvious and must be shown using advanced integration techniques. Happily, such techniques are not required knowledge for any of the results in this book. Given the excellent reference books available, one can spend a lifetime doing econometric theory without the need to learn these tricks.

An expected value defined specifically in terms of the joint distribution is the expected product. For the bivariate normal example, this is

$$\begin{aligned} \mathrm{E}(XY) &= \int_{-\infty}^{+\infty}\int_{-\infty}^{+\infty} xy\phi(x,y)\mathrm{d}x\mathrm{d}y \\ &= \int_{-\infty}^{+\infty} x\phi_X(x)\mathrm{d}x \int_{-\infty}^{+\infty} y\phi_Y(y)\mathrm{d}y \\ &= 0. \end{aligned}$$

Under independence a fundamental result, true for any bivariate distribution, is that the expected product is equal to the product of the expectations.

A very convenient fact is that expected values, being integrals and hence glorified averages, are *linear*. At its simplest, this means that for constants a and b,

$$\mathrm{E}(a + bX) = a + b\mathrm{E}(X). \tag{5.11}$$

The variance of a random variable X, written with the shorthand notation $\mathrm{Var}(X)$, is formally defined as the expected squared deviation from the mean. Multiplying out, using linearity, and remembering that $\mathrm{E}(X)$ is a constant,

$$\begin{aligned} \mathrm{Var}(X) &= \mathrm{E}(X - \mathrm{E}(X))^2 \\ &= \mathrm{E}(X^2) - \mathrm{E}(X\mathrm{E}(X)) - \mathrm{E}(\mathrm{E}(X)X) + \mathrm{E}(X)^2 \\ &= \mathrm{E}(X^2) - \mathrm{E}(X)^2. \end{aligned} \tag{5.12}$$

In words, "the variance is the expected square less the square of the expectation".

If $\mathrm{E}(Z) = 0$ and $\mathrm{E}(Z^2) = 1$, consider for constants μ and $\sigma > 0$ the random variable

$$X = \sigma Z + \mu.$$

Linearity gives the results

$$\begin{aligned} \mathrm{E}(X) &= \sigma\mathrm{E}(Z) + \mu \\ &= \mu \end{aligned}$$

and

$$\begin{aligned} \mathrm{Var}(X) &= \mathrm{E}(\sigma Z + \mu)^2 - \mu^2 \\ &= \sigma^2\mathrm{E}(Z^2) + 2\mu\sigma\mathrm{E}(Z) + \mu^2 - \mu^2 \\ &= \sigma^2. \end{aligned}$$

In particular, $\mathrm{E}(X)$ and $\mathrm{Var}(X)$ are the two distribution parameters identifying a member of the normal family, as in (5.8).

The general rule for variances of linear functions is

$$\begin{aligned}\mathrm{Var}(a+bX) &= \mathrm{E}((a+bX)^2) - \mathrm{E}(a+bX)^2 \\ &= a^2 + 2ab\mathrm{E}(X) + b^2\mathrm{E}(X^2) - a^2 - 2ab\mathrm{E}(X) - b^2\mathrm{E}(X)^2 \\ &= b^2\mathrm{Var}(X).\end{aligned}$$

Since the random variables are expressed in mean deviations, the variance is invariant to shifts of location; thus the last formula does not depend on a.

The covariance of a pair of random variables X and Y is defined as

$$\begin{aligned}\mathrm{Cov}(X,Y) &= \mathrm{E}(X-\mathrm{E}(X))(Y-\mathrm{E}(Y)) \\ &= \mathrm{E}(XY) - \mathrm{E}(X)\mathrm{E}(Y). \qquad (5.13)\end{aligned}$$

In words, "the covariance is the expected product less the product of the expectations". As noted above, the condition of independence, such that the probability density factorizes into marginal components, implies that the covariance is zero.

The linearity property of expected values provides a simple way to analyze relationships between variables. Write

$$W = aX + bY$$

as the random variable defined in (5.9). Since X and Y are uncorrelated,

$$\begin{aligned}\mathrm{Cov}(X,W) &= \mathrm{E}(aX^2 + bXY) - a\mathrm{E}(X)^2 - b\mathrm{E}(XY) \\ &= a\mathrm{Var}(X).\end{aligned}$$

Accordingly, X and W are a correlated pair of normal variates when $a \neq 0$.

Finally, consider the mean and variance of a sum of random variables. Respectively,

$$\mathrm{E}(X+Y) = \mathrm{E}(X) + \mathrm{E}(Y) \qquad (5.14)$$

which is straightforward and, perhaps less so,

$$\mathrm{E}((X+Y)^2) = \mathrm{E}(X^2) + \mathrm{E}(Y^2) + 2\mathrm{E}(XY) \qquad (5.15)$$

so that

$$\begin{aligned}\mathrm{Var}(X+Y) &= \mathrm{E}((X+Y)^2) - \mathrm{E}(X+Y)^2 \\ &= \mathrm{E}(X^2) + \mathrm{E}(Y^2) + 2\mathrm{E}(XY) - \mathrm{E}(X)^2 - \mathrm{E}(Y)^2 - 2\mathrm{E}(X)\mathrm{E}(Y) \\ &= \mathrm{Var}(X) + \mathrm{Var}(Y) + 2\mathrm{Cov}(X,Y). \qquad (5.16)\end{aligned}$$

The mantra to remember is, "The variance of the sum of *uncorrelated* random variables is equal to the sum of the variances." The uncorrelatedness qualification should not be overlooked.

This is probably a good moment to remind the reader that the linearity property enters the story of distributions in two distinct ways, and care must be taken not to confuse them. Expected values are defined for many different distributions, and expected values of linear functions are linear functions of expected values. This is a general rule. Also, as we have seen, linear functions of jointly normal random variables are normal. These two useful properties often interact in probabilistic arguments, but the rationales that underlie them are quite different.

5.4 Discrete Random Variables

As a contrast to the normal distribution, consider a random phenomenon of an entirely different kind – the coin toss. There are just two outcomes, heads and tails, and if the coin is fair, these have equal probability of occurrence, so

$$\Pr(\text{heads}) = \Pr(\text{tails}) = 0.5.$$

It proves convenient to express the coin-toss outcome as a random variable by assigning the values 1 for heads and 0 for tails. A random variable equal to 1 with probability p and 0 with probability $1 - p$, for $0 \leq p \leq 1$, is said to have a *Bernoulli* distribution[3].

When a random variable assumes just a finite set of possible values, expected value calculations involve probability-weighted sums rather than integrals. If the possible outcomes are $x_1, x_2, \ldots$ with respective probabilities $p_1, p_2, \ldots$ such that

$$\sum_j p_j = 1$$

then the mean is

$$E(X) = \sum_j p_j x_j \tag{5.17}$$

and the variance is

$$\begin{aligned} \mathrm{Var}(X) &= \sum_j p_j (x_j - E(X))^2 \\ &= \sum_j p_j x_j^2 - E(X)^2 \end{aligned} \tag{5.18}$$

The Bernoulli distribution specifies just two possible outcomes, so the mean and variance are easily calculated, as

$$\begin{aligned} E(X) &= p \times 1 + (1 - p) \times 0 \\ &= p \end{aligned} \tag{5.19}$$

and

$$\begin{aligned} \mathrm{Var}(X) &= p \times (1 - p)^2 + (1 - p) \times (0 - p)^2 \\ &= p(1 - p). \end{aligned} \tag{5.20}$$

Given these easy calculations, one can then ask a more elaborate question, but potentially a very useful one. Given n successive, independent Bernoulli trials (e.g. coin tosses) with probability p of success ("heads"), what is the probability that k of them will be successes (the value 1) and and $n - k$ of them failures (the value 0)? The random variable X, taking possible values $k = 0, 1, 2, \ldots, n$, is said to have the *binomial distribution*, with shorthand representation $X \sim \text{binomial}(n, p)$.

With independent trials, the multiplication rule is used to calculate probabilities. With $p = 0.5$ the probability of getting "heads" twice in a row is $0.5^2 = 0.25$, and so forth. More generally, since under independence the order of occurrence does not matter, the probability of a particular sequence of Bernoulli outcomes is p raised to the power of

---

3 Named for Jacob Bernoulli, 1654-1705.

the number of successes times $1-p$ raised to the power of the number of failures. For example, suppose in nine successive trials the outcomes are 1,1,0,1,0,1,0,0,0. The probability of this occurrence is the same as the probability of 1,1,1,1,0,0,0,0,0 (or any other permutation) and is $p^4(1-p)^5$.

To find the probability of k successes out of n draws, where the order of occurrence does not matter, it is necessary to consider how many different sequences of outcomes there are containing k successes and $(n-k)$ failures, and multiply the probability of any one such draw by this number. The well-known answer to this question is the binomial coefficient, written[4]

$$\binom{n}{k} = \frac{n!}{k!(n-k)!}.$$

Putting all these considerations together results in the formula for the binomial probabilities. Under the stated conditions (n independent draws, fixed probability p of success),

$$\Pr(X = k) = \binom{n}{k} p^k (1-p)^{n-k} \tag{5.21}$$

for $k = 0, 1, 2, \ldots, n$. Adding these $n + 1$ probabilities together should give 1, since there has to be *some* number of successes in n trials. This is indeed the case according to the binomial theorem, here taking the form

$$\begin{aligned}\sum_{k=0}^{n} \binom{n}{k} p^k (1-p)^{n-k} &= (p + (1-p))^n \\ &= 1.\end{aligned}$$

Multiplying out the second member of the equality does produce collections of terms matching the binomial probabilities, as can be verified by direct calculation, at least for small values of n.

The mean and variance of the binomial(n, p) distribution might be calculated directly with formulae (5.17) and (5.18), with $x_j = k$ for $k = 0, 1, \ldots, n$ and setting the p_j from (5.21). This is potentially quite a large calculation, but there is a short cut to the results using (5.14) and (5.16). Since the trials are independent, the mean of the sum is the sum of the means, and the variance of the sum is the sum of the variances. The formulae of the constituent Bernoulli random variables, (5.19) and (5.20), yield respectively

$$\mathrm{E}(X) = np \tag{5.22}$$

and

$$\mathrm{Var}(X) = np(1-p). \tag{5.23}$$

It is not too hard to verify these calculations when n is quite a small number. When n is large, doing the calculations implied by (5.21) clearly becomes more and more burdensome. However, such calculations rarely need to be done, because something remarkable happens.

Figure 5.5 shows the binomial probabilities for the case $n = 20$ and $p = 0.5$, and superimposed on this plot, as a broken line, is the Gaussian density function with a matching mean of 10 and matching variance of 5. It is notable how closely the two plots match, and the correspondence is far from coincidental.

4 See Appendix A for the explanation of this formula.

Figure 5.5 Binomial probabilities and the normal p.d.f. *Source*: Figure 23.2 of *Stochastic Limit Theory: An Introduction for Econometricians* (Advanced Texts in Econometrics) by James Davidson (1994). Reproduced by permission of Oxford University Press.

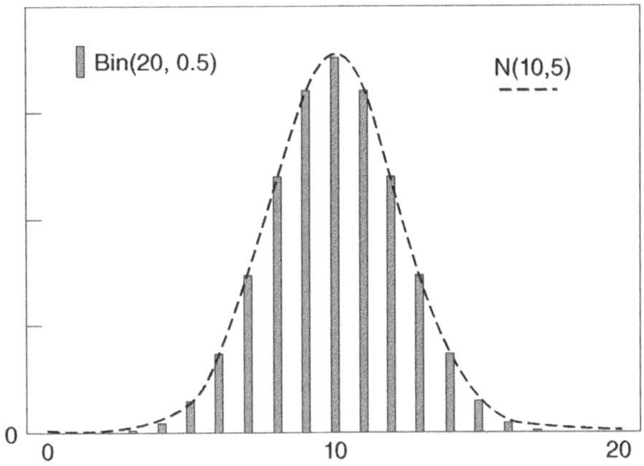

The binomial(n, p) random variable is the sum of n independent Bernoulli random variables $x_j, \ldots, x_n$ (say) and might be written as $\sum_{j=1}^{n} x_j$. Since the mean and variance of a sum grow with the number of terms, it is easiest to see what is happening after standardizing, first subtracting the mean and then dividing by the standard deviation. The famous *central limit theorem* says that as n increases, the standardized sequence

$$Z_n = \frac{\sum_{j=1}^{n}(x_j - p)}{\sqrt{np(1-p)}}, \quad n = 1, 2, 3, \ldots \tag{5.24}$$

is 'attracted to' the standard normal distribution, getting closer and closer as n increases to a N(0, 1) variate. Even though Z_n is a discrete random variable and N(0, 1) is continuous, the distribution of the discrete sequence as the number of terms tend to infinity gets closer and closer to the N(0, 1) in the sense that the standard normal tables get more and more accurate as measures of the probability of Z_n falling in a particular region. The reproductive property of the normal distribution shown in (5.10) is of course an important part of this story. Once the mean is adjusted to zero, the key part of the normalization is division by the square root of the number of trials. The rate of divergence of the sum, given that contributions can be either positive or negative after centring, is not given by the number of terms (as would be the case if all had the same sign) but by its square root. Section 13.3 gives more details on the central limit phenomenon.

Convergence towards the normal distribution is not restricted to the case $p = 0.5$; it holds true regardless of the value of p, provided this is fixed strictly above zero and below 1. The case of Figure 5.5 is especially favourable because the binomial probabilities are arranged symmetrically around the halfway point, and n as low as 20 gives a good match, as the figure shows. With p closer to 0 or 1, the binomial probabilities exhibit skewness and then a larger n is needed to get such a close match. It will, however, get there eventually.

There is another case of the binomial(n, p) with large n that does not behave in this way. This is where p is small and, specifically, gets closer to zero as n increases. Considering the sequence of binomial distributions where $p = \lambda/n$ and λ is a fixed parameter, the resulting limit as n goes to infinity is not the normal but the *Poisson* distribution[5]. To see

5 Named for Siméon Poisson, 1781-1840.

what happens here, suppose n is large relative to the number of successes k, which has a fixed finite value. Then, note that

$$\frac{n!}{(n-k)!} \approx n^k.$$

Also, setting $p = \lambda/n$, large n implies

$$\left(1 - \frac{\lambda}{n}\right)^{n-k} \approx \left(1 - \frac{\lambda}{n}\right)^{n} \approx \mathrm{e}^{-\lambda}$$

where the second of these approximations refers to the fact that e^x is the limiting case of $(1 + x/n)^n$ as $n \to \infty$, as detailed in Appendix B. Therefore, the binomial probabilities in (5.21) have the form

$$\frac{1}{k!}\frac{n!}{(n-k)!}\left(\frac{\lambda}{n}\right)^{k}\left(1 - \frac{\lambda}{n}\right)^{n-k} \to \frac{\lambda^k \mathrm{e}^{-\lambda}}{k!} \tag{5.25}$$

where the arrow denotes the fact that as n increases, the formula gets closer and closer to the limit case on the right-hand side. The Poisson distribution assigns this limit to $\Pr(X = k)$.

An interesting feature of the Poisson distribution is that the discrete outcome $X = k$ is well defined for every finite k; there is no upper limit. A discrete distribution may have an infinite number of possible outcomes provided they can be labeled by the integers $k = 0, 1, 2, \ldots$.[6] This is why the generic mean and variance formulae in (5.17) and (5.18) do not specify an upper bound for the sums. However, since the probabilities must sum to 1 over k, most of these outcomes must have probabilities arbitrarily close to zero. Indeed, the series expansion of the exponential function (see (B.2) in Appendix B) confirms that

$$\sum_{k=0}^{\infty} \frac{\lambda^k \mathrm{e}^{-\lambda}}{k!} = 1$$

as required, the terms of this sum approaching zero rapidly as k increases.

Letting X be Poisson distributed, since $\lambda = np$ for every n, it is easy to see from (5.22) that

$$\mathrm{E}(X) = \lambda. \tag{5.26}$$

Since $1 - p$ approaches 1 as n increases, (5.23) has the curious implication

$$\mathrm{Var}(X) = \lambda. \tag{5.27}$$

This match of mean and variance is a special feature of the Poisson distribution. Another special feature is a reproductive property, comparable to that of the normal in (5.10), although different. If $X_1, \ldots, X_n$ are independently distributed as Poisson(λ/n), then it can be shown that

$$\sum_{i=1}^{n} X_i \sim \text{Poisson}(\lambda).$$

6 This is called a *countable* infinity, to be distinguished from the number of points on the line (the continuum) that are said to be *uncountable* and for which continuous distributions such as the normal must be invoked. The result that uncountable infinities are strictly larger than countable infinities, due to Georg Cantor (1845-1918), is one of the most famous and controversial theorems of nineteenth-century mathematics.

The Poisson distribution suggests itself whenever a random outcome has low probability, but there are a large number of potential instances. Consider the frequency of hamburger purchases at (let's say) London's Waterloo Station branch of McDonald's. Thousands of travellers are in the station at any time, so the number of potential purchasers, n, is large. But the probability that the typical traveller is simultaneously hungry, has time on their hands, and favours McDonald's over other dining options, may be pretty small. Letting p go to zero while n goes to infinity provides an idealized approximation to this state of affairs. The mean number of purchases λ in a fixed time period (say, five minutes) could be measured by averaging the numbers over a sample of such periods. The distribution could then be used to calculate the probability of no orders being placed in the given period, or of one order, and also the probability of ten or more orders, the kind of thing the management would presumably wish to know.

A colourful if not bizarre data set in this vein is quoted in an excellent and highly recommended little book, *Lady Luck* by Warren Weaver [7]. This is the numbers of cavalrymen kicked to death by their horses in the Prussian army. The probability of such a fatal accident must have been thankfully low, but thousands of soldiers were at risk. Weaver presents the data for 14 army corps in each of 20 years, the period 1875–1894, giving a total of 280 data points. The following table shows the distribution of the recorded deaths.

Number of deaths	0	1	2	3	4	5+	Total
Army corps-years	144	91	32	11	2	0	280

The mean of this empirical distribution is

$$\frac{91 + 2 \times 32 + 3 \times 11 + 4 \times 2}{280} = 0.7$$

The plot of the relative frequencies of deaths, and Poisson probabilities with matching mean for comparison, are shown in Figure 5.6. Not an exact match, but in this relatively small number of trials, close enough be suggestive. The classic facetious question for the student to pose is, of course, how do the horses know when they've kicked enough riders to match the Poisson formula? The best answer we can give to this specifies two conditions. First, these horses and riders all behave pretty much alike, so that the probability of a fatal kick can be treated as a constant across places and times; and second, the

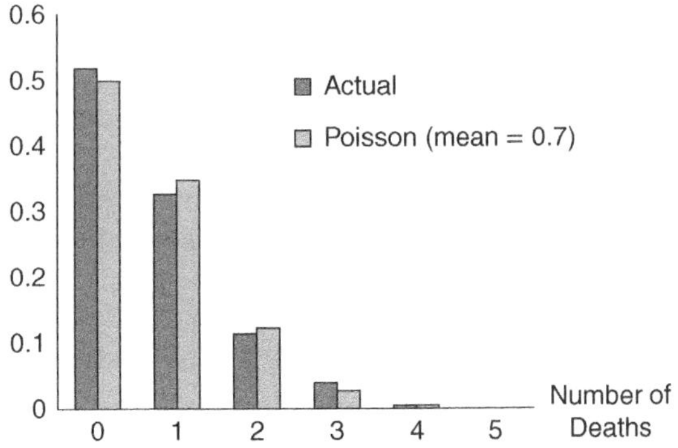

Figure 5.6 Prussian cavalry data and predictions.

7 Warren Weaver, *Lady Luck: The Theory of Probability* New York: Dover Books, 1982.

horses act independently. They do not conspire among themselves to coordinate their efforts, but just do what comes naturally. This is all that is needed to make the Poisson distribution a good model of this phenomenon.

5.5 Exercises

1 Are the following statements true or false?
   (a) If and only if random variables are independent, they are uncorrelated.
   (b) If and only if continuously distributed random variables are independent, their joint density function factorizes into marginal densities.
   (c) A normal random variable can take any value between minus infinity and plus infinity even though its variance is finite.
   (d) If X, Y, and Z are independent and normally distributed random variables and a, b, c and d are constants, then $W = a + bX + cY + dZ$ is also a normally distributed random variable.
   (e) The variance of the sample mean of a collection of n identically distributed random variables with common variance σ^2 is σ^2/n.
   (f) The sum of n independent Bernoulli-distributed random variables with probability p has the binomial(n, p) distribution.
   (g) A Poisson-distributed random variable $x = 0, 1, 2, \ldots$, with probabilities $p(k) = e^{-\lambda}\lambda^x/x!$ has $\text{E}(x) = \lambda$ and $\text{E}(x^2) = \lambda$.

2 Suppose that $X \sim \text{N}(5, 2)$, $Y \sim \text{N}(1, 3)$, and X and Y are independent of each other. Calculate the mean, the variance, and the covariance with X of
   (a) $X + Y$
   (b) $X - Y$
   (c) XY.

3 Let X and Y be independent standard normal random variables, and let a and b be constants.
   (a) Find the probability density function of the random variable $Z = aX + bY$.
   (b) Find the joint probability density function of the pair (U, V) when $U = aX$ and $V = bY$.

4 Let a pair (X, Y) of independent standard normal random variables represent a point in the plane. Using the tabulation of the normal distribution, or otherwise, calculate the following:
   (a) The probability that X falls in the interval $[1, 2]$.
   (b) The probability that (X, Y) falls in the rectangle $[1, 2] \times [-1, 0]$.
   (c) The probability that $X^2 < 2$.
   (d) The probability that $X + Y < 0$.[8]
   (e) The probability that (X, Y) lies inside a circle of radius 2.45 centred at the origin.[9]

---

8 The normal tables are no use here, but try drawing a picture.

9 The normal tables are no use here either, but use Pythagoras's theorem to express the restriction as an inequality. Then check out Section 6.3.

5 (a) If $x_1, \dots, x_T$ is a random sample with mean μ and variance σ^2, and s^2 is defined in (1.3), show that

$$E(s^2) = \sigma^2.$$

(b) If (x_t, y_t) for $t = 1, \dots, T$ is a random sample of pairs with means μ_x and μ_y and covariance σ_{xy}, and s_{xy} is defined in (1.9), show that

$$E(s_{xy}) = \sigma_{xy}.$$

6 What is the probability of having x heads appear in n successive tosses of a fair coin, in the following cases?

(a) $x = n = 1$
(b) $x = n = 5$
(c) $x = 2,\ n = 5$
(d) $x = 3,\ n = 6$

7 Let X be distributed as binomial(6, 0.2).

(a) What is the probability that $X = 3$?
(b) What is the probability that $X < 2$?
(c) What is $E(X)$?
(d) What is $\mathrm{Var}(X)$?

8 The mean of the Poisson distribution with parameter λ has the formula

$$E(X) = \sum_{k=0}^{\infty} k \frac{e^{-\lambda}\lambda^k}{k!}$$

Use the series expansion of e^{λ} (see (B.2)) to show that $E(X) = \lambda$.

6

More on Distributions

6.1 Random Vectors

The first task of this chapter is to extend the analysis of one or two random variables to an arbitrary number. The tools of matrix algebra are of course brought into play. Let

$$\boldsymbol{x} = \begin{bmatrix} x_1 \\ x_2 \\ \vdots \\ x_n \end{bmatrix}$$

be an n-vector whose elements are random variables. With a different set of conventions for matrices, note that the capital-letter convention for random variables has to be foregone here. Without enough distinct symbols to allow notational conventions to apply universally, there is no alternative to just keeping in mind how a particular object has been defined.

The new idea is the generalization of mean and variance to the vector case. The expected value of $\boldsymbol{x}$ is, straightforwardly enough, the vector whose elements are the expected values of the elements of $\boldsymbol{x}$:

$$\mathrm{E}(\boldsymbol{x}) = \begin{bmatrix} \mathrm{E}(x_1) \\ \mathrm{E}(x_2) \\ \vdots \\ \mathrm{E}(x_n) \end{bmatrix} \quad (n \times 1).$$

However, generalizing the idea of the variance requires more than a vector of variances, because the random elements don't exist in isolation. Covariances also need to be represented. The key idea is the *expected outer product* of a vector. This is the symmetric square matrix having the form

$$\mathrm{E}(\boldsymbol{x}\boldsymbol{x}') = \begin{bmatrix} \mathrm{E}(x_1^2) & \mathrm{E}(x_1 x_2) & \cdots & \mathrm{E}(x_1 x_n) \\ \mathrm{E}(x_2 x_1) & \mathrm{E}(x_2^2) & & \vdots \\ \vdots & & \ddots & \vdots \\ \mathrm{E}(x_n x_1) & \cdots & \cdots & \mathrm{E}(x_n^2) \end{bmatrix} \quad (n \times n).$$

An Introduction to Econometric Theory, First Edition. James Davidson.

Companion website: www.wiley.com/go/davidson/introecmettheory

The *covariance matrix* of $\boldsymbol{x}$ (sometimes just called the variance matrix, with notation $\mathrm{Var}(\cdot)$) is the expected outer product of the mean deviations. Written out element by element, this has the form

$$\mathrm{Var}(\boldsymbol{x}) = \begin{bmatrix} \mathrm{Var}(x_1) & \mathrm{Cov}(x_1, x_2) & \cdots & \mathrm{Cov}(x_1, x_n) \\ \mathrm{Cov}(x_2, x_1) & \mathrm{Var}(x_2) & & \vdots \\ \vdots & & \ddots & \vdots \\ \mathrm{Cov}(x_n, x_1) & \cdots & \cdots & \mathrm{Var}(x_n) \end{bmatrix}. \tag{6.1}$$

Following the rule that the expected value of a matrix is the matrix of expected values and applying the rules of matrix algebra in the usual way leads to the alternative representations

$$\begin{aligned} \mathrm{Var}(\boldsymbol{x}) &= \mathrm{E}((\boldsymbol{x} - \mathrm{E}(\boldsymbol{x}))(\boldsymbol{x} - \mathrm{E}(\boldsymbol{x}))') \\ &= \mathrm{E}(\boldsymbol{x}\boldsymbol{x}') - \mathrm{E}(\boldsymbol{x}\mathrm{E}(\boldsymbol{x})') - \mathrm{E}(\mathrm{E}(\boldsymbol{x})\boldsymbol{x}') + \mathrm{E}(\boldsymbol{x})\mathrm{E}(\boldsymbol{x})' \\ &= \mathrm{E}(\boldsymbol{x}\boldsymbol{x}') - \mathrm{E}(\boldsymbol{x})\mathrm{E}(\boldsymbol{x})'. \end{aligned}$$

6.2 The Multivariate Normal Distribution

Consider a vector $\boldsymbol{x}$ $(n \times 1)$ whose elements are independently distributed $\mathrm{N}(0, 1)$. Using the multiplication rule for independent random variables, which extends to n cases just as to the random pair, and also product rule (B.3) for exponential functions, it easy to see that the joint probability density function is

$$\begin{aligned} \phi_X(x_1, x_2, \ldots, x_n) &= \phi(x_1)\phi(x_2)\cdots\phi(x_n) \\ &= \left(\frac{1}{\sqrt{2\pi}}\right)^n \exp\left\{-\frac{1}{2}\sum_{i=1}^n x_i^2\right\}. \end{aligned}$$

However, using matrix notation an elegant way to write the same expression is

$$\phi_X(\boldsymbol{x}) = \frac{\exp\left\{-\frac{1}{2}\boldsymbol{x}'\boldsymbol{x}\right\}}{(2\pi)^{n/2}}. \tag{6.2}$$

Taking the elements pairwise, the independence implies that $\mathrm{E}(x_i) = 0$, $\mathrm{E}(x_i^2) = 1$, and $\mathrm{E}(x_i x_j) = 0$ for each $i = 1, \ldots n$ and $j \neq i$. In matrix notation, these relations become

$$\mathrm{E}(\boldsymbol{x}) = \boldsymbol{0}$$

and

$$\begin{aligned} \mathrm{Var}(\boldsymbol{x}) &= \mathrm{E}(\boldsymbol{x}\boldsymbol{x}') \\ &= \boldsymbol{I}_n. \end{aligned}$$

Now consider an affine transformation of $\boldsymbol{x}$,

$$\boldsymbol{y} = \boldsymbol{A}\boldsymbol{x} + \boldsymbol{b} \; (n \times 1) \tag{6.3}$$

where $\boldsymbol{A}$ is $n \times n$ nonsingular. In the terminology of linear algebra, an affine transformation is a linear transformation plus a translation (shift of origin) although the term linear itself is often used loosely to cover these cases. To find the density function of $\boldsymbol{y}$ in (6.3) the procedure is to invert the transformation. Write

$$\boldsymbol{x} = \boldsymbol{A}^{-1}(\boldsymbol{y} - \boldsymbol{b}) \tag{6.4}$$

where the distribution of $\boldsymbol{x}$ is known. Defining the positive definite $n \times n$ matrix

$$\boldsymbol{\Sigma} = \boldsymbol{A}\boldsymbol{A}' \tag{6.5}$$

the rules for transposes and products of inverse matrices give

$$\begin{aligned}(\boldsymbol{A}^{-1})'\boldsymbol{A}^{-1} &= (\boldsymbol{A}')^{-1}\boldsymbol{A}^{-1}\\ &= (\boldsymbol{A}\boldsymbol{A}')^{-1}\\ &= \boldsymbol{\Sigma}^{-1}\end{aligned} \tag{6.6}$$

and hence,

$$\begin{aligned}\boldsymbol{x}'\boldsymbol{x} &= (\boldsymbol{y} - \boldsymbol{b})'(\boldsymbol{A}^{-1})'\boldsymbol{A}^{-1}(\boldsymbol{y} - \boldsymbol{b})\\ &= (\boldsymbol{y} - \boldsymbol{b})'\boldsymbol{\Sigma}^{-1}(\boldsymbol{y} - \boldsymbol{b}).\end{aligned} \tag{6.7}$$

Substituting (6.7) into (6.2) yields the required formula apart from a modified scale factor, generalizing the modification in (5.7), to ensure that integrating ϕ_X over $-\infty < x_i < \infty$ for each $i = 1, \cdots, n$ yields unity. The factor required is the absolute value of the determinant $|\boldsymbol{A}^{-1}|$, which is called the "Jacobian of the inverse transformation." The general rule is that if $\boldsymbol{y} = \boldsymbol{A}\boldsymbol{x} + \boldsymbol{b}$, then the density function ϕ_Y of $\boldsymbol{y}$ is related to ϕ_X by the formula

$$\phi_Y(\boldsymbol{y}) = ||\boldsymbol{A}^{-1}||\phi_X(\boldsymbol{A}^{-1}(\boldsymbol{y} - \boldsymbol{b})). \tag{6.8}$$

(This rather awkward notation, bars on bars to denote the absolute value of the determinant, might be avoided by writing $\det \boldsymbol{A}^{-1}$ instead of $|\boldsymbol{A}^{-1}|$.)

The result in (6.8) calls for a thorough study of multivariate calculus to be properly appreciated, and since its proof is peripheral to the development of regression theory, for present purposes it must be taken on trust. However, note that, using the rules for determinants of products and inverses from Section 3.3,

$$|\boldsymbol{A}^{-1}| = \frac{1}{|\boldsymbol{A}|}$$

and the absolute value of $|\boldsymbol{A}|$ is

$$\begin{aligned}||\boldsymbol{A}|| &= \sqrt{|\boldsymbol{A}|^2}\\ &= \sqrt{|\boldsymbol{A}\boldsymbol{A}'|}\\ &= \sqrt{|\boldsymbol{\Sigma}|}.\end{aligned}$$

Therefore, with the appropriate renormalization the joint Gaussian density function takes the form

$$\phi_Y(\boldsymbol{y}) = \frac{\exp\left\{-\frac{1}{2}(\boldsymbol{y} - \boldsymbol{b})'\boldsymbol{\Sigma}^{-1}(\boldsymbol{y} - \boldsymbol{b})\right\}}{(2\pi)^{n/2}\sqrt{|\boldsymbol{\Sigma}|}}. \tag{6.9}$$

This is the general formula for the multivariate normal density. It shows that $\boldsymbol{y}$ belongs to the multivariate normal family and that *every* normal vector can be reduced to the standard normal case (6.2) by an affine transformation.

Using linearity in (6.3), the mean of $\boldsymbol{y}$ is

$$\mathrm{E}(\boldsymbol{y}) = \boldsymbol{b}$$

and the variance is therefore

$$\begin{aligned}\mathrm{Var}(\boldsymbol{y}) &= \mathrm{E}(\boldsymbol{y} - \boldsymbol{b})(\boldsymbol{y} - \boldsymbol{b})' \\ &= \mathrm{E}(\boldsymbol{A}\boldsymbol{x}\boldsymbol{x}'\boldsymbol{A}'). \end{aligned} \tag{6.10}$$

The $n \times n$ matrix following the second equality of (6.10) is the expected outer product of the n-vector $\boldsymbol{Ax}$ whose elements have the form $\sum_{k=1}^{n} a_{ik}x_k$, for $i = 1, \dots, n$. It may be helpful to write out the typical element explicitly. Considering row i and column j,

$$\begin{aligned}\mathrm{E}\left(\sum_{k=1}^{n} a_{ik}x_k \sum_{l=1}^{n} a_{jl}x_l\right) &= \sum_{k=1}^{n}\sum_{l=1}^{n} a_{ik}\mathrm{E}(x_k x_l)a_{jl} \\ &= \sum_{k=1}^{n} a_{ik}a_{jk} \end{aligned} \tag{6.11}$$

where the first equality uses linearity of the expected values and the second one the fact that $\mathrm{E}(x_k x_l) = 1$ when $k = l$ and 0 otherwise. The last member of (6.11) is just the $(i, j)^{\text{th}}$ element of $\boldsymbol{AA}'$. These calculations can be reassembled into matrix form as

$$\begin{aligned}\mathrm{E}(\boldsymbol{A}\boldsymbol{x}\boldsymbol{x}'\boldsymbol{A}') &= \boldsymbol{A}\mathrm{E}(\boldsymbol{x}\boldsymbol{x}')\boldsymbol{A}' \\ &= \boldsymbol{AA}'. \end{aligned}$$

In short, it has been shown that the variance matrix of $\boldsymbol{y}$ is

$$\mathrm{Var}(\boldsymbol{y}) = \boldsymbol{\Sigma}.$$

A key fact about the multivariate normal distribution is that relationships between the vector coordinates are completely described by their covariances. If they are uncorrelated, with off-diagonal elements of $\boldsymbol{\Sigma}$ equal to zero, they are independently distributed. It is this fact that allows linear transformations to define any member of the normal family. A fact not to be overlooked is that it is possible to construct random variables whose marginal distributions are normal but that are *not* multivariate normal. Such variables do not have the linearity property of the multivariate normal, and they can be uncorrelated without being independent. The formulation of the *joint* distribution of a vector is therefore critical.

While the transformation in (6.3) is invertible according to (6.4), making it possible to transform to the standard Gaussian distribution and back again on a one-to-one basis, linearity also extends to noninvertible transformations. If (6.3) defines $\boldsymbol{y}$, the m-vector

$$\boldsymbol{z} = \boldsymbol{C}\boldsymbol{y} + \boldsymbol{d}$$

where $\boldsymbol{C}$ is a fixed $m \times n$ matrix is also Gaussian. The mean is

$$\mathrm{E}(\boldsymbol{z}) = \boldsymbol{Cb} + \boldsymbol{d},$$

and the $m \times m$ variance matrix is

$$\mathrm{Var}(\boldsymbol{z}) = \boldsymbol{C\Sigma C}'.$$

If $m \leq n$ and $\boldsymbol{C}$ has rank m, the joint density function of $\boldsymbol{z}$ is

$$\phi_Z(\boldsymbol{z}) = \frac{\exp\left\{-\frac{1}{2}(\boldsymbol{z} - \boldsymbol{Cb} - \boldsymbol{d})'(\boldsymbol{C\Sigma C}')^{-1}(\boldsymbol{z} - \boldsymbol{Cb} - \boldsymbol{d})\right\}}{(2\pi)^{m/2}\sqrt{|\boldsymbol{C\Sigma C}'|}}. \tag{6.12}$$

In the case $m < n$, one can view $\boldsymbol{z}$ as simply a subvector of an n-vector obtained via an invertible transformation. On the other hand, if $m > n$ the variance matrix is singular with rank n, and no density function is defined for $\boldsymbol{z}$. A Gaussian density function *can* however be specified for any full-rank linear combination of $\boldsymbol{z}$ of order not exceeding n. In these cases, the distribution of $\boldsymbol{z}$ is called *singular Gaussian.*

6.3 Other Continuous Distributions

The assumption that the data have a Gaussian distribution is fundamental to the classical theory of statistical inference, as explained in later chapters. The practical consequence of this assumption is to determine the distributions of various functions of the data, especially test statistics. If the functions are linear so much the better, since Gaussianity is preserved, and it is just a matter of computing the new mean and variance. However, non-linear transformations also arise, especially involving squares. Working out and tabulating the distributions of particular functions of the normal was a crucial step in the development of statistical inference techniques.

Consider an n-vector $\boldsymbol{x}$ of independent standard normals, having the density specified in (6.2). The sum of squares of these elements, in other words the inner product $\boldsymbol{x}'\boldsymbol{x}$, has a distribution known as the *chi-squared with n degrees of freedom.* This is written either as $\chi^2(n)$ or sometimes as χ^2_n. Considering the cases $n = 1, 2, 3, \ldots$ defines the chi-squared family of distributions. The terminology "degrees of freedom" is explained in Section 7.5, but it relates essentially to the context in which these distributions are applied.

Being sums of squares, these random variables have positive probability density on (are 'supported on' in statistical jargon) the non-negative part of the line only. The density functions are truncated below at zero. Unlike the normal density, they are asymmetric curves with right-hand tails extending to infinity, the actual shapes depending on n. Using the rule (5.15), it is easy to see that the expected value of $\chi^2(n)$ is n. It is less obvious that the variance is $2n$, but this is a fact to be elucidated in Section 6.4.

One way that a chi-squared random variable can be generated is as a quadratic form in a normal vector with the inverted covariance matrix. If

$$\boldsymbol{x} \sim \mathrm{N}(\boldsymbol{b},\ \boldsymbol{\Sigma})$$

$(n \times 1)$ and the positive definite matrix $\boldsymbol{\Sigma}$ has the decomposition $\boldsymbol{\Sigma} = \boldsymbol{AA}'$ as in (6.5), invert transformation (6.3) using

$$\boldsymbol{A}^{-1}\boldsymbol{\Sigma}(\boldsymbol{A}')^{-1} = \boldsymbol{I}_n$$

and so write

$$\boldsymbol{z} = \boldsymbol{A}^{-1}(\boldsymbol{x} - \boldsymbol{b}) \sim \mathrm{N}(\boldsymbol{0},\ \boldsymbol{I}_n).$$

Applying (6.6) therefore gives

$$(\boldsymbol{x}-\boldsymbol{b})'\boldsymbol{\Sigma}^{-1}(\boldsymbol{x}-\boldsymbol{b}) = \boldsymbol{z}'\boldsymbol{z}$$
$$\sim \chi^2(n). \tag{6.13}$$

This kind of development often arises in the sequel.

Sums of squares and sample variances often arise as standardizing factors in the construction of test statistics. The family of *Student's t* distributions show how this standardization might be implemented. Student's t with ν degrees of freedom, which is written variously as $t(\nu)$ or t_ν, is the distribution of the ratio of two independently drawn random variables. The numerator is a standard normal, and the denominator is the square root of a chi-squared with ν degrees of freedom, normalized to have mean of unity. In symbols write

$$t_\nu \sim \frac{\mathrm{N}(0,1)}{\sqrt{\chi^2(\nu)/\nu}} \tag{6.14}$$

although this notation leaves implicit the crucial condition, not to be overlooked, that the two components are independently drawn. Student was the pseudonym of the inventor of the distribution, W. S. Gosset, who chose not to publish his 1908 paper with the result under his own name, since he was at the time an employee of Guinness Breweries in Dublin.

The case $\nu = 1$ is of special interest because t_1 is nothing but the ratio of one standard normal to the absolute value (square root of the square) of another, independently drawn, standard normal. Taking the absolute value is optional, since it amounts to a random change of sign with probability 0.5. Such a switch does not change the distribution of a random variable that is symmetrically distributed about zero. Hence, t_1 is in effect the distribution of a ratio of independent standard normals. This is the standard case of the *Cauchy distribution.*[1] The Cauchy(m,γ) family of distributions has probability density function

$$f(x) = \frac{1}{\pi\gamma\left(1+\left(\frac{x-m}{\gamma}\right)^2\right)} \tag{6.15}$$

which may be of interest to compare with (5.7). The standard Cauchy, otherwise the t_1, is the case $m = 0$ and $\gamma = 1$. This function is sketched in Figure 6.1.

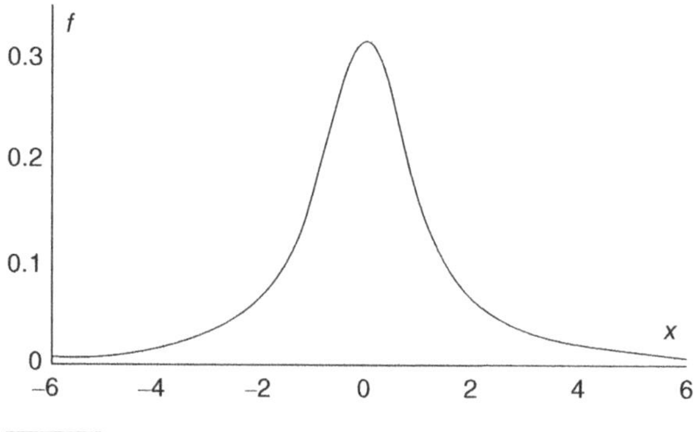

Figure 6.1 The standard Cauchy p.d.f.

1 Named for Augustin-Louis Cauchy, 1789-1857

At the other end of the scale, as ν increases $\chi^2(\nu)/\nu$ is getting closer and closer to its expected value, the constant 1. This is due to a phenomenon called the *law of large numbers*, to be discussed in detail in Section 13.1. It suffices here to note, using linearity of the expectation, that

$$\text{Var}\left(\frac{\chi^2(\nu)}{\nu}\right) = \frac{2\nu}{\nu^2}$$

which converges to zero as ν get larger. When ν is large, t_ν is correspondingly close to the N(0,1) distribution and attains this limiting case as $\nu \to \infty$.

The next important cases are the *Fisher's F* family of distributions, also sometimes called the Fisher-Snedecor distributions. R. A. Fisher (1890-1962) was the British biologist and mathematician to whom much of the theory of statistical inference is due, and the designation '*F*' is in his honour. The members of the family are designated $F(n_1, n_2)$, being the distributions of the ratios of independently drawn pairs of chi-squared random variables having n_1 and n_2 degrees of freedom, respectively, and standardized to have means of unity. Symbolically,

$$F(n_1, n_2) \sim \frac{\chi^2(n_1)/n_1}{\chi^2(n_2)/n_2}.$$

where the independence of the components is taken as implicit.

One final example of a continuous distribution is exceptionally simple, although not in this case derived from the normal. The *uniform distribution* on the unit interval, with abbreviation U[0, 1], has the simple density function

$$f(x) = \begin{cases} 1, & 0 \le x \le 1, \\ 0, & \text{elsewhere.} \end{cases}$$

It is easily verified that

$$\int_0^1 f(x)dx = 1$$

since this just the area of the unit square. The mean is $\frac{1}{2}$, and the variance is calculated as

$$\begin{aligned} \int_0^1 x^2 dx - \left(\frac{1}{2}\right)^2 &= \frac{1}{3} - \frac{1}{4} \\ &= \frac{1}{12}. \end{aligned}$$

Why is this case interesting? Chiefly because it is very easy to generate pseudorandom variables with a uniform distribution on the computer. The trick is to generate an effectively random string of decimal digits (members of the set 0, 1, … , 9). On the computer, multiply two large numbers together to give a still larger number, and discard the leading digits to give a remainder that is impossible to distinguish from a genuinely random collection. Then put a zero and a decimal point at the front of the string, to define a number between zero and one. Voila! The longer the string the better, within the limit set by the precision of the computer.

This trick leads to various techniques of generating normal pseudorandom variables on the computer. The simplest approach would be to randomly select a probability

$p \sim \mathrm{U}[0, 1]$, as described, and then use the normal tabulation to find z such that

$$\Pr(Z \le z) = p$$

for standard normal Z. It may be intuitively clear that z so selected is a random drawing from the normal distribution. More sophisticated methods in common use replace the tabulation with a formula, but the basic idea is the same.

6.4 Moments

The statistical term *moments* refers to the expected values of the positive integer powers of a random variable. This sequence of constants, typically written μ_k for $k = 1, 2, 3, \dots$, is a convenient way to describe the characteristics of the distribution. The first moment μ_1 is the mean, although in this case simply μ is a common notation. For powers two and greater, it is usual to consider the *centred* moments, for the random variable expressed as a mean deviation. Thus, for $k \ge 2$,

$$\mu_k = \mathrm{E}((X - \mu)^k).$$

The case $k = 2$ is of course the variance. The case $k = 3$ is the *skewness*, taking the value zero when the distribution is symmetric about its mean, and otherwise positive or negative depending on the respective profiles of the left- and right-hand tails of the distribution. The case $k = 4$ is the *kurtosis*, which captures the relation between the areas under the body and the tails of the distribution and hence the propensity of the distribution to exhibit outliers.

The normal distribution is distinctive because its odd-order centred moments are all zero, thanks to its symmetry, and the even-order moments depend only on the variance. This reflects the fact that the mean and variance completely specify the distribution. The general formula for even values of k is

$$\mu_k = \frac{k!}{2^{k/2}(k/2)!}\sigma^k.$$

The first few members of the sequence are $\mu_2 = \sigma^2$, $\mu_4 = 3\sigma^4$, $\mu_6 = 15\sigma^6$, and $\mu_8 = 105\sigma^8$. This sequence is finite for all finite k, an important property of the normal being that all its moments exist. The case μ_4 yields the promised explanation of the variance of a chi-squared distributed random variable. Applying the formula $\mathrm{E}(X^4) = 3$ and using the independence of the terms,

$$\begin{aligned}\mathrm{E}\left(\sum_{i=1}^{n} X_i^2\right)^2 &= \sum_{i=1}^{n} \mathrm{E}(X_i^4) + \sum_{i=1}^{n}\sum_{j\neq i} \mathrm{E}(X_i^2)\mathrm{E}(X_j^2) \\ &= 3n + n(n-1).\end{aligned}$$

Hence, using (5.12),

$$\begin{aligned}\mathrm{Var}(\chi^2(n)) &= 3n + n(n-1) - n^2 \\ &= 2n.\end{aligned}$$

However, there are important cases for which moments cannot be constructed. It can be shown for the Student's t_v family that for $v > 2$

$$\mathrm{Var}(t_v) = \frac{v}{v-2}.$$

For $\nu = 1$ and $\nu = 2$, the variance is, in effect, infinite, and the same is true for all the higher even-order moments. Similarly, the kurtosis exists for $\nu > 4$ but not otherwise, and in general the kth moment exists for $\nu > k$. In the case $\upsilon = 1$, which is the Cauchy(0,1) distribution, there is no finite mean, but here the argument is a little different. It is not that the mean is infinite, but that it is not a well-defined object. Using (6.15), the integral that would define it, if it did exist, would be the limiting case as $M \to \infty$ of

$$\begin{aligned}\int_{-M}^{M} \frac{x}{\pi(1+x^2)}\mathrm{d}x &= \int_{0}^{M} \frac{x}{\pi(1+x^2)}\mathrm{d}x - \int_{0}^{M} \frac{x}{\pi(1+x^2)}\mathrm{d}x \\ &= 0.\end{aligned}$$

However, calculus gives the result[2]

$$\begin{aligned}\int_{0}^{M} \frac{x}{\pi(1+x^2)}\mathrm{d}x &= \frac{\log(M^2+1)}{2\pi} \\ &\to \infty\end{aligned}$$

as $M \to \infty$. The expected value has the form $\infty - \infty$, which is neither zero nor infinity, but an undefined number. One can of course compute the average of a sample of Cauchy variates, but if $X_1, \dots, X_n$ are independent Cauchy(0, 1) variates, then

$$\frac{1}{n}\sum_{i=1}^{n} X_i \sim \text{Cauchy}(0, 1). \tag{6.16}$$

The mean has the same distribution as the terms of the sum! This is another example of a reproductive property of the kind already seen in the case of the Gaussian and the Poisson, but when comparing (6.16) with (5.10), note the different normalization in the two cases.

Compare the Cauchy density in Figure 6.1 with the Gaussian density in Figure 5.4. The key difference is that the Gaussian tails converge at an exponential rate to zero, as in formula (5.6), while the Cauchy tails converge only at the rate of the square of the argument, as in (6.15). These different rates of approach to zero make the difference between the existence of finite moments of all orders and no finite moments of any order.

So, while the moment concept is often a useful one, it cannot supply a complete picture of the properties of distributions. There are other ways to define attributes such as central tendency that don't involve calculating integrals. The *median* of a distribution is the value m such that

$$\Pr(X \leq m) = 0.5 \tag{6.17}$$

which is well defined for the Cauchy distribution, corresponding to the parameter bearing that symbol in (6.15).

A key question is to always determine whether the mean and variance exist, and the useful concept for this purpose is that of the *absolute moments,* defined as $\mathrm{E}(|X|^{\delta})$ for any $\delta > 0$. In this case, there is no need for δ to be an integer. A random variable X is said to be *integrable* if $\mathrm{E}(|X|) < \infty$, and this is a condition that should always be checked before attempting calculations involving moments. *Square integrability* is the case with $\delta = 2$ and corresponds to a finite variance.

2 To verify this formula, differentiate it using the chain rule and compare with equation (C.1).

6.5 Conditional Distributions

In multivariate distributions, the possibility always exists of random variables being observed in sequence. Suppose a random pair are not the vertical and horizontal deviations of an arrow strike, generated simultaneously, but the prices of a stock on successive days. The possibility of observing part of the outcome and using this partial information to modify predictions of the other part is obvious, and a problem of obvious interest to economists and forecasters.

Let X and Y be a continuously distributed pair of random variables with joint density function $f(x, y)$. The *conditional density function* of $Y|X$ (say "Y given X") is defined as

$$f(y|x) = \frac{f(x,y)}{f_X(x)}. \tag{6.18}$$

where f_X is the marginal density of X. The conditional density depends on x and y, but unlike the joint density its application would be to computing probabilities or expected values for Y, treating $X = x$ as a datum. Since

$$\int_{-\infty}^{\infty} f(x,y)\mathrm{d}y = f_X(x),$$

the conditional density possesses the required property that for any x,

$$\int_{-\infty}^{\infty} f(y|x)\mathrm{d}y = 1.$$

Formula (6.18) represents a univariate distribution for Y but in general a different one from the marginal density $f_Y(y)$. The exception to this rule is when the two random variables are independently distributed. In this case, the usual factorization of $f(x, y)$ yields the result $f(y|x) = f_Y(y)$ for any x.

The best-known case of these formulae, chiefly because the calculations are relatively easy to do, is the bivariate Gaussian distribution. Just for simplicity, let the pair (X, Y) have means of zero and covariance matrix

$$\boldsymbol{\Sigma} = \begin{bmatrix} \sigma_{XX} & \sigma_{XY} \\ \sigma_{YX} & \sigma_{YY} \end{bmatrix}.$$

where of course $\sigma_{YX} = \sigma_{XY}$. Taking the two-dimensional case of formula (6.9) and applying the determinant and inverse formulae for the 2×2 covariance matrix, the joint density is

$$\phi(x,y) = \frac{1}{2\pi}\frac{1}{\sqrt{\begin{vmatrix} \sigma_{XX} & \sigma_{XY} \\ \sigma_{YX} & \sigma_{YY} \end{vmatrix}}}\exp\left\{-\frac{1}{2}\begin{bmatrix} x & y \end{bmatrix}\begin{bmatrix} \sigma_{XX} & \sigma_{XY} \\ \sigma_{YX} & \sigma_{YY} \end{bmatrix}^{-1}\begin{bmatrix} x \\ y \end{bmatrix}\right\}$$

$$= \frac{1}{2\pi}\frac{1}{\sqrt{\sigma_{XX}}\sqrt{\sigma_{YY} - \dfrac{\sigma_{XY}^2}{\sigma_{XX}}}}\exp\left\{-\frac{1}{2}\frac{\sigma_{YY}x^2 + \sigma_{XX}y^2 - 2\sigma_{XY}xy}{\sigma_{XX}\left(\sigma_{YY} - \dfrac{\sigma_{XY}^2}{\sigma_{XX}}\right)}\right\}. \tag{6.19}$$

Note how the determinant $\sigma_{YY}\sigma_{XX} - \sigma_{XY}^2$ has been factorized in the last member of (6.19).

The function itself is factorized into conditional and marginal components with the use of a trick called "completing the square". Consider the identity

$$\sigma_{YY}x^2 + \sigma_{XX}y^2 - 2\sigma_{XY}xy = \sigma_{XX}\left(y - \frac{\sigma_{XY}}{\sigma_{XX}}x\right)^2 + \left(\sigma_{YY} - \frac{\sigma_{XY}^2}{\sigma_{XX}}\right)x^2.$$

To verify this, multiply out the square on the right-hand side and simplify, to check that it matches the left-hand side. Substituting this version of the numerator in the exponential term of (6.19) and then factorizing the latter leads to

$$\phi(x, y) = \phi_X(x)\phi(y|x),$$

where

$$\phi(y|x) = \frac{1}{\sqrt{2\pi\left(\sigma_{YY} - \dfrac{\sigma_{XY}^2}{\sigma_{XX}}\right)}} \exp\left\{-\frac{\left(y - \dfrac{\sigma_{XY}}{\sigma_{XX}}x\right)^2}{2\left(\sigma_{YY} - \dfrac{\sigma_{XY}^2}{\sigma_{XX}}\right)}\right\}$$

and the marginal component has the familiar form,

$$\phi_X(x) = \frac{1}{\sqrt{2\pi\sigma_{XX}}} \exp\left\{-\frac{x^2}{2\sigma_{XX}}\right\}.$$

Modifying these formulae to allow for nonzero means under the joint distribution is straightforward; just replace x by $x - \mu_X$ and y by $y - \mu_Y$ throughout.

Note the interesting features of the conditional density expression. Clearly this is a Gaussian density, but the conditional mean and variance have novel formulae. Allowing for nonzero means, the conditional mean takes the form

$$E(Y|x) = \mu_Y + \frac{\sigma_{XY}}{\sigma_{XX}}(x - \mu_X), \tag{6.20}$$

which is a function of x. This shows that knowledge that $X = x$ provides a modified prediction of Y. Further,

$$\text{Var}(Y|x) = \sigma_{YY} - \frac{\sigma_{XY}^2}{\sigma_{XX}},$$

which is not a function of x but is in general smaller than the marginal (or unconditional) variance σ_{YY}. If X and Y are independent with covariance $\sigma_{XY} = 0$, the conditional distribution reduces to the marginal distribution of Y.

The property that independence is equivalent to zero covariance is, as has been mentioned, unique to the Gaussian distribution. This is a good point in the story to give a statement of the general sufficient condition for independence. From (5.13), the condition of zero covariance is that the expected product equals the product of expectations,

$$E(XY) = E(X)E(Y).$$

Independence of X and Y holds if the same relation applies for *all eligible transformations* of X and Y. In other words, for all $g(X)$ and $h(Y)$ such that the expected values are well defined and finite, independence implies that

$$E(g(X)h(Y)) = E(g(X))E(h(Y)).$$

While eligibility depends on both the form of the transformation and the distributions of the variables, possible cases include X^k for integers k, $|X|^\delta$ for any δ, $\log(X)$, e^X, $\cos(X)$, $\sin(X)$, and more.

6.6 Exercises

1 Are the following statements true or false?
  (a) If $\boldsymbol{u} \sim \mathrm{N}(\boldsymbol{0}, \boldsymbol{\Sigma})$ $(n \times 1)$ where $\boldsymbol{\Sigma}$ is nonsingular then $\boldsymbol{u}'\boldsymbol{\Sigma}^{-1}\boldsymbol{u} \sim \chi^2(n)$.
  (b) If a sample $x_1 \dots, x_n$ is identically and independently distributed as $\mathrm{N}(0, \sigma^2)$, then if $\bar{x}$ denotes the sample mean and s^2 the sample variance, the statistic $\sqrt{n}\bar{x}/s$ is Student's t-distributed with $n - 1$ degrees of freedom.
  (c) If random variables X and Y are jointly normally distributed with marginal densities $\phi_X(x)$ and $\phi_Y(y)$, the conditional density function $\phi(y|x)$ equals $\phi_X(x)$ if and only if $\mathrm{Cov}(X, Y) = 0$.
  (d) The $F(n_1, n_2)$ distribution is the distribution of the ratio of a pair of chi-squared random variables, having n_1 and n_2 degrees of freedom respectively.
  (e) The probability density function of the uniform distribution is the unit square.
  (f) A random variable may have a central tendency but no mean.
  (g) In the distribution of the normal pair (X, Y), the conditional variance of Y given X is the same as the unconditional variance, not depending on X.

2 Let X and Y be independent standard normal random variables, and let

$$Z = aX + bY$$

where a and b are constants. What is the probability density function of the random vector $\begin{bmatrix} Z \\ X \end{bmatrix}$?

3 If $\boldsymbol{y}$ is a normal n-vector and $\boldsymbol{y}'\boldsymbol{A}\boldsymbol{y}$ has the $\sigma^2\chi^2(n)$ distribution for positive constant σ^2, what can you say about
  (a) the rank of $\boldsymbol{A}$?
  (b) The definiteness of $\boldsymbol{A}$?
  (c) The mean of $\boldsymbol{y}$?
  (d) The variance matrix of $\boldsymbol{y}$?
  (e) The mean of $\boldsymbol{y}'\boldsymbol{A}\boldsymbol{y}$?
  (f) The variance of $\boldsymbol{y}'\boldsymbol{A}\boldsymbol{y}$?

4 Let X and Y be a pair of independent standard normal random variables.
  (a) What is the mean of XY?
  (b) What is the variance of XY?
  (c) Explain why $\frac{Y}{X}$ has the same distribution as $\frac{Y}{|X|}$.
  (d) What is this distribution?
  (e) What can you say about the mean of $\frac{Y}{X}$?

5 Let $\boldsymbol{x}$ $(n \times 1)$ be a standard normal random vector.

(a) What is the joint density function of the m-vector $\boldsymbol{y} = \boldsymbol{Ax} + \boldsymbol{b}$ where $\boldsymbol{A}$ $(m \times n)$ is a fixed matrix with rank m and $\boldsymbol{b}$ is a fixed vector?

(b) Consider the vectors $\boldsymbol{u} = \boldsymbol{Ax}$ and $\boldsymbol{v} = \boldsymbol{Bx}$ where $\boldsymbol{A}$ $(m \times n)$ and $\boldsymbol{B}$ $(p \times n)$ are fixed matrices. Show that if $\boldsymbol{AB}' = \boldsymbol{0}$, then $\boldsymbol{u}$ and $\boldsymbol{v}$ are distributed independently of each other.

(c) Consider in particular the cases $\boldsymbol{A} = n^{-1}\boldsymbol{\iota}'$ where $\boldsymbol{\iota}'$ denotes the row n-vector of ones, and $\boldsymbol{B} = \boldsymbol{I}_n - n^{-1}\boldsymbol{\iota\iota}'$ $(n \times n)$. Show that these matrices satisfy the condition in part (b) and interpret the result.

(d) Does it follow from the result in part (c) that the sample mean and sample variance of a normal random sample are independent random variables? Explain.

6 Suppose that the $n_1 + n_2$-vector $\boldsymbol{x} = \begin{bmatrix} \boldsymbol{x}_1 \\ \boldsymbol{x}_2 \end{bmatrix} \begin{matrix} n_1 \\ n_2 \end{matrix}$ is multivariate normal with mean zero and covariance matrix $\boldsymbol{\Omega} = \begin{bmatrix} \boldsymbol{\Omega}_{11} & \boldsymbol{\Omega}_{12} \\ \boldsymbol{\Omega}_{21} & \boldsymbol{\Omega}_{22} \end{bmatrix}$ where $\boldsymbol{\Omega}_{21} = \boldsymbol{\Omega}_{12}'$.

(a) Write out the marginal density function of $\boldsymbol{x}_2$.

(b) Write out the joint density function of $\boldsymbol{x}$ in partitioned form, using the partitioned inverse and determinant formulae. (Tip: To make this operation more tractable, use the substitutions $\boldsymbol{E} = (\boldsymbol{\Omega}_{11} - \boldsymbol{\Omega}_{12}\boldsymbol{\Omega}_{22}^{-1}\boldsymbol{\Omega}_{21})^{-1}$ and $\boldsymbol{B} = \boldsymbol{\Omega}_{12}\boldsymbol{\Omega}_{22}^{-1}$.)

(c) Show that this function factorizes into the product of the marginal density of $\boldsymbol{x}_2$ and conditional density of $\boldsymbol{x}_1|\boldsymbol{x}_2$. Hence show that the conditional mean of $\boldsymbol{x}_1|\boldsymbol{x}_2$ is $\boldsymbol{Bx}_2$ and the conditional variance of $\boldsymbol{x}_1|\boldsymbol{x}_2$ is $\boldsymbol{E}^{-1}$.

(d) Comment on any linkages you see between your formulae and multiple regression.

7 Consider a pair of random variables generated in the following way. X is standard normal (mean 0, variance 1), and $Y = WX$ where W is an independently drawn discrete random variable, taking the values 1 and -1 with equal probabilities of 0.5.

(a) Is the marginal distribution of Y standard normal?

(b) What is the covariance of X and Y?

(c) What is the covariance of X^2 and Y^2?

(d) What can be said about the distribution of $X + Y$?

(e) Discuss your findings, and consider the proposition that X and Y are normal but not jointly normal.

7

The Classical Regression Model

7.1 The Classical Assumptions

Chapters 1 to 4 of this book have developed the mathematics of the linear regression model, but were careful to avoid any statistical context. Deliberately, the issue was treated wholly as a line-fitting exercise. In particular, the residual was treated simply as the unexplained part of the dependent variable, with the property, implicit in the least squares fit, of orthogonality with the regressors, but otherwise simply expected to be small in a well-fitting regression.

Now that the key concepts of distribution theory have been introduced in Chapters 5 and 6, it is possible to return to these procedures and view them in a new light. The *classical* model defines what has been taught to students, at least at an elementary level, ever since econometrics became a regular component of the economics syllabus. It has some features that are not very appropriate in an economics context, but it has the benefit of delivering interesting results using quite elementary techniques.

Begin with the full-sample matrix representation of the regression model in (4.12). Section 4.2 should be consulted for the relevant definitions and notation. The new ingredient is the treatment of the vector $\boldsymbol{u}$, and by extension the observed vector $\boldsymbol{y}$, as random in the sense that a distribution with some known properties will be assigned to it. Putting restrictions on this distribution will become a way of imposing a form on the model of what is commonly referred to as the *data generation process*.

However, before developing these ideas further there are two fundamental issues to be addressed. The first is the supposed source of the randomness. In the target-shooting example of Section 5.1, there was the unambiguous concept of a repeated random experiment generating a predictable pattern. The regression model example, by contrast, is generalized and abstract. Without having a specific mechanism in mind, the usual recourse is to the concept of a thought experiment. What is called the *sampling distribution* is the hypothetical random mechanism that throws up a vector $\boldsymbol{u}$ to produce the sample data observed.

In a classic case in economics, the data consist of a randomly selected sample of households whose attributes and behaviour, including incomes, and expenditures on some commodities such as food, are recorded. Such data are used to measure elasticities of expenditure with respect to income, by regressing (in logarithmic form, usually) the latter variables on the former. The Living Costs and Food Survey conducted by the UK Office for National Statistics (formerly, the Family Expenditure Survey) is an annual exercise, a leading purpose of which is to estimate the weights used in the construction

An Introduction to Econometric Theory, First Edition. James Davidson.

Companion website: www.wiley.com/go/davidson/introecmettheory

of inflation measures such as the Retail Prices Index. The survey collects information from around 5000 households out of the total of around 26 million in the United Kingdom, selected by a randomization technique designed to ensure they are representative of the population.

Randomization will involve similar techniques to those used to select lottery winners, in this case applied to post codes rather than lottery tickets.[1] The key requirement is that the selections cannot be predicted in advance, whether from knowledge of previous selections, or otherwise. This random draw could of course be repeated any number of times, each such repetition throwing up a different sample of 5000 households whose membership cannot be predicted from previous draws. It is this possibility of repetition that defines the sampling distribution, establishing the link between the single sample that is in fact drawn and the population as a whole. Knowing the form of the sampling distribution allows us to quantify the information contained in the sample about the population, in particular, to know how reliable it is. The thought-experiment approach may appear somewhat counterintuitive, given that no more than one drawing from the population is ever seen in practice. Suffice it to say that this is an approach that practitioners generally find useful.

However, having established the key idea of the sampling distribution, the classical regression model introduces an idea that is odd and unappealing. This is to impose the condition that the matrix $\boldsymbol{X}$ is fixed. In other words, in the repeated sampling framework, every drawing should feature the same explanatory variables, and only the $\boldsymbol{y}$ vectors should be sampled afresh. The reason for this assumption, simply enough, is that without it the statistical reasoning to be developed in this chapter will not be strictly valid. It is possible to envisage cases in which the assumption is perfectly reasonable, such as the analysis of experimental data. If $\boldsymbol{y}$ represents to outcome of a set of experiments in which different conditions are set, then $\boldsymbol{X}$ can represent those conditions, and $\boldsymbol{u}$ the random influences determining the experimental outcomes. Our thought experiment readily allows us to conceive of rerunning the same set of experiments with independent random influences determining each of the outcomes. Indeed, $\boldsymbol{X}$ is often referred to in textbooks as the 'design matrix' to emphasize this interpretation of the model. A classic example might be plant breeding experiments, in which agronomists sow different varieties of some crop in experimental plots, subject to different treatments of fertilizer and irrigation, and then measure the yield from each. The random factors in the experiment will be due to weather, soil variations, and the like, varying randomly from one experiment to another, while the treatments are replicated.

However, it is equally clear that this setup is quite unlike nearly every observational context in economics, which is mainly a nonexperimental discipline. The sampled households of the Living Costs and Food survey come as a package of measures. Repeated sampling has no hope of drawing new households whose incomes and other attributes match those of the last survey, case for case. Fixed $\boldsymbol{X}$ is clearly a nonsensical notion in this context.

And yet the classical regression model has been taught to generations of students of economics, very, very few of whom ever question its sphere of application. This fact

---

1 In practice, methods known as *cluster sampling* and *stratified sampling* are used to increase the representativeness of a small sample by nonrandom selections. Nonetheless, randomization remains the core feature of the sampling procedure.

must show that the concept is rarely well understood, whether by students or their teachers. We develop it here, regardless, simply because it allows the construction of powerful tools of statistical inference using elementary statistical ideas. The attractions of this wilful distortion of reality are undeniable, gross though it is. Redemption will be sought in Chapter 12, where it will be shown with the use of some slightly more advanced concepts that the classical regression model can, very nearly, describe the sampling environment appropriate to much economic data – although equally, there are cases to which it does not apply where different techniques are needed. These different techniques are sketched very briefly in Chapters 13 and 14, although more advanced treatments than this book can offer will be needed to do them full justice. Meanwhile, the reader is asked to persevere with the somewhat eccentric approach to statistical modelling developed in the next five chapters. If at any point doubts creep in, it might be a good idea to skip ahead and check out just the first section of Chapter 12. This will hopefully supply the missing context and give an idea how the difficulties will be resolved.

7.2 The Model

The term *model* , as it appears in this context, now requires explanation. The regression calculations described in Chapter 1 and Chapter 4 did not require the concept of a model to justify them, even though such an idea might exist in the minds of investigators carrying them out. These were simply line-fitting exercises, which might be performed on any set of variables whatever, related or otherwise. The regression residual u_t was simply the part of y_t not explained by $\boldsymbol{x}_t$. A good fit (large R^2, small residuals) might be more suggestive of an underlying relationship than a poor fit, but nothing beyond this can really be said.

Now, by contrast, we examine the consequences of assuming some rather specific properties for the u_t. With these strict conditions some powerful and elegant properties of the least squares coefficients can be demonstrated. The regression model postulates the existence of a specific causal relationship between the observables that, moreover, has linear functional form. The equation is conceived of as representing the data generation process for $\boldsymbol{y}$. Keeping the experimental context in mind, think of the yield of the agronomists' plots as driven by the selection of fertilizer and irrigation, with an added random noise that, however, contains no pattern of its own that might be regarded as an additional explanation. Once $\boldsymbol{X}$ is known, there is no systematic way to improve the prediction of outcome $\boldsymbol{y}$.

Here, then, are the assumptions governing the equations

$$\boldsymbol{y} = \boldsymbol{X}\boldsymbol{\beta} + \boldsymbol{u} \quad (T \times 1) \tag{7.1}$$

in the classical regression model.

Assumptions CRM

(i) $\boldsymbol{X}$ $(T \times k)$ is a fixed matrix of rank $k \leq T$.
(ii) $\mathrm{E}(\boldsymbol{u}) = \boldsymbol{0}$.
(iii) $\mathrm{E}(\boldsymbol{u}\boldsymbol{u}') = \sigma^2 \boldsymbol{I}_T$.

Recalling that

$$\mathrm{E}(\boldsymbol{u}) = \begin{bmatrix} \mathrm{E}(u_1) \\ \vdots \\ \mathrm{E}(u_T) \end{bmatrix}$$

and

$$\mathrm{E}(\boldsymbol{u}\boldsymbol{u}') = \begin{bmatrix} \mathrm{E}(u_1^2) & \cdots & \mathrm{E}(u_1 u_T) \\ \vdots & \ddots & \vdots \\ \mathrm{E}(u_T u_1) & \cdots & \mathrm{E}(u_T^2) \end{bmatrix},$$

assumptions CRM(ii) and (iii) are equivalent respectively to

$$\mathrm{E}(u_t) = 0 \text{ for } t = 1, \ldots, T$$

and

$$\mathrm{E}(u_t u_s) = \begin{cases} \sigma^2, & t = s \\ 0, & t \neq s \end{cases}, \quad \text{for } t, s = 1, \ldots, T.$$

In the context of these assumptions, it is usual to speak of *disturbances* or *errors* and also *shocks* to refer to $\boldsymbol{u}$, rather than residuals where the latter has the connotation of something 'left over' rather than active components of the model. Assumption CRM(ii) says something stronger than that the regression residuals are 'zero on average' over the sample. The least squares residuals have the property of summing to zero by construction, provided an intercept is included in the model, but this fact says nothing whatever about the relationship between the observables. Assumption CRM(ii) says that u_t has a mean of zero for each t, when these are viewed as drawings from the sampling distribution. This is a fairly trivial assumption if the u_t are all drawn from the same distribution, since if the mean of this distribution is not zero, a simple redefinition of the intercept coefficient can make it so. It is therefore the possibility that the u_t have different means for different t that is strictly being ruled out here. If this were true, it would imply that one or more relevant variables has been omitted from $\boldsymbol{X}$, and hence that the specified model is incorrect.

Assumption CRM(iii) says that u_t has a common variance of σ^2 for each t and also says that these random variables are uncorrelated across the sample. It is the variations with respect to the sampling distribution that are assumed to be uncorrelated for each pair of cases, t and s, $s \neq t$. This is a stronger condition than that the $\frac{1}{2}T(T-1)$ products $u_t u_s$ for $t \neq s$ are zero on average in the given sample, although this fact would be an implication of assumption CRM(iii).

These assumptions are saying something quite specific about the relations between $\boldsymbol{X}$ and $\boldsymbol{y}$ in the population, element by element, which will be reflected in any given sample drawing, but being conditions on the sampling distribution, they cannot be verified by examining a single sample. More exactly, we should say that under certain conditions they can be seen to fail in a single sample, but they cannot be proved to hold. They are however jointly ensured if the disturbances are identically and independently distributed. This fundamental characterization of the sampling process is often abbreviated to 'i.i.d.'.

It is often assumed that $\boldsymbol{u}$ has a multivariate normal distribution, but this is not a requirement here. For the results of this chapter, $\boldsymbol{u}$ can have any distribution such that the mean and variance are well defined. Normality will be formally introduced in Chapter 10, at the point where the results to be derived depend on it. Where normality does hold, the uncorrelatedness part of assumption CRM(iii) is *equivalent* to the disturbances being independently drawn, according to the results of Section 6.2. Without normality it is possible for uncorrelatedness to coexist with some other form of dependence, although it is difficult to think of practical cases where this situation could arise. It is natural to think of sample disturbances satisfying assumption CRM(iii) as drawn independently of one another, whether Gaussian or not.

Assumption CRM(i) specifies the fixed $\boldsymbol{X}$ assumption and also a rank condition that ensures that the regression is well defined and can be calculated. The key point to be appreciated is that the sampling distribution is defined for the specific $\boldsymbol{X}$ and hence in particular for a specific sample size T. The operation of observing additional data points defines a new model, so that the results with different T, and hence different design matrices, are not strictly comparable. It is important to emphasize this point because, as will be shown in Chapter 13, there is an alternative approach to interpreting the regression model in which the thought experiment of repeated sampling with fixed sample size T is replaced by the thought experiment of letting T increase without limit. This powerful technique, known as *asymptotic theory*, is fundamentally incompatible with the CRM, since letting the sample size change redefines the repeated sampling framework.

7.3 Properties of Least Squares

In the context of model (7.1) and assumptions CRM, consider again the least squares solution, copied from (4.16):

$$\hat{\boldsymbol{\beta}} = (\boldsymbol{X}'\boldsymbol{X})^{-1}\boldsymbol{X}'\boldsymbol{y}. \tag{7.2}$$

In this context, $\hat{\boldsymbol{\beta}}$ is known as an *estimator* of $\boldsymbol{\beta}$ in (7.1), a significant designation because assumptions CRM confer a certain status on the vector $\boldsymbol{\beta}$. It is the vector of weights that, given observations $\boldsymbol{y}$ and $\boldsymbol{X}$, uniquely endows $\boldsymbol{u} = \boldsymbol{y} - \boldsymbol{X}\boldsymbol{\beta}$ with properties CRM(ii) and (iii). Making inferences about these elements is of course a primary aim of regression analysis. To be precise the term estimator refers to the *rule*, in this case a formula such as (7.2), that generates an *estimate* of unknown parameters from a data set. The estimate is the actual vector of values produced by the given sample.

The first property of $\hat{\boldsymbol{\beta}}$ that follows from assumption CRM is *existence*, specifically the existence of a solution to the normal equations through the invertibility of the matrix $\boldsymbol{X}'\boldsymbol{X}$. This follows from assumption CRM(i) thanks to rule (4.9).

The next step is to calculate the expected value of $\hat{\boldsymbol{\beta}}$. First, use the distributive rule of matrix algebra, and then cancellation, to get the decomposition

$$\begin{aligned}\hat{\boldsymbol{\beta}} &= (\boldsymbol{X}'\boldsymbol{X})^{-1}\boldsymbol{X}'(\boldsymbol{X}\boldsymbol{\beta} + \boldsymbol{u}) \\ &= \boldsymbol{\beta} + (\boldsymbol{X}'\boldsymbol{X})^{-1}\boldsymbol{X}'\boldsymbol{u}.\end{aligned} \tag{7.3}$$

Note the application of two essential identities, $(\boldsymbol{X}'\boldsymbol{X})^{-1}\boldsymbol{X}'\boldsymbol{X} = \boldsymbol{I}_k$ and $\boldsymbol{I}_k\boldsymbol{\beta} = \boldsymbol{\beta}$. These kinds of manipulations will be used repeatedly in the sequel, without further comment.

Taking the expected value of (7.3) gives

$$\begin{aligned}\mathrm{E}(\hat{\boldsymbol{\beta}}) &= \boldsymbol{\beta} + \mathrm{E}((\boldsymbol{X}'\boldsymbol{X})^{-1}\boldsymbol{X}'\boldsymbol{u}) \\ &= \boldsymbol{\beta} + (\boldsymbol{X}'\boldsymbol{X})^{-1}\boldsymbol{X}'\mathrm{E}(\boldsymbol{u}) \\ &= \boldsymbol{\beta}. \end{aligned} \tag{7.4}$$

This is the property of *unbiasedness*. The expected value of the least squares estimator is the true value $\boldsymbol{\beta}$.

The calculation in (7.4) uses CRM(i) and CRM(ii) plus the linearity property of expectations. To see just how this works, element by element, define the matrix

$$\boldsymbol{L} = (\boldsymbol{X}'\boldsymbol{X})^{-1}\boldsymbol{X}' \tag{7.5}$$

of dimension $k \times T$, fixed by assumption. Then, the second term of (7.3) is the k-vector $\boldsymbol{Lu}$. Verify using the matrix multiplication rule that the elements of this vector are of the form

$$\{\boldsymbol{Lu}\}_i = l_{i1}u_1 + l_{i2}u_2 + \cdots + l_{iT}u_T$$

for $i = 1, \dots, k$. The linearity property of expectations then yields, for each i,

$$\begin{aligned}\mathrm{E}(l_{i1}u_1 + l_{i2}u_2 + \cdots + l_{iT}u_T) &= l_{i1}\mathrm{E}(u_1) + l_{i2}\mathrm{E}(u_2) + \cdots + l_{iT}\mathrm{E}(u_T) \\ &= 0. \end{aligned} \tag{7.6}$$

The fixed $\boldsymbol{X}$ assumption, translating into fixed $\boldsymbol{L}$, is critical for this calculation. If $\boldsymbol{X}$ was to be viewed as a random matrix sampled on the same basis as $\boldsymbol{y}$, as in the expenditure survey data in Section 7.1, then the calculation in (7.6) would be invalid as it stands. This is, essentially, why CRM(i) is needed to make progress.

Next, consider the variance matrix of $\hat{\boldsymbol{\beta}}$. In view of (7.4), write

$$\mathrm{Var}(\hat{\boldsymbol{\beta}}) = \mathrm{E}((\hat{\boldsymbol{\beta}} - \boldsymbol{\beta})(\hat{\boldsymbol{\beta}} - \boldsymbol{\beta})')$$

where in view of (7.3),

$$\hat{\boldsymbol{\beta}} - \boldsymbol{\beta} = (\boldsymbol{X}'\boldsymbol{X})^{-1}\boldsymbol{X}'\boldsymbol{u}. \tag{7.7}$$

The variance calculation therefore proceeds by the following sequence of steps:

$$\begin{aligned}\mathrm{Var}(\hat{\boldsymbol{\beta}}) &= \mathrm{E}((\boldsymbol{X}'\boldsymbol{X})^{-1}\boldsymbol{X}'\boldsymbol{uu}'\boldsymbol{X}(\boldsymbol{X}'\boldsymbol{X})^{-1}) \\ &= (\boldsymbol{X}'\boldsymbol{X})^{-1}\boldsymbol{X}'\mathrm{E}(\boldsymbol{uu}')\boldsymbol{X}(\boldsymbol{X}'\boldsymbol{X})^{-1} \\ &= (\boldsymbol{X}'\boldsymbol{X})^{-1}\boldsymbol{X}'(\sigma^2\boldsymbol{I}_T)\boldsymbol{X}(\boldsymbol{X}'\boldsymbol{X})^{-1} \\ &= \sigma^2(\boldsymbol{X}'\boldsymbol{X})^{-1}\boldsymbol{X}'\boldsymbol{I}_T\boldsymbol{X}(\boldsymbol{X}'\boldsymbol{X})^{-1} \\ &= \sigma^2(\boldsymbol{X}'\boldsymbol{X})^{-1}. \end{aligned} \tag{7.8}$$

Consider these equalities one at a time. The first one substitutes from (7.7), noting how the rule for transposition of products gets applied. The second one uses linearity of expectations, and is most easily deconstructed by noting that it is the expected outer product of the vector $\boldsymbol{Lu}$ where $\boldsymbol{L}$ is given by (7.5). The $(i, j)^{\text{th}}$ element of the $k \times k$ matrix $\boldsymbol{Luu}'\boldsymbol{L}'$ is a double sum of T^2 terms, with T squares and $T(T-1)$ cross products, thus:

$$\begin{aligned}&(l_{i1}u_1 + l_{i2}u_2 + \cdots + l_{iT}u_T)(l_{j1}u_1 + l_{j2}u_2 + \cdots + l_{jT}u_T) \\ &\quad = l_{i1}l_{j1}u_1^2 + \cdots + l_{i1}l_{jT}u_1u_T + l_{i1}l_{j2}u_1u_2 + l_{i2}l_{j2}u_2^2 + \cdots \\ &\quad = \sum_{t=1}^{T}\sum_{s=1}^{T} l_{it}l_{js}u_tu_s. \end{aligned}$$

Taking expected values, linearity means that the expectation of the sum is the sum of the expectations, so the typical element of $\mathrm{E}(\boldsymbol{Luu'L'})$ has the form

$$\begin{aligned}
&\mathrm{E}((l_{i1}u_1+l_{i2}u_2+\cdots+l_{iT}u_T)(l_{j1}u_1+l_{j2}u_2+\cdots+l_{jT}u_T)) \\
&\quad=\sum_{t=1}^{T}\sum_{s=1}^{T} l_{it}l_{js}\mathrm{E}(u_t u_s).
\end{aligned} \tag{7.9}$$

In view of the rule for multiplication, the matrix containing these elements can be written

$$\mathrm{E}(\boldsymbol{Luu'L'}) = \boldsymbol{L}\mathrm{E}(\boldsymbol{uu'})\boldsymbol{L'}.$$

Next, apply assumption CRM(iii) to obtain the third equality of (7.8). Elementwise, the terms in (7.9) where $t \neq s$ vanish and

$$\begin{aligned}
&\mathrm{E}((l_{i1}u_1+l_{i2}u_2+\cdots+l_{iT}u_T)(l_{j1}u_1+l_{j2}u_2+\cdots+l_{jT}u_T)) \\
&\quad= \sigma^2(l_{i1}l_{j1}+\cdots+l_{iT}l_{jT})
\end{aligned}$$

where $l_{i1}l_{j1}+\cdots+l_{iT}l_{jT}$ is the $(i,j)^{\text{th}}$ element of the square $k \times k$ matrix $\boldsymbol{LL'}$. By definition of the inverse,

$$\begin{aligned}
\boldsymbol{LL'} &= (\boldsymbol{X'X})^{-1}\boldsymbol{X'X}(\boldsymbol{X'X})^{-1} \\
&= (\boldsymbol{X'X})^{-1}
\end{aligned}$$

as in the last equality of (7.8).

This sequence of arguments is highly typical of the way that matrix formulae are manipulated in regression analysis. The same kind of thing in different contexts will be done throughout the rest of this book, and the style of (7.8) will generally be adopted without comment. Knowing what the matrix expressions mean in terms of the individual elements is simply a matter of applying the rules of matrix algebra. If in doubt, Chapter 2 contains all the relevant information.

The formula in (7.8) contains an unknown parameter σ^2, and for it to be of use, σ^2 will have to be replaced by an estimator. This will be derived in Section 7.5.

7.4 The Projection Matrices

The least squares prediction of $\boldsymbol{y}$ is a linear combination of the columns of $\boldsymbol{X}$ with weights $\hat{\boldsymbol{\beta}}$. This may be written as

$$\begin{aligned}
\hat{\boldsymbol{y}} &= \boldsymbol{X}\hat{\boldsymbol{\beta}} \\
&= \boldsymbol{X}(\boldsymbol{X'X})^{-1}\boldsymbol{X'y} \\
&= \boldsymbol{Qy}
\end{aligned} \tag{7.10}$$

where

$$\boldsymbol{Q} = \boldsymbol{X}(\boldsymbol{X'X})^{-1}\boldsymbol{X'}. \tag{7.11}$$

$\boldsymbol{Q}$ is a symmetric matrix of dimension $T \times T$ whose column space is spanned by the columns of $\boldsymbol{X}$, in the terminology of Section 4.1. Under assumption CRM(i), it has rank k.[2] The corresponding linear transformation from T-vector $\boldsymbol{y}$ to T-vector $\hat{\boldsymbol{y}}$ is

2 This fact can be deduced from (4.8) and (4.10), but see Section 9.5 for a different approach.

called a *projection*, because its effect is to 'project' $\boldsymbol{y}$ into the space spanned by $\boldsymbol{X}$, and $\boldsymbol{Q}$ is accordingly known as the *least squares projection matrix*. Your shadow on the wall is a two-dimensional projection of a three-dimensional object. Here, an object $\boldsymbol{y}$ from the set of all possible T-vectors is used to define an object $\hat{\boldsymbol{y}}$ belonging to a smaller set of T-vectors, those that can be formed as linear combinations of the columns of $\boldsymbol{X}$. $\hat{\boldsymbol{y}}$ is the prediction of the dependent variable generated by the regression from the information contained in $\boldsymbol{X}$. Note in particular that $\boldsymbol{QX} = \boldsymbol{X}$, the columns of $\boldsymbol{X}$ being the best predictions of themselves.

Also consider the least squares residuals, which can be written as

$$\begin{aligned}\hat{\boldsymbol{u}} &= \boldsymbol{y} - \boldsymbol{X}\hat{\boldsymbol{\beta}} \\ &= \boldsymbol{My} \end{aligned} \tag{7.12}$$

where

$$\boldsymbol{M} = \boldsymbol{I} - \boldsymbol{X}(\boldsymbol{X}'\boldsymbol{X})^{-1}\boldsymbol{X}'. \tag{7.13}$$

$\boldsymbol{M}$ is another symmetric $T \times T$ matrix, sometimes called the *orthogonal projection matrix* because it projects $\boldsymbol{y}$ into the complementary space of vectors that are orthogonal to the columns of $\boldsymbol{X}$. The word orthogonal is sometimes interpreted geometrically, as meaning "at right-angles to". It can also describe a matrix whose null space is spanned by $\boldsymbol{X}$, and so has nullity k under CRM(i), and rank $T - k$. The property $\boldsymbol{MX} = \boldsymbol{0}$ (a $T \times k$ matrix of zeros) is easily verified by direct calculation.

Both $\boldsymbol{Q}$ and $\boldsymbol{M}$ have the important property known as *idempotency*. An idempotent matrix $\boldsymbol{A}$ is a square matrix satisfying the identity

$$\boldsymbol{AA} = \boldsymbol{A}.$$

The one example of an idempotent matrix so far encountered is the identity matrix $\boldsymbol{I}$, and this one has the distinction of being the only case having full rank. All other idempotent matrices are singular. It is easily verified by direct calculation that the property holds for $\boldsymbol{Q}$ and $\boldsymbol{M}$. The reader should do this before going any further. An immediate feature of a symmetric idempotent matrix is positive semidefiniteness, noting that

$$\boldsymbol{z}'\boldsymbol{Az} = \boldsymbol{z}'\boldsymbol{A}'\boldsymbol{Az}$$

and comparing with Property 1 of Section 4.3. The final property to verify is the orthogonality relation $\boldsymbol{QM} = \boldsymbol{0}$ ($T \times T$ matrix of zeros) which, by symmetry, implies $\boldsymbol{MQ} = \boldsymbol{0}$ as well.

It may perhaps be worth remarking that although matrices such as $\boldsymbol{Q}$ and $\boldsymbol{M}$ feature very prominently in least squares theory, they are of course large (T^2 elements) and are never actually evaluated and stored when doing econometric computations. They always appear in the guise of products, such as (7.10) and (7.12), or quadratic forms. All that matters is their special properties in forming functions of the data.

7.5 The Trace

The *trace* of a square matrix is the sum of its diagonal elements. If $\boldsymbol{A}$ is $n \times n$, then

$$\operatorname{tr} \boldsymbol{A} = \sum_{i=1}^{n} a_{ii}.$$

The trace obeys the following rules. The rule for sums is very obvious. If $\boldsymbol{A}$ and $\boldsymbol{B}$ are square and conformable for addition, then

$$\text{tr}(\boldsymbol{A}+\boldsymbol{B}) = \text{tr}\boldsymbol{A} + \text{tr}\boldsymbol{B}.$$

If $\boldsymbol{A}$ is $m \times n$ and $\boldsymbol{B}$ is $n \times m$, then both the products $\boldsymbol{AB}$ $(m \times m)$ and $\boldsymbol{BA}$ $(n \times n)$ exist. The important multiplication rule for the trace is

$$\text{tr}\boldsymbol{AB} = \text{tr}\boldsymbol{BA}, \tag{7.14}$$

which is easily verified by noting that the diagonal elements of $\boldsymbol{AB}$ are given by $\sum_{j=1}^{n} a_{ij}b_{ji}$ for $i = 1, \dots, m$ and the diagonal elements of $\boldsymbol{BA}$ are $\sum_{i=1}^{m} b_{ji}a_{ij}$ for $j = 1, \dots, n$. Since scalar multiplication is commutative, adding up the first set of terms with respect to i leads to the same result as adding up the second set of terms with respect to j.

A useful fact for the reader to verify is that for any matrix $\boldsymbol{A}$, tr $\boldsymbol{A}'\boldsymbol{A}$ is the sum of the squares of all the elements of $\boldsymbol{A}$. The measure of magnitude

$$\|\boldsymbol{A}\| = \sqrt{\text{tr}\,\boldsymbol{A}'\boldsymbol{A}}$$

sometimes called the *Frobenius norm* of the matrix, is the natural generalization of the Euclidean norm of a vector, see (2.5).

A leading application of the trace is to estimating the variance of the regression disturbances. The least squares residuals, on substituting for $\boldsymbol{y}$ in (7.12), become

$$\begin{aligned}\hat{\boldsymbol{u}} &= \boldsymbol{MX}\beta + \boldsymbol{Mu}\\ &= \boldsymbol{Mu}\end{aligned} \tag{7.15}$$

since $\boldsymbol{MX} = \boldsymbol{0}$. Here, $\boldsymbol{u}$ is the vector of the true, unobserved disturbances, and the last equality is tantalizing, but since $\boldsymbol{M}$ is singular with rank $T-k$, the equation cannot be inverted to get $\boldsymbol{u}$ from $\hat{\boldsymbol{u}}$. However, using the by now familiar linearity arguments for the expected value, together with assumption CRM(iii) and the symmetry and idempotency of $\boldsymbol{M}$,

$$\begin{aligned}\text{E}(\hat{\boldsymbol{u}}\hat{\boldsymbol{u}}') &= \text{E}(\boldsymbol{Muu}'\boldsymbol{M})\\ &= \boldsymbol{M}(\sigma^2\boldsymbol{I}_T)\boldsymbol{M}\\ &= \sigma^2\boldsymbol{M}.\end{aligned} \tag{7.16}$$

This means that the least squares residuals have a singular distribution. Knowing $T-k$ of them, it is possible to deduce the remaining k elements exactly, knowing $\boldsymbol{X}$ and using the orthogonality relations $\boldsymbol{X}'\hat{\boldsymbol{u}} = \boldsymbol{0}$ $(k \times 1)$.

A further result from idempotency and symmetry is

$$\hat{\boldsymbol{u}}'\hat{\boldsymbol{u}} = \boldsymbol{u}'\boldsymbol{Mu}. \tag{7.17}$$

At this point, a clever argument is introduced. $\boldsymbol{u}'\boldsymbol{Mu}$ is a scalar quadratic form, and a scalar can be interpreted as a matrix of dimension 1×1. The single element is of necessity a diagonal element, and so it is equal to its own trace. Using the multiplication rule for the trace gives the neat result

$$\begin{aligned}\boldsymbol{u}'\boldsymbol{Mu} &= \text{tr}\,\boldsymbol{u}'\boldsymbol{Mu}\\ &= \text{tr}\,\boldsymbol{Muu}'.\end{aligned}$$

Inverting the order of multiplication of $\boldsymbol{u}'$ and $\boldsymbol{Mu}$ gives on the one hand a scalar and on the other hand a $T \times T$ matrix of rank 1, but both products are well defined and (7.14) gives the second equality. The expected value of the residual sum of squares can now be calculated. Using linearity in the usual way, along with assumption CRM(iii), gives

$$\begin{aligned}\mathrm{E}(\hat{\boldsymbol{u}}'\hat{\boldsymbol{u}}) &= \mathrm{E}(\mathrm{tr}\,\boldsymbol{M}\boldsymbol{u}\boldsymbol{u}')\\ &= \mathrm{tr}\,\boldsymbol{M}\mathrm{E}(\boldsymbol{u}\boldsymbol{u}')\\ &= \sigma^2\mathrm{tr}\,\boldsymbol{M}.\end{aligned}$$

The remaining question is to determine the trace of $\boldsymbol{M}$, but the sum and product rules together provide this result:

$$\begin{aligned}\mathrm{tr}\,\boldsymbol{M} &= \mathrm{tr}\,\boldsymbol{I}_T - \mathrm{tr}\,\boldsymbol{X}(\boldsymbol{X}'\boldsymbol{X})^{-1}\boldsymbol{X}'\\ &= T - \mathrm{tr}\,\boldsymbol{X}'\boldsymbol{X}(\boldsymbol{X}'\boldsymbol{X})^{-1}\\ &= T - k.\end{aligned}$$

The trace of $\boldsymbol{M}$ turns out to be equal to its rank, and this is in fact a general property of idempotent matrices, as will be shown in Section 9.5.

What has been shown here is that

$$\mathrm{E}(\hat{\boldsymbol{u}}'\hat{\boldsymbol{u}}) = \sigma^2(T-k)$$

and it follows directly that an unbiased estimator for σ^2 is

$$s^2 = \frac{\hat{\boldsymbol{u}}'\hat{\boldsymbol{u}}}{T-k}. \tag{7.18}$$

$T-k$, the number of observations less the number of fitted parameters, is the *degrees of freedom* of the regression. It is evident that the degrees of freedom must be positive, with at least one more observation than the number of regression coefficients, to be able to estimate σ^2. If $\boldsymbol{X}$ is square with rank $T=k$ the residuals are identically zero, as shown in (4.26). However, the relation between the degrees of freedom and the expected value of the residual sum of squares is an interesting revelation. This result explains formula (1.3) which it was promised to elucidate, since fitting the mean of a series uses up one degree of freedom. A series expressed in mean deviations is equivalent to the residuals from a regression in which the single explanatory variable is the intercept term, as can be deduced from (1.28) and (1.29).

The practical application of (7.18) is that it provides the means to make formula (7.8) operational, replacing the unknown σ^2 by the unbiased estimator s^2. Conventionally s^2 is called the "least squares residual variance", although take care to note that it does not itself solve a sum of squares minimization. It is merely constructed from components which do this.

7.6 Exercises

1 Are the following statements true or false?
 (a) If the square matrix $\boldsymbol{A}$ is idempotent, then the matrix $\boldsymbol{I}-\boldsymbol{A}$ is also idempotent.
 (b) If the square matrix $\boldsymbol{A}$ is idempotent, then the matrix $\boldsymbol{A}-\boldsymbol{I}$ is also idempotent.
 (c) If two square matrices are orthogonal, they must be singular.
 (d) If $\boldsymbol{A}$ and $\boldsymbol{B}$ are $n\times n$, and $\boldsymbol{B}$ is nonsingular,

$$\mathrm{tr}\,\boldsymbol{B}\boldsymbol{A}\boldsymbol{B}^{-1} = \mathrm{tr}\,\boldsymbol{A}$$

(e) If A is $n \times m$ with rank $A = m$, rank $A(A'A)^{-1}A' = \mathrm{tr}A(A'A)^{-1}A'$.
(f) For any matrix A, the trace of $A'A$ is equal to the sum of squares of all the matrix elements.
(g) The degrees of freedom of a regression is equal to the number of observations less the number of slope coefficients.

2 Are these matrices idempotent?

(a)
$$\begin{bmatrix} -\frac{1}{2} & \frac{1}{2} \\ \frac{1}{2} & -\frac{1}{2} \end{bmatrix}$$

(b)
$$\begin{bmatrix} 0 & 0 \\ 0 & 1 \end{bmatrix}$$

(c)
$$\begin{bmatrix} \frac{2}{3} & -\frac{1}{3} & -\frac{1}{3} \\ -\frac{1}{3} & \frac{2}{3} & -\frac{1}{3} \\ -\frac{1}{3} & -\frac{1}{3} & \frac{2}{3} \end{bmatrix}$$

(d)
$$\begin{bmatrix} \frac{1}{3} & \frac{1}{3} & \frac{1}{3} \\ \frac{1}{3} & \frac{1}{3} & \frac{1}{3} \\ \frac{1}{3} & \frac{1}{3} & \frac{1}{3} \end{bmatrix}$$

(e)
$$\begin{bmatrix} \frac{1}{2} & 0 & \frac{1}{2} \\ 0 & 0 & 0 \\ \frac{1}{2} & 0 & \frac{1}{2} \end{bmatrix}$$

3 For *all* choices of A and B such that the following matrices exist, are the matrices (i) symmetric? (ii) idempotent? (iii) positive definite or semidefinite?

(a) $A(A'A)^{-1}A'$
(b) $AB^{-1}A'$
(c) $A(B'A)^{-1}B'$
(d) $A(A'BA)^{-1}A'B$
(e) $BA(A'A)^{-1}A'B^{-1}$
(f) $A(A'A)^{-1}B'[B(A'A)^{-1}B']^{-1}B(A'A)^{-1}A'$

4 Consider the multiple regression equation

$$y = X\beta + u$$

Suppose that the independent variables are subjected to a linear transformation

$$Z = XA$$

where the matrix A is square and nonsingular. In the regression

$$y = Z\boldsymbol{\delta} + \boldsymbol{v}$$

(a) What is the relationship between the OLS estimate $\hat{\boldsymbol{\delta}}$ and the estimate $\hat{\boldsymbol{\beta}}$ from the original equation?
(b) What is the relationship between the residuals $\hat{\boldsymbol{v}}$ from the transformed equation, and $\hat{\boldsymbol{u}}$ from the original equation?

5 Let $\hat{\boldsymbol{\beta}}$ be defined in (7.2) and let assumptions CRM hold.
(a) Let $\boldsymbol{a}$ be a k-vector of constants. What are the mean and variance of $\boldsymbol{a}'\hat{\boldsymbol{\beta}}$?
(b) Let $\boldsymbol{A}$ be a $r \times k$ matrix of constants. What are the mean vector and variance matrix of $\boldsymbol{A}\hat{\boldsymbol{\beta}}$?
(c) In part (b), suppose $r > k$ and $\boldsymbol{A}$ has rank k. Show that there exists a perfectly predictable (zero variance) linear combination of the elements of $\boldsymbol{A}\hat{\boldsymbol{\beta}}$.

6 Let $\boldsymbol{Q} = \boldsymbol{X}(\boldsymbol{X}'\boldsymbol{X})^{-1}\boldsymbol{X}'$ where $\boldsymbol{X}$ $(T \times k)$ has rank k.
(a) Show that $\boldsymbol{Q}$ has rank k.
(b) Show that $\boldsymbol{M} = \boldsymbol{I} - \boldsymbol{Q}$ has rank $T - k$.

7 In the regression model $\boldsymbol{y} = \boldsymbol{X}\boldsymbol{\beta} + \boldsymbol{u}$ where $\boldsymbol{X} = (\boldsymbol{x}_1\ \boldsymbol{x}_2\ \cdots\ \boldsymbol{x}_T)'$, assume $\mathrm{E}(\boldsymbol{u}) = \boldsymbol{0}$ and $\mathrm{E}(\boldsymbol{u}\boldsymbol{u}') = \sigma^2\boldsymbol{I}_T$.
(a) What is the variance of $\hat{u}_t$, the tth element of the vector $\hat{\boldsymbol{u}}$ of least squares residuals?
(b) What is the covariance of $\hat{u}_t$ with $\hat{u}_s$ when t is different from s?
(c) What do your formulae imply about the validity of using $\hat{\boldsymbol{u}}$ as an estimator of $\boldsymbol{u}$?
(d) If the regression contains an intercept, the last column of $\boldsymbol{X}$ is $\boldsymbol{\iota} = (1, 1, \ldots, 1)'$. Show that in this case the residuals sum to zero, that is, $\hat{\boldsymbol{u}}'\boldsymbol{\iota} = 0$.

8 Consider the quadratic form $\boldsymbol{u}'\boldsymbol{M}\boldsymbol{u}$, where $\boldsymbol{M}$ is defined by (7.13) and $\boldsymbol{X}$ is $T \times k$ with rank k.
(a) Show that this is a sum of squares.
(b) In the case when $k = 1$ and $\boldsymbol{X}$ $(T \times 1)$ is the unit column $\boldsymbol{\iota} = (1, 1, \ldots, 1)'$, write out $\boldsymbol{u}'\boldsymbol{M}\boldsymbol{u}$ in 'sigma' notation.
(c) Show that if $T - k$ of the elements of $\hat{\boldsymbol{u}} = \boldsymbol{M}\boldsymbol{u}$ are known, and $\boldsymbol{X}$ is known, the remaining k elements can be calculated exactly. Show how this calculation might be done.

8

The Gauss-Markov Theorem

8.1 A Simple Example

The Gauss-Markov theorem is named by tradition after two mathematicians, one German and one Russian,[1] who were however not collaborators and whose lives did not even overlap. It is the famous result that the least squares estimator is *efficient* in the class of linear unbiased estimators in the regression model.

The efficiency of an estimator is the property that its variance with respect to the sampling distribution is the smallest in the specified class. The comparison is between alternative estimators based on a given sample. Thus, it is incorrect usage to say that least squares in a large sample is more efficient than in a small sample, even though the variance may be smaller in the former case. The task is to compare the sampling distributions of different estimators of $\boldsymbol{\beta}$ in (7.1) for a given design matrix $\boldsymbol{X}$.

These ideas will be developed first in the simplest possible example, the mean μ of a random sample $y_1, \dots, y_T$. If $\mathrm{E}(y_t) = \mu$ and $\mathrm{Var}(y_t) = \sigma^2$ for each t and $\mathrm{Cov}\,(y_t, y_s) = 0$ for $t \neq s$, assumptions CRM of Section 7.2 hold, where $\boldsymbol{X}$ $(T \times 1)$ is the column of ones. Recall from (1.29) that

$$\bar{y} = \frac{1}{T}\sum_{t=1}^{T} y_t$$

is the least squares estimator in the regression model

$$y_t = \mu + u_t.$$

That $\bar{y}$ is unbiased follows from

$$\begin{aligned}\mathrm{E}(\bar{y}) &= \frac{1}{T}\sum_{t=1}^{T}\mathrm{E}(y_t)\\ &= \mu.\end{aligned}$$

The variance of $\bar{y}$ is therefore calculated as

$$\mathrm{E}(\bar{y} - \mu)^2 = \frac{1}{T^2}\mathrm{E}\left(\sum_{t=1}^{T}(y_t - \mu)\right)^2$$

1 Carl Friedrich Gauss, 1777–1855 and Andrey Andreyevich Markov, 1856–1922.

An Introduction to Econometric Theory, First Edition. James Davidson.

Companion website: www.wiley.com/go/davidson/introecmettheory

$$= \frac{1}{T^2}\left(\sum_{t=1}^{T} \mathrm{E}(y_t - \mu)^2 + 2\sum_{t=2}^{T}\sum_{s=1}^{t-1} \mathrm{E}(y_t - \mu)(y_s - \mu)\right)$$

$$= \frac{\sigma^2}{T} \tag{8.1}$$

since $\mathrm{E}(y_t - \mu)(y_s - \mu) = \mathrm{Cov}(y_t, y_s) = 0$ for all $t \neq s$, by independence.

Take careful note of the form of the calculation in (8.1), for the square of a sum is an object that arises repeatedly in regression theory. Multiplying out the square of T terms results in T^2 terms, of which T are squares, and the other $T(T-1)$ are the so-called cross products, equal in pairs since scalar multiplication is commutative, swapping t and s giving the same result. The terms in (8.1) are the elements of the covariance matrix of the vector $\boldsymbol{y} = (y_1, \ldots, y_T)'$, as represented in (6.1). Since the matrix is symmetric, it is only necessary to add up the triangular array of elements below the main diagonal and multiply by two, as shown in (8.1) where the summation is first by rows and then by columns.

Consider the class of linear estimators of the mean. These are weighted sums of the series elements and take the generic form

$$m_a = \sum_{t=1}^{T} a_t y_t \tag{8.2}$$

for some collection of fixed weights $a_1, \ldots, a_T$. The least squares estimator $\bar{y}$ is the member of the class with $a_t = 1/T$ for every t. Two properties of m_a are easily established. First,

$$\mathrm{E}(m_a) = \sum_{t=1}^{T} a_t \mathrm{E}(y_t)$$

$$= \mu \sum_{t=1}^{T} a_t,$$

so that unbiasedness of m_a is the property

$$\sum_{t=1}^{T} a_t = 1.$$

Second, the variance of m_a, subject to the unbiasedness condition, is

$$\mathrm{E}(m_a - \mu)^2 = \mathrm{E}\left(\sum_{t=1}^{T} a_t(y_t - \mu)\right)^2$$

$$= \sum_{t=1}^{T} a_t^2 \mathrm{E}(y_t - \mu)^2 + 2\sum_{t=2}^{T}\sum_{s=1}^{t-1} a_t a_s \mathrm{E}(y_t - \mu)(y_s - \mu)$$

$$= \sigma^2 \sum_{t=1}^{T} a_t^2.$$

At this point we resort to a neat trick. Clearly, one can write

$$a_t = 1/T + (a_t - 1/T)$$

and hence

$$a_t^2 = \frac{1}{T^2} + \left(a_t - \frac{1}{T}\right)^2 + \frac{2}{T}\left(a_t - \frac{1}{T}\right).$$

If m_a is unbiased, the cross-product terms sum to zero, and

$$\begin{aligned}\sum_{t=1}^{T} a_t^2 &= \frac{1}{T} + \sum_{t=1}^{T}\left(a_t - \frac{1}{T}\right)^2 + \frac{2}{T}\sum_{t=1}^{T}\left(a_t - \frac{1}{T}\right) \\ &= \frac{1}{T} + \sum_{t=1}^{T}\left(a_t - \frac{1}{T}\right)^2 \\ &\geq \frac{1}{T}.\end{aligned}$$

Since all the terms in the second sum are zero or positive, this inequality becomes an equality only if $a_t = 1/T$ for every t, which is the case $m_a = \bar{y}$. This shows that under assumption CRM, least squares has smaller variance than any other linear unbiased estimator and is said to be the efficient member of the indicated class. This is the simplest instance of the Gauss-Markov theorem.

8.2 Efficiency in the General Model

The task in this section is to consider efficient estimation of $\boldsymbol{\beta}$ in the model (7.1). The chief complication here is the need to compare, not two variances, but two variance *matrices*. For comparison with the least squares estimator $\hat{\boldsymbol{\beta}}$ ("beta-hat"), consider the general class of linear unbiased estimators, of which the generic member will be designated by $\check{\boldsymbol{\beta}}$. We might say this as "beta-upside down hat", but perhaps "beta-moon" is neater and equally descriptive.

What is meant by a 'linear' estimator of $\boldsymbol{\beta}$? This is simply answered. The elements of the estimator vector must be linear functions of $\boldsymbol{y}$, or

$$\check{\boldsymbol{\beta}} = \boldsymbol{L}\boldsymbol{y}, \tag{8.3}$$

where $\boldsymbol{L}$ is a some $k \times T$ matrix of constants. Ordinary least squares (OLS) is the case $\boldsymbol{L} = (\boldsymbol{X}'\boldsymbol{X})^{-1}\boldsymbol{X}'$, as in (7.2). The expected value of the estimator under (7.1) and assumption CRM(ii) is calculated as

$$\begin{aligned}\mathrm{E}(\check{\boldsymbol{\beta}}) &= \boldsymbol{L}\mathrm{E}(\boldsymbol{y}) \\ &= \boldsymbol{L}\boldsymbol{X}\boldsymbol{\beta} + \boldsymbol{L}\mathrm{E}(\boldsymbol{u}) \\ &= \boldsymbol{L}\boldsymbol{X}\boldsymbol{\beta}.\end{aligned} \tag{8.4}$$

The unbiasedness condition is found as

$$\boldsymbol{L}\boldsymbol{X} = \boldsymbol{I}_k, \tag{8.5}$$

which is of course satisfied by OLS, since $(\boldsymbol{X}'\boldsymbol{X})^{-1}\boldsymbol{X}'\boldsymbol{X} = \boldsymbol{I}_k$.

Next consider the variance matrix of the linear unbiased estimator, to be denoted $\boldsymbol{V}(\check{\boldsymbol{\beta}})$ $(k \times k)$. Under unbiasedness,

$$\check{\boldsymbol{\beta}} = \boldsymbol{\beta} + \boldsymbol{L}\boldsymbol{u},$$

and the standard set of arguments leads under assumption CRM(iii) to

$$\begin{aligned} V(\check{\boldsymbol{\beta}}) &= \mathrm{E}((\check{\boldsymbol{\beta}} - \boldsymbol{\beta})(\check{\boldsymbol{\beta}} - \boldsymbol{\beta})') \\ &= \mathrm{E}(\boldsymbol{L}\boldsymbol{u}\boldsymbol{u}'\boldsymbol{L}') \\ &= \sigma^2 \boldsymbol{L}\boldsymbol{L}'. \end{aligned}$$

Thus, consider two linear unbiased estimators of $\boldsymbol{\beta}$ in (7.1), say $\hat{\boldsymbol{\beta}}$ and $\check{\boldsymbol{\beta}}$, with variance matrices $V(\hat{\boldsymbol{\beta}})$ and $V(\check{\boldsymbol{\beta}})$. How can these be compared? How can one variance matrix be "smaller" than another? To require every element of one matrix to be smaller than its counterpart in the other might be an unnecessarily stringent condition. Perhaps it would be enough to compare the individual variances (diagonal elements) and not worry about covariances?

In fact, there is an extremely neat way to do the comparison. Let this be stated formally as follows:

Efficiency criterion: $\hat{\boldsymbol{\beta}}$ is more efficient than (at least as efficient as) $\check{\boldsymbol{\beta}}$ if the matrix $V(\check{\boldsymbol{\beta}}) - V(\hat{\boldsymbol{\beta}})$ is positive definite (positive semidefinite).

The rationale for the definition is straightforward. Consider estimating a linear combination of $\boldsymbol{\beta}$, say $\boldsymbol{a}'\boldsymbol{\beta}$, where $\boldsymbol{a}$ is a chosen k-vector of constants. Let the estimator of the scalar $\boldsymbol{a}'\boldsymbol{\beta}$ be $\boldsymbol{a}'\check{\boldsymbol{\beta}}$. Clearly this is a linear estimator with the form $\boldsymbol{a}'\boldsymbol{L}\boldsymbol{y}$. Further, if $\check{\boldsymbol{\beta}}$ is unbiased then

$$\begin{aligned} \mathrm{E}(\boldsymbol{a}'\check{\boldsymbol{\beta}}) &= \boldsymbol{a}'\mathrm{E}(\check{\boldsymbol{\beta}}) \\ &= \boldsymbol{a}'\boldsymbol{\beta}, \end{aligned}$$

so this is also an unbiased estimator. The variance is

$$\begin{aligned} \mathrm{Var}(\boldsymbol{a}'\check{\boldsymbol{\beta}}) &= \mathrm{E}(\boldsymbol{a}'\check{\boldsymbol{\beta}} - \boldsymbol{a}'\boldsymbol{\beta})^2 \\ &= \mathrm{E}(\boldsymbol{a}'(\check{\boldsymbol{\beta}} - \boldsymbol{\beta}))^2 \\ &= \boldsymbol{a}'\mathrm{E}((\check{\boldsymbol{\beta}} - \boldsymbol{\beta})(\check{\boldsymbol{\beta}} - \boldsymbol{\beta})')\boldsymbol{a} \\ &= \boldsymbol{a}'V(\check{\boldsymbol{\beta}})\boldsymbol{a}. \end{aligned}$$

Observe the neat trick of taking the square of a matrix expression that evaluates to a scalar and replacing it by the product of the expression with its transpose. In other words, for a given random vector $\boldsymbol{z}$,

$$\begin{aligned} \mathrm{E}(\boldsymbol{a}'\boldsymbol{z})^2 &= \mathrm{E}(\boldsymbol{a}'\boldsymbol{z}\boldsymbol{z}'\boldsymbol{a}) \\ &= \boldsymbol{a}'\mathrm{E}(\boldsymbol{z}\boldsymbol{z}')\boldsymbol{a}. \end{aligned}$$

The trick is neat because while $\boldsymbol{z}\boldsymbol{z}'$ is an outer product matrix having rank 1, its expected value is a variance matrix of rank k. This change of rank may appear unexpected, but of course the expected value represents an average over the population of all the possible $\boldsymbol{z}\boldsymbol{z}'$ matrices, a very different object from the single drawing. Therefore, consider comparing the variances of two scalar unbiased estimators:

$$\begin{aligned} \mathrm{Var}(\boldsymbol{a}'\check{\boldsymbol{\beta}}) - \mathrm{Var}(\boldsymbol{a}'\hat{\boldsymbol{\beta}}) &= \boldsymbol{a}'V(\check{\boldsymbol{\beta}})\boldsymbol{a} - \boldsymbol{a}'V(\hat{\boldsymbol{\beta}})\boldsymbol{a} \\ &= \boldsymbol{a}'(V(\check{\boldsymbol{\beta}}) - V(\hat{\boldsymbol{\beta}}))\boldsymbol{a}. \end{aligned}$$

If $V(\check{\boldsymbol{\beta}}) - V(\hat{\boldsymbol{\beta}})$ is positive definite, this difference is positive, and the estimator $\boldsymbol{a}'\hat{\boldsymbol{\beta}}$ is more efficient than $\boldsymbol{a}'\check{\boldsymbol{\beta}}$.

This result holds for any choice of $\boldsymbol{a}$. For example, if $\boldsymbol{a}$ were to have a 1 in the first position and 0 in all other positions, then $\boldsymbol{a}'\boldsymbol{\beta} = \beta_1$. More generally, set $\boldsymbol{a} = (0, \ldots, 1, \ldots, 0)'$ (1 in the ith position, 0 otherwise) to pick out β_i for any i. This shows that the criterion applies to the estimators of any individual element. As another example, setting $\boldsymbol{a} = (1, -1, 0, \ldots, 0)'$ gives $\boldsymbol{a}'\boldsymbol{\beta} = \beta_1 - \beta_2$, and so forth. Any linear function of the coefficients is estimated more efficiently by $\hat{\boldsymbol{\beta}}$ than by $\check{\boldsymbol{\beta}}$. The efficiency criterion does not extend to non-linear functions, for example it cannot be claimed that β_1/β_2 is more efficiently estimated by $\hat{\beta}_1/\hat{\beta}_2$ than by $\check{\beta}_1/\check{\beta}_2$, but in any case these derived estimators are neither linear nor unbiased.

To demonstrate the required efficiency result, another neat trick is employed, generalizing the argument for the sample mean. Define the matrix

$$\boldsymbol{D} = \boldsymbol{L} - (\boldsymbol{X}'\boldsymbol{X})^{-1}\boldsymbol{X}',$$

and observe that $\boldsymbol{DX} = \boldsymbol{0}$ when $\check{\boldsymbol{\beta}}$ is unbiased, according to (8.5). Then,

$$\begin{aligned} \boldsymbol{LL}' &= ((\boldsymbol{X}'\boldsymbol{X})^{-1}\boldsymbol{X}' + \boldsymbol{D})(\boldsymbol{X}(\boldsymbol{X}'\boldsymbol{X})^{-1} + \boldsymbol{D}') \\ &= (\boldsymbol{X}'\boldsymbol{X})^{-1}\boldsymbol{X}'\boldsymbol{X}(\boldsymbol{X}'\boldsymbol{X})^{-1} + (\boldsymbol{X}'\boldsymbol{X})^{-1}\boldsymbol{X}'\boldsymbol{D}' + \boldsymbol{DX}(\boldsymbol{X}'\boldsymbol{X})^{-1} + \boldsymbol{DD}' \\ &= (\boldsymbol{X}'\boldsymbol{X})^{-1} + \boldsymbol{DD}' \end{aligned} \tag{8.6}$$

and

$$V(\check{\boldsymbol{\beta}}) - V(\hat{\boldsymbol{\beta}}) = \sigma^2\boldsymbol{DD}'.$$

$\boldsymbol{DD}'$ is positive semidefinite by construction, according to Property 1 of Section 4.3. Since $\sigma^2 > 0$, the same is true of $\sigma^2\boldsymbol{DD}'$, and the Gauss-Markov theorem is shown to hold for the general regression model under assumption CRM. Conventionally, OLS is said to be BLUE – Best in the class of Linear Unbiased Estimators.

8.3 Failure of the Assumptions

The discussion has made clear that assumptions CRM are quite stringent. Some powerful and useful properties for the OLS estimator have been demonstrated, but they depend on the model being correct and complete in the specific ways described. Suppose the assumptions are false? As discussed, CRM(i) is intrinsic to the classical regression approach. The failure of CRM(ii) would imply the omission of explanatory variables, for which there can be no remedy except correcting the specification. But that leaves the possibility that CRM(ii) holds but CRM(iii) fails.

Suppose this is the case, and write the modified assumptions as

$$\begin{aligned} \mathrm{E}(\boldsymbol{u}) &= \boldsymbol{0} \\ \mathrm{E}(\boldsymbol{uu}') &= \sigma^2\boldsymbol{\Omega}, \end{aligned}$$

where $\boldsymbol{\Omega}$ is a $T \times T$ positive definite matrix. Consider the properties of OLS in this case. As before,

$$\begin{aligned} \mathrm{E}(\hat{\boldsymbol{\beta}}) &= \boldsymbol{\beta} + (\boldsymbol{X}'\boldsymbol{X})^{-1}\boldsymbol{X}'\mathrm{E}(\boldsymbol{u}) \\ &= \boldsymbol{\beta}, \end{aligned}$$

so the estimator is still unbiased. However, the usual arguments yield

$$\begin{aligned}\text{Var}(\hat{\boldsymbol{\beta}}) &= \text{E}((\boldsymbol{X}'\boldsymbol{X})^{-1}\boldsymbol{X}'\boldsymbol{u}\boldsymbol{u}'\boldsymbol{X}(\boldsymbol{X}'\boldsymbol{X})^{-1}) \\ &= (\boldsymbol{X}'\boldsymbol{X})^{-1}\boldsymbol{X}'\text{E}(\boldsymbol{u}\boldsymbol{u}')\boldsymbol{X}(\boldsymbol{X}'\boldsymbol{X})^{-1} \\ &= \sigma^2(\boldsymbol{X}'\boldsymbol{X})^{-1}\boldsymbol{X}'\boldsymbol{\Omega}\boldsymbol{X}(\boldsymbol{X}'\boldsymbol{X})^{-1}. \end{aligned} \tag{8.7}$$

The Gauss-Markov theorem fails to hold in this case. The generic variance matrix of the linear unbiased class becomes

$$\text{Var}(\check{\boldsymbol{\beta}}) = \sigma^2\boldsymbol{L}\boldsymbol{\Omega}\boldsymbol{L}',$$

and equation (8.6) becomes

$$\begin{aligned}\boldsymbol{L}\boldsymbol{\Omega}\boldsymbol{L}' &= (\boldsymbol{X}'\boldsymbol{X})^{-1}\boldsymbol{X}'\boldsymbol{\Omega}\boldsymbol{X}(\boldsymbol{X}'\boldsymbol{X})^{-1} \\ &\quad + \boldsymbol{D}\boldsymbol{\Omega}\boldsymbol{X}(\boldsymbol{X}'\boldsymbol{X})^{-1} + (\boldsymbol{X}'\boldsymbol{X})^{-1}\boldsymbol{X}'\boldsymbol{\Omega}\boldsymbol{D}' + \boldsymbol{D}\boldsymbol{\Omega}\boldsymbol{D}'.\end{aligned}$$

The matrix $\boldsymbol{D}\boldsymbol{\Omega}\boldsymbol{X}(\boldsymbol{X}'\boldsymbol{X})^{-1}$ and its transpose do not vanish, so nothing can be said about the positive definiteness of the matrix $\text{Var}(\check{\boldsymbol{\beta}}) - \text{Var}(\hat{\boldsymbol{\beta}})$. Even worse, if practitioners are not aware of this failure of the assumptions they would typically use the OLS formula $s^2(\boldsymbol{X}'\boldsymbol{X})^{-1}$ to estimate coefficient variances and perform inferences. This is clearly not a valid estimator for (8.7). Hence, OLS estimation would be flawed on two distinct counts.

8.4 Generalized Least Squares

There is an elegant even if idealized solution to this problem. Idealized, because $\boldsymbol{\Omega}$ must be known, which is rarely the case in a practical situation. The basic solution can potentially be combined with advanced techniques incorporating estimators of $\boldsymbol{\Omega}$, although these would take us beyond the framework of the classical regression model. The focus of the present discussion is limited to improving understanding of the properties of least squares.

Since $\boldsymbol{\Omega}$ is positive definite, it has a Cholesky decomposition according to Property 2 of Section 4.3. There exists a nonsingular matrix $\boldsymbol{K}$ $(T \times T)$ such that

$$\boldsymbol{\Omega} = \boldsymbol{K}\boldsymbol{K}'. \tag{8.8}$$

Premultiplying both sides of this equation by $\boldsymbol{K}^{-1}$ and then postmultiplying by the transpose gives

$$\boldsymbol{K}^{-1}\boldsymbol{\Omega}(\boldsymbol{K}')^{-1} = \boldsymbol{I}_T.$$

In view of this identity, consider transforming the data matrices. Let $\boldsymbol{y}^* = \boldsymbol{K}^{-1}\boldsymbol{y}$ and $\boldsymbol{X}^* = \boldsymbol{K}^{-1}\boldsymbol{X}$. Accordingly write a transformed version of the model as

$$\boldsymbol{y}^* = \boldsymbol{X}^*\boldsymbol{\beta} + \boldsymbol{u}^*. \tag{8.9}$$

Since both sides of the equation $\boldsymbol{y} = \boldsymbol{X}\boldsymbol{\beta} + \boldsymbol{u}$ have been multiplied by $\boldsymbol{K}^{-1}$, it follows necessarily that $\boldsymbol{u}^* = \boldsymbol{K}^{-1}\boldsymbol{u}$. Then observe that

$$\begin{aligned}\text{E}(\boldsymbol{u}^*\boldsymbol{u}^{*\prime}) &= \boldsymbol{K}^{-1}\text{E}(\boldsymbol{u}\boldsymbol{u}')(\boldsymbol{K}')^{-1} \\ &= \sigma^2\boldsymbol{K}^{-1}\boldsymbol{\Omega}(\boldsymbol{K}')^{-1} \\ &= \sigma^2\boldsymbol{I}_T.\end{aligned} \tag{8.10}$$

Evidently, the transformed model (8.9) satisfies assumption CRM(iii).

Using the rule for inversion of a product, note that

$$\begin{aligned}(\boldsymbol{K}')^{-1}\boldsymbol{K}^{-1} &= (\boldsymbol{K}\boldsymbol{K}')^{-1}\\ &= \boldsymbol{\Omega}^{-1}.\end{aligned} \tag{8.11}$$

Therefore, the OLS estimator applied to this model takes the form

$$\begin{aligned}\tilde{\boldsymbol{\beta}} &= (\boldsymbol{X}^{*\prime}\boldsymbol{X}^{*})^{-1}\boldsymbol{X}^{*\prime}\boldsymbol{y}^{*}\\ &= (\boldsymbol{X}'(\boldsymbol{K}')^{-1}\boldsymbol{K}^{-1}\boldsymbol{X})^{-1}\boldsymbol{X}'(\boldsymbol{K}')^{-1}\boldsymbol{K}^{-1}\boldsymbol{y}\\ &= (\boldsymbol{X}'\boldsymbol{\Omega}^{-1}\boldsymbol{X})^{-1}\boldsymbol{X}'\boldsymbol{\Omega}^{-1}\boldsymbol{y}.\end{aligned} \tag{8.12}$$

This is called the *generalized least squares* (GLS) estimator, otherwise known as Aitken's estimator. Note the use of the tilde decoration instead of the hat, to distinguish this estimator from OLS. It should perhaps be noted that the last formula of (8.12), while often quoted, is never used for computation since the $T \times T$ matrix $\boldsymbol{\Omega}$ would be awkward to construct and store. GLS is always implemented in practice by running OLS on transformed variables.

The properties of GLS are found by application of the usual techniques. Unbiasednessholds just as before, with

$$\begin{aligned}\mathrm{E}(\tilde{\boldsymbol{\beta}}) &= \boldsymbol{\beta} + (\boldsymbol{X}'\boldsymbol{\Omega}^{-1}\boldsymbol{X})^{-1}\boldsymbol{X}'\boldsymbol{\Omega}^{-1}\mathrm{E}(\boldsymbol{u})\\ &= \boldsymbol{\beta}.\end{aligned}$$

The variance matrix of GLS is found very similarly to (7.8), as

$$\begin{aligned}\mathrm{E}[(\tilde{\boldsymbol{\beta}} - \boldsymbol{\beta})(\tilde{\boldsymbol{\beta}} - \boldsymbol{\beta})'] &= (\boldsymbol{X}'\boldsymbol{\Omega}^{-1}\boldsymbol{X})^{-1}\boldsymbol{X}'\boldsymbol{\Omega}^{-1}\mathrm{E}(\boldsymbol{u}\boldsymbol{u}')\boldsymbol{\Omega}^{-1}\boldsymbol{X}(\boldsymbol{X}'\boldsymbol{\Omega}^{-1}\boldsymbol{X})^{-1}\\ &= (\boldsymbol{X}'\boldsymbol{\Omega}^{-1}\boldsymbol{X})^{-1}\boldsymbol{X}'\boldsymbol{\Omega}^{-1}\sigma^2\boldsymbol{\Omega}\boldsymbol{\Omega}^{-1}\boldsymbol{X}(\boldsymbol{X}'\boldsymbol{\Omega}^{-1}\boldsymbol{X})^{-1}\\ &= \sigma^2(\boldsymbol{X}'\boldsymbol{\Omega}^{-1}\boldsymbol{X})^{-1}.\end{aligned}$$

Contrast this formula with the OLS variance matrix (8.7). GLS is obtained by applying OLS to a model that satisfies assumptions CRM; thus, according the Gauss-Markov theorem, GLS must be efficient in the class of linear unbiased estimators. In particular, it must be the case that the matrix

$$(\boldsymbol{X}'\boldsymbol{X})^{-1}\boldsymbol{X}'\boldsymbol{\Omega}\boldsymbol{X}(\boldsymbol{X}'\boldsymbol{X})^{-1} - (\boldsymbol{X}'\boldsymbol{\Omega}^{-1}\boldsymbol{X})^{-1} \tag{8.13}$$

is positive semidefinite, and positive definite unless $\boldsymbol{\Omega} = \boldsymbol{I}_T$. Although the Gauss-Markov theorem establishes this fact indirectly, it would be nice to demonstrate it by direct calculation. This can be done as follows but is strictly optional for the development. Skip unless curious.

Using Property 6 of positive definite matrices from Section 4.3 and the rules for inversion of products, what has to be shown is the positive definiteness of

$$\boldsymbol{X}'\boldsymbol{\Omega}^{-1}\boldsymbol{X} - \boldsymbol{X}'\boldsymbol{X}(\boldsymbol{X}'\boldsymbol{\Omega}\boldsymbol{X})^{-1}\boldsymbol{X}'\boldsymbol{X}. \tag{8.14}$$

Substituting the decompositions (8.8) and (8.11) into (8.14) and gathering the terms in the difference produces

$$\begin{aligned}&\boldsymbol{X}'\boldsymbol{K}'^{-1}\boldsymbol{K}^{-1}\boldsymbol{X} - \boldsymbol{X}'\boldsymbol{X}(\boldsymbol{X}'\boldsymbol{K}\boldsymbol{K}'\boldsymbol{X})^{-1}\boldsymbol{X}'\boldsymbol{X}\\ &\qquad = \boldsymbol{X}'\boldsymbol{K}'^{-1}\boldsymbol{M}_{KX}\boldsymbol{K}^{-1}\boldsymbol{X}\\ &\qquad = \boldsymbol{A}'\boldsymbol{A},\end{aligned} \tag{8.15}$$

where

$$M_{KX} = I_T - K'X(X'KK'X)^{-1}X'K$$

is symmetric and idempotent with rank $T - k$ and

$$A = M_{KX}K^{-1}X \quad (T \times k).$$

$A'A$ is positive semidefinite by Property 1 from Section 4.3. It is also positive definite if A has full rank k, and this is the case unless there exists a vector in the column space of $K^{-1}X$ that is also in the column space of $K'X$ and hence orthogonal to M_{KX}. However, $K^{-1} = K'$ implies $\Omega = I_T$.

8.5 Weighted Least Squares

The GLS estimator is generally impractical because of the requirement to know all the elements of the large matrix Ω, but if the disturbances are independently distributed and just their variances differ, this case could prove feasible to implement. Representing the matrix in terms of its elements, as $\Omega = \{\omega_{ts}\}$, this is the diagonal case where $\omega_{ts} = 0$ for $t \neq s$, but $\omega_{tt} \neq \omega_{ss}$. The technical term for this condition is *heteroscedasticity*.[2] A case sometimes invoked is where a variable $w_1, \dots, w_T$ is observed and fixed in repeated samples, such that $\omega_{tt} = w_t^2$. GLS in this case is called weighted least squares (WLS).

The following result has already been shown to be true, being a case of the general result of the last section, but it is included to contribute some extra intuition for a simple case. By comparison with the somewhat obscure demonstration that (8.13) is positive semidefinite, here a neat and transparent argument is available, worth knowing in its own right.

For clarity, let the model be a simple regression where the intercept is suppressed, perhaps because the data are expressed in deviations from the mean, although the notation will not show this explicitly. The equation is

$$y_t = \beta x_t + u_t, \quad t = 1, \dots, T$$

where $\mathrm{E}(u_t) = 0$ and $\mathrm{Cov}\,(u_t, u_s) = 0$ for $t \neq s$ but $\mathrm{Var}(u_t) = \sigma^2 w_t^2$. The WLS method is to divide through both sides of the equation by the absolute value of w_t (square root of the square) and fit this equation by OLS. The OLS estimator of β in the equation

$$\frac{y_t}{|w_t|} = \beta\frac{x_t}{|w_t|} + \frac{u_t}{|w_t|}$$

is

$$\begin{aligned}\tilde{\beta} &= \frac{\sum_{t=1}^T x_t y_t / w_t^2}{\sum_{t=1}^T x_t^2 / w_t^2} \\ &= \beta + \frac{\sum_{t=1}^T x_t u_t / w_t^2}{\sum_{t=1}^T x_t^2 / w_t^2}.\end{aligned} \tag{8.16}$$

2 Sometimes spelt *heteroskedasticity* in deference to the Greek root of the word.

The unbiasedness of $\tilde{\beta}$ is immediate from the assumption $\mathrm{E}(u_t) = 0$ for each t, and the variance is the expected square of the second term on the right-hand side of (8.16). Since the cross-product terms all vanish, this is just the sum of the expected squares and simplifies to

$$\begin{aligned}\mathrm{Var}(\tilde{\beta}) &= \sigma^2 \frac{\sum_{t=1}^{T} x_t^2 w_t^2 / w_t^4}{\left(\sum_{t=1}^{T} x_t^2 / w_t^2\right)^2} \\ &= \frac{\sigma^2}{\sum_{t=1}^{T} x_t^2 / w_t^2}.\end{aligned} \tag{8.17}$$

The proposition is that this is the smallest value attainable by a linear unbiased estimator and, in particular, is smaller than the variance of the OLS estimator. To show that WLS improves on OLS, write the latter as

$$\begin{aligned}\hat{\beta} &= \frac{\sum_{t=1}^{T} x_t y_t}{\sum_{t=1}^{T} x_t^2} \\ &= \beta + \frac{\sum_{t=1}^{T} x_t u_t}{\sum_{t=1}^{T} x_t^2}\end{aligned}$$

and observe that

$$\mathrm{Var}(\hat{\beta}) = \sigma^2 \frac{\sum_{t=1}^{T} x_t^2 w_t^2}{\left(\sum_{t=1}^{T} x_t^2\right)^2}. \tag{8.18}$$

Comparing the formulae in (8.17) and (8.18), it is easily seen that the condition for $\mathrm{Var}(\hat{\beta}) > \mathrm{Var}(\tilde{\beta})$ is

$$\sum_{t=1}^{T} x_t^2 w_t^2 \sum_{t=1}^{T} \frac{x_t^2}{w_t^2} > \left(\sum_{t=1}^{T} x_t^2\right)^2. \tag{8.19}$$

Multiplying out the left-hand side of (8.19) and rearranging gives

$$\begin{aligned}\sum_{t=1}^{T} x_t^2 w_t^2 \sum_{s=1}^{T} \frac{x_s^2}{w_s^2} &= \sum_{t=1}^{T} \sum_{s=1}^{T} x_t^2 x_s^2 \frac{w_t^2}{w_s^2} \\ &= \sum_{t=1}^{T} x_t^4 + \sum_{t=2}^{T} \sum_{s=1}^{t-1} x_t^2 x_s^2 \left(\frac{w_t^2}{w_s^2} + \frac{w_s^2}{w_t^2}\right).\end{aligned} \tag{8.20}$$

Of these T^2 terms, in addition to the T cases with $t = s$, there are $T(T-1)$ cross products that in the last member of (8.20) are organized in pairs, the cases with $t > s$, as shown, matched with the cases $s > t$. Note that $x_s^2 x_t^2 = x_t^2 x_s^2$ but each ratio of weights is paired with its reciprocal. By contrast, the right-hand side of (8.19) after multiplying out is

$$\left(\sum_{t=1}^{T} x_t^2\right)^2 = \sum_{t=1}^{T} x_t^4 + 2 \sum_{t=2}^{T} \sum_{s=1}^{t-1} x_t^2 x_s^2.$$

Therefore, the inequality is proved if it can be shown that

$$\frac{w_t^2}{w_s^2} + \frac{w_s^2}{w_t^2} > 2$$

whenever $w_t^2 \neq w_s^2$. Considering the case $w_t^2 > w_s^2$ without loss of generality, the inequality corresponds to

$$x + 1/x > 2$$

for $x > 1$, which is easily demonstrated by rearranging the inequality

$$x(x-1) > (x-1).$$

Inequality (8.19) is therefore shown to hold unless $w_t^2 = w_s^2$ for every $t \neq s$, which is the homoscedastic case.

8.6 Exercises

1 Are the following statements true or false?
  (a) 'Efficiency' is the property of an estimator of having a smaller variance than any other estimator.
  (b) If the difference of the covariance matrices of two alternative estimators of coefficient vector $\boldsymbol{\beta}$ is positive definite, this means that the sum of the estimated coefficients has a smaller variance in the second case than in the first case.
  (c) If the sum of the estimated coefficients has a smaller variance in the case of Estimator 2 of $\boldsymbol{\beta}$ than in the case of Estimator 1, this means that the difference of the two covariance matrices is positive definite.
  (d) The Gauss-Markov theorem compares the variances of linear functions of the regression coefficients. It has nothing to tell us about non-linear functions.
  (e) If the assumption of uncorrelated disturbances fails, the least squares variance formula is smaller than it should be.
  (f) Generalized least squares is a feasible estimator if and only if the covariance matrix of the disturbances is a known function of the regressors $\boldsymbol{X}$.
  (g) Weighted least squares is the case of generalized least squares where the disturbances are uncorrelated.

2 In the model

$$y_t = \beta x_t + u_t, \quad t = 1, \dots, T$$

where $u_t \sim$ i.i.d. with $\mathrm{E}(u_t) = 0$ and $\mathrm{E}(u_t^2) = \sigma^2$,
  (a) Obtain $\hat{\beta}$, the least squares estimator of the parameter β.
  (b) Show that $\hat{\beta}$ is best in the class of linear unbiased estimators.

3 In the model of Question 2, suppose that $\mathrm{E}(u_t) = 0$, $\mathrm{E}(u_t^2) = \sigma^2 w_t^2$, and $\mathrm{E}(u_t u_s) = 0$ for $t \neq s$, where w_t is an observed data series, fixed in repeated samples.
  (a) Show that the weighted least squares estimator of β has a lower variance than the OLS estimator.

(b) Show that the weighted least squares estimator is efficient in the class of linear unbiased estimators of β.

4 A 'random coefficient' model of the relationship between a random series $y_1, \dots, y_T$ and $a_1, \dots, a_T$, a collection of observed constants, is

$$y_t = a_t(\beta + u_t),$$

where $u_t \sim$ i.i.d.$(0, \sigma^2)$. Compare and contrast the following proposed estimators of β.

(a) The sample mean of the series $y_1/a_1, \cdots, y_T/a_T$.
(b) Least squares regression of y_t onto a_t.
(c) The ratio $\frac{\bar{y}}{\bar{a}}$, where $\bar{y}$ and $\bar{a}$ are the sample means of the two series.

5 In the regression model $\boldsymbol{y} = \boldsymbol{X\beta} + \boldsymbol{u}$ $(T \times 1)$, $\boldsymbol{X}$ $(T \times k)$ is fixed with rank k, $\mathrm{E}(\boldsymbol{u}) = \boldsymbol{0}$, and $\mathrm{E}(\boldsymbol{uu}') = \sigma^2\boldsymbol{\Omega}$.

(a) Consider the function

$$S(\boldsymbol{b}) = (\boldsymbol{y} - \boldsymbol{Xb})'\boldsymbol{\Omega}^{-1}(\boldsymbol{y} - \boldsymbol{Xb}).$$

Given a vector $\tilde{\boldsymbol{\beta}}$, define $\tilde{\boldsymbol{u}} = \boldsymbol{y} - \boldsymbol{X}\tilde{\boldsymbol{\beta}}$. Show that if

$$\boldsymbol{X}'\boldsymbol{\Omega}^{-1}\tilde{\boldsymbol{u}} = \boldsymbol{0}, \tag{8.21}$$

then S is minimized by setting $\boldsymbol{b} = \tilde{\boldsymbol{\beta}}$.

(b) Obtain the formula for $\tilde{\boldsymbol{\beta}}$ by solving equation (1) in part (a). Obtain the mean and the variance matrix of $\tilde{\boldsymbol{\beta}}$.

6 In the model $\boldsymbol{y} = \boldsymbol{X\beta} + \boldsymbol{u}$ where $\boldsymbol{X}$ $(T \times k)$ is fixed with rank k, consider transforming the data as $\boldsymbol{y}^* = \boldsymbol{Py}$ and $\boldsymbol{X}^* = \boldsymbol{PX}$, where $\boldsymbol{P}$ is a $T \times T$ lower triangular nonsingular matrix.

(a) Show that the generalized least squares estimator can be computed by running the OLS regression of $\boldsymbol{y}^*$ onto $\boldsymbol{X}^*$ where $\boldsymbol{P}$ is suitably chosen, and explain how $\boldsymbol{P}$ is related to $\boldsymbol{\Omega}$.
(b) If $\mathrm{E}(\boldsymbol{u}) = \boldsymbol{0}$ and $\mathrm{E}(\boldsymbol{uu}') = \sigma^2\boldsymbol{\Omega}$, obtain the variance matrix of $\boldsymbol{u}^* = \boldsymbol{Pu}$. Is the GLS estimator efficient in the class of linear unbiased estimators of $\boldsymbol{\beta}$? Explain your answer.

7 Suppose that

$$y_t = \mu + u_t, \quad t = 1, \dots, T$$

where $\mathrm{E}(u_t) = 0$ but $\mathrm{E}(u_t^2) = \sigma_t^2$, and it is known that the observations fall into two groups, having more and less dispersion. In the 'noisy' group labelled $t = 1, \dots, T_1$, $\sigma_t^2 = 4$, while in the group labelled $t = T_1 + 1, \dots, T$, $\sigma_t^2 = 1$.

(a) Find the efficient estimator of μ.
(b) Compare the efficient estimator with the sample mean of the observations.

Part III

Testing

9

Eigenvalues and Eigenvectors

This chapter represents something of a change of gear in the study of matrices. So far, we have learned how to do various calculations using matrix notation and exploit the fairly simple rules of matrix algebra. Most importantly, we have used linearity to calculate the expected values of matrix functions of random variables and so computed means and variances of estimators. However, all these calculations could in principle have been done using 'sigma' notation with scalar quantities. Matrix algebra simply confers the benefits of simplicity and economy in what would otherwise be seriously complicated calculations.

What happens in this chapter is different in kind because the methods don't really have any counterparts in scalar algebra. One enters a novel and rather magical world where seemingly intractable problems turn out to have feasible solutions. Careful attention to detail will be necessary to keep abreast of the new ideas. This is a relatively technical chapter, and some of the arguments are quite intricate. This material does not all need to be completely absorbed in order to make use of the results in the chapters to come, and readers who are happy to take such results on trust may want to skip or browse it at first reading. The material essential for understanding least squares inference relates to the diagonalization of symmetric idempotent matrices.

9.1 The Characteristic Equation

Let $\boldsymbol{A}$ be square $n \times n$, and consider for a scalar λ the scalar equation

$$|\boldsymbol{A} - \lambda \boldsymbol{I}| = 0. \tag{9.1}$$

This is the determinant of the matrix formed from $\boldsymbol{A}$ by subtracting λ from each of its diagonal elements. It is known as the *characteristic equation* of $\boldsymbol{A}$. By considering the form of the determinant, as in (3.8), this is found to be a nth-order polynomial in λ. The determinant is a sum of terms, of which one is the product of the diagonal elements. When multiplied out, it must contain the term λ^n, and in general, powers of λ of all orders up to n appear in one term or another. The roots (or zeros) of the characteristic equation are the values of λ for which (9.1) holds. There are n of these, denoted $\lambda_1, \dots, \lambda_n$, although they are not necessarily distinct and repeated roots are possible. These roots are sometimes called the *characteristic values* of $\boldsymbol{A}$ but more commonly the *eigenvalues* of $\boldsymbol{A}$.

An Introduction to Econometric Theory, First Edition. James Davidson.

Companion website: www.wiley.com/go/davidson/introecmettheory

Since the coefficient of λ^n is always 1, the characteristic polynomial can be written in factored form as

$$|A - \lambda I| = (\lambda - \lambda_1)(\lambda - \lambda_2)\cdots(\lambda - \lambda_n) \tag{9.2}$$

such that putting λ equal to any of the roots sets (9.2) to zero. One evident feature of equation (9.1) is that $\lambda = 0$ is a solution if and only if $|A| = 0$. A singular matrix must have at least one zero eigenvalue.

Beyond this simple fact, the interpretation of the eigenvalues can appear as a rather opaque problem. The roots of a higher-order polynomial usually have to be calculated numerically. To see what is going on, it is helpful to consider initially a 2×2 matrix, where

$$\begin{aligned} |A - \lambda I| &= \begin{vmatrix} a_{11} - \lambda & a_{12} \\ a_{21} & a_{22} - \lambda \end{vmatrix} \\ &= (a_{11} - \lambda)(a_{22} - \lambda) - a_{12}a_{21} \\ &= \lambda^2 - (a_{11} + a_{22})\lambda + |A| \end{aligned}$$

and $|A| = a_{11}a_{22} - a_{12}a_{21}$. In this case, (9.1) is a quadratic equation having two roots, say λ_1 and λ_2.

Writing a quadratic function in generic notation as

$$\lambda^2 + b\lambda + c = (\lambda - \lambda_1)(\lambda - \lambda_2)$$

and multiplying out shows that

$$\lambda_1 + \lambda_2 = -b \tag{9.3}$$

and

$$\lambda_1\lambda_2 = c. \tag{9.4}$$

The roots are found by inverting this pair of equations, and the well-known solutions, easily verified by substituting them back into (9.3) and (9.4) and simplifying, are

$$\lambda_1 = -\frac{1}{2}\left(b + \sqrt{b^2 - 4c}\right) \tag{9.5}$$

$$\lambda_2 = -\frac{1}{2}\left(b - \sqrt{b^2 - 4c}\right). \tag{9.6}$$

In fact, this form of solution arises in the general case, since (9.2) with $n > 2$ can always be viewed as the product of quadratic factors, times $(\lambda - \lambda_n)$ if n is odd. These quadratic pairs must then have solutions with the general form of (9.5) and (9.6). The well-known difficulty is the existence of cases where $4c > b^2$, so that the number under the square root signs in (9.5) and (9.6) is negative. In this case, no real solutions of (9.5) and (9.6) exist, and the only way to proceed is to invoke the theory of complex numbers. Fortunately, complex eigenvalues do not generally arise in the theory of regression, but a proper understanding of *why* this is so requires some grasp of the theory.

9.2 Complex Roots

To handle the case $4c > b^2$ in (9.5) and (9.6), what is done is to write

$$\sqrt{b^2 - 4c} = \mathrm{i}\sqrt{4c - b^2}$$

where the square root can now be evaluated and $i = \sqrt{-1}$, the well-known *imaginary number*. The eigenvalues in this case are so-called complex numbers with the forms

$$\lambda_1 = -\frac{1}{2}\left(b + i\sqrt{4c - b^2}\right) \tag{9.7}$$

$$\lambda_2 = -\frac{1}{2}\left(b - i\sqrt{4c - b^2}\right). \tag{9.8}$$

A complex number is the sum of two terms of which one, the imaginary part, contains the factor i. Numbers without imaginary parts, the familiar case, are called real numbers in this context.

The pair (9.7) and (9.8) are the same in all respects apart from the signs of the imaginary parts, and such pairs are called *complex conjugates*. Complex solutions of (9.1) can only arise as conjugate pairs, because while the zeros of (9.2) may be complex-valued, the elements of $\boldsymbol{A}$ are real and the determinant itself must be real-valued if evaluated at a real λ. For simplicity of notation, write $\lambda_1 = A + iB$ and $\lambda_2 = A - iB$, and verify, using the fact that $i^2 = -1$ by definition, that

$$\lambda_1 + \lambda_2 = 2A$$

and

$$\begin{aligned}\lambda_1\lambda_2 &= (A + iB)(A - iB)\\ &= A^2 + iAB - iAB - (i^2)B^2\\ &= A^2 + B^2.\end{aligned}$$

The conjugacy ensures that b and c in (9.3) and (9.4) are always real numbers.

The square root of the product of a complex number with its complex conjugate is called the *modulus* of the number and is the counterpart for complex numbers of the absolute value of a real number. If $Z = A + iB$, the modulus is

$$|Z| = \sqrt{A^2 + B^2}.$$

The real and imaginary parts of a complex number are often visualized as defining a point in the plane, with the real part defining the horizontal distance from the origin (0,0) and the imaginary part the vertical distance. The resulting plot is called an 'Argand diagram'. By Pythagoras's theorem, the modulus is the length of the hypotenuse of the right-angled triangle with sides A and B; in other words, of the line connecting the point to the origin.

A fact that proves useful below is that the complex conjugate of a product of complex numbers is equal to the product of their complex conjugates. Thus, if Z and W are complex numbers and Z^* and W^* denote their complex conjugates,

$$(ZW)^* = Z^*W^*.$$

To see that this is true, put $Z = A + iB$ and $W = C + iD$, and use the identity $i^2 = -1$ wherever required to get

$$\begin{aligned}[(A + iB)(C + iD)]^* &= [(AC - BD) + i(AD + BC)]^*\\ &= (AC - BD) - i(AD + BC)\\ &= (A - iB)(C - iD).\end{aligned} \tag{9.9}$$

9.3 Eigenvectors

Because $\boldsymbol{A} - \lambda_j \boldsymbol{I}$ is by construction a singular matrix for each $j = 1, \ldots, n$, there exist nonzero n-vectors $\boldsymbol{c}_1, \ldots, \boldsymbol{c}_n$ such that

$$\boldsymbol{A}\boldsymbol{c}_j = \lambda_j \boldsymbol{c}_j, \quad j = 1, \ldots, n. \tag{9.10}$$

These are called the *eigenvectors* of the matrix $\boldsymbol{A}$. Being the solutions of homogeneous systems, these vectors are not unique, since if $\boldsymbol{c}_j$ is a solution so is $a\boldsymbol{c}_j$, for any scalar $a \neq 0$. To resolve this indeterminacy, the vectors are given unit length, requiring $\boldsymbol{c}_j'\boldsymbol{c}_j = 1$. Premultiplying equation (9.10) by $\boldsymbol{c}_j'$ reveals the representation

$$\lambda_j = \boldsymbol{c}_j'\boldsymbol{A}\boldsymbol{c}_j. \tag{9.11}$$

If the eigenvalues are all distinct, the eigenvectors form a linearly independent set. This means that the square $n \times n$ matrix

$$\boldsymbol{C} = [\boldsymbol{c}_1 \ \ \boldsymbol{c}_2 \ \ \ldots \ \ \boldsymbol{c}_n] \tag{9.12}$$

is nonsingular. This proposition is sufficiently important that a demonstration is desirable, although this is a slightly technical argument, so the reader in a hurry might wish to skip the next paragraph at first reading.

The approach is a classic proof by contradiction. Suppose the eigenvectors are linearly dependent. This means that a collection of between 2 and n of the vectors must form a linearly dependent set. Let the *smallest* such collection (where the vectors can be chosen in any order) be $\boldsymbol{c}_1, \ldots, \boldsymbol{c}_J$, such that dropping any one of these vectors leaves a linearly independent collection. Then there must exist the linear combination

$$b_1\boldsymbol{c}_1 + b_2\boldsymbol{c}_2 + \cdots + b_J\boldsymbol{c}_J = \boldsymbol{0} \tag{9.13}$$

where $b_1, \ldots, b_J$ are not all zero. Premultiply (9.13) by $\boldsymbol{A}$, and then use (9.10) to write

$$b_1\lambda_1\boldsymbol{c}_1 + \cdots + b_J\lambda_J\boldsymbol{c}_J = \boldsymbol{0}. \tag{9.14}$$

But also, multiply (9.13) through by λ_J (note that the order of the columns is arbitrary) to get

$$b_1\lambda_J\boldsymbol{c}_1 + \cdots + b_J\lambda_J\boldsymbol{c}_J = \boldsymbol{0}. \tag{9.15}$$

Subtracting (9.14) from (9.15) produces

$$b_1(\lambda_1 - \lambda_J)\boldsymbol{c}_1 + \cdots + b_{J-1}(\lambda_{J-1} - \lambda_J)\boldsymbol{c}_{J-1} = \boldsymbol{0}.$$

But this is a contradiction. Since the eigenvalues are distinct, at least one of the weights in this sum is nonzero. If $J = 2$, then $b_1(\lambda_1 - \lambda_2) \neq 0$, whereas if $J > 2$, $\boldsymbol{c}_1, \ldots, \boldsymbol{c}_{J-1}$ is revealed as a linearly dependent set, contrary to what was assumed. Therefore, no linearly dependent set of eigenvalues exists. QED

There is nothing to stop eigenvectors as well as eigenvalues being complex valued, even when the matrix $\boldsymbol{A}$ is real valued. Allowing for this possibility, write $\lambda_1^*, \ldots, \lambda_n^*$ and $\boldsymbol{c}_1^*, \ldots, \boldsymbol{c}_n^*$ to be the complex conjugates of $\lambda_1, \ldots, \lambda_n$ and $\boldsymbol{c}_1, \ldots, \boldsymbol{c}_n$, where since the $\boldsymbol{c}_j$ are vectors, the complex conjugate is the vector in which each element has the sign of its imaginary part reversed. Of course, if λ_j and $\boldsymbol{c}_j$ are real valued then there are no imaginary parts, so in this case $\lambda_j^* = \lambda_j$ and $\boldsymbol{c}_j^* = \boldsymbol{c}_j$.

One of the most important results to be made use of later on is that the eigenvalues of symmetric matrices are always real valued. To see why this must be so (skip this paragraph to take it on trust!), consider equation (9.10). The same equation must hold for the complex conjugate, which just has the signs of the imaginary parts switched for each element. For any $j = 1, \dots, n$,

$$(\boldsymbol{A}\boldsymbol{c}_j)^* = (\lambda_j \boldsymbol{c}_j)^*.$$

However, since $\boldsymbol{A}$ is real, $(\boldsymbol{A}\boldsymbol{c}_j)^* = \boldsymbol{A}\boldsymbol{c}_j^*$, and in view of (9.9), $(\lambda_j \boldsymbol{c}_j)^* = \lambda_j^* \boldsymbol{c}_j^*$, so

$$\boldsymbol{A}\boldsymbol{c}_j^* = \lambda_j^* \boldsymbol{c}_j^*. \tag{9.16}$$

Now premultiply (9.10) by $\boldsymbol{c}_j^{*\prime}$ to get

$$\boldsymbol{c}_j^{*\prime}\boldsymbol{A}\boldsymbol{c}_j = \lambda_j \boldsymbol{c}_j^{*\prime}\boldsymbol{c}_j, \tag{9.17}$$

and also premultiply (9.16) by $\boldsymbol{c}_j'$ to get

$$\boldsymbol{c}_j'\boldsymbol{A}\boldsymbol{c}_j^* = \lambda_j^* \boldsymbol{c}_j'\boldsymbol{c}_j^*. \tag{9.18}$$

Note that these are scalars. Subtracting (9.18) from (9.17) yields

$$\boldsymbol{c}_j^{*\prime}\boldsymbol{A}\boldsymbol{c}_j - \boldsymbol{c}_j'\boldsymbol{A}\boldsymbol{c}_j^* = (\lambda_j - \lambda_j^*)\boldsymbol{c}_j^{*\prime}\boldsymbol{c}_j, \tag{9.19}$$

noting that the inner product on the right-hand side is a scalar, invariant to transposition. If $\boldsymbol{A}$ is symmetric, the left-hand side of (9.19) is zero, again because the terms are scalars and invariant to transposition. It follows that in this case $\lambda_j = \lambda_j^*$, which can only mean that there is no imaginary part and the eigenvalue is real. QED

There is an especially elegant way to present the relationship between the matrix $\boldsymbol{A}$ and its eigenvectors, by defining the $n \times n$ diagonal matrix

$$\boldsymbol{\Lambda} = \begin{bmatrix} \lambda_1 & 0 & \cdots & 0 \\ 0 & \lambda_2 & & \vdots \\ \vdots & & \ddots & 0 \\ 0 & \cdots & 0 & \lambda_n \end{bmatrix}, \tag{9.20}$$

which is also written compactly as $\boldsymbol{\Lambda} = \text{diag}\{\lambda_1, \dots, \lambda_n\}$. Then the n column vectors defined in (9.10) can be stacked side by side into a square matrix equation, taking the form

$$\boldsymbol{A}\boldsymbol{C} = \boldsymbol{C}\boldsymbol{\Lambda} \tag{9.21}$$

where $\boldsymbol{C}$ is defined by (9.12).

This form introduces the notion of a transformation of $\boldsymbol{A}$ that shares its eigenvalues. Given *any* $n \times n$ nonsingular matrix $\boldsymbol{P}$, let

$$\boldsymbol{B} = \boldsymbol{P}\boldsymbol{A}\boldsymbol{P}^{-1}. \tag{9.22}$$

Note first that

$$\boldsymbol{P}\boldsymbol{A}\boldsymbol{C} = \boldsymbol{P}\boldsymbol{A}\boldsymbol{P}^{-1}\boldsymbol{P}\boldsymbol{C} = \boldsymbol{B}\boldsymbol{P}\boldsymbol{C}. \tag{9.23}$$

Note second, from (9.21), that

$$\boldsymbol{P}\boldsymbol{A}\boldsymbol{C} = \boldsymbol{P}\boldsymbol{C}\boldsymbol{\Lambda}. \tag{9.24}$$

Hence it follows that from (9.23) and (9.24) that

$$BPC = PC\Lambda.$$

Comparing this equation with (9.21), it is evident that $\boldsymbol{B}$ has the same eigenvalues as $\boldsymbol{A}$ and its eigenvectors are the columns of $\boldsymbol{PC}$. This is called a similarity transformation, and $\boldsymbol{A}$ and $\boldsymbol{B}$ are said to be *similar* matrices.

9.4 Diagonalization

Assume the eigenvalues of $\boldsymbol{A}$ are distinct, so that $\boldsymbol{C}$ is nonsingular. In this case $\boldsymbol{A}$ and $\boldsymbol{\Lambda}$ are similar matrices, with $\boldsymbol{P} = \boldsymbol{C}$ and

$$A = C\Lambda C^{-1}. \tag{9.25}$$

This is called the *diagonalization* of $\boldsymbol{A}$, although more properly the diagonalization is the similarity transformation of $\boldsymbol{A}$ by $\boldsymbol{P} = \boldsymbol{C}^{-1}$,

$$\Lambda = C^{-1}AC.$$

The eigenvalues of a diagonal matrix are identical with the diagonal elements by definition, and the eigenvector matrix of $\boldsymbol{\Lambda}$ is of course $\boldsymbol{I}_n$.

Matrices with repeated eigenvalues have a less tidy representation in general. A form comparable to (9.25) does exist, but $\boldsymbol{\Lambda}$ may not be diagonal. The so-called Jordan canonical form features elements equal to 1 in cells of the upper second diagonal adjacent to a repeating pair. Happily, such cases are confined to non-symmetric matrices and do not arise in the applications covered in this book.

In the case of a symmetric matrix $\boldsymbol{A}$, a particularly interesting property reveals itself. Premultiply (9.10) by $\boldsymbol{c}_k'$ for some $k \neq j$ to get

$$c_k'Ac_j = \lambda_j c_k'c_j. \tag{9.26}$$

Interchanging j and k in (9.26) gives

$$c_j'Ac_k = \lambda_k c_j'c_k. \tag{9.27}$$

Since $\boldsymbol{A}$ is symmetric the left-hand sides of (9.26) and (9.27) are equal, being invariant to transposition. However, if λ_j and λ_k are different, since the inner product of the eigenvectors is also invariant to transposition, it follows that

$$(\lambda_j - \lambda_k)c_j'c_k = 0.$$

The conclusion is that if λ_j and λ_k are different, $\boldsymbol{c}_j'\boldsymbol{c}_k = 0$. The two eigenvectors have zero inner product and are said to be *orthogonal*.

Recalling that eigenvectors have length 1, this fact has a remarkable consequence. Orthogonal vectors of unit length are called *orthonormal*. If the eigenvalues are all different, then the eigenvector matrix has the property

$$C'C = I. \tag{9.28}$$

Moreover, premultiplying (9.28) by $\boldsymbol{C}$ gives

$$CC'C = C \tag{9.29}$$

and C is nonsingular, so postmultiply (9.29) by C^{-1} to get

$$CC' = I. \tag{9.30}$$

Taking (9.28) and (9.30) together and comparing with (3.2) shows that $C^{-1} = C'$. An orthonormal matrix is one whose inverse is equal to its transpose. When A is symmetric with distinct eigenvalues, the diagonalization takes the form

$$A = C\Lambda C'. \tag{9.31}$$

However, the story does not end here. It turns out that for symmetric matrices (9.31) holds generally, with or without repeated roots. The demonstration is different in the repeated root case, and there may be not just one but an infinity of valid choices of eigenvector. This is another fairly tricky argument, and to take the result on trust at first reading, just skip to the end of this section.

Suppose that λ_j has multiplicity 2, with $\lambda_{j+1} = \lambda_j$. The argument works by constructing a similarity transform. There is an eigenvector c_j satisfying (9.10), so let Y denote a $n \times n-1$ matrix with the property that $Y'Y = I_{n-1}$ and $Y'c_j = 0$, and hence define the orthonormal $n \times n$ matrix

$$B = [c_j \;\; Y].$$

By the partitioned product rule (2.10), the similarity transformation of A is

$$\begin{aligned} B'AB &= \begin{bmatrix} c_j'Ac_j & c_j'AY \\ Y'Ac_j & Y'AY \end{bmatrix} \\ &= \begin{bmatrix} \lambda_j & 0' \\ 0 & Y'AY \end{bmatrix}, \end{aligned}$$

where the second equality follows from (9.11) and

$$\begin{aligned} Y'Ac_j &= \lambda_j Y'c_j \\ &= 0. \end{aligned}$$

Matrix $B'AB$ has the same eigenvalues as A, and the characteristic equation, applying (3.31), is

$$|B'AB - \lambda I_n| = (\lambda_j - \lambda)|Y'AY - \lambda I_{n-1}|.$$

Since root λ_j is repeated, it must be the case that $|Y'AY - \lambda_j I_{n-1}| = 0$, but if $Y'AY - \lambda_j I_{n-1}$ is singular, its rank cannot exceed $n-2$, and the same is true of $B'AB - \lambda_j I_n$. In other words, the nullity of

$$B'AB - \lambda_j I_n = B'(A - \lambda_j I_n)B$$

is at least 2, and since B has full rank by construction, this is also the nullity of $A - \lambda_j I_n$. Therefore, the null space of $A - \lambda_j I_n$ contains a vector c_{j+1} that is linearly independent of, and orthogonal to, c_j. QED

If the multiplicity is 3 and $\lambda_{j+2} = \lambda_{j+1} = \lambda_j$, this argument can be applied again with

$$B = [c_j \; c_{j+1} \; Y],$$

where now Y is $n \times n-2$, and similarly for as many repeated eigenvalues as may exist. This concludes the demonstration that the diagonalization (9.31) exists for any set of real eigenvalues whatever.

The reader may wonder about the claim that sets of orthonormal vectors can be constructed as required, but this is no mystery. Let $\boldsymbol{C}_1$ be any $n \times m$ orthonormal matrix with $m < n$ such that $\boldsymbol{C}_1'\boldsymbol{C}_1 = \boldsymbol{I}_m$, and define $\boldsymbol{M}_1 = \boldsymbol{I}_n - \boldsymbol{C}_1\boldsymbol{C}_1'$ so that

$$\boldsymbol{M}_1\boldsymbol{C}_1 = \boldsymbol{C}_1'\boldsymbol{M}_1 = \boldsymbol{0}.$$

If $\boldsymbol{e}$ is *any* n-vector that is linearly independent of the columns of $\boldsymbol{C}_1$, the vector

$$\boldsymbol{c}_2 = \frac{\boldsymbol{M}_1\boldsymbol{e}}{\|\boldsymbol{M}_1\boldsymbol{e}\|}$$

where (2.5) defines $\|\cdot\|$ has the properties $\boldsymbol{C}_1'\boldsymbol{c}_2 = \boldsymbol{0}$ and $\boldsymbol{c}_2'\boldsymbol{c}_2 = 1$. This construction, known as the *Gram-Schmidt* procedure, can be applied sequentially to add orthonormal columns to an existing set for any $m \geq 1$.

9.5 Other Properties

Diagonalization is a trick with a host of applications, of which the most basic are simply to relate the eigenvalues of a matrix to its already familiar properties. Consider the determinant. Using rules (3.19) and (3.20),

$$\begin{aligned}
|\boldsymbol{A}| &= |\boldsymbol{C}||\boldsymbol{C}^{-1}||\boldsymbol{\Lambda}| \\
&= |\boldsymbol{\Lambda}| \\
&= \lambda_1 \times \lambda_2 \times \cdots \times \lambda_n.
\end{aligned}$$

The determinant is the product of the eigenvalues, confirming that if one or more eigenvalues are zero, the matrix is singular. On the other hand, the trace is the *sum* of the eigenvalues. Using the product rule (7.14),

$$\begin{aligned}
\operatorname{tr} \boldsymbol{A} &= \operatorname{tr} \boldsymbol{C}\boldsymbol{\Lambda}\boldsymbol{C}^{-1} \\
&= \operatorname{tr} \boldsymbol{\Lambda}\boldsymbol{C}^{-1}\boldsymbol{C} \\
&= \operatorname{tr} \boldsymbol{\Lambda} \\
&= \lambda_1 + \lambda_2 + \cdots + \lambda_n.
\end{aligned}$$

The diagonalization can be used to show that the number of nonzero eigenvalues of a symmetric matrix equals its rank. Suppose $\boldsymbol{A}$ $(n \times n)$ is singular and symmetric with $n - m$ zero eigenvalues. The eigenvalue matrix has the partition

$$\boldsymbol{\Lambda} = \begin{bmatrix} \boldsymbol{\Lambda}_1 & \boldsymbol{0} \\ \boldsymbol{0} & \boldsymbol{0} \end{bmatrix}$$

where $\boldsymbol{\Lambda}_1$ is $m \times m$. Since $\boldsymbol{\Lambda}_1$ and hence also $\boldsymbol{\Lambda}$ has rank m and $\boldsymbol{C}$ is nonsingular, it follows by (4.8) that m is also the rank of $\boldsymbol{A}$. Partition $\boldsymbol{C}$ by columns, conformably, as $[\boldsymbol{C}_1 \;\; \boldsymbol{C}_2]$. The diagonalization has the form

$$\begin{aligned}
\boldsymbol{A} &= [\boldsymbol{C}_1 \;\; \boldsymbol{C}_2] \begin{bmatrix} \boldsymbol{\Lambda}_1 & \boldsymbol{0} \\ \boldsymbol{0} & \boldsymbol{0} \end{bmatrix} \begin{bmatrix} \boldsymbol{C}_1' \\ \boldsymbol{C}_2' \end{bmatrix} \\
&= \boldsymbol{C}_1\boldsymbol{\Lambda}_1\boldsymbol{C}_1'. \qquad (9.32)
\end{aligned}$$

An interesting fact is that $\boldsymbol{A}$ does not depend in any way on $\boldsymbol{C}_2$. *Any* orthonormal set of vectors that is also orthogonal to $\boldsymbol{C}_1$ can serve as well as any other here.

Incidentally, there is no loss of generality in grouping the nonzero eigenvalues together, as is done in (9.32) for notational clarity. Observe that with $\boldsymbol{C}$ partitioned by columns as in (9.12), an alternative form of (9.31) is

$$\boldsymbol{A} = \sum_{j=1}^{n} \lambda_j \boldsymbol{c}_j \boldsymbol{c}_j'. \tag{9.33}$$

Diagonalization is invariant to the ordering of the eigenvalues.

The eigenvalues of a symmetric matrix are all positive (non-negative) if and only if the matrix is positive (semi-)definite. To see this, consider

$$\begin{aligned} \boldsymbol{x}'\boldsymbol{A}\boldsymbol{x} &= \boldsymbol{x}'\boldsymbol{C}\boldsymbol{\Lambda}\boldsymbol{C}'\boldsymbol{x} \\ &= \boldsymbol{z}'\boldsymbol{\Lambda}\boldsymbol{z} \\ &= \sum_{j=1}^{n} \lambda_j z_j^2, \end{aligned}$$

where $\boldsymbol{z} = \boldsymbol{C}'\boldsymbol{x}$ and all possible $\boldsymbol{z} \neq \boldsymbol{0}$ can be so obtained by choice of $\boldsymbol{x}$ since $\boldsymbol{C}$ is nonsingular. The sum is positive (non-negative) for every $\boldsymbol{x} \neq \boldsymbol{0}$ if and only if $\lambda_j > 0$ (≥ 0) for all j.

Finally, consider the case where $\boldsymbol{A} = \boldsymbol{C}\boldsymbol{\Lambda}\boldsymbol{C}^{-1}$ is idempotent. Then,

$$\begin{aligned} \boldsymbol{A} &= \boldsymbol{A}\boldsymbol{A} \\ &= \boldsymbol{C}\boldsymbol{\Lambda}\boldsymbol{C}^{-1}\boldsymbol{C}\boldsymbol{\Lambda}\boldsymbol{C}^{-1} \\ &= \boldsymbol{C}\boldsymbol{\Lambda}^2\boldsymbol{C}^{-1}. \end{aligned}$$

It follows that $\boldsymbol{\Lambda} = \boldsymbol{\Lambda}^2$, where $\boldsymbol{\Lambda}^2$ is another notation for $\boldsymbol{\Lambda}\boldsymbol{\Lambda}$, and since the matrix is diagonal, $\boldsymbol{\Lambda}^2$ is the diagonal matrix having the squares of the diagonal elements of $\boldsymbol{\Lambda}$ on the diagonal. The only numbers invariant under squaring are 0 and 1. All idempotent matrices other than $\boldsymbol{I}$ are singular, and so in any other case there is always at least one zero eigenvalue, and the nonzero eigenvalues must equal 1. Another useful fact following from this is that the rank of a symmetric idempotent matrix, being the number of nonzero eigenvalues, equals its trace. This is how we knew in Section 7.5 that rank $\boldsymbol{M} = T - k$.

9.6 An Interesting Result

If $\boldsymbol{A}$ is a symmetric and positive definite matrix and $\boldsymbol{B}$ is *any* symmetric positive definite or semidefinite matrix of the same dimension, there exists a matrix $\boldsymbol{P}$ and a diagonal matrix $\boldsymbol{\Delta}$ such that

$$\begin{aligned} \boldsymbol{A} &= \boldsymbol{P}\boldsymbol{P}' \\ \boldsymbol{B} &= \boldsymbol{P}\boldsymbol{\Delta}\boldsymbol{P}'. \end{aligned}$$

Note that $\boldsymbol{A}$ and $\boldsymbol{B}$ need have no other connection than what is stated, yet the diagonal elements of $\boldsymbol{\Delta}$ are sufficient to map from one to the other.

The demonstration of this unlikely-sounding result employs an ingenious trick with diagonalization. Define

$$A = C\Lambda C'$$

where $CC' = I$ and, by positive definiteness, Λ is diagonal with all diagonal elements positive. Hence define the matrix

$$T = \Lambda^{-1/2}C'BC\Lambda^{-1/2}, \tag{9.34}$$

where $\Lambda^{1/2}$ is the diagonal matrix having the square roots of the eigenvalues of A (all positive by assumption) on its diagonal and $\Lambda^{-1/2}$ has these diagonal elements inverted. T is symmetric and also positive semidefinite using Property 4 in Section 4.3. Equality (9.34) can be rearranged, premultiplying by $C\Lambda^{1/2}$ and postmultiplying by$\Lambda^{1/2}C'$, to give

$$B = C\Lambda^{1/2}\,T\Lambda^{1/2}C'. \tag{9.35}$$

Diagonalize T as

$$T = D\Delta D',$$

where $DD' = I$, so defining D and Δ. Letting

$$P = C\Lambda^{1/2}D,$$

observe that

$$\begin{aligned} PP' &= C\Lambda^{1/2}DD'\Lambda^{1/2}C' \\ &= C\Lambda C' \\ &= A \end{aligned}$$

and from (9.35),

$$\begin{aligned} P\Delta P' &= C\Lambda^{1/2}D\Delta D'\Lambda^{1/2}C' \\ &= C\Lambda^{1/2}T\Lambda^{1/2}C' \\ &= B. \qquad\qquad \text{QED} \end{aligned}$$

As an application, consider Property 6 of definite matrices from Section 4.3. If A and B are positive definite with the same dimension and $A - B$ is positive definite or positive semidefinite, then the same property holds for $B^{-1} - A^{-1}$. To show this, start by writing

$$\begin{aligned} A - B &= PP' - P\Delta P' \\ &= P(I - \Delta)P'. \end{aligned}$$

Therefore, a quadratic form in $A - B$ can be written as

$$\begin{aligned} z'(A - B)z &= y'(I - \Delta)y \\ &= \sum_{i=1}^{n}(1 - \Delta_i)y_i^2, \end{aligned} \tag{9.36}$$

where $y = P'z$ with elements $y_1, \dots, y_n$ and $\Delta = \text{diag}\{\Delta_1, \dots, \Delta_n\}$. It follows that if and only if $A - B$ is positive definite, $\Delta_i < 1$ for all i. If this is true, it is also the case that the diagonal elements of $\Delta^{-1} - I$ are all positive. But

$$\begin{aligned} B^{-1} - A^{-1} &= P'^{-1}\Delta^{-1}P^{-1} - P'^{-1}P^{-1} \\ &= Q(\Delta^{-1} - I)Q' \end{aligned}$$

where $Q = P'^{-1}$. This matrix is positive definite by the same argument just applied to (9.36). If $\boldsymbol{\Delta}$ has one or more diagonal elements equal to unity, then $A - B$ is singular, but the same argument goes through with 'positive semidefinite' substituted for 'positive definite'. QED

9.7 Exercises

1 Are the following statements true or false?
   (a) The eigenvalues of a symmetric matrix are always real.
   (b) Odd numbers of complex-valued eigenvalues of real-valued matrices cannot occur.
   (c) The eigenvalues of an idempotent matrix include at least one zero in every case.
   (d) Eigenvectors of idempotent matrices are always orthonormal.
   (e) Orthonormal vectors are always linearly independent.
   (f) If a matrix is singular, the characteristic equation has a zero-order term of zero.
   (g) Every square matrix is similar to a diagonal matrix.

2 Obtain the eigenvalues and eigenvectors of the following 2×2 matrices. In each case, determine whether the matrix is: (i) positive definite, (ii) positive semidefinite, (iii) idempotent.
   (a) $$\begin{bmatrix} 2 & 1 \\ 1 & 2 \end{bmatrix}$$
   (b) $$\begin{bmatrix} 1 & 2 \\ 2 & 4 \end{bmatrix}$$
   (c) $$\begin{bmatrix} \frac{1}{2} & \frac{1}{2} \\ \frac{1}{2} & \frac{1}{2} \end{bmatrix}$$
   (d) $$\begin{bmatrix} \frac{1}{2} & -\frac{1}{2} \\ -\frac{1}{2} & \frac{1}{2} \end{bmatrix}$$

3 Obtain the eigenvalues and eigenvectors of the following 3×3 matrices. In each case, determine whether the matrix is: (i) positive definite, (ii) positive semidefinite, (iii) idempotent.
   (a) $$\begin{bmatrix} 1 & 0 & 1 \\ 0 & 1 & 0 \\ 1 & 0 & 1 \end{bmatrix}$$
   (b) $$\begin{bmatrix} 2 & 1 & 1 \\ 1 & 2 & 0 \\ 1 & 0 & 2 \end{bmatrix}$$

4 Consider the matrix

$$A = \begin{bmatrix} \frac{1}{3} & \frac{1}{3} & \frac{1}{3} \\ \frac{1}{3} & \frac{1}{3} & \frac{1}{3} \\ \frac{1}{3} & \frac{1}{3} & \frac{1}{3} \end{bmatrix}$$

(a) Show that the eigenvalues of $\boldsymbol{A}$ are $\lambda_1 = 1$ and $\lambda_2 = \lambda_3 = 0$.
(b) Find eigenvectors $\boldsymbol{c}_1$ for λ_1 and $\boldsymbol{c}_2$ for λ_2. Verify that these vectors are mutually orthogonal. Normalize them to have unit length.
(c) Find an eigenvector $\boldsymbol{e}_3$ for λ_3, being an element of the null space of $\boldsymbol{A}$ linearly independent of $\boldsymbol{c}_2$.
(d) Project $\boldsymbol{e}_3$ into the space orthogonal to $\boldsymbol{c}_1$, and $\boldsymbol{c}_2$, and normalize it to unit length. Call this vector $\boldsymbol{c}_3$, and show that the resulting vectors form an orthonormal matrix $\boldsymbol{C}$ that diagonalizes $\boldsymbol{A}$.

5 Consider the matrix

$$B = \begin{bmatrix} \frac{2}{3} & -\frac{1}{3} & -\frac{1}{3} \\ -\frac{1}{3} & \frac{2}{3} & -\frac{1}{3} \\ -\frac{1}{3} & -\frac{1}{3} & \frac{2}{3} \end{bmatrix}$$

(a) Show that $\boldsymbol{B}$ has eigenvalues $\lambda_1 = \lambda_2 = 1$ and $\lambda_3 = 0$.
(b) Find eigenvectors $\boldsymbol{c}_1$ for λ_1 and $\boldsymbol{c}_3$ for λ_3. Verify that these vectors are mutually orthogonal, and normalize them to have unit length.
(c) Find an eigenvector $\boldsymbol{e}_2$ for λ_2, being an element of the null space of $\boldsymbol{B} - \boldsymbol{I}$ linearly independent of $\boldsymbol{c}_1$.
(d) Project $\boldsymbol{e}_2$ into the space orthogonal to $\boldsymbol{c}_1$ and $\boldsymbol{c}_3$, and normalize it to have unit length. Call this $\boldsymbol{c}_2$, and show that the resulting vectors form an orthonormal matrix $\boldsymbol{C}$ that diagonalizes $\boldsymbol{B}$.
(e) Compare and contrast the properties of $\boldsymbol{B}$ with those of $\boldsymbol{A}$ in Question 4.

10

The Gaussian Regression Model

10.1 Testing Hypotheses

In this chapter, a key extra assumption is added to the classical regression model (CRM) specified in Section 7.2. Like the CRM itself, this is not necessarily a realistic assumption as it stands, but it often holds as an approximation and yields powerful results – not less than a complete theory of statistical inference. The Gaussian classical regression model (GCRM) shares assumptions GCRM(i)–(iii) with CRM(i)–(iii) and adds the following

Assumption GCRM(iv): $\boldsymbol{u} \sim \mathrm{N}(\boldsymbol{0}, \sigma^2 \boldsymbol{I}_T)$.

$\mathrm{N}(\boldsymbol{0}, \sigma^2 \boldsymbol{I}_T)$ means that the disturbances are jointly normally distributed, with density function

$$\phi(\boldsymbol{u}) = \left(\frac{1}{\sqrt{2\pi}\sigma}\right)^T \exp\left\{-\frac{\boldsymbol{u}'\boldsymbol{u}}{2\sigma^2}\right\}.$$

If $\boldsymbol{A}$ is any fixed conformable matrix and $\boldsymbol{b}$ a fixed conformable vector, GCRM(iv) and the linearity property of the normal distribution implies that

$$\boldsymbol{A}\boldsymbol{u} + \boldsymbol{b} \sim \mathrm{N}(\boldsymbol{b}, \sigma^2 \boldsymbol{A}\boldsymbol{A}').$$

In particular, since by (7.2) and (7.1)

$$\hat{\boldsymbol{\beta}} = \boldsymbol{\beta} + (\boldsymbol{X}'\boldsymbol{X})^{-1}\boldsymbol{X}'\boldsymbol{u} \tag{10.1}$$

and

$$(\boldsymbol{X}'\boldsymbol{X})^{-1}\boldsymbol{X}'\boldsymbol{X}(\boldsymbol{X}'\boldsymbol{X})^{-1} = (\boldsymbol{X}'\boldsymbol{X})^{-1},$$

it follows that

$$\hat{\boldsymbol{\beta}} \sim \mathrm{N}(\boldsymbol{\beta},\ \sigma^2(\boldsymbol{X}'\boldsymbol{X})^{-1}). \tag{10.2}$$

This is the basic result permitting inferences from the sample data about the values of the unknown $\boldsymbol{\beta}$.

By way of introduction to this chapter, here is a brief summary of the way such inferences are commonly performed and the relevant terminology. A restriction on an econometric model may be given the designation of the *null hypothesis* and the symbol H_0.

An Introduction to Econometric Theory, First Edition. James Davidson.

Companion website: www.wiley.com/go/davidson/introecmettheory

The terminology is traditional and indicates that under the hypothesis some coefficient or coefficients, or maybe a function or functions of coefficients, take the value zero. The null hypothesis represents a restricted form of the model in question, which is given the name *maintained hypothesis*. The cases for which the maintained hypothesis is true but the null hypothesis is false are gathered under the name *alternative hypothesis*, often called H_1. This form of words is to emphasize that usually the null hypothesis is a special case, 'nested' within the alternative. The two are on an equivalent footing only in special cases. The maintained hypothesis will include conditions that are by no means trivial, such as assumptions GCRM(i)–(iv). Never overlook the fact that test procedures are typically misleading if the maintained hypothesis is false.

Tests are decision-making procedures in which the null hypothesis is either rejected or accepted, based on the sample evidence. There are broadly three stages.

1. A function of the sample data called a *test statistic* is calculated. This is designed to have the property that when the null hypothesis is true, it has a known distribution and, equally important, it has a different distribution when the null hypothesis is false.
2. A *rejection region* is formulated, being a set of real values such that if the test statistic falls in it, the null hypothesis will be rejected. The boundaries of this region, called *critical values*, are calculated on the basis that if the null hypothesis is true, the probability of rejection is no greater than a known value called the *significance level* of the test.
3. The decision to accept or reject the null hypothesis follows on comparison of the statistic with the rejection region.

Statistical tests can return the wrong result, and the idea underlying the test procedure is that the probability of making at least one form of error is controlled. The error of rejecting a true null is called Type I error, while Type II error is the error of failing to reject a false null. The bound on the probability of a Type I error is called the *size* of the test. In simple hypotheses that fix all parameters at given values, the size matches the significance level. If (as is often the case) the null hypothesis is specified to include some unrestricted parameters, the size is defined as the largest Type I error probability over the possible variants. However, in all our applications the test statistics are *pivotal*, meaning that the null distribution is a known, tabulated case regardless of nuisance parameters.

The probability of correctly rejecting the null hypothesis is called the *power* of the test, although since the power is likely to depend on the relevant case of the alternative, there is more commonly a power *function*, typically larger for alternatives remote from the null than for those near the null.

This chapter reviews methods for generating statistics whose null distributions are known, although these results are often used in different contexts from straightforward decision-making. For example, a *confidence interval* computed from sample data assigns a known probability to an unknown parameter lying within it, and so provides a measure of the uncertainty associated with the estimate. Nonetheless, a confidence interval always has a test procedure naturally associated with it, with a decision based on whether or not the hypothesized parameter value lies in the interval. Another approach, rather than reporting a decision whether or not to reject at a given significance level, is simply to report the smallest significance level under which the test leads to a rejection, giving readers of the research the opportunity to choose their own decision rule. This is called the *p-value* of the test.

10.2 Idempotent Quadratic Forms

This section develops some technical results that are the key to exact inference in the GCRM, 'exact' meaning that the size of the test is known exactly. The problem to be solved is to compute pivotal test statistics, that have known distributions when the null hypothesis to be tested is true, regardless of the values of $\boldsymbol{X}$ and σ^2. These are the F and Student's t distributions reviewed in Section 6.3. Quantiles of these distributions – that is, values that are exceeded with a given probability – are tabulated in appendices of the popular statistics and econometrics textbooks, and are easily found online.

The solution to the problem exploits the properties of the idempotent projection matrices introduced in Section 7.4. The important results derived in Chapter 9 are as follows. A symmetric idempotent $T \times T$ matrix $\boldsymbol{A}$, having rank $r < T$, has the diagonalization

$$\boldsymbol{A} = \boldsymbol{C}\boldsymbol{\Lambda}_r\boldsymbol{C}',$$

where $\boldsymbol{C}$ is a $T \times T$ orthonormal matrix of eigenvectors having the property

$$\boldsymbol{C}'\boldsymbol{C} = \boldsymbol{C}\boldsymbol{C}' = \boldsymbol{I}_T$$

and the eigenvalue matrix is

$$\boldsymbol{\Lambda}_r = \begin{bmatrix} \boldsymbol{I}_r & \boldsymbol{0} \\ \boldsymbol{0} & \boldsymbol{0} \end{bmatrix}.$$

Partitioning $\boldsymbol{C}$ by columns as $[\boldsymbol{C}_1 \ \boldsymbol{C}_2]$ so that $\boldsymbol{C}_1$ is $T \times r$, these results imply the representation

$$\boldsymbol{A} = \boldsymbol{C}_1\boldsymbol{C}_1'.$$

Now, for a random T-vector $\boldsymbol{u} \sim \mathrm{N}(\boldsymbol{0}, \sigma^2\boldsymbol{I}_T)$ define the T-vector

$$\boldsymbol{z} = \frac{\boldsymbol{C}'\boldsymbol{u}}{\sigma}$$

so that

$$\begin{aligned}\mathrm{E}(\boldsymbol{z}\boldsymbol{z}') &= \frac{\boldsymbol{C}'\mathrm{E}(\boldsymbol{u}\boldsymbol{u}')\boldsymbol{C}}{\sigma^2} \\ &= \boldsymbol{C}'\boldsymbol{C} \\ &= \boldsymbol{I}_T.\end{aligned}$$

Thus, $\boldsymbol{z}$ is a standard normal vector, and in particular its first r elements form the vector

$$\begin{aligned}\boldsymbol{z}_1 &= \frac{\boldsymbol{C}_1'\boldsymbol{u}}{\sigma} \\ &\sim \mathrm{N}(\boldsymbol{0}, \boldsymbol{I}_r).\end{aligned}$$

Assuming momentarily that σ^2 is known, construct the quadratic form in $\boldsymbol{A}$ with the vector $\boldsymbol{u}/\sigma$, and note that

$$\begin{aligned}\frac{\boldsymbol{u}'\boldsymbol{A}\boldsymbol{u}}{\sigma^2} &= \frac{\boldsymbol{u}'\boldsymbol{C}_1\boldsymbol{C}_1'\boldsymbol{u}}{\sigma^2}\\ &= \boldsymbol{z}_1'\boldsymbol{z}_1\\ &= \sum_{j=1}^{r} z_j^2\\ &\sim \chi^2(r).\end{aligned}$$

The quadratic form behaves exactly like the sum of squares of r independent standard normal variates, and so it has the chi-squared distribution with r degrees of freedom. This result holds true for any symmetric idempotent matrix $\boldsymbol{A}$ with rank r, regardless of its particular form.

The problem with making practical use of these properties of quadratic forms is that σ^2 is unknown. However, at this point a bit of cleverness is exploited. The ratio of two such quadratic forms in $\boldsymbol{u}$ would not depend on σ^2. Thus, let $\boldsymbol{B}\,(T \times T)$ be another symmetric idempotent matrix, this time with rank $s < T$, which satisfies the orthogonality condition

$$\boldsymbol{A}\boldsymbol{B} = \boldsymbol{0}.$$

By the same argument as before,

$$\begin{aligned}\boldsymbol{B} &= \boldsymbol{D}\boldsymbol{\Lambda}_s\boldsymbol{D}'\\ &= \boldsymbol{D}_1\boldsymbol{D}_1',\end{aligned}$$

where

$$\boldsymbol{D}'\boldsymbol{D} = \boldsymbol{D}\boldsymbol{D}' = \boldsymbol{I}_T$$

and

$$\boldsymbol{\Lambda}_s = \begin{bmatrix}\boldsymbol{I}_s & \boldsymbol{0}\\ \boldsymbol{0} & \boldsymbol{0}\end{bmatrix}.$$

Then,

$$\begin{aligned}\boldsymbol{w}_1 &= \frac{\boldsymbol{D}_1'\boldsymbol{u}}{\sigma}\\ &\sim \mathrm{N}(\boldsymbol{0}, \boldsymbol{I}_s)\end{aligned}$$

and

$$\begin{aligned}\frac{\boldsymbol{u}'\boldsymbol{B}\boldsymbol{u}}{\sigma^2} &= \frac{\boldsymbol{u}'\boldsymbol{D}_1\boldsymbol{D}_1'\boldsymbol{u}}{\sigma^2}\\ &= \boldsymbol{w}_1'\boldsymbol{w}_1\\ &\sim \chi^2(s).\end{aligned}$$

The object is now to show that these two quadratic forms are distributed independently of each other. The reasoning goes as follows. Consider the $T \times T$ matrix of $\boldsymbol{C}_1$ with columns augmented by zeros,

$$\begin{aligned}[C_1 \;\; \mathbf{0}] &= C\Lambda_r \\ &= C\Lambda_r C'C \\ &= AC\end{aligned}$$

and similarly

$$\begin{aligned}[D_1 \;\; \mathbf{0}] &= D\Lambda_s \\ &= D\Lambda_s D'D \\ &= BD.\end{aligned}$$

If $AB = \mathbf{0}$, then necessarily $C'ABD = \mathbf{0}$, and

$$\begin{aligned}C'ABD &= \begin{bmatrix} C_1' \\ \mathbf{0} \end{bmatrix} \begin{bmatrix} D_1 & \mathbf{0} \end{bmatrix} \\ &= \begin{bmatrix} C_1'D_1 & \mathbf{0} \\ \mathbf{0} & \mathbf{0} \end{bmatrix}.\end{aligned}$$

In particular, the orthogonality has the implication

$$C_1'D_1 = \mathbf{0}.$$

Hence

$$\begin{aligned}\mathrm{E}(z_1 w_1') &= \frac{\mathrm{E}(C_1'uu'D_1)}{\sigma^2} \\ &= \frac{C_1'\mathrm{E}(uu')D_1}{\sigma^2} \\ &= C_1'D_1 \\ &= \mathbf{0}.\end{aligned}$$

In other words, the elements of the vectors z_1 and w_1 are mutually uncorrelated.

This is where the second major piece of cleverness enters the picture, Since these are Gaussian vectors, the fact that they have zero covariances means that they are distributed independently of one another. This equivalence of uncorrelatedness and independence is a special attribute of the normal distribution, so assumption GCRM(iv) is critical at this point. However, if it holds, then any functions of these vectors are also independent, subject only to the condition that their joint distribution is well defined.

The functions in question are the two quadratic forms. $AB = \mathbf{0}$ means that $u'Au$ and $u'Bu$ are independent random variables, notwithstanding that they are functions of the *same* vector u. Recall from Section 6.3 that the F distribution is defined as the ratio of two independently distributed chi-squared variates, standardized by degrees of freedom. Since the σ^2 cancels,

$$\frac{u'Au}{u'Bu}\frac{s}{r} \sim F(r, s).$$

This is a tabulated distribution depending only on the two integers r and s. This works for any choice of idempotent matrices A and B satisfying the assumptions – quite a remarkable result.

10.3 Confidence Regions

As the reader has guessed by now, the last derivation can be applied to the projection matrices

$$Q = X(X'X)^{-1}X'$$

having rank k, the column rank of X, and

$$M = I - Q$$

having rank $T - k$ and satisfying $QM = 0$. The quadratic forms in question are

$$\begin{aligned} u'Qu &= u'X(X'X)^{-1}X'u \\ &= (\hat{\beta} - \beta)'X'X(\hat{\beta} - \beta) \end{aligned}$$

from (10.1), and

$$\begin{aligned} u'M\,u &= \hat{u}'\hat{u} \\ &= (T - k)s^2 \end{aligned}$$

from (7.17). The reasoning of Section 10.2 has shown that

$$\frac{(\hat{\beta} - \beta)'X'X(\hat{\beta} - \beta)}{ks^2} \sim F(k, T - k). \tag{10.3}$$

Note how the denominator quadratic form after normalization plays the role of estimator of the unknown σ^2, corresponding to the s^2 defined in (7.18). The deeper role of the degrees of freedom normalization by $T - k$ may now be appreciated. It is not merely that s^2 is unbiased for σ^2, but that it yields the desired pivotal distribution when used to replace σ^2 in the formula.

In expression (10.3), $\hat{\beta}$, X, and s^2 depend on the sample observations and can be regarded, after the event of drawing the sample, as fixed quantities. On the other hand, β is the unknown true value of the regression model parameter vector. This expression summarizes the information about β that is contained in the sample. Let $F^*_\alpha(k, T - k)$ denote the critical value from the tabulation of the F distribution, such that

$$\Pr\left(F(k, T - k) > F^*_\alpha(k, T - k)\right) = \alpha.$$

Then, (10.3) lets us assert that, under assumptions GCRM(i)–(iv),

$$\Pr\left(\frac{(\hat{\beta} - \beta)'X'X(\hat{\beta} - \beta)}{ks^2} \le F^*_\alpha(k, T - k)\right) = 1 - \alpha. \tag{10.4}$$

Consider the representation in Figure 10.1, which shows the case $k = 2$, so that the vector $\beta = (\beta_1, \beta_2)'$ represents a point in the plane and the numerator in (10.3) can be written as

$$(\hat{\beta}_1 - \beta_1)^2 \sum_{t=1}^{T} x_{1t}^2 + (\hat{\beta}_2 - \beta_2)^2 \sum_{t=1}^{T} x_{2t}^2 + 2(\hat{\beta}_1 - \beta_1)(\hat{\beta}_2 - \beta_2) \sum_{t=1}^{T} x_{1t}x_{2t}. \tag{10.5}$$

The ellipses are centred on $(\hat{\beta}_1, \hat{\beta}_2)'$ and plot the values of β over which the quadratic form is constant; hence, they play the role of contour lines. The probability that the true β lies within the inner ellipse is $1 - \alpha_1$, and the probability that it lies within the outer ellipse is $1 - \alpha_2$, with $\alpha_1 > \alpha_2$. When s^2 is small, the sample is the more informative about β, the range of values that do not violate the inequality in (10.4) is smaller, and the

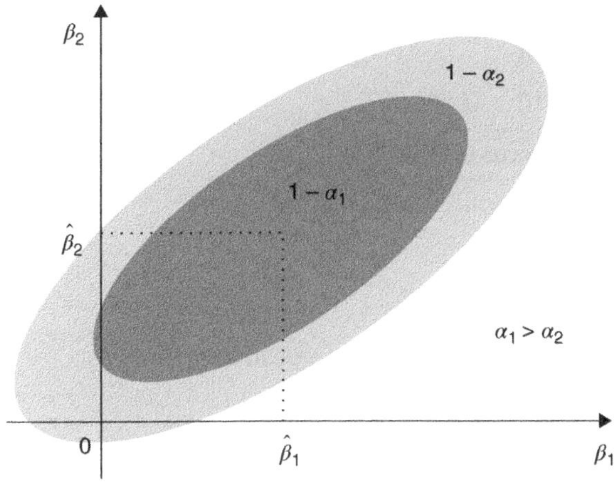

Figure 10.1 Regression confidence regions, $k = 2$. *Source*: Figure 2.1 of *Econometric Theory* by James Davidson, Blackwell Publishers 2000. Reproduced by permission of Wiley-Blackwell.

contours correspondingly tighter. The shape and orientation of the ellipses depend on the contributions of the terms of (10.5). A negative cross product produces the lower-left to upper-right orientation illustrated. When $\hat{\beta}_1 - \beta_1$ and $\hat{\beta}_2 - \beta_2$ have the same sign, there is an offsetting effect, since the regressors, assumed to have zero means,[1] are varying in opposing directions. There is more uncertainty about possible true values when the pairs are on the same sides of the point estimates, above or below; hence the contours are elongated in these directions. When the cross-product term is positive, the opposite effect applies, the offsetting effect being obtained when $\beta_1 - \hat{\beta}_1$ and $\beta_2 - \hat{\beta}_2$ have different signs. Then the contours would be oriented upper-left to lower-right, with greater uncertainty about cases on different sides of the point estimates.

In higher-dimensional models, the regions defined by (10.4) are called *confidence ellipsoids*. They can no longer be plotted on a graph, but evaluating the ratio at any specified value of $\boldsymbol{\beta}$ allows a level of confidence to be assigned to it. It is important not to overlook that $\boldsymbol{\beta}$ is unknown but fixed, while repeated sampling generates a distribution of random ellipsoids, centred on the random $\hat{\boldsymbol{\beta}}$ and scaled by the random s^2. The 'confidence' measured here is the probability that the random ellipsoid contains the true $\boldsymbol{\beta}$. This is a fact worth emphasizing because of the rather prevalent mistake of thinking that (10.4) and diagrams such as Figure 10.1 are describing a distribution of random $\boldsymbol{\beta}$ values.

10.4 *t* Statistics

While the confidence regions of the foregoing section provide the most complete information about the parameters contained in the sample, they are difficult to construct and interpret and are not much used in practice. It is much simpler to look at the regression coefficients one at a time, and this is the customary way of evaluating a regression. Instead of a multi-dimensional confidence region, confidence *intervals* are the usual yardsticks of choice.

1 The mechanics of expressing regressors in mean deviation form to avoid including an intercept are explained in Section 11.2.

Therefore, assume interest focuses on β_i for any $1 \leq i \leq k$. To pick out this element, define the selection vector

$$\boldsymbol{r}_i = (0, \dots, 1, \dots, 0)' \quad (k \times 1), \tag{10.6}$$

having a 1 in position i, zeros elsewhere, so that

$$\beta_i = \boldsymbol{r}_i'\boldsymbol{\beta}.$$

For economy of notation, let

$$\boldsymbol{A} = (\boldsymbol{X}'\boldsymbol{X})^{-1}$$

so that the ith diagonal element of this matrix can be written as

$$\boldsymbol{r}_i'(\boldsymbol{X}'\boldsymbol{X})^{-1}\boldsymbol{r}_i = a_{ii}. \tag{10.7}$$

Hence, define the fixed T-vector

$$\boldsymbol{c}_i = \frac{\boldsymbol{X}(\boldsymbol{X}'\boldsymbol{X})^{-1}\boldsymbol{r}_i}{\sqrt{a_{ii}}},$$

constructed to have unit length such that

$$\boldsymbol{c}_i'\boldsymbol{c}_i = 1.$$

Under assumptions GCRM(i)–(iv),

$$\begin{aligned}\mathrm{E}(\boldsymbol{c}_i'\boldsymbol{u})^2 &= \boldsymbol{c}_i'\mathrm{E}(\boldsymbol{u}\boldsymbol{u}')\boldsymbol{c}_i \\ &= \sigma^2,\end{aligned}$$

and so

$$\boldsymbol{c}_i'\boldsymbol{u} \sim \mathrm{N}(0, \sigma^2).$$

However, in view of (10.1), it is also the case that

$$\boldsymbol{c}_i'\boldsymbol{u} = \frac{\hat{\beta}_i - \beta_i}{\sqrt{a_{ii}}}.$$

Next, recall from (7.15) and (7.16) that under GCRM(i)–(iv),

$$\hat{\boldsymbol{u}} \sim \mathrm{N}(\boldsymbol{0}, \sigma^2\boldsymbol{M}) \tag{10.8}$$

where $\boldsymbol{M} = \boldsymbol{I}_T - \boldsymbol{X}(\boldsymbol{X}'\boldsymbol{X})^{-1}\boldsymbol{X}'$. This is a singular Gaussian distribution, as described in Section 6.2. Since $\boldsymbol{X}'\boldsymbol{M} = \boldsymbol{0}$,

$$\begin{aligned}\boldsymbol{c}_i'\boldsymbol{M} &= \frac{1}{\sqrt{a_{ii}}}\boldsymbol{r}_i'(\boldsymbol{X}'\boldsymbol{X})^{-1}\boldsymbol{X}'\boldsymbol{M} \\ &= \boldsymbol{0},\end{aligned}$$

and it follows that

$$\begin{aligned}\mathrm{E}\left(\frac{\hat{\beta}_i - \beta_i}{\sqrt{a_{ii}}}\hat{\boldsymbol{u}}'\right) &= \mathrm{E}(\boldsymbol{c}_i'\boldsymbol{u}\boldsymbol{u}'\boldsymbol{M}) \\ &= \sigma^2\boldsymbol{c}_i'\boldsymbol{M} \\ &= \boldsymbol{0}.\end{aligned}$$

In words, this says that the scalar $c_i'u$ is uncorrelated with each of the elements of $\hat{u}$. Since $c_i'u$ and $\hat{u}$ are jointly Gaussian, the same trick used to derive (10.3) works here. Uncorrelatedness implies independence, and if $c_i'u$ and $\hat{u}$ are distributed independently of one another, then the same is true of $c_i'u$ and $s = \sqrt{\hat{u}'\hat{u}/(T-k)}$. It follows that s and $(\hat{\beta}_i - \beta_i)/\sqrt{a_{ii}}$ are independent random variables and from (7.17) that

$$\hat{u}'\hat{u} \sim \sigma^2\chi^2(T-k).$$

The definition of the Student's t distribution in (6.14) then leads to

$$\frac{\hat{\beta}_i - \beta_i}{s\sqrt{a_{ii}}} \sim t_{T-k}. \tag{10.9}$$

This fundamental result is the basis for constructing confidence intervals. Define t^{α}_{T-k} to be the critical value from the tabulation of Student's t with $T-k$ degrees of freedom, such that

$$\Pr(t_{T-k} > t^{\alpha}_{T-k}) = \alpha.$$

Noting that the Student distribution is symmetric about 0, the confidence interval for β_i takes the form

$$\Pr(\hat{\beta}_i - s\sqrt{a_{ii}}t^{\alpha/2}_{T-k} \le \beta_i \le \hat{\beta}_i + s\sqrt{a_{ii}}t^{\alpha/2}_{T-k}) = 1-\alpha. \tag{10.10}$$

This formula defines an interval, centred on $\hat{\beta}_i$, within which the unknown β_i lies with probability $1-\alpha$ when assumptions GCRM(i)–(iv) hold.

As with the confidence ellipsoid, it is important not to misinterpret (10.10). While unknown, β_i is not random. It is the interval whose location and width varies randomly from one sample drawing to another. The distribution has the property that for the case $\alpha = 0.05$ (say), in repeated sampling nineteen out of twenty of these random intervals contain β_i.

The width of the interval depends on two factors: the critical value that reflects the Gaussianity assumption and the regression *standard error*, the quantity $s\sqrt{a_{ii}}$ often written as s.e. $(\hat{\beta}_i)$. This is the square root of the ith diagonal element of the matrix $s^2(X'X)^{-1}$, the estimated counterpart of the variance matrix (7.8). The customary choice of α in empirical work is 0.05, and unless $T-k$ is very small, $t^{\alpha/2}_{T-k}$ is close to 2 and approaches the normal critical value of 1.96 as T approaches infinity. We often speak loosely of the "two standard error rule" to define the "ninety five percent" confidence interval. The 95% interval is in fact of the order of four standard errors in width, centred on the point estimate.

It is of interest to compare this approach to assigning probabilities to that based on (10.4). Consider again the two-parameter regression model. The pair of confidence intervals for β_1 and β_2 define a rectangular region of the plane. What is the probability that a pair (β_1, β_2) lies outside this rectangle? This is the probability that either the first interval does not contain β_1 or the second interval does not contain β_2, or both. Calling these events A_1 and A_2 respectively, with $\Pr(A_1) = \Pr(A_2) = \alpha$, the best that can be said is

$$\begin{aligned}\Pr(A_1 \text{ or } A_2) &= \Pr(A_1) + \Pr(A_2) - \Pr(A_1 \text{ and } A_2)\\ &\le 2\alpha.\end{aligned}$$

Enlarging the intervals to have individual confidence levels of $1 - \alpha/2$ defines a rectangular region such that the probability of (β_1, β_2) lying outside is *at most* α. It is not possible to be more precise, because the intervals do not take the possible correlation of the two coefficients into account. By contrast, the probability that (β_1, β_2) lies outside of the $1 - \alpha$-level confidence region in (10.4) is exactly α.

The result for which (10.9) is most frequently used is to provide a *test of significance*, by consideration of the ratio in the case $\beta_i = 0$. Symmetry of the distribution about zero means that the probability that the absolute value of the statistic exceeds $t_{T-k}^{\alpha/2}$ is equal to the probability of it lying outside the $1 - \alpha$ confidence interval. The quantity

$$t_{\text{calc}} = \frac{\hat{\beta}_i}{\text{s.e.}(\hat{\beta}_i)} \tag{10.11}$$

is commonly called the "t ratio" and is normally printed by default in the output of estimation software. When $|t_{\text{calc}}|$ exceeds the neighbourhood of 2, the coefficient is said to be 'significant'. The same distribution is used to test the null hypothesis that β_i assumes any given value, say β_i^*. The 'two-sided' statistic

$$\frac{|\hat{\beta}_i - \beta_i^*|}{\text{s.e.}(\hat{\beta}_i)}$$

is used when there is no prior knowledge as to where the case of the alternative hypothesis $\beta_i \neq \beta_i^*$ might lie. When prior knowledge rules out one set of alternatives, such as $\beta_i < \beta_i^*$, the sign of the t ratio may be retained, and then negative values would be regarded as supporting the null hypothesis. In such a one-sided test, the rejection region lies entirely above β_i^*, and a test with significance level of $100\alpha\%$ should use the critical value t_{T-k}^{α}.

10.5 Tests of Linear Restrictions

Consider the null hypothesis

$$\boldsymbol{R\beta} = \boldsymbol{c} \tag{10.12}$$

where $\boldsymbol{R}$ $(r \times k)$ is a fixed, known matrix of rank r and $\boldsymbol{c}$ a known r-vector. This equation expresses one or more linear restrictions on the parameter vector. The number of restrictions is r and often $r = 1$; for example, "$\beta_1 = \beta_2$" is embodied in the specification

$$\boldsymbol{R} = \begin{bmatrix} 1 & -1 & 0 & \cdots & 0 \end{bmatrix}, \quad \boldsymbol{c} = [0], \tag{10.13}$$

whereas "$\beta_1 + \beta_2 + \beta_3 = 1$" is imposed with

$$\boldsymbol{R} = \begin{bmatrix} 1 & 1 & 1 & 0 & \cdots & 0 \end{bmatrix}, \quad \boldsymbol{c} = [1]. \tag{10.14}$$

Economic models not infrequently embody restrictions of this sort.

Another important class of cases are multiple significance tests. Suppose there are r regressors out of k whose role in the model is uncertain. Putting these elements of $\boldsymbol{\beta}$ (with no loss of generality) at the front of the vector, capture their exclusion by setting

$$\boldsymbol{R} = [\boldsymbol{I}_r \quad \boldsymbol{0}], \quad \boldsymbol{c} = \boldsymbol{0}. \tag{10.15}$$

Testing the significance of these elements one at a time, using t tests, is of course another option. However, a different result is generally obtained by testing the restrictions jointly, and the joint test is always preferred. This is the counterpart of the contrast between confidence intervals and confidence regions discussed in the preceding section. The joint significance test takes correlations between the estimators into account in evaluating the evidence, as t-tests cannot.

Consider the distribution of the vector of restrictions evaluated at the unrestricted least squares estimator. Substituting

$$\hat{\boldsymbol{\beta}} \sim \mathrm{N}(\boldsymbol{\beta}, \sigma^2(\boldsymbol{X}'\boldsymbol{X})^{-1})$$

into (10.12) yields the normal r-vector

$$\boldsymbol{R}\hat{\boldsymbol{\beta}} - \boldsymbol{c} \sim \mathrm{N}(\boldsymbol{R}\boldsymbol{\beta} - \boldsymbol{c},\ \sigma^2\boldsymbol{R}(\boldsymbol{X}'\boldsymbol{X})^{-1}\boldsymbol{R}'). \tag{10.16}$$

Substituting from (10.1), this vector can also be written as

$$\boldsymbol{R}\hat{\boldsymbol{\beta}} - \boldsymbol{c} = \boldsymbol{R}\boldsymbol{\beta} - \boldsymbol{c} + \boldsymbol{R}(\boldsymbol{X}'\boldsymbol{X})^{-1}\boldsymbol{X}'\boldsymbol{u}. \tag{10.17}$$

Suppose that assumptions GCRM(i)–(iv) hold and the hypothesis $\boldsymbol{R}\boldsymbol{\beta} = \boldsymbol{c}$ is true. In this case, (10.17) is just a linear combination of the disturbances, and the quadratic form of (10.17) with the inverse covariance matrix from (10.16) is chi-squared distributed with r degrees of freedom. But now look!

$$\begin{aligned}
&(\boldsymbol{R}\hat{\boldsymbol{\beta}} - \boldsymbol{c})'(\sigma^2\boldsymbol{R}(\boldsymbol{X}'\boldsymbol{X})^{-1}\boldsymbol{R}')^{-1}(\boldsymbol{R}\hat{\boldsymbol{\beta}} - \boldsymbol{c}) \\
&\quad = \sigma^{-2}\boldsymbol{u}'\boldsymbol{X}(\boldsymbol{X}'\boldsymbol{X})^{-1}\boldsymbol{R}'[\boldsymbol{R}(\boldsymbol{X}'\boldsymbol{X})^{-1}\boldsymbol{R}']^{-1}\boldsymbol{R}(\boldsymbol{X}'\boldsymbol{X})^{-1}\boldsymbol{X}'\boldsymbol{u} \\
&\quad = \sigma^{-2}\boldsymbol{u}'\boldsymbol{P}\boldsymbol{u}
\end{aligned} \tag{10.18}$$

where the last equality defines the matrix $\boldsymbol{P}$. $\boldsymbol{P}$ is a $T \times T$ matrix easily verified to be symmetric and idempotent. Its rank is r, the dimension and rank of the inverse matrix in the centre of the expression. Its most important attribute is the identity

$$\boldsymbol{P}\boldsymbol{M} = \boldsymbol{0} \tag{10.19}$$

where $\boldsymbol{M} = \boldsymbol{I}_T - \boldsymbol{X}(\boldsymbol{X}'\boldsymbol{X})^{-1}\boldsymbol{X}'$, easily verified because $\boldsymbol{X}'$ is the right-hand factor of the matrix $\boldsymbol{P}$. As has already been remarked, while the matrix expressions generated in least squares theory are often complicated in appearance, the non-commutativity of matrix multiplication means that a property such as orthogonality depends entirely on the left- or right-hand factor in a product. Determining such properties by inspection is easier than might be imagined.

It follows from (10.19) that just as in (10.3) and (10.9), s^2 can be substituted for the unknown σ^2 in (10.18). The test statistic, with division by r to match the F tabulation, has the form

$$\begin{aligned}
W &= \frac{(\boldsymbol{R}\hat{\boldsymbol{\beta}} - \boldsymbol{c})'[\boldsymbol{R}(\boldsymbol{X}'\boldsymbol{X})^{-1}\boldsymbol{R}']^{-1}(\boldsymbol{R}\hat{\boldsymbol{\beta}} - \boldsymbol{c})}{rs^2} \\
&= \frac{\boldsymbol{u}'\boldsymbol{P}\boldsymbol{u}}{\boldsymbol{u}'\boldsymbol{M}\boldsymbol{u}}\frac{T-k}{r}.
\end{aligned} \tag{10.20}$$

The test is then implemented using the fact that

$$W \sim F(r, T-k)$$

when assumptions GCRM(i)–(iv) *and* the restrictions hypothesis hold. Hypothesis tests based on the distribution of a constraint function evaluated at the unconstrained estimates are known in the literature as *Wald tests.*

Since this test statistic in its general formulation is quite a complicated object, it will be useful to see how the procedure works out for a simple and familiar case. Consider the simple restriction $\beta_i = 0$ for some $i \leq k$, previously considered for a t-test. The relevant ingredients are $r = 1$, $c = 0$, and $\boldsymbol{R} = \boldsymbol{r}_i'$ defined by (10.6). Then $\boldsymbol{R}\hat{\boldsymbol{\beta}} - \boldsymbol{c} = \hat{\beta}_i$ and $\boldsymbol{R}(\boldsymbol{X}'\boldsymbol{X})^{-1}\boldsymbol{R}' = a_{ii}$ as defined in (10.7). The test statistic (10.20) now reduces to

$$W = \frac{\hat{\beta}_i^2}{s^2 a_{ii}},$$

which is of course the square of the usual t ratio. From the definitions of these distributions, it is evident that

$$(t_{T-k})^2 \sim F(1, T-k).$$

It follows that the t-test of $\beta_i = 0$ against the two-tailed alternative $\beta_i \neq 0$, based on the statistic $|t_{\text{calc}}|$ from (10.11), is identical with the F test. Where the two procedures are not comparable is that the t-test has a 'one-tail' variant, where the sign as well as the magnitude of the statistic can determine the outcome. Such alternatives are not available in the F test framework.

10.6 Constrained Least Squares

An alternative to forming a test statistic from the unrestricted least squares estimator of $\boldsymbol{\beta}$ is to construct an estimator satisfying the restrictions and compare this with the unrestricted case. Minimizing the sum of squares function subject to constraints is achieved by finding a stationary point of the so-called Lagrangian function

$$\frac{1}{2}S(\boldsymbol{b}) + \boldsymbol{\lambda}'(\boldsymbol{R}\boldsymbol{b} - \boldsymbol{c}) \tag{10.21}$$

where S is defined by (4.13). Here, the r-vector $\boldsymbol{\lambda}$ is the vector of *Lagrangian multipliers*, forming an additional set of arguments. The first-order conditions for a stationary point, equating the first derivatives of (10.21) with respect to both $\boldsymbol{b}$ and $\boldsymbol{\lambda}$ to zero, are

$$\boldsymbol{X}'(\boldsymbol{y} - \boldsymbol{X}\dot{\boldsymbol{\beta}}) + \boldsymbol{R}'\dot{\boldsymbol{\lambda}} = \boldsymbol{0} \tag{10.22}$$

$$\boldsymbol{R}\dot{\boldsymbol{\beta}} - \boldsymbol{c} = \boldsymbol{0}, \tag{10.23}$$

where the solutions are denoted respectively $\dot{\boldsymbol{\beta}}$ and $\dot{\boldsymbol{\lambda}}$. The factor of $\frac{1}{2}$ in (10.21) is included solely to avoid carrying a factor of 2 through the solutions. The derivatives with respect to $\boldsymbol{\lambda}$ are of course nothing but the deviations from the constraint relations, so that the constraints are required to bind at the solution.

It is worth spending a bit of time reflecting on the way these solutions work in different cases. There has to be a trade-off between the terms of (10.21), and reducing S by choice of $\boldsymbol{\beta}$ has to be balanced against changes in the value of the constraint. The optimal trade-off is found at the stationary point of the Lagrangian function, and the form of the solution depends on the form of the constraint. Suppose each constraint contains just one coefficient, fixing it to a given value. This is the case in particular for (10.15), where $\boldsymbol{R} = [\boldsymbol{I}_r \;\; \boldsymbol{0}]$. Then, equations (10.22) show that $\dot{\boldsymbol{\lambda}}$ is just the negative of the gradient of $\frac{1}{2}S$ with respect to $(\beta_1, \cdots, \beta_r)'$ at the point where these vector elements are zero. Coefficients $(\beta_{r+1}, \cdots, \beta_k)'$ are chosen to minimize $\frac{1}{2}S$ without restriction, so in these dimensions the gradient elements are zero, although generally at a different point from the fully unrestricted minimization.

A more subtle case is where a constraint involves two or more of the coefficients, as in the examples (10.13) and (10.14). The difference is that more than one set of coefficient values satisfy the constraint, or constraints, and a true trade-off exists. Condition (10.22) imposes the condition for the constrained minimum of S, that the gradient of $\frac{1}{2}S$ at the solution matches the rate of change of the constraint with $\boldsymbol{\beta}$ (that is, $\boldsymbol{R}$) weighted by $\boldsymbol{\lambda}$, where $\boldsymbol{\lambda}$ is adjusted so that the constraint just binds at the point of trade-off. If changing $\boldsymbol{\beta}$ moved the *rescaled* constraint vector at a lower rate than it reduced S, this would indicate that S could be reduced further while maintaining equality (10.23). Equation (10.22) is the condition under which no such adjustment is available.

To solve the Lagrangian equations, start by premultiplying equation (10.22) by $(\boldsymbol{X}'\boldsymbol{X})^{-1}$ and rearranging. Recalling the definition of $\hat{\boldsymbol{\beta}}$, the result is

$$\dot{\boldsymbol{\beta}} = \hat{\boldsymbol{\beta}} + (\boldsymbol{X}'\boldsymbol{X})^{-1}\boldsymbol{R}'\dot{\boldsymbol{\lambda}}, \tag{10.24}$$

which reveals the relationship between the constrained and unconstrained least squares estimators. Next, premultiply (10.24) by $\boldsymbol{R}$, which yields the solution

$$\dot{\boldsymbol{\lambda}} = -[\boldsymbol{R}(\boldsymbol{X}'\boldsymbol{X})^{-1}\boldsymbol{R}']^{-1}\boldsymbol{R}(\hat{\boldsymbol{\beta}} - \dot{\boldsymbol{\beta}}),$$

and remembering that $\dot{\boldsymbol{\beta}}$ satisfies (10.23), an equivalent solution is

$$\dot{\boldsymbol{\lambda}} = -[\boldsymbol{R}(\boldsymbol{X}'\boldsymbol{X})^{-1}\boldsymbol{R}']^{-1}(\boldsymbol{R}\hat{\boldsymbol{\beta}} - \boldsymbol{c}).$$

Finally, substituting back into (10.24) yields

$$\dot{\boldsymbol{\beta}} = \hat{\boldsymbol{\beta}} + (\boldsymbol{X}'\boldsymbol{X})^{-1}\boldsymbol{R}'[\boldsymbol{R}(\boldsymbol{X}'\boldsymbol{X})^{-1}\boldsymbol{R}']^{-1}(\boldsymbol{R}\hat{\boldsymbol{\beta}} - \boldsymbol{c}). \tag{10.25}$$

It turns out, pleasingly, that the distribution of the difference between the two estimators depends on a vector whose distribution is known, $\boldsymbol{R}\hat{\boldsymbol{\beta}} - \boldsymbol{c}$. In fact, from (10.25) it is easy to verify that

$$\begin{aligned}(\dot{\boldsymbol{\beta}} - \hat{\boldsymbol{\beta}})'\boldsymbol{X}'\boldsymbol{X}(\dot{\boldsymbol{\beta}} - \hat{\boldsymbol{\beta}}) &= (\boldsymbol{R}\hat{\boldsymbol{\beta}} - \boldsymbol{c})'[\boldsymbol{R}(\boldsymbol{X}'\boldsymbol{X})^{-1}\boldsymbol{R}']^{-1}(\boldsymbol{R}\hat{\boldsymbol{\beta}} - \boldsymbol{c}). \\ &= \boldsymbol{u}'\boldsymbol{P}\boldsymbol{u},\end{aligned} \tag{10.26}$$

where the second equality is from (10.18).

The conclusion, intriguingly enough, is that the F-test based on the difference of the two estimators is identical to the Wald test of (10.20). This is basically due to the fact that both the regression model and constraint function are linear in $\boldsymbol{\beta}$. Non-linear regression models and non-linear constraints are both possible, but do not have these convenient properties.

There is one further surprising revelation to come. Consider the residuals from the constrained estimator. Since $\hat{\boldsymbol{u}} = \boldsymbol{y} - \boldsymbol{X}\hat{\boldsymbol{\beta}}$, these have the form

$$\begin{aligned}\dot{\boldsymbol{u}} &= \boldsymbol{y} - \boldsymbol{X}\dot{\boldsymbol{\beta}} \\ &= \hat{\boldsymbol{u}} + \boldsymbol{X}(\hat{\boldsymbol{\beta}} - \dot{\boldsymbol{\beta}}).\end{aligned} \tag{10.27}$$

Of course, $\dot{\boldsymbol{u}}$ is not orthogonal to $\boldsymbol{X}$, for this is exclusively the attribute of the unconstrained least squares case. However, consider the sum of squares of these residuals. Equation (10.27) yields the result

$$\begin{aligned}\dot{\boldsymbol{u}}'\dot{\boldsymbol{u}} &= \hat{\boldsymbol{u}}'\hat{\boldsymbol{u}} + 2\hat{\boldsymbol{u}}'\boldsymbol{X}(\hat{\boldsymbol{\beta}} - \dot{\boldsymbol{\beta}}) + (\hat{\boldsymbol{\beta}} - \dot{\boldsymbol{\beta}})'\boldsymbol{X}'\boldsymbol{X}(\hat{\boldsymbol{\beta}} - \dot{\boldsymbol{\beta}}) \\ &= \hat{\boldsymbol{u}}'\hat{\boldsymbol{u}} + \boldsymbol{u}'\boldsymbol{P}\boldsymbol{u}\end{aligned}$$

in view of (10.26) and the familiar fact that $\boldsymbol{X}'\hat{\boldsymbol{u}} = \boldsymbol{0}$. This is a third route to computing $\boldsymbol{u}'\boldsymbol{P}\boldsymbol{u}$, in this case as the difference of the two sums of squares, of the constrained least squares residuals and the unconstrained least squares residuals.

Here for comparison, from (10.20) and (10.26), are the three different forms of the F statistic, where in the last case s^2 has been substituted to emphasize the simplicity of the formula.

$$\begin{aligned}W &= \frac{(\boldsymbol{R}\hat{\boldsymbol{\beta}} - \boldsymbol{c})'[\boldsymbol{R}(\boldsymbol{X}'\boldsymbol{X})^{-1}\boldsymbol{R}']^{-1}(\boldsymbol{R}\hat{\boldsymbol{\beta}} - \boldsymbol{c})}{rs^2} \\ &= \frac{(\dot{\boldsymbol{\beta}} - \hat{\boldsymbol{\beta}})'\boldsymbol{X}'\boldsymbol{X}(\dot{\boldsymbol{\beta}} - \hat{\boldsymbol{\beta}})}{rs^2} \\ &= \frac{\dot{\boldsymbol{u}}'\dot{\boldsymbol{u}} - \hat{\boldsymbol{u}}'\hat{\boldsymbol{u}}}{\hat{\boldsymbol{u}}'\hat{\boldsymbol{u}}}\frac{T-k}{r}. \end{aligned} \tag{10.28}$$

All of these versions may have their uses in particular applications, but the last one is plainly the most attractive for many purposes. For example, to perform a multiple significance test, run two regressions, one excluding the variables under test and the other including them. The F statistic is then obtained as the function of the two sums of squares in the last member of (10.28), a trivial calculation.

A test statistic often quoted in the output of regression packages is the "test of the regression", which is the test for joint significance of all the regressors. The null hypothesis in this test is that $\beta_1 = \cdots = \beta_{k-1} = 0$ and hence that

$$\boldsymbol{y} \sim \mathrm{N}(\beta_k \boldsymbol{\iota}, \sigma^2 \boldsymbol{I}_T)$$

where $\boldsymbol{\iota}$ $(T \times 1)$ is the column of ones, representing the intercept. In this case

$$\dot{\boldsymbol{u}}'\dot{\boldsymbol{u}} = \boldsymbol{y}'\boldsymbol{y} - T\bar{y}^2,$$

and referring to (4.24) shows that the statistic (10.28) has the simple form

$$W = \frac{R^2}{1 - R^2}\frac{T-k}{k-1}.$$

Despite its ubiquity in applied work, this test should be used with caution. The hypothesis that none of the chosen regressors significantly explains $\boldsymbol{y}$ is not strictly equivalent to the hypothesis that $\boldsymbol{y}$ is identically and independently distributed. The possibility of an incorrect maintained hypothesis needs to be taken into account to avoid the pitfall of a false positive.

10.7 Exercises

1 Are the following statements true or false?

(a) The size of a test is the probability of rejecting the null hypothesis when it is true. If there are different cases of the null hypothesis on which the probability depends, the size is the largest such probability.

(b) The least squares estimator is normally distributed thanks to the fact that linear functions of expected values are linear.

(c) The derivation of pivotal test statistics depends on having different functions of the same data set that are independent of each other.

(d) F and t statistics are ratios, and the validity of F and t tests depends on the numerator and denominator being uncorrelated random variables.

(e) If $k = T$ and X has rank k, the regression model fits the data exactly.

(f) The solution to the constrained minimum of the sum of squares entails setting the Lagrangian multipliers to zero.

(g) It is a special feature of linear regression that three different testing principles – comparing constraints, comparing constrained with unconstrained estimators, and comparing sums of squares – all lead to the same statistic.

2 In the regression model

$$y_t = \beta_1 x_{1t} + \beta_2 x_{2t} + u_t, \quad t = 1, \dots, 12,$$

x_{1t} and x_{2t} are fixed in repeated samples and are expressed as deviations from their sample means, and $u_t \sim \mathrm{N}(0, \sigma^2)$. The following is the moment matrix of the data:

$$\begin{bmatrix} \sum y_t^2 & \sum x_{1t}y_t & \sum x_{2t}y_t \\ \sum x_{1t}y_t & \sum x_{1t}^2 & \sum x_{1t}x_{2t} \\ \sum x_{2t}y_t & \sum x_{1t}x_{2t} & \sum x_{2t}^2 \end{bmatrix} = \begin{bmatrix} 4/3 & 1 & 1 \\ 1 & 2 & 1 \\ 1 & 1 & 2 \end{bmatrix}$$

Construct statistics to test the hypotheses

(a) $\beta_1 = 0$, and $\beta_2 = 0$.

(b) $\beta_1 = \beta_2 = 0$.

Comment on your results.

3 Consider the linear regression model

$$y_t = \boldsymbol{\beta}'\boldsymbol{x}_t + u_t, \quad t = 1, \dots, T,$$

where y_t and $\boldsymbol{x}_t$ ($k \times 1$) are observed and u_t is a random disturbance. The following assumptions are made about this model:

(i) $\mathrm{E}(u_t) = 0$ for each t.

(ii) $\mathrm{E}(u_t^2) = \sigma^2$ (constant) for each t.

(iii) $\mathrm{E}(u_t u_s) = 0$ for each t and $s \neq t$.

(iv) $u_1, \dots, u_T$ are jointly normally distributed.

(v) $\boldsymbol{x}_1, \dots, \boldsymbol{x}_T$ are fixed in repeated samples.

Let

$$V = s^2\left(\sum_{t=1}^{T} \boldsymbol{x}_t\boldsymbol{x}_t'\right)^{-1}$$

$(k \times k)$ where

$$s^2 = \frac{1}{T-k}\sum_{t=1}^{T}(y_t - \hat{\boldsymbol{\beta}}'\boldsymbol{x}_t)^2$$

and $\hat{\boldsymbol{\beta}}$ is the least squares estimator. Let β_j denote the jth element of $\boldsymbol{\beta}$, $\hat{\beta}_j$ the corresponding element of $\hat{\boldsymbol{\beta}}$, and v_{jj} the corresponding diagonal element of $\boldsymbol{V}$.

(a) Derive from $\hat{\beta}_j$ a statistic having the Student's t distribution.
(b) Explain the roles of each of assumptions (i)–(v) in validating the result of part (a). Should the assumption of random sampling have been included in this list?
(c) Does the result of part (a) depend on having $x_{kt} = 1$ for each t (inclusion of an intercept)? Explain your answer.
(d) Explain how the hypothesis $\beta_j = 0$ is tested using the result of part (a).

4 In the model $\boldsymbol{y} = \boldsymbol{X\beta} + \mathbf{u}$ $(T \times 1)$ where $\boldsymbol{X}$ is $T \times k$, consider the test statistic

$$W = \frac{(\boldsymbol{R}\hat{\boldsymbol{\beta}} - \mathbf{c})'(\boldsymbol{R}(\boldsymbol{X}'\boldsymbol{X})^{-1}\boldsymbol{R}')^{-1}(\boldsymbol{R}\hat{\boldsymbol{\beta}} - \mathbf{c})}{rs^2}$$

where $\boldsymbol{R}$ $(r \times k)$ and $\mathbf{c}$ $(r \times 1)$ are fixed and $s^2 = \hat{\boldsymbol{u}}'\hat{\boldsymbol{u}}/(T-k)$.

(a) For W to have the $F(r, T-k)$ distribution requires that the numerator and denominator are distributed independently. State definitions of the quantities $\hat{\boldsymbol{\beta}}$ and $\hat{\boldsymbol{u}}$ and appropriate assumptions under which this condition holds, and explain the underlying reasoning.
(b) Also justify, under the same definitions/assumptions, the claim that the numerator and denominator have rescaled chi-squared distributions.

5 Consider the following two-variable model with $T = 21$ observations, where the data are expressed in sample mean-deviation form.

$$\boldsymbol{y} = \boldsymbol{x}_1\beta_1 + \boldsymbol{x}_2\beta_2 + \boldsymbol{u}$$

(a) If $\boldsymbol{x}_1'\boldsymbol{x}_1 = 3$, $\boldsymbol{x}_2'\boldsymbol{x}_2 = 2$, $\boldsymbol{x}_1'\boldsymbol{x}_2 = \boldsymbol{x}_1'\boldsymbol{y} = \boldsymbol{x}_2'\boldsymbol{y} = 1$, and $\boldsymbol{y}'\boldsymbol{y} = 4/5$, calculate
   i. The least squares coefficients $\hat{\beta}_1$ and $\hat{\beta}_2$.
   ii. The coefficient of determination R^2.
   iii. The t-statistic to test the hypothesis $\beta_1 = 0$.
   iv. The F-statistic to test the hypothesis $\beta_1 = \beta_2 = 0$.
(b) Explain the assumptions under which the statistics in parts iii. and iv. of part (a) have their nominal distributions under the respective null hypotheses.

6 The regression model

$$y_t = \beta_1 x_{1t} + \beta_2 x_{2t} + u_t, \quad t = 1, \dots, T$$

is estimated by constrained least squares, subject to the restriction $\beta_2 = 0$.

(a) Find the constrained least squares estimators $\dot{\beta}_1$ and $\dot{\beta}_2$.
(b) Find the formula for the Lagrangian multiplier $\dot{\lambda}$.
(c) Show that

$$\dot{\beta}_1 - \hat{\beta}_1 = \hat{\Lambda}\hat{\beta}_2$$

where $\hat{\beta}_2$ is the unconstrained least squares estimator of β_2, giving a formula for $\hat{\Lambda}$.
(d) Find the formula for the Wald test statistic for this restriction, and show how it is related to $\dot{\lambda}$.

11

Partitioning and Specification

11.1 The Partitioned Regression

In nearly every modelling exercise, explanatory variables fall into two groups. There are the *focus* variables, the significance, sign, or magnitude of whose coefficients are the object of the analysis. And there are also what are often called *nuisance* variables, which are included because they help to explain $\boldsymbol{y}$, although there is no particular interest in their coefficients. Focus and nuisance parameters may be spoken of in the same vein. The intercept term is perhaps the most frequently encountered of the latter type. This is a natural motivation for partitioning the regressor matrix by columns and the coefficient vector to match. Choosing k_1 and k_2 such that $k_1 + k_2 = k$, write

$$\boldsymbol{X} = [\boldsymbol{X}_1 \quad \boldsymbol{X}_2]$$

where $\boldsymbol{X}_1$ is $T \times k_1$ and $\boldsymbol{X}_2$ is $T \times k_2$, partition $\boldsymbol{\beta}$ conformably, and hence write

$$\begin{aligned} \boldsymbol{y} &= \boldsymbol{X}\boldsymbol{\beta} + \boldsymbol{u} \\ &= [\boldsymbol{X}_1 \quad \boldsymbol{X}_2] \begin{bmatrix} \boldsymbol{\beta}_1 \\ \boldsymbol{\beta}_2 \end{bmatrix} + \boldsymbol{u}. \end{aligned} \tag{11.1}$$

The partition of the inner product matrix follows the outer product pattern as in (2.10),

$$\boldsymbol{X}'\boldsymbol{X} = \begin{bmatrix} \boldsymbol{X}_1' \\ \boldsymbol{X}_2' \end{bmatrix} [\boldsymbol{X}_1 \ \boldsymbol{X}_2] = \begin{bmatrix} \boldsymbol{X}_1'\boldsymbol{X}_1 & \boldsymbol{X}_1'\boldsymbol{X}_2 \\ \boldsymbol{X}_2'\boldsymbol{X}_1 & \boldsymbol{X}_2'\boldsymbol{X}_2 \end{bmatrix}.$$

Hence the least squares normal equations

$$\boldsymbol{X}'\boldsymbol{X}\hat{\boldsymbol{\beta}} = \boldsymbol{X}'\boldsymbol{y}$$

can be written in partitioned form as

$$\begin{bmatrix} \boldsymbol{X}_1'\boldsymbol{X}_1 & \boldsymbol{X}_1'\boldsymbol{X}_2 \\ \boldsymbol{X}_2'\boldsymbol{X}_1 & \boldsymbol{X}_2'\boldsymbol{X}_2 \end{bmatrix} \begin{bmatrix} \hat{\boldsymbol{\beta}}_1 \\ \hat{\boldsymbol{\beta}}_2 \end{bmatrix} = \begin{bmatrix} \boldsymbol{X}_1'\boldsymbol{y} \\ \boldsymbol{X}_2'\boldsymbol{y} \end{bmatrix}. \tag{11.2}$$

To get formulae for $\hat{\boldsymbol{\beta}}_1$ and $\hat{\boldsymbol{\beta}}_2$, write these equations as the pair

$$\boldsymbol{X}_1'\boldsymbol{X}_1\hat{\boldsymbol{\beta}}_1 + \boldsymbol{X}_1'\boldsymbol{X}_2\hat{\boldsymbol{\beta}}_2 = \boldsymbol{X}_1'\boldsymbol{y} \tag{11.3}$$

$$\boldsymbol{X}_2'\boldsymbol{X}_1\hat{\boldsymbol{\beta}}_1 + \boldsymbol{X}_2'\boldsymbol{X}_2\hat{\boldsymbol{\beta}}_2 = \boldsymbol{X}_2'\boldsymbol{y} \tag{11.4}$$

An Introduction to Econometric Theory, First Edition. James Davidson.

Companion website: www.wiley.com/go/davidson/introecmettheory

to be solved in sequence. First, invert $X_2'X_2$, and so from (11.4) obtain

$$\hat{\beta}_2 = (X_2'X_2)^{-1}(X_2'y - X_2'X_1\hat{\beta}_1). \tag{11.5}$$

Substituting this expression for $\hat{\beta}_2$ into (11.3) gives an equation containing only $\hat{\beta}_1$. Collecting terms in $\hat{\beta}_1$ and inverting the resulting $k_1 \times k_1$ matrix yields the solution,

$$\hat{\beta}_1 = (X_1'X_1 - X_1'X_2(X_2'X_2)^{-1}X_2'X_1)^{-1}(X_1'y - X_1'X_2(X_2'X_2)^{-1}X_2'y).$$

This formula might appear somewhat intractable, until it is noticed that after collecting terms the orthogonal projection matrix

$$M_2 = \mathrm{I} - X_2(X_2'X_2)^{-1}X_2'$$

appears twice. The formula simplifies to the very tractable

$$\hat{\beta}_1 = (X_1'M_2X_1)^{-1}X_1'M_2y. \tag{11.6}$$

The same stepwise solution approach yields the companion solution

$$\hat{\beta}_2 = (X_2'M_1X_2)^{-1}X_2'M_1y \tag{11.7}$$

with the obvious definition for M_1.

Another approach to solving (11.2) is to make use of the partitioned inverse formula (3.29). Defining

$$\begin{aligned} E &= (X_1'X_1 - X_1'X_2(X_2'X_2)^{-1}X_2'X_1)^{-1} \\ &= (X_1'M_2X_1)^{-1} \end{aligned}$$

this gives

$$\begin{aligned} &\begin{bmatrix} X_1'X_1 & X_1'X_2 \\ X_2'X_1 & X_2'X_2 \end{bmatrix}^{-1} \\ &= \begin{bmatrix} E & -EX_1'X_2(X_2'X_2)^{-1} \\ -(X_2'X_2)^{-1}X_2'X_1E & (X_2'X_2)^{-1} + (X_2'X_2)^{-1}X_2'X_1EX_1'X_2(X_2'X_2)^{-1} \end{bmatrix} \end{aligned}$$

It easy to see from

$$\begin{bmatrix} \hat{\beta}_1 \\ \hat{\beta}_2 \end{bmatrix} = \begin{bmatrix} X_1'X_1 & X_1'X_2 \\ X_2'X_1 & X_2'X_2 \end{bmatrix}^{-1} \begin{bmatrix} X_1'y \\ X_2'y \end{bmatrix}$$

that the solution

$$\hat{\beta}_1 = EX_1'y - EX_1'X_2(X_2'X_2)^{-1}X_2'y$$

matches (11.6). The formula for $\hat{\beta}_2$ from this solution looks a bit terrifying, but with rearrangement it simplifies to equation (11.5). It might also be arrived at directly using the alternative partitioned inverse (3.30).

Also consider the partitioned representation of the least squares residuals,

$$\begin{aligned} \hat{u} &= y - X_1\hat{\beta}_1 - X_2\hat{\beta}_2 \\ &= y - X_1\hat{\beta}_1 - X_2(X_2'X_2)^{-1}(X_2'y - X_2'X_1\hat{\beta}_1) \\ &= M_2y - M_2X_1\hat{\beta}_1 \\ &= (M_2 - M_2X_1(X_1'M_2X_1)^{-1}X_1'M_2)y. \end{aligned} \tag{11.8}$$

Note the rather striking implication of (11.8), that

$$M = M_2 - M_2X_1(X_1'M_2X_1)^{-1}X_1'M_2, \tag{11.9}$$

where M is defined in (7.13). Both terms in this decomposition of M are symmetric and idempotent, with ranks respectively of $T - k_2$ and k_1, as can be verified by computing the trace of each. The formula does of course have a further variant in which the subscripts '1' and '2' are interchanged throughout.

11.2 Frisch-Waugh-Lovell Theorem

Since M_2 is idempotent and symmetric, (11.6) can also be written in the form

$$\begin{aligned}\hat{\beta}_1 &= (X_1'M_2'M_2X_1)^{-1}X_1'M_2'y \\ &= (X_1^{*\prime}X_1^*)^{-1}X_1^{*\prime}y,\end{aligned}$$

where $X_1^* = M_2X_1$. The curiosity of these formulae is that the variables are the residuals obtained after regressing the columns of X_1 onto X_2. What has become known as the Frisch-Waugh-Lovell (FWL) theorem is the result that the partitioned regression can be calculated by a sequence of regular regressions. If X_2 are the nuisance variables and X_1 are the focus variables, the procedure is to regress the focus variables onto the nuisance set and obtain the residuals from these regressions. The final stage is to do the regression for the focus variables alone, but using the residuals in place of the raw data series. This might be described as 'purging' the focus variables of the effects of the nuisance variables, as an alternative to including the latter in the multiple regression. We also speak of 'partialling out' the effect of nuisance variables.

The 'Frisch' whose name is attached to this result is Ragnar Frisch, founder of the Econometric Society and the journal *Econometrica* and first recipient of the Nobel Prize in economics. Frisch was a pioneer of regression analysis in the 1930s, before the invention of digital computers. Then, such calculations were performed by research assistants using mechanical calculators. Indeed, in its original meaning the term "computer" referred to a person, not a machine. Frisch's problem was that the inversion of matrices by hand was a time-consuming procedure, with the burden growing at the rate of the cube of the dimension of the matrix (see Section 3.6). Keeping the dimension of the problem small was of paramount importance, and a natural expedient was to store one's data in the form of residuals from regressions on nuisance variables.

Consider the intercept. Let $X_2 = \iota$, the T-vector with all elements 1. Verify that

$$\begin{aligned}M_2X_1 &= X_1 - \iota(\iota'\iota)^{-1}\iota'X_1 \\ &= X_1 - \iota\bar{x}_1'\end{aligned}$$

where

$$\bar{x}_1' = \frac{\iota'X_1}{T}$$

is the row k-vector containing the sample means of the columns of X_1. Thus, M_2X_1 here represents the data expressed in mean deviation form. The FWL theorem says that multiple regression including an intercept is equivalent to regression without an intercept but with the data in mean-deviation form. Working with these series makes the intercept unnecessary, with a corresponding reduction in computational burden.

Another nice application of the FWL theorem is to provide a formula for any individual element of the multiple regression coefficient vector. Take the case of the ith coefficient, for any $i = 1, \ldots, k$,

$$\hat{\beta}_i = \frac{\sum_{t=1}^{T} \tilde{x}_{it} y_t}{\sum_{t=1}^{T} \tilde{x}_{it}^2}, \tag{11.10}$$

where $\tilde{x}_{it}$ is the residual from the regression of x_{it} on all the other regressors *except* x_{it}. Comparing this formula with (1.27), the 'covariance over variance' formulation evidently has a quite general application. In the case of simple regression in Section 1.5, it is simply a matter of putting the data in mean deviations, but this is revealed as just an instance of the general principle of partialling out the 'other' regressors.

Formula (11.10) appears to allow multiple regression to be performed without any resort to matrix algebra. However, while in principle the formula could be used to execute such calculations by hand, the amount of labour involved must be apparent. This is a recursive formula involving multiple regressions of lower dimension, not unlike the determinant recursion (3.8) which in a sense it must replicate. The most useful application of (11.10) is as an aid to explaining how multiple regression works to students with no knowledge of matrix algebra.

11.3 Misspecification Analysis

A vital application of partitioning is to study the consequences of misspecifying the regression model. One form of misspecification is the omission of regressors that should be included, which means in particular that assumptions CRM(ii) and CRM(iii) are both violated.

Suppose that the true model has the form

$$\boldsymbol{y} = \boldsymbol{X\beta} + \boldsymbol{Z\delta} + \boldsymbol{u}$$

where the columns of the matrices $\boldsymbol{X}$ $(T \times k)$ and $\boldsymbol{Z}$ $(T \times m)$ are linearly independent, the coefficient vector $\boldsymbol{\delta}$ is different from zero and $\mathrm{E}(\boldsymbol{u}) = \boldsymbol{0}$. If $\boldsymbol{Z}$ is omitted from the regression, the fitted equation is

$$\boldsymbol{y} = \boldsymbol{X\beta} + \boldsymbol{e}$$

where

$$\boldsymbol{e} = \boldsymbol{Z\delta} + \boldsymbol{u}$$

and $\mathrm{E}(\boldsymbol{e}) = \boldsymbol{Z\delta}$. OLS applied to this assumed model yields the estimator

$$\begin{aligned} \dot{\boldsymbol{\beta}} &= (\boldsymbol{X}'\boldsymbol{X})^{-1}\boldsymbol{X}'\boldsymbol{y} \\ &= \boldsymbol{\beta} + (\boldsymbol{X}'\boldsymbol{X})^{-1}\boldsymbol{X}'\boldsymbol{Z\delta} + (\boldsymbol{X}'\boldsymbol{X})^{-1}\boldsymbol{X}'\boldsymbol{u}. \end{aligned} \tag{11.11}$$

The consequence of omitting variables is that the OLS estimator of $\boldsymbol{\beta}$ is no longer centred on the true value. The *bias* due to omitted variables is

$$\mathrm{E}(\dot{\boldsymbol{\beta}}) - \boldsymbol{\beta} = \hat{\boldsymbol{\Lambda}}\boldsymbol{\delta} \tag{11.12}$$

where

$$\hat{\boldsymbol{\Lambda}} = (\boldsymbol{X}'\boldsymbol{X})^{-1}\boldsymbol{X}'\boldsymbol{Z}. \tag{11.13}$$

The bias formula has quite a useful interpretation. Using the partitioned regression formula (11.5) where $\boldsymbol{X}_2$ is the counterpart of $\boldsymbol{X}$ and $\boldsymbol{X}_1$ the counterpart of $\boldsymbol{Z}$, the estimator of $\boldsymbol{\beta}$ in the correctly specified model is

$$\begin{aligned}\hat{\boldsymbol{\beta}} &= (\boldsymbol{X}'\boldsymbol{X})^{-1}(\boldsymbol{X}'\boldsymbol{y} - \boldsymbol{X}'\boldsymbol{Z}\hat{\boldsymbol{\delta}})\\ &= \dot{\boldsymbol{\beta}} - \hat{\boldsymbol{\Lambda}}\hat{\boldsymbol{\delta}}\end{aligned} \tag{11.14}$$

where

$$\hat{\boldsymbol{\delta}} = (\boldsymbol{Z}'\boldsymbol{M}_X\boldsymbol{Z})^{-1}\boldsymbol{Z}'\boldsymbol{M}_X\boldsymbol{y}$$

is the unbiased estimator of $\boldsymbol{\delta}$. In other words, the effect of including $\boldsymbol{Z}$ in the regression is to introduce a correction term whose expected value (since $\mathrm{E}(\hat{\boldsymbol{\delta}}) = \boldsymbol{\delta}$) is the negative of the bias due to its exclusion.

So much is fairly apparent, but the bias term has a further useful interpretation. Rearranging (11.12), or equivalently taking expectations of (11.14), gives the interesting decomposition

$$\boldsymbol{\beta} = \mathrm{E}(\dot{\boldsymbol{\beta}}) - \hat{\boldsymbol{\Lambda}}\boldsymbol{\delta}, \tag{11.15}$$

showing how the true $\boldsymbol{\beta}$ is made up. One part is unbiasedly estimated by $\dot{\boldsymbol{\beta}}$ and evidently has the interpretation of the 'direct' effect of $\boldsymbol{X}$ on $\boldsymbol{y}$. The second part is the product of two factors, one the prediction of $\boldsymbol{Z}$ by $\boldsymbol{X}$, which is $\hat{\boldsymbol{\Lambda}}$, and the other the coefficient of $\boldsymbol{Z}$ in the true model. This latter term is the 'indirect' effect on $\boldsymbol{y}$, as $\boldsymbol{X}$ has an effect on $\boldsymbol{Z}$ which in turn affects $\boldsymbol{y}$. There is no need to take literally the idea of $\boldsymbol{X}$ *causing* $\boldsymbol{Z}$, in this context, since $\hat{\boldsymbol{\Lambda}}$ represents nothing but the best prediction of $\boldsymbol{Z}$ by $\boldsymbol{X}$, which depends on $\boldsymbol{X}$ unless the two matrices are orthogonal.

This version of formula (11.12) helps interpretation of the biased estimator. Suppose $\boldsymbol{Z}$ is unobserved, so that its omission is inevitable. Then $\dot{\boldsymbol{\beta}}$ has the virtue that it is giving the best possible prediction of $\boldsymbol{y}$ from $\boldsymbol{X}$ alone. That is,

$$\begin{aligned}\mathrm{E}(\boldsymbol{X}\dot{\boldsymbol{\beta}}) &= \boldsymbol{X}\boldsymbol{\beta} + \mathbf{X}\hat{\boldsymbol{\Lambda}}\boldsymbol{\delta}\\ &= \boldsymbol{X}\boldsymbol{\beta} + \mathrm{Q}_X\boldsymbol{Z}\boldsymbol{\delta}\end{aligned}$$

where $\boldsymbol{Q}_X = \boldsymbol{X}(\boldsymbol{X}'\boldsymbol{X})^{-1}\boldsymbol{X}'$. Contrast this with the mean forecast from the true model,

$$\mathrm{E}(\boldsymbol{y}) = \boldsymbol{X}\boldsymbol{\beta} + \boldsymbol{Z}\boldsymbol{\delta}.$$

When $\mathbf{Z}$ is unavailable, the biased estimator is providing the best available proxy, the projection of $\boldsymbol{Z}$ into the space spanned by $\boldsymbol{X}$. Thus, biased estimation is not necessarily a useless exercise. When the object of the exercise is prediction, rather than testing hypotheses about $\boldsymbol{\beta}$, it makes the best of a bad job.

However, there is a downside. Even if $\dot{\boldsymbol{\beta}}$ is assigned a useful interpretation, inference is still compromised by the failure of assumption CRM(iii). Note that

$$\begin{aligned}\mathrm{E}(\boldsymbol{e}\boldsymbol{e}') &= \mathrm{E}(\boldsymbol{u} + \boldsymbol{Z}\boldsymbol{\delta})(\boldsymbol{u} + \boldsymbol{Z}\boldsymbol{\delta})'\\ &= \sigma^2\boldsymbol{I}_T + \boldsymbol{Z}\boldsymbol{\delta}\boldsymbol{\delta}'\boldsymbol{Z}'.\end{aligned}$$

The addition of the fixed matrix means that the computed standard errors for this model will not in general have a useful interpretation. Attempted inference on $\boldsymbol{\beta}$ will inevitably be misleading.

Having learned of the dangers of omitting important variables from the model, we may wish to adopt a "if in doubt, include" strategy, so it would be as well to investigate the consequences of incorrect inclusion. Now, let the true model be

$$\boldsymbol{y} = \boldsymbol{X}\boldsymbol{\beta} + \boldsymbol{u}, \tag{11.16}$$

satisfying assumptions CRM(i)–(iii), but assume that the fitted equation is

$$\boldsymbol{y} = \boldsymbol{X}\boldsymbol{\beta} + \boldsymbol{Z}\boldsymbol{\delta} + \boldsymbol{u}$$

where $\boldsymbol{\delta} = \boldsymbol{0}$. The unrestricted OLS estimator of $\boldsymbol{\beta}$ in the latter model is

$$\hat{\boldsymbol{\beta}} = (\boldsymbol{X}'\boldsymbol{M}_Z\boldsymbol{X})^{-1}\boldsymbol{X}'\boldsymbol{M}_Z\boldsymbol{y} \tag{11.17}$$

where

$$\boldsymbol{M}_Z = \boldsymbol{I} - \boldsymbol{Z}(\boldsymbol{Z}'\boldsymbol{Z})^{-1}\boldsymbol{Z}'.$$

Substituting from (11.16) into (11.17) gives

$$\hat{\boldsymbol{\beta}} = \boldsymbol{\beta} + (\boldsymbol{X}'\boldsymbol{M}_Z\boldsymbol{X})^{-1}\boldsymbol{X}'\boldsymbol{M}_Z\boldsymbol{u},$$

where, by a now often-rehearsed argument, the assumptions imply

$$\begin{aligned} \mathrm{E}(\hat{\boldsymbol{\beta}}) &= \boldsymbol{\beta} + (\boldsymbol{X}'\boldsymbol{M}_Z\boldsymbol{X})^{-1}\boldsymbol{X}'\boldsymbol{M}_Z\mathrm{E}(\boldsymbol{u}) \\ &= \boldsymbol{\beta}. \end{aligned}$$

Including irrelevant regressors does not bias the estimates of the focus parameters.

However, there is also the issue of efficiency to consider. The efficient estimator is correctly specified OLS, which in this case is the restricted estimator

$$\dot{\boldsymbol{\beta}} = (\boldsymbol{X}'\boldsymbol{X})^{-1}\boldsymbol{X}'\boldsymbol{y}.$$

This follows by the Gauss-Markov theorem, where the rival case of (8.3) has

$$\boldsymbol{L} = (\boldsymbol{X}'\boldsymbol{M}_Z\boldsymbol{X})^{-1}\boldsymbol{X}'\boldsymbol{M}_Z,$$

and its covariance matrix is

$$\mathrm{Var}(\hat{\boldsymbol{\beta}}) = \sigma^2(\boldsymbol{X}'\boldsymbol{M}_Z\boldsymbol{X})^{-1}.$$

Therefore,

$$\mathrm{Var}(\hat{\boldsymbol{\beta}}) - \mathrm{Var}(\dot{\boldsymbol{\beta}}) = \sigma^2(\boldsymbol{X}'\boldsymbol{M}_Z\boldsymbol{X})^{-1} - \sigma^2(\boldsymbol{X}'\boldsymbol{X})^{-1}. \tag{11.18}$$

To see that this difference of matrices is positive semidefinite, note first that $\boldsymbol{X}'\boldsymbol{X}$ and $\boldsymbol{X}'\boldsymbol{M}_Z\boldsymbol{X}$ are both positive definite, and by Property 6 of Section 4.3, the positive semidefiniteness of (11.18) follows from that of

$$\boldsymbol{X}'\boldsymbol{X} - \boldsymbol{X}'\boldsymbol{M}_Z\boldsymbol{X} = \boldsymbol{X}'\boldsymbol{Q}_Z\boldsymbol{X} \tag{11.19}$$

where

$$\boldsymbol{Q}_Z = \boldsymbol{Z}(\boldsymbol{Z}'\boldsymbol{Z})^{-1}\boldsymbol{Z}'.$$

Since $\boldsymbol{Q}_Z$ is symmetric and idempotent, (11.19) is positive semidefinite by Property 1 of Section 4.3. The interesting question is whether $\boldsymbol{X}'\boldsymbol{Q}_Z\boldsymbol{X}$ $(k \times k)$ has full rank k and hence is positive definite, in which case this is also true of (11.18). Note that $\boldsymbol{Q}_Z\boldsymbol{X}$ is the projection of $\boldsymbol{X}$ into the space spanned by $\boldsymbol{Z}$. The columns of $\boldsymbol{X}$ and $\boldsymbol{Z}$ ($T \times m$) must be linearly independent (note that otherwise $\boldsymbol{X}'\boldsymbol{M}_Z\boldsymbol{X}$ would be singular), so in the case $m \geq k$, $\boldsymbol{X}'\boldsymbol{Z}$ has rank k, and hence

$$\boldsymbol{X}'\boldsymbol{Q}_Z\boldsymbol{X} = (\boldsymbol{X}'\boldsymbol{Z})(\boldsymbol{Z}'\boldsymbol{Z})^{-1}(\boldsymbol{X}'\boldsymbol{Z})'$$

is positive definite according to Property 4 of Section 4.3. Otherwise, this matrix is positive semidefinite but is singular with rank m. The correctly specified estimator is unambiguously more efficient than the overspecified case when the irrelevant regressors are numerous enough, but is never less efficient.

The choice between inclusion and exclusion of doubtful variables may involve a trade-off of bias versus efficiency, and it is sometimes suggested to base the decision on a comparison of mean squared errors. From (11.11), note that

$$\mathrm{E}(\dot{\boldsymbol{\beta}} - \boldsymbol{\beta})(\dot{\boldsymbol{\beta}} - \boldsymbol{\beta})' = \sigma^2(\boldsymbol{X}'\boldsymbol{X})^{-1} + \hat{\boldsymbol{\Lambda}}\boldsymbol{\delta}\boldsymbol{\delta}'\hat{\boldsymbol{\Lambda}}',$$

which is to be compared with

$$\mathrm{E}(\hat{\boldsymbol{\beta}} - \boldsymbol{\beta})(\hat{\boldsymbol{\beta}} - \boldsymbol{\beta})' = \sigma^2(\boldsymbol{X}'\boldsymbol{M}_Z\boldsymbol{X})^{-1}.$$

However, it is important not to overlook the issue of valid inferences. If restrictions on the model are to be tested, the importance of a correct maintained hypothesis is critical.

11.4 Specification Testing

There is clearly an important issue with the selection of explanatory variables, with costs entailed by both errors of omission and errors of inclusion. It is standard practice to make decisions on the inclusion of nuisance variables on the basis of statistical tests. These are often referred to as *diagnostic* tests. A useful exercise is to review the F testing framework of Section 10.5 in this context.

Consider testing the hypothesis $\boldsymbol{\delta} = \boldsymbol{0}$ ($m \times 1$) in the model

$$\boldsymbol{y} = \boldsymbol{X}\boldsymbol{\beta} + \boldsymbol{Z}\boldsymbol{\delta} + \boldsymbol{u}, \tag{11.20}$$

which under the maintained hypothesis is assumed to satisfy assumptions GCRM(i)–(iv). This is often referred to in the literature as a *variable addition* test. Expressed as a linear restriction on the parameters, the hypothesis may be written as the m-vector

$$\begin{bmatrix} \boldsymbol{0} & \boldsymbol{I}_m \end{bmatrix} \begin{bmatrix} \boldsymbol{\beta} \\ \boldsymbol{\delta} \end{bmatrix} = \boldsymbol{0}.$$

The F statistic (10.20) for this hypothesis takes the form

$$\begin{aligned} W &= \frac{1}{ms^2}\hat{\boldsymbol{\delta}}' \left(\begin{bmatrix} \boldsymbol{0} & \boldsymbol{I}_m \end{bmatrix} \begin{bmatrix} \boldsymbol{X}'\boldsymbol{X} & \boldsymbol{X}'\boldsymbol{Z} \\ \boldsymbol{Z}'\boldsymbol{X} & \boldsymbol{Z}'\boldsymbol{Z} \end{bmatrix}^{-1} \begin{bmatrix} \boldsymbol{0} \\ \boldsymbol{I}_m \end{bmatrix} \right)^{-1} \hat{\boldsymbol{\delta}} \\ &= \frac{\hat{\boldsymbol{\delta}}'\boldsymbol{Z}'\boldsymbol{M}_X\boldsymbol{Z}\hat{\boldsymbol{\delta}}}{ms^2}, \end{aligned} \tag{11.21}$$

where the fact that the lower-right block of the inverse matrix is $(\boldsymbol{Z}'\boldsymbol{M}_X\boldsymbol{Z})^{-1}$ follows by the second partitioned inverse formula, (3.30).

The partitioned regression formula gives the unrestricted estimator of $\boldsymbol{\delta}$ as

$$\hat{\boldsymbol{\delta}} = (\boldsymbol{Z}'\boldsymbol{M}_X\boldsymbol{Z})^{-1}\boldsymbol{Z}'\boldsymbol{M}_X\boldsymbol{y}.$$

From (11.9), the sum of squared residuals from the unrestricted regression has the partitioned form

$$\boldsymbol{y}'\boldsymbol{M}_X\boldsymbol{y} - \boldsymbol{y}'\boldsymbol{M}_X\boldsymbol{Z}(\boldsymbol{Z}'\boldsymbol{M}_X\boldsymbol{Z})^{-1}\boldsymbol{Z}'\boldsymbol{M}_X\boldsymbol{y}, \tag{11.22}$$

where $\boldsymbol{M}_X = \boldsymbol{I}_T - \boldsymbol{X}(\boldsymbol{X}'\boldsymbol{X})^{-1}\boldsymbol{X}'$ and the first term is the sum of squared residuals from the restricted regression containing $\boldsymbol{X}$ alone. The second term in (11.22) is none other than the numerator in (11.21), which therefore has the form

$$\frac{\hat{\boldsymbol{\delta}}'\boldsymbol{Z}'\boldsymbol{M}_X\boldsymbol{Z}\hat{\boldsymbol{\delta}}}{ms^2} = \frac{\boldsymbol{y}'\boldsymbol{M}_X\boldsymbol{Z}(\boldsymbol{Z}'\boldsymbol{M}_X\boldsymbol{Z})^{-1}\boldsymbol{Z}'\boldsymbol{M}_X\boldsymbol{y}}{\boldsymbol{y}'(\boldsymbol{M}_X - \boldsymbol{M}_X\boldsymbol{Z}(\boldsymbol{Z}'\boldsymbol{M}_X\boldsymbol{Z})^{-1}\boldsymbol{Z}'\boldsymbol{M}_X)\boldsymbol{y}}\frac{T-k-m}{m}. \tag{11.23}$$

It can easily be verified that the matrices of these quadratic forms are symmetric, idempotent, and mutually orthogonal. When the maintained hypothesis and the null hypothesis $\boldsymbol{\delta} = \boldsymbol{0}$ both hold, the $\boldsymbol{y}$ in these formulae is replaced by $\boldsymbol{u}$, and the statistic is distributed like $F(m, T-k-m)$. Notice that the numerator in (11.23), according to (11.22), is just the difference between the restricted and unrestricted sums of squares as in (10.28), and this is certainly the simplest way to compute the statistic.

In some circumstances, it is computationally convenient to convert linear restrictions into zero restrictions by transforming the data set and then to perform a variable addition test. After reordering the coefficients if necessary, it is always possible to partition $\boldsymbol{R}$ in (10.12) as $[\boldsymbol{R}_1\ \ \boldsymbol{R}_2]$ where $\boldsymbol{R}_2$ is $r \times r$ and invertible, and partition $\boldsymbol{\beta}$ conformably into its first $k-r$ and last r elements, as $(\boldsymbol{\beta}_1', \boldsymbol{\beta}_2')'$. Then the restrictions can be written in solved form as

$$\boldsymbol{S}\boldsymbol{\beta}_1 + \boldsymbol{\beta}_2 = \boldsymbol{d} \tag{11.24}$$

where $\boldsymbol{S} = \boldsymbol{R}_2^{-1}\boldsymbol{R}_1$ and $\boldsymbol{d} = \boldsymbol{R}_2^{-1}\boldsymbol{c}$. If $[\boldsymbol{X}_1\ \boldsymbol{X}_2]$ is the corresponding partition of the regressors into $k-r$ and r columns, observe that $\boldsymbol{y} = \boldsymbol{X}\boldsymbol{\beta} + \boldsymbol{u}$ can be written equivalently as

$$\boldsymbol{y} - \boldsymbol{X}_2\boldsymbol{d} = (\boldsymbol{X}_1 - \boldsymbol{X}_2\boldsymbol{S})\boldsymbol{\beta}_1 + \boldsymbol{X}_2(\boldsymbol{S}\boldsymbol{\beta}_1 + \boldsymbol{\beta}_2 - \boldsymbol{d}) + \boldsymbol{u} \tag{11.25}$$

The disturbances of this manufactured regression, of $\boldsymbol{y} - \boldsymbol{X}_2\boldsymbol{d}$ onto $\boldsymbol{X}_1 - \boldsymbol{X}_2\boldsymbol{S}$ and $\boldsymbol{X}_2$, are identical to those of the original. The regressors have been subjected to an invertible transformation, and the least squares residuals are likewise identical to the originals. To test restrictions (11.24) in (11.25), simply do the variable addition test for $\boldsymbol{X}_2$, as above. This may look like a relatively elaborate scheme, but it all depends on the form of the restrictions. The available estimation software, a spreadsheet for example, may be better adapted to transforming columns of data than to constructing matrix expressions on the lines of (10.18).

11.5 Stability Analysis

Consider a partition of the regression model by *rows*. Write

$$\boldsymbol{y} = \begin{bmatrix} \boldsymbol{y}_1 \\ \boldsymbol{y}_2 \end{bmatrix}$$

and similarly

$$X = \begin{bmatrix} X_1 \\ X_2 \end{bmatrix},$$

where the partition is into T_1 rows and $T_2 = T - T_1$ rows, where $T_1 > k$ and also $T_2 > k$. The regression model takes the form

$$\begin{bmatrix} y_1 \\ y_2 \end{bmatrix} = \begin{bmatrix} X_1 \\ X_2 \end{bmatrix} \beta + \begin{bmatrix} u_1 \\ u_2 \end{bmatrix}. \tag{11.26}$$

With this setup, consider the maintained hypothesis that the model is different for the first T_1 and the last T_2 observations, specifically that the coefficient vector $\boldsymbol{\beta}$ takes respective values $\boldsymbol{\beta}_1$ and $\boldsymbol{\beta}_2$. In this case the model becomes

$$\begin{bmatrix} y_1 \\ y_2 \end{bmatrix} = \begin{bmatrix} X_1 & \mathbf{0} \\ \mathbf{0} & X_2 \end{bmatrix} \begin{bmatrix} \beta_1 \\ \beta_2 \end{bmatrix} + \begin{bmatrix} u_1 \\ u_2 \end{bmatrix}. \tag{11.27}$$

The object is now to test whether some or all of the elements of the two vectors $\boldsymbol{\beta}_1$ and $\boldsymbol{\beta}_2$ are in fact equal. This can be done as a variable addition test by fitting a transformed version of the model as in (11.25). In this case, it can be verified that $\boldsymbol{S} = -\boldsymbol{I}_k$ and $\boldsymbol{d} = \mathbf{0}$ in (11.24), so the transformation of (11.27) takes the form

$$\begin{bmatrix} y_1 \\ y_2 \end{bmatrix} = \begin{bmatrix} X_1 & \mathbf{0} \\ X_2 & X_2 \end{bmatrix} \begin{bmatrix} \beta_1 \\ \delta \end{bmatrix} + \begin{bmatrix} u_1 \\ u_2 \end{bmatrix}, \tag{11.28}$$

where

$$\delta = \beta_2 - \beta_1.$$

With this setup, the significance of elements of $\boldsymbol{\delta}$ can be tested either individually by t-tests or by an F test.

If the object is to test all the coefficients in (11.27) for equality, the problem assumes an interesting form. Fitting the extended model turns out to be equivalent to running the regression on the two subsamples separately, noting that

$$\begin{aligned}
\begin{bmatrix} \hat{\beta}_1 \\ \hat{\beta}_2 \end{bmatrix} &= \left(\begin{bmatrix} X_1 & \mathbf{0} \\ \mathbf{0} & X_2 \end{bmatrix} \begin{bmatrix} X_1 & \mathbf{0} \\ \mathbf{0} & X_2 \end{bmatrix} \right)^{-1} \begin{bmatrix} X_1' & \mathbf{0} \\ \mathbf{0} & X_2' \end{bmatrix} \begin{bmatrix} y_1 \\ y_2 \end{bmatrix} \\
&= \begin{bmatrix} X_1'X_1 & \mathbf{0} \\ \mathbf{0} & X_2'X_2 \end{bmatrix}^{-1} \begin{bmatrix} X_1'y_1 \\ X_2'y_2 \end{bmatrix} \\
&= \begin{bmatrix} (X_1'X_1)^{-1}X_1'y_1 \\ (X_2'X_2)^{-1}X_2'y_2 \end{bmatrix}.
\end{aligned}$$

The sum of squared residuals of the unrestricted regression is simply the sum of the subsample sums of squares, $\hat{u}_1'\hat{u}_1 + \hat{u}_2'\hat{u}_2$ where $\hat{u}_1 = y_1 - X_1\hat{\beta}_1$ and $\hat{u}_2 = y_2 - X_2\hat{\beta}_2$. An F test of the hypothesis $\boldsymbol{\beta}_1 = \boldsymbol{\beta}_2$ can be implemented with the 'difference of sums of squares' formula, as in (10.28). The statistic is

$$W = \frac{\dot{u}'\dot{u} - \hat{u}_1'\hat{u}_1 - \hat{u}_2'\hat{u}_2}{\hat{u}_1'\hat{u}_1 + \hat{u}_2'\hat{u}_2} \frac{T - 2k}{k}, \tag{11.29}$$

where $\hat{\boldsymbol{u}}$ represents the residuals from the restricted regression including all the observations. This test is known as the *Chow stability test*,[1] having the $F(k, T-2k)$ distribution when the stability hypothesis is true.

These tests are of course subject to the requirement that the unrestricted model satisfies assumptions GCRM(i)–(iv), assuming in particular that σ^2 takes the same value for both subsamples. However, this hypothesis can also be tested. Let the disturbance variances for the two subsamples be σ_1^2 and σ_2^2 respectively, estimated by the least squares residual variances s_1^2 and s_2^2. Let the null hypothesis to be tested be $\mathrm{H}_0 : \sigma_1^2 = \sigma_2^2$, against the one-sided alternative $\sigma_1^2 > \sigma_2^2$. Define

$$\boldsymbol{M}_j = \boldsymbol{I}_{T_j} - \boldsymbol{X}_j(\boldsymbol{X}_j'\boldsymbol{X}_j)^{-1}\boldsymbol{X}_j' \quad (T_j \times T_j)$$

for $j = 1$ and $j = 2$. Assuming $s_1^2 > s_2^2$, the test statistic is

$$\frac{s_1^2}{s_2^2} = \frac{\boldsymbol{y}_1'\boldsymbol{M}_1\boldsymbol{y}_1}{\boldsymbol{y}_2'\boldsymbol{M}_2\boldsymbol{y}_2}\frac{T_2 - k}{T_1 - k}. \tag{11.30}$$

In case the ratio in (11.30) is smaller than 1, simply interchange the subscripts and test against the other one-sided alternative. If the null hypothesis is true, this ratio is distributed as $F(T_1 - k, T_2 - k)$, and the tabulation of the F distribution can be used to decide at the 5% significance level whether it is too large to be a drawing from the null distribution.

This is a version of the *Goldfeld-Quandt test*[2] for homoscedasticity. The rationale is that under the null hypothesis, the numerator and denominator in (11.30) are respectively $\sigma^2\chi^2(T_1 - k)/(T_1 - k)$ and $\sigma^2\chi^2(T_2 - k)/(T_2 - k)$ and that these two random variables are independent. However, the independence is not, in this case, because of orthogonality of the idempotent matrices, but simply because of random sampling. Assumption GCRM(iii) implies $\mathrm{E}(\boldsymbol{u}_1\boldsymbol{u}_2') = \boldsymbol{0}$. The Chow test and its variants should ideally be performed only in the event that the homoscedasticity test does not lead to a rejection.

11.6 Prediction Tests

Now consider a different approach to the stability question, which is to test whether individual observations in a group are drawn from the same distribution as the remainder. The question posed is whether observations to which the regression has not been fitted are as well predicted by the equation as those used to construct the fit. Without loss of generality, let the test observations be the last m of the sample. Unlike the stability test, m can be smaller than k and can be 1. This can be done as a variable addition test where in this case the test regressors in (11.20) have the form

$$\underset{T\times m}{\boldsymbol{Z}} = \begin{bmatrix} \boldsymbol{0} \\ \boldsymbol{I}_m \end{bmatrix} \begin{matrix} T-m \\ m \end{matrix}.$$

These m columns are set to 1 at position $T - j$ for $j = 0, \ldots, m-1$ and zero everywhere else. Each of the m final observations is explained by an individual 'shift dummy' and

1 Chow, Gregory C. (1960). "Tests of Equality Between Sets of Coefficients in Two Linear Regressions". *Econometrica* 28 (3): 591–605.

2 Goldfeld, Stephen M. and Quandt, R. E. (June 1965). "Some Tests for Homoscedasticity". *Journal of the American Statistical Association* 60 (310): 539–547.

hence, in effect, removed from the sample. Under the maintained hypothesis, the coefficients $\boldsymbol{\delta}$ represent possible intercept shifts, in case the observations in question are drawn from a different distribution.

In the unrestricted regression, the corresponding residuals are identically zero. To see that this is so, there is no loss of generality in considering the case $m = 1$ so that $\boldsymbol{Z}$ is just a selection vector for element T with 1 in the last position, and can be written $\boldsymbol{z}$, and δ is a scalar. Let tildes denote unrestricted estimators. In this notation,

$$\begin{aligned}\tilde{\delta} &= \frac{\boldsymbol{z}'\boldsymbol{M}_X\boldsymbol{y}}{\boldsymbol{z}'\boldsymbol{M}_X\boldsymbol{z}} \\ &= \frac{\hat{u}_T}{m_{TT}},\end{aligned}$$

where $\hat{\boldsymbol{u}} = \boldsymbol{M}_X\boldsymbol{y}$ is the vector of residuals from the regression excluding $\boldsymbol{z}$ and $\hat{u}_T$ is its Tth element, $\boldsymbol{M}_X$ being the orthogonal projection matrix for $\boldsymbol{X}$ and

$$m_{TT} = 1 - \boldsymbol{x}_T'(\boldsymbol{X}'\boldsymbol{X})^{-1}\boldsymbol{x}_T$$

its Tth diagonal element. The unrestricted estimator of $\boldsymbol{\beta}$ in the regression including $\boldsymbol{z}$ is found from formula (11.5), where $\boldsymbol{X}_2 = \boldsymbol{X}, \boldsymbol{X}_1 = \boldsymbol{z}$, and $\hat{\boldsymbol{\beta}}_1 = \tilde{\delta}$. This is

$$\tilde{\boldsymbol{\beta}} = \hat{\boldsymbol{\beta}} - (\boldsymbol{X}'\boldsymbol{X})^{-1}\boldsymbol{x}_T\frac{\hat{u}_T}{m_{TT}}.$$

The Tth residual in the unrestricted regression is therefore

$$\begin{aligned}\tilde{u}_T &= y_T - \boldsymbol{x}_T'\tilde{\boldsymbol{\beta}} - \tilde{\delta} \\ &= \hat{u}_T + \boldsymbol{x}_T'(\boldsymbol{X}'\boldsymbol{X})^{-1}\boldsymbol{x}_T\frac{\hat{u}_T}{m_{TT}} - \tilde{\delta} \\ &= \hat{u}_T\frac{m_{TT} + (1 - m_{TT}) - 1}{m_{TT}} \\ &= 0.\end{aligned}$$

The same argument holds for any of m such cases. Simply move the observation in question to position T, and let the other dummies be included in $\boldsymbol{X}$. It follows that the unrestricted residual sum of squares with m shift dummies matches that of the regression fitted to the first $T - m$ observations only.

This makes it straightforward to set up the F test of the hypothesis $\boldsymbol{\delta} = \boldsymbol{0}$. Fit the regression to the full sample of size T for the restricted sum of squares and to the first $T - m$ observations for the unrestricted sum of squares, then compute the F statistic by formula (10.28), with m and $T - k - m$ degrees of freedom. This is the *Chow prediction test*. This test was proposed in the same paper as Chow's stability test cited above and should not be confused with it.

11.7 Exercises

1 Are the following statements true or false?

(a) Multiple regressions can be computed by a recursive sequence of simple regressions.

(b) If regressors are in mean deviation form, including an intercept in the regression leaves the regression coefficients unchanged.

(c) Omitted variable bias vanishes if the omitted regressors are orthogonal to the included regressors.
(d) If omitted regressors are orthogonal to the included regressors, their omission is harmless.
(e) Including unnecessary regressors is always a better thing to do than omitting important regressors.
(f) Diagnostic tests are exactly like significance tests but performed on nuisance variables, not focus variables.
(g) Chow's prediction test is the same as Chow's stability test if there are enough observations to fit the regression to the prediction period.

2 In the regression model

$$y_t = \beta_1 x_{1t} + \beta_2 x_{2t} + \beta_3 + u_t, \qquad (1)$$

the multiple least squares estimator of β_1 can be written as

$$\hat{\beta}_1 = \frac{\sum_{t=1}^{T} \tilde{x}_{1t} y_t}{\sum_{t=1}^{T} \tilde{x}_{1t}^2}. \qquad (2)$$

(a) Give a definition of $\tilde{x}_{1t}$ under which this formula is valid.
(b) In formula (2), suppose that y_t is replaced by $\tilde{y}_t$ where the transformation is the same as that applied to x_{1t}. How does this change the result?
(c) Suppose that in model (1) the intercept is omitted, but x_{1t} and x_{2t} are replaced by mean deviations $x_{1t} - \bar{x}_1$ and $x_{2t} - \bar{x}_2$. How does this change the result in (2)?

3 The multiple regression model in partitioned matrix notation is

$$\boldsymbol{y} = \boldsymbol{x}_1 \beta_1 + \boldsymbol{X}_2 \boldsymbol{\beta}_2 + \boldsymbol{u} \quad (T \times 1),$$

where $\boldsymbol{x}_1$ is $T \times 1$, and $\boldsymbol{X}_2$ is $T \times k - 1$, and the multiple least squares estimator of β_1 is

$$\hat{\beta}_1 = \frac{\boldsymbol{x}_1' \boldsymbol{M}_2 \boldsymbol{y}}{\boldsymbol{x}_1' \boldsymbol{M}_2 \boldsymbol{x}_1}.$$

(a) Show that for the case $k = 3$, where the model contains an intercept, this formula is identical to (2) in Question 2.
(b) Derive a significance test for β_1, assuming fixed regressors and normal and independently distributed disturbances with mean zero and variance σ^2.

4 Consider the regression

$$y = \alpha \boldsymbol{\iota} + \boldsymbol{X\beta} + \boldsymbol{u}$$

where $\boldsymbol{\iota}$ is the column of ones and $\boldsymbol{X}$ contains other regressors.
(a) If the columns of $\boldsymbol{X}$ are in mean deviation form, what is the least squares estimator of α?
(b) If the columns of $\boldsymbol{X}$ are not in mean deviation form, how does this modify the answer to part (a)?
(c) If $\boldsymbol{\iota}$ is one of the columns of $\boldsymbol{X}$, how does this modify the answer to part (b)?

5 Consider the following two regressions:

$$y = X\beta + Z\delta + v, \qquad (1)$$

where y is $T \times 1$, X is $T \times k$ and includes the column of ones representing the intercept, Z is $T \times l$, and

$$\hat{u} = X\theta + Z\delta + e, \qquad (2)$$

where $\hat{u} = y - X\hat{\beta}$ is the vector of least squares residuals from the regression of y on X.

(a) Show that the two regressions yield identical results, except that $\hat{\theta} = \tilde{\beta} - \hat{\beta}$ where $\tilde{\beta}$ is the estimator of β in (1).

(b) Show that the Wald test statistics for the hypothesis $\delta = 0$ in the two regressions are identical.

(c) Show that in regression (2), the test statistic for the hypothesis $\delta = 0$ can be computed as

$$\frac{R^2}{1-R^2}\frac{T-k-l}{l}$$

where R^2 is the coefficient of determination.

6 Linear restrictions on the coefficients of a regression model can be represented as zero restrictions for implementation of a significance test with the statistic (11.21), by linear transformations of the variables. If the equation is

$$y_t = \beta_1 x_{1t} + \beta_2 x_{2t} + \beta_3 x_{3t} + \beta_4 + u_t,$$

show how to construct equations in new variables allowing tests of the following restrictions:

(a) $\beta_1 = \beta_2$

(b) $\beta_2 + \beta_3 = 0$

(c) $\beta_1 + \beta_2 + \beta_3 = 1$.

7 In model (11.27) where $\beta_1 = \beta_2$, define the estimators

$$\dot{\beta} = (X_1'X_1 + X_2'X_2)^{-1}(X_1'y_1 + X_2'y_2)$$

(from fitting (11.26)) and

$$\hat{\beta}_2 = (X_2'X_2)^{-1}X_2'y_2.$$

(a) Show that both estimators are unbiased and that

$$\text{Var}(\hat{\beta}_2 - \dot{\beta}) = \sigma^2((X_2'X_2)^{-1} - ((X_1'X_1 + X_2'X_2)^{-1})).$$

(b) Consider applying the significance test in (11.21) to the hypothesis $\delta = 0$ in (11.28). Show that for this case

$$\hat{\delta}'Z'M_X Z\hat{\delta} = (\hat{\beta}_2 - \dot{\beta})'((X_2'X_2)^{-1} - ((X_1'X_1 + X_2'X_2)^{-1}))^{-1}(\hat{\beta}_2 - \dot{\beta}).$$

(c) Explain why s^2 can be estimated from the residuals of either regression (11.27) or regression (11.28) with identical results.

8 (a) Show that if $\boldsymbol{A}$ $(n \times n)$ is a nonsingular matrix and $\boldsymbol{b}$ any n-vector, then $\boldsymbol{A} + \boldsymbol{b}\boldsymbol{b}'$ is nonsingular and

$$(\boldsymbol{A} + \boldsymbol{b}\boldsymbol{b}')^{-1} = \boldsymbol{A}^{-1} - \frac{\boldsymbol{A}^{-1}\boldsymbol{b}\boldsymbol{b}'\boldsymbol{A}^{-1}}{1 + \boldsymbol{b}'\boldsymbol{A}^{-1}\boldsymbol{b}}$$

(the Sherman-Morrison formula).

(b) Let

$$\hat{\boldsymbol{\beta}}_T = (\boldsymbol{X}'\boldsymbol{X})^{-1}\boldsymbol{X}'\boldsymbol{y}$$

be the least squares regression from a sample of T observations. Show how the result in part (a) can be used to add an extra observation $(y_{T+1}, \boldsymbol{x}_{T+1})$ to the data set, and so calculate $\hat{\boldsymbol{\beta}}_{T+1}$ given $(\boldsymbol{X}'\boldsymbol{X})^{-1}$ but without needing to calculate a further matrix inverse. Comment on your formula.

Part IV

Extensions

12

Random Regressors

12.1 Conditional Probability

At this point, get ready for another major change of gear. Chapters 7 to 11 have explored the properties and implications of the classical regression model, although not before explaining how this framework has major limitations from the point of view of modelling economic phenomena. What the present chapter aims to show is that a fairly minor modification of the statistical framework can provide a new context for the results assembled up to now, one much more appropriate to economics, and most of the results will hold virtually unchanged. However, some additional statistical theory is needed to make sense of the new approach. This needs to be developed with some care.

In elementary probability theory, Bayes' Rule is a well-known formula for assigning a probability to an unobserved event A when another event B has been observed to occur. This is denoted $\Pr(A|B)$, and the rule is

$$\Pr(A|B) = \frac{\Pr(A \text{ and } B)}{\Pr(B)}. \tag{12.1}$$

Simply enough, if we know B has occurred, then the probability of A, given this information, must depend on the probability of their joint occurrence. Hence the numerator in this ratio. However, this needs to be normalized so that (e.g.) in the case $A = \Omega$, the sample space,[1]

$$\Pr(\Omega \text{ and } B) = \Pr(B)$$

so the the rule gives

$$\begin{aligned}\Pr(\Omega|B) &= \Pr(\Omega)\\ &= 1\end{aligned}$$

as required, because knowing that B has happened cannot change the probability that *something* happens. Bayes rule also embodies the multiplicative rule for the joint probability of independent events. If A and B are independent, then the product rule for probabilities holds

$$\Pr(A \text{ and } B) = \Pr(A)\Pr(B)$$

1 'Sample space' is statistical jargon for all the possible outcomes of a random experiment, the event that includes all others.

An Introduction to Econometric Theory, First Edition. James Davidson.

Companion website: www.wiley.com/go/davidson/introecmettheory

which implies directly,

$$\Pr(A|B) = \Pr(A).$$

This equality in effect defines the concept of statistical independence. Knowing that B has occurred supplies no information about the prospects for A occurring, so the events must be unconnected.

Already, the alert reader may have formed the opinion that conditional probability is a tricky concept. There are two grounds for potential disquiet. The first is the 'frequentist' interpretation that motivates probability in terms of the distribution of outcomes in many independent repetitions of a random experiment. The idea that random events have a timing, falling earlier or later, sits awkwardly with such an interpretation. The alternative interpretation of probability as representing a subjective 'degree of belief' on the part of an observer is more natural as an underpinning of Bayes's rule and is the basis of so-called *Bayesian statistics*, in which unknown model parameters are regarded as having a distribution in the mind of an observer. By contrast, in this book and in classical statistics generally, parameters are treated as fixed characteristics of a data generation mechanism. This approach is linked to the frequentist interpretation in spite of making serious use of the conditional probability idea.

The second puzzle is with conditioning under continuous distributions. Positive probability appears to be an important attribute of event B for formula (12.1) to make sense. The coin toss of Section 5.4 is an example where the event "heads" consists of a single outcome, having a positive probability, but in general the symbols A and B stand for random events which are *collections* of random outcomes. In the archery example of Section 5.1 a region of the target with positive extent could be a conditioning event, whereas individual outcomes have probability zero under a continuous distribution. Section 6.5 introduced the Gaussian conditional distribution, conditioning the probability density of a random variable Y on another random variable X. The conditional density function (6.18) has as its argument a point value x. But if the event $X = x$ has probability zero, how is the conditional density function to be interpreted? This is a fair question, in spite of the statement "$f(y|x)$ is the probability density of Y when $X = x$" appearing a perfectly reasonable one.

Sorting out these paradoxes proves difficult using the naive approach of elementary statistics, and advanced mathematical ideas are needed to resolve them. However, the mathematics does provide the desired conclusion, that conditioning theory is formally valid and internally consistent. The theory also has useful applications that can be quite remote from these issues of subjective interpretation. It is in this spirit that we apply it.

12.2 Conditional Expectations

Probabilities and expectations are the two key concepts in statistical theory. Sections 5.1 and 5.3 provided a quick reminder of the way these objects are constructed. The close link between them can be appreciated by considering another construction called an *indicator function*. Considering the bivariate normal distribution, for example, let A be an area of the plane (a set whose elements are pairs of numbers) and so write $I_A(x, y)$ as the indicator of A. This is a function taking two possible values. If the pair (x, y) belong to A, then $I_A(x, y) = 1$, and otherwise $I_A(x, y) = 0$. Adapting the formulations of (5.2) and (5.3) produces

$$\begin{aligned}\Pr(A) &= \int_{\{x,y \text{ in } I_A\}} \phi(x, y)\mathrm{d}x\mathrm{d}y \\ &= \int_{-\infty}^{\infty}\int_{-\infty}^{\infty} I_A(x, y)\phi(x, y)\mathrm{d}x\mathrm{d}y \\ &= \mathrm{E}(I_A).\end{aligned}$$

In this manner, the probability of a random event can always be expressed equivalently as the expected value of its indicator. Conditional expectation is often treated as the fundamental concept of conditioning theory, extending the results to probabilities as required through the device of the indicator function.

Imagine a random experiment generating a pair of random variables, X and Y. Outcome $X = x$ is observed, but Y is as yet unobserved. How can this information be used to modify predictions of Y? In the absence of information, the best prediction of Y is $\mathrm{E}(Y)$, a constant, the central tendency of the marginal distribution of Y. After observing $X = x$, the best prediction from this information is a function of x. For the Gaussian case, this is formula (6.20).

However, a question often asked is the following. Before observing anything, what can be said about the *distribution* of the conditional expectation? This now has to be considered as a random variable depending on the distribution of X. In parallel with (6.20), write for the Gaussian case

$$\mathrm{E}(Y|X) = \mu_Y + \frac{\sigma_{XY}}{\sigma_{XX}}(X - \mu_X). \tag{12.2}$$

The difference is subtle but critical. The object in (12.2) is a random variable, and being a linear function of X it is also Gaussian. It has a mean of μ_Y and a variance of

$$\begin{aligned}\mathrm{E}[\mathrm{E}(Y|X) - \mu_Y]^2 &= \frac{\sigma_{XY}^2}{\sigma_{XX}^2}\mathrm{E}(X - \mu_X)^2 \\ &= \frac{\sigma_{XY}^2}{\sigma_{XX}}.\end{aligned}$$

The Gaussian distribution is a special case, but conditional expectations, regarded as a random variables, have a number of universal and important properties. Some care is necessary in these manipulations, because random variables are different from constants in critical ways. The equality

$$X = Y \tag{12.3}$$

is unambiguous when X and Y are constants. When they are random variables, however, (12.3) is asserting something about two distributions, that whenever a drawing is made from each distribution, the two drawings are equal. This is a comparatively strong statement, often stronger than needed. What matters is that any exceptions are too rare to effect the calculations, which usually involve expected values. A fundamental fact is the following:

$$\text{If } X = Y \text{ with probability 1, then } \mathrm{E}(X) = \mathrm{E}(Y). \tag{12.4}$$

This doubtless sounds a bit strange, but the mathematics requires a distinction between the case where an event has probability zero and the case where the outcomes in question are not even in the sample space. Allowing exceptions with probability zero avoids various technical complications, and there is a formality in the technical literature to signal this by appending a tag, either 'w.p.1' or, more colourfully, 'a.s.', which is short for *almost surely*. Not quite the same as surely, but near enough to validate the calculations. Such tags often get left off, but it does no harm to remind readers that we are working with random variables.

Here are four fundamental results on conditional expectations.

1. *The Law of Iterated Expectations*. Also known as the LIE, this states that

$$\mathrm{E}[\mathrm{E}(Y|X)] = \mathrm{E}(Y).$$

In words, the expectation of the prediction of Y using partial information, averaged over the distribution of that information, is the same as the expectation of Y itself. This fact has already been verified for the Gaussian case. The notation $\mathrm{E}[\,\cdot\,]$ is used here to denote the unconditional expectation, averaging over X, where inside the square brackets is a random variable whose distribution derives from that of X.

The LIE extends to results of the following sort, for predictions with more and less information. Given random variables Y, X, and Z, the prediction of Y given knowledge of X and Z is $\mathrm{E}(Y|X,Z)$, a random variable whose distribution is derived from the joint distribution of X and Z. By the LIE, the prediction of this prediction from the standpoint of an observer who observes only Z is

$$\mathrm{E}[\mathrm{E}(Y|X,Z)|Z] = \mathrm{E}(Y|Z) \text{ w.p.1.}$$

Notice the tag. This is an equality of two random variables. Exceptions with probability zero are not ruled out, but they cannot affect our calculations.

2. *Conditional Linearity*. In a conditional expectation, the conditioning variable behaves like a constant. Conditional expectations have the linearity property, which means, for example, that

$$\mathrm{E}(XY|X) = X\mathrm{E}(Y|X) \text{ w.p.1.}$$

This is frequently a useful manipulation. For example, if $\mathrm{E}(Y|X) = \mathrm{E}(Y)$ w.p.1, this implies that X and Y are uncorrelated. To show this, use linearity and the LIE, and also a variant of (12.4), to get

$$\begin{aligned}\mathrm{E}(XY) &= \mathrm{E}[\mathrm{E}(XY|X)]\\ &= \mathrm{E}[X\mathrm{E}(Y|X)]\\ &= \mathrm{E}[X\mathrm{E}(Y)]\\ &= \mathrm{E}(X)\mathrm{E}(Y).\end{aligned} \tag{12.5}$$

3. *Minimum MSE Predictor*. The conditional expectation is the 'best predictor' of Y in a special sense, that it minimizes the mean squared prediction error (MSE). The MSE is an example of a *loss function*, a measure of the cost of failing to hit a target. If minimum MSE sounds to be a fairly natural property, bear in mind that there are many different ways of defining the best predictor. One would be to minimize the mean absolute error. Loss functions can also be asymmetric, weighting overshoots differently from undershoots. That the conditional mean invokes the mean square

is basically a consequence of the linearity of expected values. The argument goes as follows. Let $F(X)$ be any predictor of Y based on knowledge of X. Then

$$\begin{aligned}
\mathrm{E}[(Y - F(X))^2] &= \mathrm{E}[(Y - \mathrm{E}(Y|X) + \mathrm{E}(Y|X) - F(X))^2] \\
&= \mathrm{E}[(Y - \mathrm{E}(Y|X))^2] + \mathrm{E}[(\mathrm{E}(Y|X) - F(X))^2] \\
&\quad + 2\mathrm{E}[(\mathrm{E}(Y|X) - F(X))(Y - \mathrm{E}(Y|X))]. \\
&\geq \mathrm{E}[(Y - \mathrm{E}(Y|X))^2].
\end{aligned}$$

Consider this formulation carefully, since it is a type of argument that is frequently invoked. The first equality is got by taking the mean squared error associated with the predictor $F(X)$ and inserting $\mathrm{E}(Y|X)$ with positive and negative signs, which of course leaves the value of the expression unchanged. Then the square of the sum of two terms is multiplied out, yielding four terms. The first of these is the mean squared error associated with $\mathrm{E}(Y|X)$. The second is the expectation of the squared difference between the predictions being compared, which must be non-negative. The third and fourth are the cross-product terms, which are equal and also equal to zero, giving rise to the inequality in the last member.

To demonstrate the last step in the argument, reason as follows. The key idea is that when considering the distribution conditional on X, the quantities $\mathrm{E}(Y|X)$ and $F(X)$ are treated as fixed. Thanks to conditional linearity,

$$\begin{aligned}
&\mathrm{E}[(\mathrm{E}(Y|X) - F(X))(Y - \mathrm{E}(Y|X))] \\
&\quad = \mathrm{E}[\mathrm{E}((\mathrm{E}(Y|X) - F(X))(Y - \mathrm{E}(Y|X))|X)] \\
&\quad = \mathrm{E}[(\mathrm{E}(Y|X) - F(X))\mathrm{E}((Y - \mathrm{E}(Y|X))|X)] \\
&\quad = \mathrm{E}[(\mathrm{E}(Y|X) - F(X)) \times 0 \text{ w.p.1}] \\
&\quad = 0. \qquad (12.6)
\end{aligned}$$

In the first equality, the LIE is used to say that the expectation equals the expectation of the conditional expectation. In the product of two terms, the first one (the difference of the two predictors) depends only on X and hence is conditionally fixed when evaluating the conditional expectation in the second term. This is moved outside the conditional expectation and then, because $\mathrm{E}(\mathrm{E}(Y|X)|X) = \mathrm{E}(Y|X)$ by the LIE,

$$\begin{aligned}
\mathrm{E}((Y - \mathrm{E}(Y|X))|X) &= \mathrm{E}(Y|X) - \mathrm{E}(Y|X) \\
&= 0 \text{ w.p.1.}
\end{aligned}$$

If a random variable is zero with probability 1, its expected value is zero, hence the final equality of (12.6). This concludes the argument.

4. *The Law of Total Variance* The conditional variance of Y given X is formally defined as

$$\mathrm{Var}(Y|X) = \mathrm{E}((Y - \mathrm{E}(Y|X))^2|X).$$

Similarly to E[.], write Var[.] to denote the unconditional variance, with averaging over X. The identity

$$\mathrm{Var}[Y] = \mathrm{E}[\mathrm{Var}(Y|X)] + \mathrm{Var}[\mathrm{E}(Y|X)]$$

can now be proved. In other words, given a conditioning variable, the variance of Y can be decomposed as the sum of two components, the mean of the conditional variance and the variance of the conditional mean.

To show this fascinating fact, the argument is closely related to the one used for the minimum MSE demonstration. Insert a new term $\mathrm{E}(Y|X)$ twice with opposing signs, multiply out the square, and evaluate the terms of the expectation separately. Thus,

$$\begin{aligned}\mathrm{Var}[Y] &= \mathrm{E}[(Y - \mathrm{E}(Y))^2]\\ &= \mathrm{E}[(Y - \mathrm{E}(Y|X) + \mathrm{E}(Y|X) - \mathrm{E}(Y))^2]\\ &= \mathrm{E}[\mathrm{E}((Y - \mathrm{E}(Y|X))^2|X)] + \mathrm{E}[(\mathrm{E}(Y|X) - \mathrm{E}(Y))^2]\\ &\quad + 2\mathrm{E}[(\mathrm{E}(Y|X) - \mathrm{E}(Y))(Y - \mathrm{E}(Y|X))].\end{aligned}$$

In the third equality, notice the use made of the LIE in the first term. The second term is $\mathrm{Var}[\mathrm{E}(Y|X)]$ by definition, using the LIE again to identify the mean of the conditional mean, and it remains to show that the cross-product term vanishes. Similarly to (12.6), with yet another application of the LIE and conditional linearity, this follows since

$$\begin{aligned}&\mathrm{E}[(\mathrm{E}(Y|X) - \mathrm{E}(Y))(Y - \mathrm{E}(Y|X))]\\ &\quad = \mathrm{E}[(\mathrm{E}(Y|X) - \mathrm{E}(Y))\mathrm{E}((Y - \mathrm{E}(Y|X))|X)]\\ &\quad = \mathrm{E}[(\mathrm{E}(Y|X) - \mathrm{E}(Y)) \times 0 \text{ w.p.1}]\\ &\quad = 0.\end{aligned}$$

12.3 Statistical Models Contrasted

We can distinguish three distinct statistical sampling frameworks, characterized by the type of random mechanism generating the data.

A: *Fixed regressors.*
B: *Random regressors with independent sampling.*
C: *Dependent Sampling.*

The classical regression model studied up to now is the leading case of framework A. As pointed out, it is mostly irrelevant to econometrics but has the virtue of yielding powerful results using comparatively elementary statistical theory. Case B is the framework to be studied in this chapter. It is mainly relevant to cross-section studies, in which the sample data are randomly drawn from a large population, for example, survey data of the type described in Section 7.1. Case C includes practically every other form of data generation mechanism, of which time series constitute much the most important category. With dependent sampling, statistical analysis has to depend on a completely different approach, that of asymptotic theory. Some of the main ideas utilized here are introduced in Section 13, but sample dependence is an advanced topic and one that is, by and large, beyond the scope of this book.

Turning then to Case B, the problem is to adapt methods appropriate to Case A to a more general context. The essence of these latter methods, used over and over again in the analysis of Parts II and III, is to exploit the linearity properties of expected values generally and also the linearity of the normal distribution. The objects generated in estimation and testing exercises have tended to be, or to depend on, linear functions of random variables with fixed coefficients. Hence, expected values have been easy to calculate. In the same kind of way, normally distributed data sets have mapped into normally distributed statistics. The clever results of Chapter 10 overcome the problem of unknown scale factors. These methods now have to be extended to functions of data where in effect everything is a random variable, and products and ratios of random variables as well as fixed-weight linear combinations enter the picture. This will require a new approach.

It will be helpful to keep in mind the household survey example of Section 7.1, where the variable set $(y_t, \boldsymbol{x}_t')'$ are randomly sampled together from the population of households, y_t is expenditure on a commodity to be explained, and $\boldsymbol{x}_t$ a k-vector of household attributes that contribute the explanation. The linear regression model

$$y_t = \boldsymbol{x}_t'\boldsymbol{\beta} + u_t$$

for $t = 1, \dots, T$, *as a statistical model*, might be understood as embodying the condition

$$\mathrm{E}(y_t|\boldsymbol{x}_t) = \boldsymbol{x}_t'\boldsymbol{\beta} \text{ w.p.1.} \tag{12.7}$$

This may be also be written as

$$\mathrm{E}(u_t|\boldsymbol{x}_t) = 0 \text{ w.p.1.}$$

This relation, it will be noted, embodies the known regression property that the disturbance is not predictable by the regressors.

The implication of (12.7) is found by premultiplying by the vector $\boldsymbol{x}_t$ and taking expected values. This gives

$$\begin{aligned} \mathrm{E}(\boldsymbol{x}_t\boldsymbol{x}_t')\boldsymbol{\beta} &= \mathrm{E}[\boldsymbol{x}_t\mathrm{E}(y_t|\boldsymbol{x}_t)] \\ &= \mathrm{E}[\mathrm{E}(\boldsymbol{x}_t y_t|\boldsymbol{x}_t)] \\ &= \mathrm{E}(\boldsymbol{x}_t y_t). \end{aligned}$$

Notice the application here of the LIE and the use of conditional linearity. If the matrix $\mathrm{E}(\boldsymbol{x}_t\boldsymbol{x}_t')$ is well-defined, finite, and nonsingular (reasonable assumptions if the model is well formulated), the equations have the solution

$$\boldsymbol{\beta} = (\mathrm{E}(\boldsymbol{x}_t\boldsymbol{x}_t'))^{-1}\mathrm{E}(\boldsymbol{x}_t y_t). \tag{12.8}$$

Expected values $\mathrm{E}(\cdot)$ here represent averaging over the sampling distribution, and (12.8) is accordingly a property of the distribution of draws $(y_t, \boldsymbol{x}_t')'$ in the population. It defines the true parameter vector $\boldsymbol{\beta}$ as a function of data first and second moments. Of course, the resemblance between (12.8) and the least squares formula

$$\hat{\boldsymbol{\beta}} = (\boldsymbol{X}'\boldsymbol{X})^{-1}\boldsymbol{X}'\boldsymbol{y} \tag{12.9}$$

is no coincidence. This provides a completely new rationale for the least squares estimator. Note that $\boldsymbol{X}'\boldsymbol{X}$ and $\sum_{t=1}^T \boldsymbol{x}_t\boldsymbol{x}_t'$ are equivalent notations and $\boldsymbol{X}'\boldsymbol{y} = \sum_{t=1}^T \boldsymbol{x}_t y_t$ similarly, and the matrix $T^{-1}\boldsymbol{X}'\boldsymbol{X}$ and vector $T^{-1}\boldsymbol{X}'\boldsymbol{y}$ are the sample counterparts of the population moments $\mathrm{E}(\boldsymbol{x}_t\boldsymbol{x}_t')$ and $\mathrm{E}(\boldsymbol{x}_t y_t)$. The factor $1/T$ would cancel in the ratio in (12.9), and least squares in effect estimates the coefficients by replacing population expectations by sample averages. This is an example of the estimation principle known as the *method of moments*.

The linear statistical model asserts a specific property of the data distribution, the linear form of the conditional mean in (12.7). This is potentially a strong assumption, often justified as an approximation adequate for small variations of some more general structure. However, a useful result can follow from a weaker assumption than (12.7). Suppose the true model takes the form

$$\mathrm{E}(y_t|\boldsymbol{x}_t) = f(\boldsymbol{x}_t),$$

where $f(.)$ is some unknown and possibly non-linear function of its argument. What is the status of linear regression in this case? To answer this question, consider the best linear approximation to $f(\cdot)$. Deploying the argument for analyzing mean squares already seen in Section 12.2, choose a vector $\boldsymbol{b}$ to minimize the mean squared approximation error,

$$\mathrm{E}[\mathrm{E}(y_t|\boldsymbol{x}_t) - \boldsymbol{b}'\boldsymbol{x}_t]^2.$$

On this occasion, let the inserted term with cancelling signs be $\boldsymbol{\beta}'\boldsymbol{x}_t$, where $\boldsymbol{\beta}$ is from (12.8). Thus,

$$\begin{aligned}\mathrm{E}[\mathrm{E}(y_t|\boldsymbol{x}_t) - \boldsymbol{b}'\boldsymbol{x}_t]^2 &= \mathrm{E}[\mathrm{E}(y_t|\boldsymbol{x}_t) - \boldsymbol{\beta}'\boldsymbol{x}_t + (\boldsymbol{\beta} - \boldsymbol{b})'\boldsymbol{x}_t]^2 \\ &= \mathrm{E}[\mathrm{E}(y_t|\boldsymbol{x}_t) - \boldsymbol{\beta}'\boldsymbol{x}_t]^2 + (\boldsymbol{\beta} - \boldsymbol{b})'\mathrm{E}(\boldsymbol{x}_t\boldsymbol{x}_t')(\boldsymbol{\beta} - \boldsymbol{b}) \\ &\quad + 2(\boldsymbol{\beta} - \boldsymbol{b})'\mathrm{E}[\boldsymbol{x}_t(\mathrm{E}(y_t|\boldsymbol{x}_t) - \boldsymbol{x}_t'\boldsymbol{\beta})] \\ &\geq \mathrm{E}[\mathrm{E}(y_t|\boldsymbol{x}_t) - \boldsymbol{\beta}'\boldsymbol{x}_t]^2.\end{aligned}$$

The inequality, which holds as a strict inequality except when $\boldsymbol{b} = \boldsymbol{\beta}$, is shown as follows. First, $\mathrm{E}(\boldsymbol{x}_t\boldsymbol{x}_t')$ is positive definite, assuming it to be invertible as in (12.8), since for any $\boldsymbol{\alpha} \neq \boldsymbol{0}$ $(k \times 1)$,

$$\begin{aligned}\boldsymbol{\alpha}'\mathrm{E}(\boldsymbol{x}_t\boldsymbol{x}_t')\boldsymbol{\alpha} &= \mathrm{E}(\boldsymbol{\alpha}'\boldsymbol{x}_t\boldsymbol{x}_t'\boldsymbol{\alpha}) \\ &= \mathrm{E}\left((\boldsymbol{\alpha}'\boldsymbol{x}_t)^2\right) \\ &> 0.\end{aligned}$$

For this expected square to be zero for a nonzero $\boldsymbol{\alpha}$ would contradict nonsingularity of the moment matrix. Also, applying conditional linearity and the LIE, the cross-product term vanishes by definition of $\boldsymbol{\beta}$ in (12.8):

$$\begin{aligned}(\boldsymbol{\beta} - \boldsymbol{b})'\mathrm{E}[\boldsymbol{x}_t(\mathrm{E}(y_t|\boldsymbol{x}_t) - \boldsymbol{x}_t'\boldsymbol{\beta})] &= (\boldsymbol{\beta} - \boldsymbol{b})'(\mathrm{E}(\boldsymbol{x}_t y_t) - \mathrm{E}(\boldsymbol{x}_t\boldsymbol{x}_t')\boldsymbol{\beta}) \\ &= 0.\end{aligned}$$

In other words, least squares has the interpretation of the method-of-moments estimator of the best linear approximation to any regression function. The assumption of a unknown regression function is too weak to validate all the properties of least squares in the linear regression, but it is nonetheless useful to know that in the linear framework, least squares appears as the best thing to do.

12.4 The Statistical Assumptions

This section is set out in parallel with the classical regression model (CRM) assumptions of Section 7.2. In the context of the full-sample representation

$$\boldsymbol{y} = \boldsymbol{X}\boldsymbol{\beta} + \boldsymbol{u}, \tag{12.10}$$

the new model will be called the random regressor model, or RRM.

Assumptions RRM

(i) X has rank k w.p.1.
(ii) $E(u|X) = 0$ w.p.1.
(iii) $E(uu'|X) = \sigma^2 I_T$ w.p.1.

These assumptions parallel those of the CRM, but now the matrix X is treated as random, and hence the expectations are conditional and the equalities have to be stated, formally, with the 'w.p.1' tag to show that probability zero exceptions are allowed. Happily, the existence of such exceptions cannot change the results to be derived. In particular, expected values (the regular kind) cannot depend on features of the distribution that arise with probability zero.

The major implication of assumptions RRM may not be immediately apparent, but is nonetheless of huge significance. The thing that matters is that the conditioning variables are the complete set of sample regressors. This is distinctly a stronger requirement than would be implied by imposing (12.7) for each $t = 1, \dots, T$. In addition to that best-predictor condition, the observations are in effect required to be independently sampled.

Assumption RRM(i) ensures that unconditional expectations over the distribution of X are well defined. One might wish to add here the condition of 'square integrability', or in other words that $E(x_t x_t') < \infty$ for each t, because without this condition (12.8) cannot be a valid representation of the coefficients. However, β is defined by (12.7), which implies (12.8) when square-integrability holds but is not equivalent to it. RRM(i) has the same implication as CRM(i), that each time the least squares estimator is computed in repeated sampling, the matrix $X'X$ will be invertible and that the estimator therefore exists. Allowing exceptions to the rank condition with probability zero is just a roundabout way of saying that they won't arise in practice.

Next consider assumption RRM(ii), taken row by row. Given that

$$u_t = y_t - x_t'\beta$$

and that

$$E(x_t'\beta | x_1, \dots, x_t, \dots, x_T) = x_t'\beta \text{ w.p.1},$$

by construction, this assumption says that

$$E(y_t | x_1, \dots, x_t, \dots, x_T) = x_t'\beta \text{ w.p.1}$$

for $t = 1, \dots, T$.

Think about this. Attempting to predict y_t from the available information, which includes all the sample observations $x_1, \dots, x_T$, the prediction $x_t'\beta$ cannot be improved on. None of that additional information on the other members of the sample, of x_s for any $s \neq t$, is helpful in explaining y_t. This is a property that in principle could come about without actual statistical independence between the observations, but it would be hard to construct a rationale for such a condition. Independence is the only simple and plausible assumption that ensures RRM(ii), and independence is ensured only by random sampling.

The most important consequence of assumptions RRM is that they *rule out* time-series data. In time series, the observations are not randomly drawn but have an ordering by date. If $t > s$, then x_t postdates u_s. Except in special cases, it is very difficult to exclude the possibility of causation running from y_{t-1} (say), and hence u_{t-1}, to $\boldsymbol{x}_t$. In a range of popular time series models, y_{t-1} is actually included as an element of $\boldsymbol{x}_t$, the so called 'lagged dependent variable'. But even without such an explicit connection, in macroeconomic and financial models it is typically hard to rule out the existence of dynamic relationships, determining the explanatory variables as functions of past shocks. Any such phenomena are liable to violate assumption RRM(ii).

Since assumption RRM(iii) specifies expected values not depending on t, the implications of random sampling (or its failure) are less manifest than in the case of RRM(ii). If the conditional variances are all equal to σ^2, not depending on any conditioning variable, then the same holds for the unconditional variances, and likewise conditional covariances of zero imply unconditional covariances of zero. It follows that assumption RRM(ii) implies

$$\mathrm{E}(u_t) = 0,$$

and RRM(iii) implies unconditional homoscedasticity and uncorrelatedness, as in

$$\mathrm{Var}(u_t) = \sigma^2 \tag{12.11}$$

for $t = 1, \dots, T$ and

$$\mathrm{Cov}(u_t, u_s) = 0 \tag{12.12}$$

for $t \neq s$. These conditions are the same as CRM(ii) and CRM(iii). However, the reverse implications do *not* hold. It cannot be deduced from (12.11) and (12.12) that the variances and covariances are not predictable from the regressor elements. RRM(ii) and RRM(iii) are needed to ensure this.

12.5 Properties of OLS

The analysis proceeds following the pattern of Section 7.3, but with conditional expectations in place of the regular kind. Thus, defining $\hat{\boldsymbol{\beta}}$ by (12.9) as usual, RRM(ii) implies

$$\begin{aligned}\mathrm{E}(\hat{\boldsymbol{\beta}}|\boldsymbol{X}) &= \boldsymbol{\beta} + (\boldsymbol{X}'\boldsymbol{X})^{-1}\boldsymbol{X}'\mathrm{E}(\boldsymbol{u}|\boldsymbol{X}) \\ &= \boldsymbol{\beta} \text{ w.p.1.}\end{aligned} \tag{12.13}$$

Notice that this result can be likened to a thought experiment. "If $\boldsymbol{X}$ was fixed in repeated samples, then $\hat{\boldsymbol{\beta}}$ would be unbiased with respect to the sampling distribution of $\boldsymbol{u}$." Moreover, cases of $\boldsymbol{X}$ where this statement does not hold have probability zero, and can be neglected. Therefore, apply the law of iterated expectations to average over these thought experiments to conclude that

$$\begin{aligned}\mathrm{E}(\hat{\boldsymbol{\beta}}) &= \mathrm{E}[\mathrm{E}(\hat{\boldsymbol{\beta}}|\boldsymbol{X})] \\ &= \mathrm{E}(\boldsymbol{\beta} \text{ w.p.1}) \\ &= \boldsymbol{\beta}.\end{aligned}$$

The final equality holds because if the conditional mean equals $\boldsymbol{\beta}$ with probability 1, this must match the unconditional mean. Thus, least squares under assumptions RRM is an unbiased estimator in the usual sense. In the feasible repeated sampling framework, that of making repeated draws of the form $(y_t, \boldsymbol{x}_t')'$ for $t = 1, \dots, T$, the central tendency of the estimator is indeed the true value. This is a new result that simply could not be anticipated from the classical regression framework.

Now consider the variance of $\hat{\boldsymbol{\beta}}$. As with the mean, $\boldsymbol{X}$ can be held conditionally fixed in a thought experiment, and then the argument of (7.8) gives

$$\mathrm{Var}(\hat{\boldsymbol{\beta}}|\boldsymbol{X}) = \sigma^2(\boldsymbol{X}'\boldsymbol{X})^{-1} \text{ w.p.1.} \tag{12.14}$$

Application of the LIE, together with the law of total variance, now yields the unconditional variance matrix. In this case, though, the conditional variance is a function of $\boldsymbol{X}$, so it is not possible for the distribution of $\hat{\boldsymbol{\beta}}$ in the random regressor model to match that in the classical model. Instead, the law of total variance gives

$$\begin{aligned}\mathrm{Var}(\hat{\boldsymbol{\beta}}) &= \mathrm{E}[\mathrm{Var}(\hat{\boldsymbol{\beta}}|\boldsymbol{X})] + \mathrm{Var}[\mathrm{E}(\hat{\boldsymbol{\beta}}|\boldsymbol{X})] \\ &= \sigma^2\mathrm{E}((\boldsymbol{X}'\boldsymbol{X})^{-1}) + \mathrm{Var}(\boldsymbol{\beta} \text{ w.p.1}) \\ &= \sigma^2\mathrm{E}((\boldsymbol{X}'\boldsymbol{X})^{-1}).\end{aligned} \tag{12.15}$$

noting that $\mathrm{Var}(\boldsymbol{\beta} \text{ w.p.1}) = \boldsymbol{0}$. A fact not to be overlooked is that

$$\mathrm{E}((\boldsymbol{X}'\boldsymbol{X})^{-1}) \neq (\mathrm{E}(\boldsymbol{X}'\boldsymbol{X}))^{-1}. \tag{12.16}$$

Interesting questions arise about the application of these formulae. Having observed a sample and computed estimates from it, almost certainly (12.14) is the formula of interest, not (12.15). Since $\boldsymbol{X}$ is observed, its characteristics provide useful information about the precision with which the various elements of $\boldsymbol{\beta}$ are estimated. This suggests that the usual sample standard error formulae are as appropriate with random regressors as in the classical model. On the other hand, for comparing different estimation procedures in the abstract, without reference to a particular sample, (12.15) is clearly the relevant formula.

Consider how the Gauss-Markov theorem applies in this context. Revisiting the argument deployed in Section 8.2, least squares can be compared with a generic linear estimator of $\boldsymbol{\beta}$,

$$\check{\boldsymbol{\beta}} = \boldsymbol{L}\boldsymbol{y}. \tag{12.17}$$

However, things are a bit different here because the matrix $\boldsymbol{L}$ must be assumed random. While leading cases depend on $\boldsymbol{X}$, the possibility of additional observations being used must be allowed for. For this purpose assumptions RRM need to be extended, as follows.

Assumptions RRM, Extended

(i) As RRM(i).
(ii) $\mathrm{E}(\boldsymbol{u}|\boldsymbol{X},\boldsymbol{L}) = \boldsymbol{0}$ w.p.1.
(iii) $\mathrm{E}(\boldsymbol{u}\boldsymbol{u}'|\boldsymbol{X},\boldsymbol{L}) = \sigma^2\boldsymbol{I}_T$ w.p.1.
(iv) $\boldsymbol{L}$ is square integrable and $\boldsymbol{L}\boldsymbol{X} = \boldsymbol{I}_k$ w.p.1.

Assumptions RRME(ii) and RRME(iii) place the elements of $\boldsymbol{L}$ alongside those of $\boldsymbol{X}$ in the category of variables with no power to predict any element of the vector $\boldsymbol{u}$. The designation here of (12.17) and least squares in particular as 'linear' estimators is not entirely straightforward. In the classical regression framework, linear means "linear function of the random data with fixed weights", whereas here the weights of the linear combination are random. What assumptions RRME(ii) and RRME(iii) ensure is that the weights can be held *conditionally* fixed. Assumption RRME(iv) had no counterpart in the classical analysis. It implies that

$$\mathrm{E}(\boldsymbol{LX}) = \boldsymbol{I}_k, \tag{12.18}$$

remembering that if $\boldsymbol{LX} \neq \boldsymbol{I}_k$ happens only with probability zero, such an event cannot affect the expected value. The square-integrability needs to be specified here since $\boldsymbol{L}$ plays a different role in the argument than $\boldsymbol{X}$, and the expected inner product needs to exist for the efficiency argument to work.

The demonstration of unbiasedness of the generic linear estimator now follows a course paralleling (8.4).

$$\begin{aligned}\mathrm{E}(\check{\boldsymbol{\beta}}) &= \mathrm{E}(\boldsymbol{Ly})\\ &= \mathrm{E}(\boldsymbol{LX})\boldsymbol{\beta} + \mathrm{E}(\boldsymbol{Lu})\\ &= \boldsymbol{\beta}\end{aligned}$$

by (12.18) and since by the LIE, (12.4), conditional linearity, and assumption RRME(ii),

$$\begin{aligned}\mathrm{E}(\boldsymbol{Lu}) &= \mathrm{E}[\mathrm{E}(\boldsymbol{Lu}|\boldsymbol{X},\boldsymbol{L})]\\ &= \mathrm{E}[\boldsymbol{L}\mathrm{E}(\boldsymbol{u}|\boldsymbol{X},\boldsymbol{L})]\\ &= \boldsymbol{0}.\end{aligned}$$

Since $\check{\boldsymbol{\beta}}$ is unbiased, assumption RRME(iii) further implies

$$\begin{aligned}\mathrm{Var}(\check{\boldsymbol{\beta}}) &= \mathrm{E}[\mathrm{Var}(\check{\boldsymbol{\beta}}|\boldsymbol{X},\boldsymbol{L})]\\ &= \mathrm{E}[\mathrm{E}(\boldsymbol{Luu}'\boldsymbol{L}'|\boldsymbol{X},\boldsymbol{L})]\\ &= \sigma^2\mathrm{E}(\boldsymbol{LL}').\end{aligned}$$

Reprising the argument from Section 8.2, let $\boldsymbol{D} = \boldsymbol{L} - (\boldsymbol{X}'\boldsymbol{X})^{-1}\boldsymbol{X}'$ so that

$$\begin{aligned}\boldsymbol{DX} &= \boldsymbol{LX} - \boldsymbol{I}_k\\ &= \boldsymbol{0} \text{ w.p.1.}\end{aligned}$$

This condition implies

$$\mathrm{E}(\boldsymbol{DX}(\boldsymbol{X}'\boldsymbol{X})^{-1}) = \boldsymbol{0}$$

by (12.4) and hence

$$\begin{aligned}\mathrm{E}(\boldsymbol{LL}') &= \mathrm{E}((\boldsymbol{X}'\boldsymbol{X})^{-1}\boldsymbol{X}'\boldsymbol{X}(\boldsymbol{X}'\boldsymbol{X})^{-1} + (\boldsymbol{X}'\boldsymbol{X})^{-1}\boldsymbol{X}'\boldsymbol{D}' + \boldsymbol{DX}(\boldsymbol{X}'\boldsymbol{X})^{-1} + \boldsymbol{DD}')\\ &= \mathrm{E}((\boldsymbol{X}'\boldsymbol{X})^{-1}) + \mathrm{E}(\boldsymbol{DD}'). \end{aligned} \tag{12.19}$$

Therefore,

$$\mathrm{Var}(\check{\boldsymbol{\beta}}) - \mathrm{Var}(\hat{\boldsymbol{\beta}}) = \sigma^2\mathrm{E}(\boldsymbol{DD}')$$

is positive semidefinite, since letting $\boldsymbol{p} = \boldsymbol{Dz}$ for any fixed $\boldsymbol{z} \neq \boldsymbol{0}$,

$$\begin{aligned}\boldsymbol{z}'\mathrm{E}(\boldsymbol{DD}')\boldsymbol{z} &= \mathrm{E}(\boldsymbol{z}'\boldsymbol{DD}'\boldsymbol{z})\\ &= \mathrm{E}(\boldsymbol{p}'\boldsymbol{p})\\ &\geq 0.\end{aligned}$$

The last inequality holds because a random sum of squares is non-negative with probability 1. This completes the proof of the following Gauss-Markov theorem counterpart in the random regressor model:

Proposition: OLS is the efficient member of the class of estimators (12.17) that satisfy assumptions RRME(i)–(iv).

All estimators in this class are unbiased, but it should be noted that there may exist unbiased estimators that do not belong to the specified class. It is sufficient for unbiasedness if the condition $\boldsymbol{LX} = \boldsymbol{I}_k$ w.p.1 is replaced by (12.18). However, while the latter condition implies

$$\mathrm{E}(\boldsymbol{DX}) = \boldsymbol{0},$$

it does *not* imply

$$\mathrm{E}(\boldsymbol{DX}(\boldsymbol{X}'\boldsymbol{X})^{-1}) = \boldsymbol{0},$$

and equality (12.19) fails. Hence, with random regressors the Gauss-Markov theorem applies only in a modified form. The existence of a linear unbiased estimator more efficient than OLS, where 'linear' is to be interpreted as 'linear in $\boldsymbol{y}$ with weights depending on conditioning variables', cannot be ruled out. The result gives no clue about how such an estimator might be constructed, and almost certainly no such estimator exists, so this limitation is unimportant in practice. It is a curiosity nonetheless.

Another contrast with the classical model is provided by the misspecification analysis of Section 11.3. Given the notation adopted there, the assumptions of model RRM need to be written in modified form. In particular, RRM(ii) becomes

Assumption RRM(ii) $\mathrm{E}(\boldsymbol{u}|\boldsymbol{X}, \boldsymbol{Z}) = \boldsymbol{0}$ w.p.1.

This is not a new assumption, note, just the same assumption in different notation with the matrix of regressors written $[\boldsymbol{X}\ \boldsymbol{Z}]$ instead of $\boldsymbol{X}$. Equation (11.14), using (12.13) and also

$$\mathrm{E}(\hat{\boldsymbol{\delta}}|\boldsymbol{X}, \boldsymbol{Z}) = \boldsymbol{\delta} \text{ w.p.1},$$

provides the relation

$$\mathrm{E}(\dot{\boldsymbol{\beta}}|\boldsymbol{X}, \boldsymbol{Z}) = \boldsymbol{\beta} + \hat{\boldsymbol{\Lambda}}\boldsymbol{\delta} \text{ w.p.1} \tag{12.20}$$

where $\hat{\boldsymbol{\Lambda}}$ is defined in (11.13). The omitted variable bias is the unconditional expectation of (12.20), and if $\mathrm{E}(\hat{\boldsymbol{\Lambda}}) = \boldsymbol{\Lambda}$ *defines* $\boldsymbol{\Lambda}$, the bias has the form

$$\mathrm{E}(\dot{\boldsymbol{\beta}}) - \boldsymbol{\beta} = \boldsymbol{\Lambda}\boldsymbol{\delta}. \tag{12.21}$$

Further, if the relations between the regressors are linear in the sense that

$$\mathrm{E}(\boldsymbol{Z}|\boldsymbol{X}) = \boldsymbol{X}\boldsymbol{\Lambda} \text{ w.p.1}, \tag{12.22}$$

then

$$\boldsymbol{\Lambda} = (\mathrm{E}(\boldsymbol{X}'\boldsymbol{X}))^{-1}\mathrm{E}(\boldsymbol{X}'\boldsymbol{Z}), \tag{12.23}$$

and reprising the arguments leading to (12.8) confirms that $\hat{\boldsymbol{\Lambda}}$ in (11.13) is unbiased for $\boldsymbol{\Lambda}$. However, if $\hat{\boldsymbol{\Lambda}}$ is merely the best linear approximation to an arbitrary regression function connecting $\boldsymbol{Z}$ with $\boldsymbol{X}$, no such conclusion can be drawn.

12.6 The Gaussian Model

The next step is to extend the assumptions in parallel with Chapter 10. The Gaussian random regressor model (GRRM) has assumptions GRRM(i)–(iii) in common with assumptions RRM(i)–(iii), and the following:

Assumption GRRM(iv): $\boldsymbol{u}|\boldsymbol{X} \sim \mathrm{N}(\mathbf{0}, \sigma^2 \boldsymbol{I}_T)$.

This assumption says that in the thought experiment in which $\boldsymbol{X}$ is held fixed in repeated samples, the sampling distribution of $\boldsymbol{u}$ is multivariate normal. It implies that the same is true *unconditionally*, or in other words that

$$\boldsymbol{u} \sim \mathrm{N}(\mathbf{0}, \sigma^2 \boldsymbol{I}_T). \tag{12.24}$$

However, this is the case only because, although conditioned on $\boldsymbol{X}$, the distribution does not depend on $\boldsymbol{X}$. The most important thing to appreciate is that (12.24) does not imply assumption GRRM(iv). The conditional means could depend on $\boldsymbol{X}$, for example, at the same time that their average over the distribution of $\boldsymbol{X}$ is zero.

Another important fact is that assumption GRRM(iv) says nothing about the distribution of $\boldsymbol{X}$, beyond the fact that the distribution of $\boldsymbol{u}$ does not depend on it. In particular, there is no requirement for $\boldsymbol{X}$ to be Gaussian. All that is needed is for the unconditional expected values of terms depending on $\boldsymbol{X}$ to be well defined.

Combining (12.8) with (12.10), assumption GRRM(iv) and linearity of the normal distribution lead directly to the result

$$\hat{\boldsymbol{\beta}}|\boldsymbol{X} \sim \mathrm{N}(\boldsymbol{\beta}, \sigma^2(\boldsymbol{X}'\boldsymbol{X})^{-1}). \tag{12.25}$$

However, this distribution depends on $\boldsymbol{X}$, and therefore the unconditional distribution of $\hat{\boldsymbol{\beta}}$ is *not* normal. In fact, it belongs to a class of multivariate distributions that are called *mixed normal*. A drawing from a mixed normal distribution is made in two steps, first drawing a variance matrix from some distribution, in this case the distribution of $\sigma^2(\boldsymbol{X}'\boldsymbol{X})^{-1}$, and then making a normal drawing with this variance. The resulting random vector will be symmetrically distributed around the mean vector $\boldsymbol{\beta}$, but the kurtosis is known to be non-normal. The tails of the density function are somewhat fatter, implying more frequent outliers than in the normal case.

However, assumption GRRM(iv) is sufficient to allow exact inferences. All the results derived in Chapter 10, apart from the distribution of $\hat{\boldsymbol{\beta}}$ itself, hold unchanged in the random regressor model. This may be a surprising fact, but it follows because although the statistics are functions of $\boldsymbol{X}$, their conditional distributions do not in fact depend on $\boldsymbol{X}$, thanks to the magic of idempotent symmetric matrices. For example, taking the relevant definitions from Chapter 10.3, the following conditional distributions hold:

$$\left.\frac{\boldsymbol{u}'\boldsymbol{Q}\boldsymbol{u}}{\sigma^2}\right|\boldsymbol{X} \sim \chi^2(k),$$

$$\left.\frac{\boldsymbol{u}'\boldsymbol{M}\boldsymbol{u}}{\sigma^2}\right|\boldsymbol{X} \sim \chi^2(T-k),$$

and hence in place of (10.3),

$$\left.\frac{(\hat{\boldsymbol{\beta}}-\boldsymbol{\beta})'\boldsymbol{X}'\boldsymbol{X}(\hat{\boldsymbol{\beta}}-\boldsymbol{\beta})}{ks^2}\right|\boldsymbol{X} \sim F(k, T-k). \tag{12.26}$$

These conditional distributions are pivotal and are the same for any $\boldsymbol{X}$, hence they hold unconditionally. Therefore (12.26) actually implies (10.3).

In the same way, using the notation from Section 10.4,

$$\left.\frac{\hat{\beta}_i}{\sigma\sqrt{a_{ii}}}\right| \boldsymbol{X} \sim \mathrm{N}(0,1), \tag{12.27}$$

and hence

$$\left.\frac{\hat{\beta}_i}{s\sqrt{a_{ii}}}\right| \boldsymbol{X} \sim t_{T-k}. \tag{12.28}$$

Again, these distributions are pivotal and do not depend on $\boldsymbol{X}$, and hence (12.28) implies (10.9). However, while they may appear just the same, there is a major difference in the ways these results are justified. Consider the ratio in (12.27). In the classical regression model, $\hat{\beta}_i$ is normally distributed, and a_{ii} (the diagonal element of $(\boldsymbol{X}'\boldsymbol{X})^{-1}$) is a constant. In the random regressor model, $\hat{\beta}_i$ is not normally distributed and a_{ii} is a random variable. However, $\hat{\beta}_i$ is mixed normal and drawn from a distribution with random variance $\sigma^2 a_{ii}$, and this normalization is just what is required to resolve the 'mixture' so the ratio is standard normal, just as in the classical case. Replacing the unknown σ by s then in effect gives the ratio of two pivotal statistics, which is in itself pivotal and tabulated as Student's t.

The results of this chapter are clearly useful and encouraging. Nearly all the properties of least squares regression that were shown to hold under the classical assumptions survive under random regressors. The one exception, that the BLUE property of OLS established by the Gauss-Markov theorem requires a minor additional assumption, has no important consequences. What is shown is the existence of a class of models appropriate to economic data, specifically randomly sampled survey data, where least squares has known and useful properties. The discouraging assessment of the classical model as a tool of economic analysis related in Section 7.1 can be mitigated, but this has not been achieved by finding an application for the classical model. Rather, the same results have been justified in a different setting, thanks to some novel statistical theory.

12.7 Exercises

1 Are the following statements true or false?
   (a) Conditional probability is defined as a "degree of belief". It has no meaning in classical statistics.
   (b) The law of iterated expectations allows us to calculate covariances using information about predictability.
   (c) The law of iterated expectations can be used to show the independence of random variables.
   (d) In the random regressor model under standard assumptions, least squares is unbiased in regression functions with arbitrary functional form.
   (e) Conditional expectations are random variables whose distribution derives from the distribution of the conditioning variables.
   (f) The square of a random variable is non-negative with probability 1.

(g) Least squares bias due to omitted variables has a known formula when relations between the variables are linear.

2 Consider the estimator $\hat{\boldsymbol{\beta}} = (\boldsymbol{X}'\boldsymbol{X})^{-1}\boldsymbol{X}'\boldsymbol{y}$ for $\boldsymbol{\beta}$ $(k \times 1)$ in the model $\boldsymbol{y} = \boldsymbol{X}\boldsymbol{\beta} + \boldsymbol{u}$ $(T \times 1)$ where $\mathrm{E}(\boldsymbol{u}|\boldsymbol{X}) = \boldsymbol{0}$ w.p.1 and $\mathrm{E}(\boldsymbol{u}\boldsymbol{u}'|\boldsymbol{X}) = \sigma^2\boldsymbol{I}_T$ w.p.1.
(a) What assumptions on $\boldsymbol{X}$ are implicit in this setup?
(b) Derive the covariance matrix of $\hat{\boldsymbol{\beta}}$, being careful to justify each step in the argument in the light of the properties of conditional expectations.
(c) How does the result of part (b) depend on the properties of the data? What might be the consequences of a failure of these properties?
(d) If $\boldsymbol{u}|\boldsymbol{X} \sim \mathrm{N}(\boldsymbol{0}, \sigma^2\boldsymbol{I}_T)$, what can be said about the distribution of $\hat{\boldsymbol{\beta}}$?
(e) Give a formula for a 95% confidence ellipsoid for $\boldsymbol{\beta}$, assuming that $k = 4$ and $T = 20$.

3 Let x_t and y_t be random variables, having mean zero, and related by

$$\mathrm{E}(y_t|x_t) = \beta x_t \text{ w.p.1.}$$

Given a random sample of the pairs (y_t, x_t), for $t = 1, \ldots, T$, consider the ordinary least squares estimator of β

$$\hat{\beta} = \frac{\sum_t x_t y_t}{\sum_t x_t^2}.$$

(a) Is $\hat{\beta}$ unbiased for β? Why? (or, Why not?)
(b) If $\mathrm{E}(u_t^2|x_t) = \sigma^2$ w.p.1, where $u_t = y_t - \beta x_t$, what is the variance of $\hat{\beta}$?
(c) If $u_t|x_t$ is normally distributed where $u_t = y_t - \beta x_t$, what can be said about the distribution of $\hat{\beta}$?
(d) Assuming $u_t|x_t$ as defined in part (c) is normally distributed, how would you perform a test of the null hypothesis $\beta = 0$?

4 In the regression model

$$y_t = \beta x_t + \gamma z_t + u_t, \quad t = 1, \ldots, T,$$

y_t, x_t, and z_t are random variables with zero means. You may assume that

$$\mathrm{E}(y_t|x_t, z_t) = \beta x_t + \gamma z_t \text{ w.p.1}$$

and also that the sample is independently drawn.
(a) What is $\mathrm{E}(u_t|x_t, z_t)$?
(b) What is $\mathrm{E}(u_t|x_1, \ldots x_T, z_1, \ldots z_T)$?
(c) Write down the formula for the least squares estimator of β.
(d) Show that this estimator is unbiased.
(e) Assuming that $\mathrm{E}(z_t|x_t) = \delta x_t$ w.p.1 where δ is a constant, find a formula for $\mathrm{Cov}(z_t, x_t)$.
(f) Using the result in part (e), show that the simple regression of y_t onto x_t alone is biased, and obtain the formula for the bias.

5 Let a non-linear regression model have the form

$$y_t = \alpha + \beta x_t + \gamma x_t^2 + u_t, \quad t = 1, \ldots, T$$

where $E(u_t|x_1, \dots, x_T) = 0$ w.p.1 and

$$E(u_t u_s|x_1, \dots, x_T) = \begin{cases} \sigma^2 & t = s \\ 0 & t \neq s \end{cases} \quad \text{w.p.1.}$$

Assume that $E(x_t) = 0$ for $t = 1, \dots, T$.

(a) What is $E(y_t|x_1, \dots, x_T)$?

(b) Find the coefficients a and b that minimize

$$E(y_t - a - bx_t)^2.$$

(c) Show that the solutions of part (b) satisfy the relations

$$a = E(y_t)$$

$$b = \frac{E(x_t y_t)}{E(x_t^2)}$$

and comment.

(d) Give an interpretation of the quantities $a - \alpha$ and $b - \beta$.

13

Introduction to Asymptotics

The statistical results developed in the chapters of this book are powerful and elegant. A comprehensive theory of statistical inference has yielded exact confidence intervals and tests for a range of hypotheses on the regression coefficients. However, there remain major limitations. The independent sampling requirement, as has been discussed extensively in Section 12.4, clearly limits the range of economic data sets that the theory covers. A great deal of econometric work involves time series and panels, yet the theory of the preceding chapters has had nothing to say about these cases.

The assumption of Gaussian disturbances is extremely conventional, and in many textbooks it barely receives comment, but it is well known that some data sets, especially in finance, exhibit a higher probability of outliers than the normal distribution predicts. Skewed disturbances can also be also encountered. However, the major problem with the Gaussianity assumption is that it is made for convenience, to allow the results of Chapter 10 and Section 12.6 to be cited. It is rarely a component of the economic or behavioural model under consideration, and in any case the theory has provided no means of establishing its truth.

These facts present a dilemma, but happily there is resolution at hand, albeit one that involves its own compromises. *Asymptotic theory* is a collection of approximation results where the adequacy of the approximation is linked to sample size. It is also known as *large sample theory*. Essentially, the method of attack is to derive certain properties that hold exactly for the case of an 'infinite' sample. Since samples are never infinite in practice, the limit case represents another type of thought experiment. However, the rate at which the limit is approached as the sample size increases, and hence the error involved in using limit results, can be evaluated in various ways; either theoretically, or by means of simulation experiments using artificial data. So-called Monte Carlo experiments, in which the empirical distributions of statistics are tabulated by randomized repetitions of a simulation, are a popular technique of econometric research.

13.1 The Law of Large Numbers

Let $y_1, \dots, y_T$ be a sample of drawings from a distribution with mean $E(y_t) = \mu$, and define the sample mean in the usual way,

$$\bar{y}_T = \frac{1}{T}\sum_{t=1}^{T} y_t. \tag{13.1}$$

An Introduction to Econometric Theory, First Edition. James Davidson.

Companion website: www.wiley.com/go/davidson/introecmettheory

Consider the behaviour of this statistic as T increases, so that bigger and bigger samples are drawn. The implied thought experiment can be contrasted with the repeated sampling exercise described in Section 7.1. Instead of repeatedly drawing samples of fixed size from a population, with replacement, to define the distribution of $\bar{y}_T$, imagine a single sample that is progressively extended, adding more and more observations. When the sampling mechanism is random, this could be done by stacking up those repeated samples into a single sample. However, the power of the limit results stems from the fact that they can be valid even under sampling mechanisms that allow dependence between successive observations.

Consider what is meant by "convergence to a limit". The sequence of numbers

$$1, \frac{1}{2}, \frac{1}{3}, \frac{1}{4}, \frac{1}{5}, \dots$$

is getting closer and closer to zero as it is extended, and $1/T$ can be made as close to zero as we please by taking T large enough. The sequence can only be of finite extent in a finite world, so 'zero' is never actually attained, but it still makes evident sense to write

$$\lim_{T\to\infty} \frac{1}{T} = 0$$

as shorthand for "getting closer to zero as T increases".

The notation $\{a_T, T = 1, 2, 3, \dots\}$, or simply $\{a_T\}$ when the context is clear, denotes the *sequence* of numbers whose *coordinates* are the a_T. The ellipsis '$\cdots$', if nothing follows it, denotes that the sequence may extend to infinity. If the sequence $\{a_T\}$ approaches a limit as $T \to \infty$, this can be defined explicitly as the value a that satisfies the following condition:

Definition: If for any positive number ε, no matter how small, there exists a positive integer T_ε with the property that

$$|a_T - a| < \varepsilon \text{ for all } T > T_\varepsilon, \tag{13.2}$$

then a is the *limit* of the sequence $\{a_T\}$.

Notice how this definition does not need to invoke the fictional '$T = \infty$' case; it just indicates what happens as T gets larger. The bars in the formula denote the absolute value, so both overshooting and undershooting are covered. This condition is written in short form using an arrow, as

$$a_T \to a.$$

Considering the sequence with coordinates (13.1) for $T = 1, 2, 3, \cdots$, the intuition is that as the sample increases in size, the amount by which $\bar{y}_T$ varies as new observations are added is getting smaller. Some rearrangement shows that

$$\bar{y}_T = \bar{y}_{T-1} + \frac{1}{T}(y_T - \bar{y}_{T-1}).$$

When T is large enough, the mean barely changes when another observation is added, and there must be a sense in which the sequence $\{\bar{y}_T\}$ converges to a limit. However, since $\bar{y}_T$ is a random variable, this sense must be carefully defined. There are in fact various ways to do this, but the most usual way is the following:

Definition: If for every $\varepsilon > 0$, no matter how small,

$$\lim_{T\to\infty} \Pr(|\bar{y}_T - \mu| \geq \varepsilon) = 0, \tag{13.3}$$

then $\{\bar{y}_T\}$ *converges in probability* to μ.

The condition specified in (13.3) is often abbreviated to

$$\bar{y}_T \xrightarrow{pr} \mu.$$

Another common notation is

$$\text{plim } \bar{y}_T = \mu,$$

which in words is rendered as "the probability limit of $\bar{y}_T$ is μ". What are actually converging here, in the sense of (13.2), are the sequences of probabilities (one for each ε) getting smaller and approaching zero as T increases. This gets around the problem that because $\bar{y}_T$ varies randomly – and the next observation added could of course be extreme – it is unrealistic to expect that condition (13.2) could be satisfied by $\bar{y}_T$ itself.

As a rule, there is another sequence associated with $\{\bar{y}_T\}$, the sequence of expected values, $\{\mathrm{E}(\bar{y}_T)\}$. A random sequence is said to obey the *law of large numbers* (LLN) if

$$\operatorname*{plim}_{T\to\infty} \bar{y}_T = \lim_{T\to\infty} \mathrm{E}(\bar{y}_T) \tag{13.4}$$

where the limit on the right-hand side of (13.4) is called the *asymptotic expectation* of the sequence. More properly, (13.4) should be designated the *weak* law of large numbers, because there is another mode of convergence defining the so-called strong law. However, for most econometrics applications the weak law is all that is needed.

If, as is often the case, the observations are all drawn from the same distribution with $\mathrm{E}(y_t) = \mu$ for every $t = 1, \ldots, T$ and every $T > 0$, then $\mathrm{E}(\bar{y}_T) = \mu$ for every T, and the limit in (13.4) is also μ. But this is not a requirement. It is permissible, even if unusual, for the observation means to be different for different t while still satisfying (13.4).

The problem is to determine whether a given sequence satisfies the law of large numbers. This is known to be true if the observations are randomly drawn. It could also hold in more general circumstances, although showing this can be tricky. A useful device in this context is the related concept of *mean square convergence.* $\{\bar{y}_T\}$ is said to converge in mean square to a limit μ if

$$\lim_{T\to\infty} \mathrm{E}(\bar{y}_T - \mu)^2 = 0. \tag{13.5}$$

The reason this condition is useful is that it is sufficient for convergence in probability to the same limit. The connection is the *Chebyshev inequality,* which says that for any random variable X and positive constant ε,

$$\Pr(|X| \geq \varepsilon) \leq \frac{\mathrm{E}(X^2)}{\varepsilon^2}. \tag{13.6}$$

This is the version for probability distributions of the rule for samples in (1.8), describing the behaviour of a random variable yet to be drawn, rather than of realized data. A simple way to show that (13.6) must be true is to use an indicator function, as defined in Section 12.2. For any point x on the line and a given $\varepsilon > 0$, let

$$I_{\{|x|\geq\varepsilon\}}(x) = \begin{cases} 1, & |x| \geq \varepsilon \\ 0, & |x| < \varepsilon \end{cases}.$$

Recalling how indicators convert probabilities to expected values, the reasoning then goes like this:

$$\begin{aligned}\varepsilon^2 \Pr(|X| \geq \varepsilon) &= \varepsilon^2 \mathrm{E}(I_{\{|X|\geq\varepsilon\}}(X)) \\ &\leq \mathrm{E}(X^2 I_{\{|X|\geq\varepsilon\}}(X)) \\ &\leq \mathrm{E}(X^2).\end{aligned}$$

Notice the trick of using linearity to move ε^2 inside the expected value in effect. The indicator function knocks out cases of X smaller in absolute value than ε, so replacing ε^2 by X^2 can only make the expected value bigger. Replacing the indicator by 1, as in the final member, must make it bigger still.

Applying (13.6) to the case $X = \bar{y}_T - \mu$, it is clear that (13.3) holds if the left-hand side of (13.6) converges to zero, for which (13.5) is sufficient. The next step is decompose the mean square into two components, as

$$\begin{aligned}\mathrm{E}(\bar{y}_T - \mu)^2 &= \mathrm{E}(\bar{y}_T - \mathrm{E}(\bar{y}_T) + \mathrm{E}(\bar{y}_T) - \mu)^2 \\ &= \mathrm{Var}(\bar{y}_T) + (\mathrm{E}(\bar{y}_T) - \mu)^2,\end{aligned}$$

where the second equality holds because, of course, $\mathrm{E}(\bar{y}_T - \mathrm{E}(\bar{y}_T)) = 0$. Consider the case where $\mathrm{E}(y_t) = \mu$ for all t, so that the second right-hand side term vanishes, and all that has to be shown is that the variance of the mean converges to zero. In particular, consider the independent sampling case. This is a calculation done in Section 8.1 for the case $\mathrm{Var}(y_t) = \sigma^2$, and the calculation in (8.1) yielded $\mathrm{Var}(\bar{y}_T) = \sigma^2/T$. This formula shows not only that $\{\bar{y}_T\}$ converges in probability but how fast this happens. Quadruple the sample size, and the standard deviation halves.

However, some more interesting calculations are also possible. Successive observations can be correlated. Suppose the sequence

$$\mathrm{Cov}(y_t, y_{t-j}) = \gamma_j,\ j = 1, 2, 3, \ldots$$

defines the *autocovariances* of the sample sequence $\{y_t\}$. This formulation, where the covariance is dependent on the separation of the observations in the ordered sample but like the variance does not depend on t, makes sense in a time series context in particular. In this case $\gamma_j = \gamma_{-j}$, and it can be verified that

$$\begin{aligned}\mathrm{Var}(\bar{y}_T) &= \mathrm{E}\left(\frac{1}{T}\sum_{t=1}^{T}(y_t - \mu)\right)^2 \\ &= \frac{1}{T^2}\left(\sum_{t=1}^{T}\mathrm{E}(y_t - \mu)^2 + 2\sum_{j=1}^{T-1}\sum_{t=j+1}^{T}\mathrm{E}(y_t - \mu)(y_{t-j} - \mu)\right) \\ &= \frac{1}{T}\sigma^2 + \frac{2}{T}\sum_{j=1}^{T-1}\left(1 - \frac{j}{T}\right)\gamma_j. \end{aligned} \tag{13.7}$$

The condition

$$\frac{1}{T}\sum_{j=1}^{T-1}\gamma_j \to 0$$

is sufficient for $\mathrm{Var}(\bar{y}_T)$ to vanish as T increases. The observations are in this case "uncorrelated on average", either by having γ_j equal to zero beyond some finite j or at least to be approaching zero fast enough as j increases, although in the latter case the rate of mean squared convergence of $\bar{y}_T$ to μ can be slower than $1/T$.

This method does not work if the variance does not exist, which is something the examples reviewed in Section 6.4 show is possible. The argument from mean squared convergence then fails, although this does not rule out the weaker condition of convergence in probability. There are alternative arguments for the law of large numbers in this case, although they are technical and beyond the scope of this chapter. However, if the mean is also undefined, then the law of large numbers itself fails. The classic counter-example is the Cauchy distribution, which has the reproductive property (6.16). The sample mean of T independent Cauchy variates is another Cauchy, with no tendency to approach a fixed limit.

Since in much of this book we have worked with the notion of 'fixed regressors' (in repeated samples), it is desirable to reconcile the classical regression paradigm with large sample theory. Is it necessary to assume a probability distribution for sequence coordinates? Clearly, any infinite sequence must have a generation *process* specified, since it is not feasible to specify each coordinate individually. Drawing repeatedly from a probability distribution is one easy way to specify such a process. However, another way would be to allow a fixed, finite sequence of finite constants to be repeated over and over. The sequence of means of such a cycling process converges to a limit in the sense of (13.2). Such a case, the intercept, is found in nearly every regression. The mean of the column of ones is always one and hence converges in a trivial sense to one. In what follows, condition (13.3) can be formally extended to the case of a 'degenerate' distribution, where $\Pr(|\bar{y}_T - \mu| \geq \varepsilon)$ is set to 0 if $|\bar{y}_T - \mu| < \varepsilon$ for the specified T and ε and to 1 otherwise.

The probability limit of a statistic is treated as the counterpart of the expected value in asymptotic analysis, and the fact that these two measures of central tendency may match is what makes the law of large numbers such an important result. However, one of the great virtues of the asymptotic approach is the flexibility available when doing calculations involving the limits. Expected values are linear, which is a useful attribute, but calculating the expected values of non-linear functions is notoriously difficult. For example,

$$\mathrm{E}\left(\frac{X}{Y}\right) \neq \frac{\mathrm{E}(X)}{\mathrm{E}(Y)}$$

in general. Similarly, for a random matrix $\boldsymbol{A}$,

$$\mathrm{E}(\boldsymbol{A}^{-1}) \neq (\mathrm{E}(\boldsymbol{A}))^{-1},$$

as has already been pointed out in (12.16). Finding the expectation of a ratio of random variables is generally an intractable problem, which is a serious handicap when it comes, for example, to working out the bias in an estimator.

However, probability limits do not suffer this limitation. The basic result is *Slutsky's theorem*,[1] of which a simple version is the following:

Proposition: Continuous functions of terms converging in probability converge to the same functions of the probability limits.

For example, the probability limit of the square of a statistic is equal to the square of the probability limit. Of course, the expected value of the square is different from the square

---

1 Eugen Slutsky, 1880-1948

of the expected value (their difference being the variance). Cases that frequently arise are ratios. If

$$\operatorname*{plim}_{T\to\infty} \bar{y}_T = \mu$$

and

$$\operatorname*{plim}_{T\to\infty} \bar{z}_T = \nu \neq 0,$$

then

$$\operatorname*{plim}_{T\to\infty} \frac{\bar{x}_T}{\bar{z}_T} = \frac{\mu}{\nu}.$$

So, while it is the case that

$$\mathrm{E}\left(\frac{\bar{x}_T}{\bar{z}_T}\right) \neq \frac{\mu}{\nu}, \tag{13.8}$$

the Slutsky theorem and the law of large numbers jointly show that the two sides of (13.8) are close to one another when the sample is large, and the larger, the closer. This is one of the most valuable approximation results available to econometrics researchers.

13.2 Consistent Estimation

Consider the simple regression equation from Section 1.4,

$$y_t = \alpha + \beta x_t + u_t. \tag{13.9}$$

In the usual way the least squares estimator of the parameter β, with its decomposition into true value and 'error of estimate' term, is

$$\begin{aligned}\hat{\beta} &= \frac{\sum_{t=1}^{T}(x_t - \bar{x})y_t}{\sum_{t=1}^{T}(x_t - \bar{x})^2} \\ &= \beta + \frac{\sum_{t=1}^{T}(x_t - \bar{x})u_t}{\sum_{t=1}^{T}(x_t - \bar{x})^2},\end{aligned} \tag{13.10}$$

where the second equality emerges on substituting for y_t from (13.9) and rearranging.

An estimator is said to be *consistent* if its probability limit is equal to the true value of the parameter in question. Consistency is often regarded as the large-sample equivalent of the unbiasedness property. There is a sense in which the estimator is "correct on average", although rather than being a property of the sampling distribution in a fixed sample size, consistency is the attribute that additional observations move the estimator closer to the true value, with high probability. In the context of econometric research, consistency may well be a more attractive property to establish, since it conveys information about the dispersion of the estimator as well as its central tendency.

Demonstrating consistency of $\hat{\beta}$ in (13.10) is primarily a matter of specifying appropriate behaviour for the sequences of observations. However, a useful place to start is to review the chain of equalities that need to be established, as follows:

$$\begin{aligned}\text{plim } \hat{\beta} &= \beta + \text{plim } \frac{\sum_{t=1}^{T}(x_t - \bar{x})u_t}{\sum_{t=1}^{T}(x_t - \bar{x})^2} \\ &= \beta + \frac{\text{plim } T^{-1}\sum_{t=1}^{T}(x_t - \bar{x})u_t}{\text{plim } T^{-1}\sum_{t=1}^{T}(x_t - \bar{x})^2} \\ &= \beta + \frac{0}{\sigma_x^2},\end{aligned} \tag{13.11}$$

where σ_x^2 denotes the probability limit of the sample variance of x_t.

The first equality here is immediate. The second equality invokes the Slutsky theorem to say that the probability limit of the ratio equals the ratio of the probability limits, but only after the critical step of converting the sums to means. Inserting the factors of T^{-1} does not of course change the value of the ratio, since they cancel out, but the substitution is critical since the sums do not possess probability limits; instead they diverge. This is a step that beginners sometimes overlook.

The final equality substitutes values for the probability limits, to be examined further. The important thing is that for the ratio to vanish in the limit requires a dual condition: that the numerator vanishes and the denominator is strictly positive. "0/0" is not zero and is not a well-defined number.

Therefore, consider the claimed values for these probability limits, which must hold by the law of large numbers. Applying the Slutsky theorem again, the numerator satisfies the equality

$$\text{plim } T^{-1}\sum_{t=1}^{T}(x_t - \bar{x})u_t = \text{plim } T^{-1}\sum_{t=1}^{T}x_t u_t - \text{plim } \bar{x} \text{ plim } \bar{u}, \tag{13.12}$$

where $\bar{u}$ is the sample mean of $u_1, \ldots, u_T$, while the denominator satisfies

$$\begin{aligned}\sigma_x^2 &= \text{plim } T^{-1}\sum_{t=1}^{T}(x_t - \bar{x})^2 \\ &= \text{plim } T^{-1}\sum_{t=1}^{T}x_t^2 - (\text{plim } \bar{x})^2.\end{aligned} \tag{13.13}$$

There are four sequences for which the law of large numbers has to be verified, respectively $\{x_t\}$, $\{u_t\}$, $\{x_t u_t\}$, and $\{x_t^2\}$. The required convergences in probability certainly hold for $\{x_t\}$ and $\{u_t\}$ if these coordinates are randomly sampled from distributions with a well-defined mean, as in Case B of Section 12.3, although random sampling is by no means a necessary condition. There are plenty of ways for either or both variables to be autocorrelated, as shown in (13.7). However, the condition of a well-defined mean is not a trivial one; failure of this requirement is a possibility, as shown in Section 6.4.

The sequences $\{x_t^2\}$ and $\{x_t u_t\}$ pose a different set of criteria. The condition $\text{E}(x_t^2) < \infty$ holds if the regressor has a finite variance. There are various conditions under which the first term of (13.13) exists and is equal to $\text{E}(x_t^2)$. Going the route of showing mean squared convergence, this would require the stronger condition $\text{E}(x_t^4) < \infty$, which would need to be shown or assumed. Happily it is known that this condition is not necessary if x_t is independently and identically distributed. Chapter 3 of *Econometric Theory*[2] provides further information. Subject to this, the probability limit in (13.13) has the required form,

$$\mathrm{E}(x_t^2) - \mathrm{E}(x_t)^2 = \mathrm{Var}(x_t).$$

If $\mathrm{E}(u_t|x_t) = 0$ with probability 1, as is implied by assumption RRM(ii) in particular, then, using the LIE and conditional linearity,

$$\begin{aligned}\mathrm{E}(x_t u_t) &= \mathrm{E}(x_t \mathrm{E}(u_t|x_t))\\ &= \mathrm{E}(x_t \times 0 \text{ w.p. } 1)\\ &= 0.\end{aligned}$$

If the numerator does converge in probability, it converges to zero. If assumption RRM(iii) holds, the mean-squared convergence argument can be used to show this, since using the same basic argument

$$\begin{aligned}\mathrm{E}(x_t^2 u_t^2) &= \mathrm{E}(x_t^2 \mathrm{E}(u_t^2|x_t))\\ &= \sigma^2 \mathrm{E}(x_t^2)\\ &< \infty.\end{aligned}$$

Putting all these components together completes the consistency demonstration for the simple regression. The notable feature of the argument is that, while it works for the random regressor model of Section 12.4, it clearly also works for a much broader class of models. There is no requirement to invoke random sampling.

The requirement that u_t be unpredictable from x_t is familiar from the bias analysis of Section 12.5, but there is a new element to the analysis here, the requirement that σ_x^2 in (13.13) be strictly positive. In a finite sample analysis this is not something to worry much about, because it could only fail if x_t showed no variation over the sample. Asymptotic conditions are trickier, because it is necessary to know something about the *process* generating the sequence, as the number of terms in the sum extends to infinity.

The following example is artificial but indicates in a simple way what might go wrong. Suppose the model has the form of (13.9) where

$$x_t = \frac{1}{t}. \tag{13.14}$$

If u_t is identically and independently distributed, this regression satisfies the classical regression model assumptions. Least squares estimation of α and β in a sample of size T is clearly unbiased and BLUE. However, the sequence of reciprocals of the natural numbers

$$\{1/t,\ t = 1, 2, 3, \ldots\}$$

has two properties that are well-known to mathematicians. These are

$$\frac{1}{\log T}\sum_{t=1}^{T}\frac{1}{t} \to 1,$$

where 'log' denotes the natural logarithm, such that $\mathrm{e}^{\log T} = T$, and

$$\sum_{t=1}^{T}\frac{1}{t^2} \to \frac{\pi^2}{6}.$$

2 James Davidson, *Econometric Theory* (Oxford: Blackwell Publishers, 2000).

Since $(\log T)/T \to 0$ as $T \to \infty$, it follows that in this case

$$\sigma_x^2 = \lim_{T\to\infty} \frac{1}{T}\sum_{t=1}^{T}\left(\frac{1}{t}\right)^2 - \lim_{T\to\infty}\left(\frac{1}{T}\sum_{t=1}^{T}\frac{1}{t}\right)^2$$
$$= 0.$$

The limit in (13.11) is therefore undefined, and there is *no* limit, whether β or anything else, to which $\hat{\beta}$ converges in probability. The sequence will not settle down to any value and will eventually diverge. This example shows how caution is always desirable in applying asymptotic results.

13.3 The Central Limit Theorem

The mean $\bar{y}_T$ of a random sample of observations $y_1, \dots, y_T$, having mean μ and variance σ^2, has a mean of μ and a variance of σ^2/T. Hence it must approach the constant μ as T tends to infinity, for the law of large numbers is certainly obeyed in this case. If $\mu = 0$, which can always be made true by subtracting the actual mean from the observations, an interesting question can be posed. Consider the random sequence

$$\sqrt{T}\bar{y}_T = \frac{1}{\sqrt{T}}\sum_{t=1}^{T} y_t. \tag{13.15}$$

It is easily verified that the mean is zero and the variance is σ^2, and this is true for any T. The normalization factor of $\sqrt{T}$ is precisely chosen, so that the variance of the rescaled sum neither collapses to zero nor diverges to infinity as T increases. This is the 'square root rule' already remarked in Section 5.2; see (5.10). The coordinates of the sequence of rescaled means remain random variables even as T increases without limit, and the interesting question is what can be said about the 'limit' case, if such a thing exists.

To appreciate just what happens, consider the change in (13.15) as the sample size goes from T to $2T$.

$$\sqrt{2T}\bar{y}_{2T} = \frac{1}{\sqrt{2T}}\sum_{t=1}^{T} y_t + \frac{1}{\sqrt{2T}}\sum_{t=T+1}^{2T} y_t.$$

If the observations are randomly drawn with variance σ^2, the two terms on the right-hand side have the same distribution with variances of $\sigma^2/2$ and are independent of each other. Observe that

$$\sqrt{2T}\bar{y}_{2T} - \sqrt{T}\bar{y}_T = \left(\frac{1}{\sqrt{2}} - 1\right)\left(\frac{1}{\sqrt{T}}\sum_{t=1}^{T} y_t\right) + \frac{1}{\sqrt{2}}\left(\frac{1}{\sqrt{T}}\sum_{t=T+1}^{2T} y_t\right)$$

and therefore

$$\mathrm{Var}\left(\sqrt{2T}\bar{y}_{2T} - \sqrt{T}\bar{y}_T\right) = \sigma^2\left[\left(\frac{1}{\sqrt{2}} - 1\right)^2 + \frac{1}{2}\right]$$
$$= \sigma^2\left(2 - \sqrt{2}\right).$$

The interesting thing about this result is that the variance of the difference does not depend on T. Doubling the sample produces a random change in the standardized mean with a variance of approximately $0.6\sigma^2$, whether $T = 1$ or $T = 1$ million!

Since the standardized mean never settles down to any unchanging value, what can be said about its distribution? If y_t is normally distributed and randomly sampled, the linearity property of the normal distribution implies that $\sqrt{T}\bar{y}_T$ is also normally distributed. However, the linearity property is not shared by most other distributions. For example, if $x_t \sim \text{N}(0, 1)$, then $y_t = (x_t^2 - 1)/\sqrt{2}$ is a standardized $\chi^2(1)$ random variable. However, in this case $\sqrt{T}\bar{y}_T$ is a standardized $\chi^2(T)$ random variable. The distribution evolves as more terms are added, and the really interesting fact is that as T increases, the distribution of this standardized sum of *squared* normals is getting closer and closer to the standard normal. This central limit phenomenon parallels the behaviour of the standardized binomial (5.24) already remarked.

The phenomenon of which these are two classic cases is called *convergence in distribution*. Another example was given in (5.25), where a sequence of binomial distributions approached a limit case, the Poisson, although that case is different in that the sequence in question was not merely a standardized sum of terms. The central limit theorem (abbreviated to CLT) is a universal law for random variables having finite variance. There are many variants of the CLT specifying different sufficient conditions. The following statement is just for the simplest and most restrictive of them. Regarding terminology, in the context of a series of observations the random sampling property is often called *serial independence*.

Proposition: If a series $u_1, \dots, u_T$ is serially independent with $\text{E}(u_t) = \mu$ and $\text{Var}(u_t) = \sigma^2$ where $0 < \sigma^2 < \infty$, then $\sqrt{T}(\bar{u}_T - \mu) \xrightarrow{d} \text{N}(0, \sigma^2)$.

Check out the notation here. The symbol "$\xrightarrow{d}$" is often used to indicate convergence in distribution, similarly to the use of "$\xrightarrow{pr}$" for convergence in probability. Care is needed in distinguishing these cases, not least because of the basis on which the phenomena in question might be verified. Given a sequence of means converging in probability, observing a sufficient number of coordinates could convince us that successive terms were approaching a fixed point. However, determining that a sequence of standardized sums is converging in distribution is not possible from observing a single sequence, no matter of what length. All that you see is a sequence constantly varying. While they do have a normal distribution beyond a certain point, successive coordinates are of course highly correlated, so they do not provide a random sample whose scatter might be tabulated. The *only* way of checking empirically that a sequence is converging in distribution to a particular limit is to observe *many* such sequences, independently generated, and consider the frequency table of the values each attains at some suitably large T.

To the susceptible mind, the central limit theorem has an almost mystical fascination. What is it about that bell-shaped curve, that it can be conjured out of completely arbitrary shocks, provided there are enough of them and they are sufficiently restrained in their behaviour to possess a finite variance? The formal proof of the theorem requires technically advanced methods, but the essential intuition stems from the linearity property, (5.9). Think of adding together two independent random variables, arbitrary but standardized to zero mean and unit variance. If their distributions are similar to the N(0, 1), then so will be the distribution of their standardized sum. If their distributions

Figure 13.1 P.d.f of the sum of three uniform r.v.s, with normal p.d.f. for comparison. *Source:* Figure 23.1 of *Stochastic Limit Theory: An Introduction for Econometricians* (Advanced Texts in Econometrics) by James Davidson (1994). Reproduced by permission of Oxford University Press.

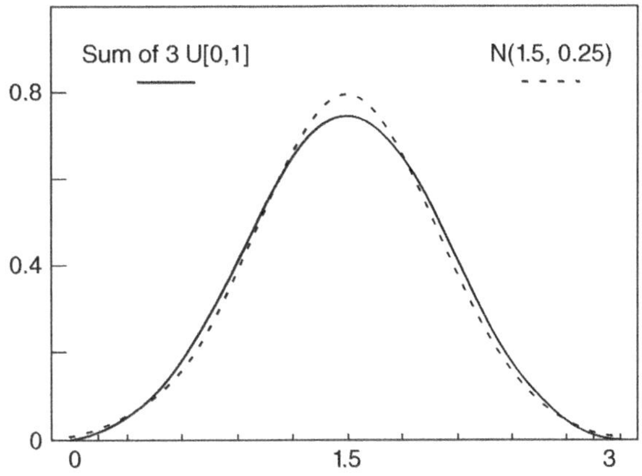

do not resemble the N(0, 1), the distribution of their sum has a range of possible forms, some resembling N(0, 1) and others not, but the former cases propagate themselves at the expense of the latter. It is easy to see how, repeating such combinations a large number of times, the normal distribution serves as an 'attractor' for random sums.

"How large is large" is of course an interesting question, and this does depend on the nature of the distributions being aggregated. In Figure 5.5, the sum of a mere 20 Bernoulli draws with success probability of $\frac{1}{2}$ reproduces the Gaussian bell shape very closely. Even more striking is the evidence in Figure 13.1, which shows the density function of the sum of just *three* independent uniformly distributed random variables, with the Gaussian curve with matching mean and variance shown for comparison. The uniform density is a rectangle, yet add three together, and something like a bell shape appears. It is true that convergence is most rapid with symmetric distributions, and by way of contrast, the standardized sum of independent squared normals requires at least 500 terms before its density function starts to look plausibly symmetric and bell shaped. However, it gets there in the end.

As with the law of large numbers, the requirement of independent sampling can be relaxed in various ways. The square root rule for normalization is valid under dependence provided the sequence of autocovariances has a finite sum, specifically so that the second term in the last member of (13.7) goes to zero at the rate $1/T$, like the first one. In this case, conditions do exist such that a central limit result holds.

There are some useful results that allow the calculation of limits in distribution of functions of random sums. *Cramér's theorem*[3] says, in essence, that given a sequence converging in distribution and another sequence converging in probability, their sum and their product have the limits in distribution one would expect, evaluated at the relevant probability limits. For example, if

$$\sqrt{T}\bar{u}_T \xrightarrow{d} \mathrm{N}(0, \sigma^2) \qquad (13.16)$$

and

$$\mathrm{plim}\ \bar{z}_T = v,$$

3 Harald Cramér, 1893-1985

then

$$\sqrt{T}\bar{u}_T + \bar{z}_T \xrightarrow{d} \mathrm{N}(\nu, \sigma^2)$$

and

$$\bar{z}_T \sqrt{T}\bar{u}_T \xrightarrow{d} \mathrm{N}(0, \nu^2\sigma^2).$$

Also, if $\nu \neq 0$,

$$\sqrt{T}\frac{\bar{u}_T}{\bar{z}_T} \xrightarrow{d} \mathrm{N}\left(0, \frac{\sigma^2}{\nu^2}\right).$$

In the context of multivariate convergence (see the next section), these basic relations generalize directly to matrix products.

The *continuous mapping theorem* is analogous to the Slutsky theorem for the convergence in distribution case. Continuous functions of sequences converging in distribution have limit distributions that are the matching transformations of the limits. Thus if (13.16) holds, then among other things

$$T\bar{u}_T^2 \xrightarrow{d} \sigma^2\chi^2(1).$$

These results may appear straightforward, and we would be surprised if anything else were to happen. It is nonetheless important that rigorous proofs are known, so that they can be applied with confidence in the context of asymptotic distribution theory. As a theory dealing in large numbers, asymptotics has a number of surprising and paradoxical features that can deceive the unwary. Happily, these should not arise in the straightforward applications treated here.

13.4 Asymptotic Normality

Consider the numerator in (13.10), after suitable normalization so that its variance does not vanish as T increases.

$$\frac{1}{\sqrt{T}}\sum_{t=1}^{T}(x_t - \bar{x})u_t = \frac{1}{\sqrt{T}}\sum_{t=1}^{T} x_t u_t - \bar{x}\frac{1}{\sqrt{T}}\sum_{t=1}^{T} u_t. \tag{13.17}$$

To show that this sequence has a Gaussian limit in distribution, it is necessary to consider the two normalized sums on the right-hand side. The presence of $\bar{x}$ in the formula is a complicating factor here, since this is a random variable depending on the complete sample, although converging in probability to a constant. What has to be shown, it turns out, is that the *joint* distribution of the two normalized sums converges to the bivariate Gaussian limit. The central limit theorem discussed in Section 13.3 only concerned scalar processes. Multivariate convergence in distribution does not just specify the marginal distributions of the two terms but requires that their interactions have Gaussian characteristics in the limit, specifically that their covariance completely defines the relationship between them. This fact cannot be inferred from the scalar convergences alone.

What is needed here is a technical result known as the *Cramér-Wold theorem*, sometimes called in the literature the "Cramér-Wold device". It is sufficient for multivariate convergence in distribution if every linear combination of the vector elements with fixed weights converges in distribution to the required scalar limit. In the present case, this means that for the convergence of the vector

$$\begin{bmatrix} \frac{1}{\sqrt{T}}\sum_{t=1}^{T} x_t u_t \\ \frac{1}{\sqrt{T}}\sum_{t=1}^{T} u_t \end{bmatrix}$$

to the bivariate normal, for every fixed finite pair of weights (α_1, α_2), with at least one different from zero, the combination

$$\alpha_1 \frac{1}{\sqrt{T}} \sum_{t=1}^{T} x_t u_t + \alpha_2 \frac{1}{\sqrt{T}} \sum_{t=1}^{T} u_t = \frac{1}{\sqrt{T}} \sum_{t=1}^{T} (\alpha_1 x_t u_t + \alpha_2 u_t) \tag{13.18}$$

must satisfy the CLT.

For simplicity, assume that both u_t and x_t are independently and identically distributed. This is certainly a sufficient condition for the CLT to operate. Under these assumptions, it is only necessary to determine the mean and variance of the sequence coordinates of (13.18), which are also the mean and variance of the normalized sum. Suppose that $\mathrm{E}(x_t) = \mu_x$ and $\mathrm{E}(x_t^2) = \sigma_x^2 + \mu_x^2$, and also that $\mathrm{E}(u_t) = 0$ and $\mathrm{E}(u_t^2) = \sigma_u^2$.[4] Then, under assumptions RRM(ii) and RRM(iii), apply the LIE to obtain

$$\begin{aligned} \mathrm{E}(x_t u_t) &= \mathrm{E}[x_t \mathrm{E}(u_t | x_t)] \\ &= \mathrm{E}[x_t \times 0 \text{ w.p.1}] \\ &= 0, \\ \mathrm{E}(x_t^2 u_t^2) &= \mathrm{E}[x_t^2 \mathrm{E}(u_t^2 | x_t)] \\ &= \mathrm{E}[x_t^2 \sigma_u^2 \text{ w.p.1}] \\ &= (\sigma_x^2 + \mu_x^2)\sigma_u^2, \end{aligned}$$

and also the covariance of the terms

$$\begin{aligned} \mathrm{E}(x_t u_t^2) &= \mathrm{E}[x_t \mathrm{E}(u_t^2 | x_t)] \\ &= \mu_x \sigma_u^2. \end{aligned}$$

It follows directly that

$$\mathrm{E}(\alpha_1 x_t u_t + \alpha_2 u_t) = 0$$

and

$$\begin{aligned} &\mathrm{E}((\alpha_1 x_t u_t + \alpha_2 u_t)^2) \\ &= (\alpha_1^2(\sigma_x^2 + \mu_x^2) + \alpha_2^2 + 2\alpha_1\alpha_2\mu_x)\sigma_u^2 \\ &< \infty. \end{aligned}$$

Given the assumptions, these arguments establish the joint CLT. It remains to consider the actual weighted combination of the two terms in (13.17) with respective weights 1 and $-\bar{x}$. Cramér's theorem allows the second of these weights to be replaced by $-\mu_x$

4 The disturbance variance is here labelled with a subscript u to distinguish it from the variance of x.

in the limit. Assigning these values to α_1 and α_2 yields $\sigma_x^2\sigma_u^2$ as the limiting variance of (13.17), and hence

$$\frac{1}{\sqrt{T}}\sum_{t=1}^{T}(x_t - \bar{x})u_t \xrightarrow{d} \mathrm{N}(0, \sigma_x^2\sigma_u^2). \tag{13.19}$$

Now consider the formula in (13.10). To get the limit result, multiply the ratio by $\sqrt{T}$ to obtain

$$\sqrt{T}(\hat{\beta} - \beta) = \frac{\frac{1}{\sqrt{T}}\sum_{t=1}^{T}(x_t - \bar{x})u_t}{\frac{1}{T}\sum_{t=1}^{T}(x_t - \bar{x})^2} \tag{13.20}$$

The denominator in (13.20) converges in probability to σ_x^2 by the law of large numbers and the Slutsky theorem, as in (13.13), and the limiting variance of the ratio is

$$\frac{\sigma_x^2\sigma_u^2}{(\sigma_x^2)^2} = \frac{\sigma_u^2}{\sigma_x^2}.$$

By (13.19) and Cramér's theorem, the final conclusion is

$$\sqrt{T}(\hat{\beta} - \beta) \xrightarrow{d} \mathrm{N}\left(0, \frac{\sigma_u^2}{\sigma_x^2}\right). \tag{13.21}$$

The practical interpretation of this limit result is that in a sample of finite size T that is "large enough", $\hat{\beta}$ is approximately normally distributed, with mean β and variance $\sigma_u^2/(T\sigma_x^2)$. The normalized variance σ_u^2/σ_x^2 is consistently estimated by $Ts_{\hat{\beta}}^2$ where

$$s_{\hat{\beta}}^2 = \frac{s^2}{\sum_{t=1}^{T}(x_t - \bar{x})^2},$$

with s^2 the usual residual variance estimator as in (7.18). An approximate confidence interval for β can therefore be constructed as

$$\Pr(\hat{\beta} - 1.96s_{\hat{\beta}} \le \beta \le \hat{\beta} + 1.96s_{\hat{\beta}}) \approx 0.95,$$

where the approximation is better as T is larger. Similarly, the usual t-ratio $\hat{\beta}/s_{\hat{\beta}}$ can be compared with the normal tabulation to test the null hypothesis $\mathrm{H}_0 : \beta = 0$.

What has been done, in the event, is to set up a new justification for the usual inference procedures in least squares. The key novelty is that there is no assumption of normality of the observations. The normal distribution is conjured out of the averaging procedures of the estimator using the central limit theorem. In developing these results, the RRM assumption of serial independence of the observations has been retained, but this was really for simplicity and tidiness. There are all kinds of directions in which these assumptions can be relaxed. However, the details are often technical and involve advanced methods from probability theory, taking us beyond the scope of this book. Chapters 6 and 7 of *Econometric Theory* are recommended readings for those wishing to know more.

There is no simple answer to the question "How large is large?" in respect of T because, as pointed out in Section 13.3, it all depends on the actual distribution of the observations. If this is symmetric and higher moments exist, the convergence can be very fast. Nothing is guaranteed, but most practitioners are pretty happy using the classical inference procedures when T is at least 30, and very happy when T is bigger than 100. Indeed, many practitioners don't worry about the sample size at all but just happily assume the Gaussian classical model applies regardless, as they have often been taught. These careless people have their bacon saved by the magic of asymptotic theory.

13.5 Multiple Regression

The results of Sections 13.2 and 13.4 are a case of the general regression model

$$\boldsymbol{y} = \boldsymbol{X\beta} + \boldsymbol{u},$$

and extending to the general case is largely a question of suitable notation. Take assumptions RRM(i)–(iii), which strictly should now be prefaced by the statement "For each $T \geq k$", and append the following:

Assumption RRM (iv) The matrix

$$\text{plim}\ \frac{1}{T}\boldsymbol{X}'\boldsymbol{X} = \boldsymbol{M}_{XX} \tag{13.22}$$

exists, and is finite and positive definite.

This asserts that the law of large numbers holds for each element of the matrix, means of squares and means of products. It certainly holds when successive observations are random and independently drawn with fixed and finite variances. 'Fixed regressors', such as the intercept, are accommodated as explained on page 191. The positive definiteness requirement serves to rule out anomalous cases such as (13.14), while the finiteness requirement rules out a different kind of dependence of the data on position in the sample, such as $x_t = t$. The latter case represents a *time trend*, when the data have a time dimension. Such things arise in econometric modelling and suffice it to say that there are ways of dealing with them, but these will not be considered further here. Chapter 7.2 of *Econometric Theory* gives a full account. As emphasized previously, some serial dependence in the regressors may be permissible, but in this case assumptions about their dynamic generation processes would have to be introduced.

Under assumptions RRM(i)–(iv),

$$\text{plim}\ \frac{1}{T}\boldsymbol{X}'\boldsymbol{u} = \boldsymbol{0} \tag{13.23}$$

follows by extending the analysis of Section 13.2. The general consistency demonstration for least squares then proceeds as follows:

$$\begin{aligned}
\text{plim}\ \hat{\boldsymbol{\beta}} &= \text{plim}\ (\boldsymbol{X}'\boldsymbol{X})^{-1}\boldsymbol{X}'\boldsymbol{y} \\
&= \boldsymbol{\beta} + \text{plim}\ (\boldsymbol{X}'\boldsymbol{X})^{-1}\boldsymbol{X}'\boldsymbol{u} \\
&= \boldsymbol{\beta} + \text{plim}\ \left(\frac{\boldsymbol{X}'\boldsymbol{X}}{T}\right)^{-1}\frac{\boldsymbol{X}'\boldsymbol{u}}{T} \\
&= \boldsymbol{\beta} + \left(\text{plim}\ \frac{\boldsymbol{X}'\boldsymbol{X}}{T}\right)^{-1}\text{plim}\ \frac{\boldsymbol{X}'\boldsymbol{u}}{T} \\
&= \boldsymbol{\beta} + \boldsymbol{M}_{XX}^{-1}.\boldsymbol{0} \\
&= \boldsymbol{\beta}.
\end{aligned}$$

Note the application of the Slutsky theorem to evaluate the probability limit of the inverse matrix. The final step invokes assumptions RRM to insert (13.22) and (13.23) and deliver the final result. While under assumptions RRM least squares is unbiased in any finite sample, this is not a necessary condition for (13.23) to hold. There exist models, usually involving some form of dependent sampling, in which least squares is biased, but the bias is "of small order in T" so it does not contradict (13.23). These are cases where the sequence of expected values depends on T but converges to a limit, the asymptotic expectation.

Asymptotic normality of the estimator entails the multivariate convergence in distribution of the vector $\boldsymbol{X}'\boldsymbol{u}/\sqrt{T}$. Under assumptions RRM, the mean vector is zero for every T, and the variance matrix is

$$\begin{aligned}\frac{\mathrm{E}(\boldsymbol{X}'\boldsymbol{u}\boldsymbol{u}'\boldsymbol{X})}{T} &= \frac{\mathrm{E}[\boldsymbol{X}'\mathrm{E}(\boldsymbol{u}\boldsymbol{u}'|\boldsymbol{X})\boldsymbol{X}]}{T} \\ &= \sigma^2\mathrm{E}\left(\frac{\boldsymbol{X}'\boldsymbol{X}}{T}\right) \\ &\to \sigma^2\boldsymbol{M}_{XX}\end{aligned}$$

by the law of large numbers, under (13.22). Similarly to (13.18), it is required to show that

$$\frac{\boldsymbol{\alpha}'\boldsymbol{X}'\boldsymbol{u}}{\sqrt{T}} \xrightarrow{d} \mathrm{N}(\boldsymbol{0}, \sigma^2\boldsymbol{\alpha}'\boldsymbol{M}_{XX}\boldsymbol{\alpha})$$

for every k-vector $\boldsymbol{\alpha} \neq \boldsymbol{0}$, which is sufficient according to the Cramér-Wold theorem for

$$\frac{\boldsymbol{X}'\boldsymbol{u}}{\sqrt{T}} \xrightarrow{d} \mathrm{N}(\boldsymbol{0}, \sigma^2\boldsymbol{M}_{XX}). \tag{13.24}$$

It then follows by the multivariate generalization of the Cramér theorem that

$$\begin{aligned}\sqrt{T}(\hat{\boldsymbol{\beta}} - \boldsymbol{\beta}) &= \left(\frac{\boldsymbol{X}'\boldsymbol{X}}{T}\right)^{-1}\frac{\boldsymbol{X}'\boldsymbol{u}}{\sqrt{T}} \\ &\xrightarrow{d} \mathrm{N}(\boldsymbol{0}, \boldsymbol{V})\end{aligned} \tag{13.25}$$

where

$$\begin{aligned}\boldsymbol{V} &= \boldsymbol{M}_{XX}^{-1}(\sigma^2\boldsymbol{M}_{XX})\boldsymbol{M}_{XX}^{-1} \\ &= \sigma^2\boldsymbol{M}_{XX}^{-1}.\end{aligned}$$

The interpretation of this result is that $\hat{\boldsymbol{\beta}}$ is *approximately* normally distributed with mean $\boldsymbol{\beta}$ and variance matrix $\sigma^2(T\boldsymbol{M}_{XX})^{-1}$, and a consistent estimator of this matrix is given by the usual OLS formula, $\hat{\boldsymbol{V}} = s^2(\boldsymbol{X}'\boldsymbol{X})^{-1}$.

It is of interest to compare the general result with the special case of (13.21). Things appear simpler here, in that the convergence in (13.24) does not require invocation of Cramér's theorem. The role of the law of large numbers in (13.25) is confined, in combination with the Slutsky theorem, to the elements of the matrix inverse. By contrast, the ratio in (13.10) is an instance of the partitioned regression formula (11.6) and illustrates how (13.25) works on an element-by-element basis.

In practice, inference procedures based on asymptotic criteria are little different from exact inference. Regression 't statistics' may not be Student's t_{T-k} distributed under the null hypothesis, but they are asymptotically $N(0, 1)$ distributed. When $T - k$ is large, which in practice means anything over around 30, the difference in the critical values is negligible, so it is really unimportant which tabulation is used. If the sample is small enough that the difference is sufficient to change the outcome of a test, then strictly neither critical value can be relied on, but if there is a possibility that the disturbances are close to being normal, the 'pseudo-exact' criteria appear the safer bet.

In multiple restriction tests, $F(r, T - k)$ random variables converge in distribution to $\chi^2(r)/r$. The statistic from (10.20) may be rewritten as

$$W_T = \frac{\left(\sqrt{T}(\boldsymbol{R}\hat{\boldsymbol{\beta}} - \boldsymbol{c})\right)' \left[\boldsymbol{R}\left(\frac{\boldsymbol{X}'\boldsymbol{X}}{T}\right)^{-1}\boldsymbol{R}'\right]^{-1} \left(\sqrt{T}(\boldsymbol{R}\hat{\boldsymbol{\beta}} - \boldsymbol{c})\right)}{rs^2}$$

$$\underset{asy}{\sim} \frac{\left(\sqrt{T}(\boldsymbol{R}\hat{\boldsymbol{\beta}} - \boldsymbol{c})\right)' [\boldsymbol{R}\boldsymbol{M}_{XX}^{-1}\boldsymbol{R}']^{-1} \left(\sqrt{T}(\boldsymbol{R}\hat{\boldsymbol{\beta}} - \boldsymbol{c})\right)}{r\sigma^2}$$

where '$\underset{asy}{\sim}$' is conventional shorthand for "has the same asymptotic distribution as", noting that

$$s^2 \xrightarrow{pr} \sigma^2.$$

Under the null hypothesis, this is a quadratic form in an asymptotically normal vector, the normalized restrictions. The central limit theorem, the continuous mapping theorem, and the Cramér theorem together supply the result that

$$W_T \xrightarrow{d} \frac{\chi^2(r)}{r}.$$

As with the case of t tests, the question of whether to consult the F table or the chi-squared table to obtain a critical value has no hard and fast answer. It will rarely yield a different outcome except in samples too small for asymptotics to be reliable, but in favour of the chi-squared approach is that the 5% critical values are not too hard to remember. For $r = 1, 2, 3$, and 4, these are respectively 3.84, 5.99, 7.81, and 9.48. The one thing not to forget, if referring to the chi-squared table, is to multiply W_T by r before doing the comparison.

13.6 Exercises

1 Are the following statements true or false?

(a) The probability limit of a sequence of ratios is equal to the ratio of the probability limits of the respective sequences, when these exist and the limit of the denominator is nonzero.

(b) A sequence of ratios is distributed in the limit like the ratio of the limits in distribution of the respective sequences, where these exist and the denominator is positive with probability 1.

(c) In most cases, the normalized sum of 50 or more independent observations with finite variance has the normal distribution.

(d) Consistency of an estimator can fail either by the sequence converging to the wrong limit or by not converging at all.
(e) The variance of a sum of T independent and identically distributed random variables normalized by $1/\sqrt{T}$ is equal to the variance of the individual terms.
(f) The asymptotic expectation of a statistic matches the probability limit if and only if the law of large numbers holds.
(g) Asymptotic confidence intervals are the same as exact finite sample confidence intervals under the usual assumptions.

2 If $x_1, x_2, \dots, x_T$ is a random sample from a distribution with mean μ and variance σ^2 and $\bar{x}_T = T^{-1} \sum_{t=1}^{T} x_t$, show that
(a) $\mathrm{E}(\bar{x}_T) = \mu$
(b) $\mathrm{Var}(\bar{x}_T) = \sigma^2/T$
(c) $\operatorname{plim} \bar{x}_T = \mu$

3 Show that a $F(m, n)$-distributed random variable converges in distribution to $\chi^2(m)/m$ as $n \to \infty$.

4 Consider a random sequence $X_1, X_2, \dots, X_N, \dots$. generated by the rule

$$X_N = N \text{ with probability } 1/N$$

$$X_N = 0 \text{ with probability } 1 - 1/N.$$

(a) What is the expected value of X_N?
(b) What is the variance of X_N?
(c) What is the probability limit of X_N as $N \to \infty$?
(d) Comment.

5 Consider the model

$$\boldsymbol{y} = \boldsymbol{X\beta} + \boldsymbol{u},$$

where $\boldsymbol{y}$ is $T \times 1$, $\boldsymbol{\beta}$ is a $k \times 1$ vector of parameters, and $\boldsymbol{X}$ $(T \times k)$ is a stochastic matrix having full column rank with probability 1; $\mathrm{E}(\boldsymbol{u}|\boldsymbol{X}) = \boldsymbol{0}$ w.p. 1 and $\mathrm{E}(\boldsymbol{uu}'|\boldsymbol{X}) = \sigma^2 \boldsymbol{I}_T$ w.p. 1; and $\operatorname{plim} \frac{1}{T}\boldsymbol{X}'\boldsymbol{X} = \boldsymbol{Q}$ $(k \times k)$ is a finite positive definite matrix. Let $\hat{\boldsymbol{\beta}}$ be the OLS estimator and $\hat{\boldsymbol{u}} = \boldsymbol{y} - \boldsymbol{X}\hat{\boldsymbol{\beta}}$ the vector of residuals from the above regression.
(a) Show that $\hat{\boldsymbol{\beta}}$ is a consistent estimator for $\boldsymbol{\beta}$.
(b) Obtain the limiting distribution of $\sqrt{T}(\hat{\boldsymbol{\beta}} - \boldsymbol{\beta})$, stating clearly any additional assumptions or standard results you employ.
(c) Let $s^2 = \dfrac{\hat{\boldsymbol{u}}'\hat{\boldsymbol{u}}}{T-k}$ be the estimated disturbance variance. Show that s^2 is a consistent estimator of σ^2.

6 Consider a regression model

$$y_t = \boldsymbol{x}_t'\boldsymbol{\beta} + u_t \quad t = 1, \dots, T$$

where u_t is identically and independently distributed with mean 0 and variance σ^2, and $\boldsymbol{x}_t = (1\ r_t)$ where $r_t = t$ modulo 5. This means that r_t is the remainder after dividing t by 5, so it takes the values 1, 2, 3, 4, and 0 in sequence.

(a) Show, by citing the relevant results from asymptotic theory, that the regression of y_t on $\boldsymbol{x}_t$, with estimator $\hat{\boldsymbol{\beta}}$, is consistent for $\boldsymbol{\beta}$.
(b) Show, similarly, that $\sqrt{T}(\hat{\boldsymbol{\beta}} - \boldsymbol{\beta})$ is asymptotically normally distributed.
(c) Find the asymptotic variance of $\hat{\boldsymbol{\beta}}$.

7 Consider a regression model

$$y_t = \boldsymbol{x}_t'\boldsymbol{\beta} + u_t \quad t = 1, \dots, T$$

where u_t is identically and independently distributed with mean 0 and variance σ^2 and $\boldsymbol{x}_t$ (2×1) is the vector with elements 1 and t.
(a) Does the matrix $T^{-1}\sum \boldsymbol{x}_t\boldsymbol{x}_t'$ converge to a finite limit?
(b) Is the least squares estimator $\hat{\boldsymbol{\beta}}$ a consistent estimator of $\boldsymbol{\beta}$?
(c) Construct a diagonal matrix $\boldsymbol{K}_T$, depending on T, such that $\boldsymbol{K}_T(\hat{\boldsymbol{\beta}} - \boldsymbol{\beta})$ has a non-degenerate distribution with finite variance as $T \to \infty$.
(d) Is this limiting distribution normal? (Intelligent guess called for.)
Hint: two well-known identities are

$$\sum_{t=1}^{T} t = \frac{T(T+1)}{2}, \quad \sum_{t=1}^{T} t^2 = \frac{T(T+1)(2T+1)}{6}.$$

14

Asymptotic Estimation Theory

14.1 Large Sample Efficiency

The preceding chapter introduced the idea of estimators with desirable properties in large samples. These are estimators that are *consistent* and *asymptotically normal*, henceforth abbreviated to CAN. Least squares is a member of the CAN class under standard assumptions, and naturally enough, this raises the question of efficiency. An estimator is said to be *asymptotically efficient* in the CAN class if for any other CAN estimator, the difference of the asymptotic variance matrices is positive semidefinite. The term *asymptotic variance* here refers to a matrix such as $\boldsymbol{V}$ in (13.25), relating to the normalized error-of-estimate and hence well defined in the limit.

The comparison parallels that of the Gauss-Markov theorem in Sections 8.2 and 12.5 except that in large samples the conditions for fixed and random regressors become in effect unified. For the regression model

$$\boldsymbol{y} = \boldsymbol{X}\boldsymbol{\beta} + \boldsymbol{u}, \tag{14.1}$$

let the linear CAN class be defined by

$$\check{\boldsymbol{\beta}} = \boldsymbol{L}\boldsymbol{y} \tag{14.2}$$

where $\boldsymbol{L}$ is a $k \times T$ random matrix and the following assumptions hold:

Assumptions CANR

(i) $\text{plim}\ \boldsymbol{L}\boldsymbol{u} = \boldsymbol{0}$.
(ii) $\text{plim}\ \boldsymbol{L}\boldsymbol{X} = \boldsymbol{I}_k$.
(iii) $\text{plim}\ T\boldsymbol{L}\boldsymbol{L}' = \boldsymbol{M}_{LL}$, finite and positive definite.
(iv) $\sqrt{T}\boldsymbol{L}\boldsymbol{u} \xrightarrow{d} \text{N}(\boldsymbol{0}, \sigma^2\boldsymbol{M}_{LL})$.

These are comparatively 'high-level' assumptions, specifying required properties but not conditions sufficient to ensure those properties. Assumptions RRME of Section 12.5 are sufficient if these hold for every $T \geq k$, but there are other ways to impose them, not entailing independent sampling. However, given that appeal is being made to the law of large numbers, a restriction implied by CANR(iv) is

$$\text{E}(u_t^2\boldsymbol{l}_t\boldsymbol{l}_t') = \sigma^2\text{E}(\boldsymbol{l}_t\boldsymbol{l}_t'),$$

with $\boldsymbol{l}_t$ denoting the tth column of $\boldsymbol{L}$. This uncorrelatedness condition can follow from assumption RRME(iii) and variants thereof.

An Introduction to Econometric Theory, First Edition. James Davidson.

Companion website: www.wiley.com/go/davidson/introecmettheory

Consistency of the estimator holds under assumptions CANR(i) and CANR(ii), with

$$\begin{aligned}\text{plim } \check{\boldsymbol{\beta}} &= \text{plim } \boldsymbol{LX\beta} + \text{plim } \boldsymbol{Lu} \\ &= \boldsymbol{\beta}.\end{aligned}$$

If least squares is a member of the class, with $\boldsymbol{L} = (\boldsymbol{X}'\boldsymbol{X})^{-1}\boldsymbol{X}'$ and satisfying assumption CANR(i) in particular, then defining as before

$$\boldsymbol{D} = \boldsymbol{L} - (\boldsymbol{X}'\boldsymbol{X})^{-1}\boldsymbol{X}',$$

assumption CANR(ii) implies that

$$\text{plim } \boldsymbol{DX} = \boldsymbol{0}. \tag{14.3}$$

It follows that

$$\begin{aligned}\boldsymbol{M}_{LL} &= \text{plim } T((\boldsymbol{X}'\boldsymbol{X})^{-1}\boldsymbol{X}' + \boldsymbol{D})(\boldsymbol{X}(\boldsymbol{X}'\boldsymbol{X})^{-1} + \boldsymbol{D}') \\ &= \boldsymbol{M}_{XX}^{-1} + \text{plim } T\boldsymbol{DD}'.\end{aligned}$$

The conclusion follows directly:

Proposition: Least squares is asymptotically efficient in the linear CAN class.

14.2 Instrumental Variables

This technique of analysis raises a further interesting possibility, that of dealing with cases in which least squares estimation of $\boldsymbol{\beta}$ is not CAN. The assumption that has been carried throughout this book is of orthogonality between regressors and disturbance, and it was noted in Section 12.3 how this assumption leads to the characterization of the coefficients of model (14.1) having representation (12.8). In the exact inference framework, no theory exists to deal with any other case, but now it is possible to explore the consequences of the condition

$$\text{plim } \frac{1}{T}\boldsymbol{X}'\boldsymbol{u} \neq \boldsymbol{0}. \tag{14.4}$$

There are a number of important scenarios in which orthogonality could fail. In a system of simultaneous equations, two or more variables in an equation may be jointly determined and hence correlated with the shocks driving the system. Omission of unobserved variables may also produce bias in least squares as in (12.21) when the omissions are correlated with the included regressors. Measurement errors in the explanatory variables are another problematic case. In such cases, least squares does not belong to the CAN class so the issue of its efficiency does not arise. The question is whether CAN alternatives exist.

A class of estimators that it may be fruitful to consider have the form (14.2), where

$$\boldsymbol{L} = \boldsymbol{P}_T\boldsymbol{W}'$$

with $\boldsymbol{P}_T$ a matrix of dimension $k \times m$ and $\boldsymbol{W}$ a matrix of variables, of dimension $T \times m$ for $m \geq k$. Least squares is the case where $\boldsymbol{P}_T = (\boldsymbol{X}'\boldsymbol{X})^{-1}$ and $\boldsymbol{W} = \boldsymbol{X}$, but under condition (14.4), a CAN estimator will need to specify a different set of observed variables satisfying

$$\text{plim } \frac{1}{T}\boldsymbol{W}'\boldsymbol{u} = \boldsymbol{0}. \tag{14.5}$$

These are commonly called *instrumental variables*. The instrumental variables (IV) estimator is denoted

$$\tilde{\boldsymbol{\beta}} = \boldsymbol{P}_T \boldsymbol{W}' \boldsymbol{y}. \tag{14.6}$$

Assumption CANR(i) is satisfied if (14.5) holds together with

$$\text{plim } T\boldsymbol{P}_T = \boldsymbol{P}$$

where $\boldsymbol{P}$ is a finite matrix of rank k, generally a function of population moments of the variables. Defining

$$\boldsymbol{M}_{WX} = \text{plim } \frac{\boldsymbol{W}'\boldsymbol{X}}{T}, \tag{14.7}$$

assumption CANR(ii) requires that

$$\begin{aligned} \text{plim } \boldsymbol{P}_T \boldsymbol{W}'\boldsymbol{X} &= \boldsymbol{P}\boldsymbol{M}_{WX} \\ &= \boldsymbol{I}_k, \end{aligned} \tag{14.8}$$

which in the case $m = k$ makes $\boldsymbol{P}_T = (\boldsymbol{W}'\boldsymbol{X})^{-1}$ the only realistic choice. However, if $m > k$, a wider range of possibilities is available. Assumptions CANR(iii) and CANR(iv) define the asymptotic covariance matrix of the estimator to have the form

$$\boldsymbol{V}_{\tilde{\beta}} = \sigma^2 \boldsymbol{P}\boldsymbol{M}_{WW}\boldsymbol{P}'$$

where

$$\boldsymbol{M}_{WW} = \text{plim } \frac{\boldsymbol{W}'\boldsymbol{W}}{T}$$

is a finite positive definite matrix, requiring that the columns of $\boldsymbol{W}$ be linearly independent in the limit. Assumptions CANR(i) and (ii) imply that $\boldsymbol{\beta}$ has the representation

$$\boldsymbol{\beta} = \boldsymbol{P}\text{E}(\boldsymbol{w}_t y_t). \tag{14.9}$$

IV is an example of a method of moments estimator in which the theoretical quantities in (14.9) are replaced by their sample counterparts to give (14.6).

Consistency of the method of moments generally follows from the conditions for the law of large numbers being satisfied and an application of Slutsky's theorem. The key idea of IV is that an orthogonality exists between the instruments and the disturbance that can be exploited to identify the linear relationship. In least squares the regressors play the role of instruments, being the efficient choice when orthogonality holds. Otherwise, valid instruments are typically 'exogenous' variables, generated outside the system being modelled, while at the same time having some relation with the explanatory variables.

Assumptions CANR(i) and CANR(ii) are the essential conditions to be jointly satisfied. The latter condition needs the existence of correlations between instruments and regressors as surely as the absence of such correlations with the disturbances. The failure of this condition is called *underidentification*. The matrix $\boldsymbol{M}_{WX}$ must have rank k, which calls for a minimum of k linearly independent instruments. When the rank condition is satisfied, the case $m = k$ is called *just-identification*, while $m > k$ is the case of *overidentification*. The condition that $\boldsymbol{W}$ has at least k columns is known as the 'order condition for identification', necessary but of course not sufficient. The rank condition requires sufficient correlations between instruments and explanatory variables to exist in the limit.

In the overidentified case, unlike the just-identified case, there is a choice of $\boldsymbol{P}_T$. Thinking of $\boldsymbol{W}\boldsymbol{P}_T'$ $(T \times k)$ as a matrix whose columns are linear combinations of the instruments, the issue is the efficient use of the information contained in them. In other words, $\boldsymbol{P}$ should be chosen to minimize the asymptotic covariance matrix $\sigma^2 \boldsymbol{P}\boldsymbol{M}_{WW}\boldsymbol{P}'$, subject to (14.8). Letting $\boldsymbol{M}_{XW} = \boldsymbol{M}_{WX}'$ for convenience of notation, the solution to this problem is to set $\boldsymbol{P}$ equal to

$$\boldsymbol{P}^* = (\boldsymbol{M}_{XW}\boldsymbol{M}_{WW}^{-1}\boldsymbol{M}_{WX})^{-1}\boldsymbol{M}_{XW}\boldsymbol{M}_{WW}^{-1}. \tag{14.10}$$

Note that $\boldsymbol{P}^*\boldsymbol{M}_{WX} = \boldsymbol{I}_k$, as in (14.8). To show this to be the efficient case, define

$$\boldsymbol{H} = \boldsymbol{P}^* - \boldsymbol{P}.$$

$\boldsymbol{P}\boldsymbol{M}_{WX} = \boldsymbol{I}_k$ also holds, as is required by CANR(ii), and hence

$$\boldsymbol{H}\boldsymbol{M}_{WX} = \boldsymbol{0}. \tag{14.11}$$

This is the condition analogous to (14.3) above. Since (14.10) and (14.11) imply that

$$\begin{aligned}\boldsymbol{H}\boldsymbol{M}_{WW}\boldsymbol{P}^{*\prime} &= \boldsymbol{H}\boldsymbol{M}_{WX}(\boldsymbol{M}_{XW}\boldsymbol{M}_{WW}^{-1}\boldsymbol{M}_{WX})^{-1} \\ &= \boldsymbol{0},\end{aligned}$$

it follows directly that

$$\begin{aligned}\boldsymbol{P}\boldsymbol{M}_{WW}\boldsymbol{P}' &= (\boldsymbol{P}^* - \boldsymbol{H})\boldsymbol{M}_{WW}(\boldsymbol{P}^* - \boldsymbol{H})' \\ &= \boldsymbol{P}^*\boldsymbol{M}_{WW}\boldsymbol{P}^{*\prime} + \boldsymbol{H}\boldsymbol{M}_{WW}\boldsymbol{H}',\end{aligned}$$

where $\boldsymbol{H}\boldsymbol{M}_{WW}\boldsymbol{H}'$ is at least positive semidefinite by Property 4 of Section 4.3.

The estimator based on instruments $\boldsymbol{W}$ that has $\sigma^2\boldsymbol{P}^*\boldsymbol{M}_{WW}\boldsymbol{P}^{*\prime}$ for its asymptotic variance matrix, and hence is the asymptotically efficient member of the CAN class, is

$$\tilde{\boldsymbol{\beta}} = (\boldsymbol{X}'\boldsymbol{W}(\boldsymbol{W}'\boldsymbol{W})^{-1}\boldsymbol{W}'\boldsymbol{X})^{-1}\boldsymbol{X}'\boldsymbol{W}(\boldsymbol{W}'\boldsymbol{W})^{-1}\boldsymbol{W}'\boldsymbol{y}. \tag{14.12}$$

This is the well-known estimator often referred to as *two-stage least squares.* A convenient method of computation, if no dedicated software is available, is to regress the columns of $\boldsymbol{X}$ unrestrictedly onto $\boldsymbol{W}$, and so obtain at the first stage the least squares predictions

$$\hat{\boldsymbol{X}} = \boldsymbol{W}(\boldsymbol{W}'\boldsymbol{W})^{-1}\boldsymbol{W}'\boldsymbol{X}.$$

The second stage is to regress $\boldsymbol{y}$ onto $\hat{\boldsymbol{X}}$, noting that

$$\tilde{\boldsymbol{\beta}} = (\hat{\boldsymbol{X}}'\hat{\boldsymbol{X}})^{-1}\hat{\boldsymbol{X}}'\boldsymbol{y}$$

is identical to (14.12), thanks to the symmetry and idempotency of the projection matrix $\boldsymbol{W}(\boldsymbol{W}'\boldsymbol{W})^{-1}\boldsymbol{W}'$. In the just-identified case when $\boldsymbol{W}'\boldsymbol{X}$ is square and invertible, the formula reduces conveniently to

$$\tilde{\boldsymbol{\beta}} = (\boldsymbol{W}'\boldsymbol{X})^{-1}\boldsymbol{W}'\boldsymbol{y}.$$

14.3 Maximum Likelihood

Until now this book has dealt exclusively with linear models to explain data that we typically conceive as continuously distributed. No clues have been offered about cases not falling into this category. The method of maximum likelihood (or ML) provides a universal estimation technique that in principle can be applied to any data distribution whatever.

Here are some examples that lie at some remove from the linear regression paradigm. Let X be a discrete random variable, and consider the probability of the event "$X = x$" where x is a postulated outcome. Suppose that

$$\Pr(X = x) = p(x, \theta),$$

where θ is a parameter on which the probability depends and that the form of the function $p(x, \cdot)$ is known while θ is unknown. Further suppose that in N independent draws from this distribution, the outcomes are $x_1, x_2, \ldots, x_N$. Using the multiplicative rule for independent events, the probability of this sample being drawn is

$$\Pr(x_1, \ldots, x_N) = p(x_1, \theta) \times p(x_2, \theta) \times \cdots \times p(x_N, \theta).$$

When this function is treated as a function of θ for fixed $x_1, \ldots, x_N$, it is known as the *likelihood function* of the sample. It is natural to assume the observed sample is 'likely' to have arisen, since it *did* arise. Therefore an appealing way to estimate θ is by the value that makes the likelihood of the sample as large as possible.

Consider tossing a bent coin, where the unknown parameter in question is the probability of heads. Write Pr(heads) $= p$, where in this case $\theta = p$ and so Pr(tails) $= 1 - p$. Suppose a sample of N tosses yields N_1 heads and $N - N_1$ tails. Since the tosses are independent, the order in which they arise is irrelevant, and the probability of drawing the sample is

$$\Pr(x_1, \ldots, x_N) = p^{N_1}(1-p)^{N-N_1}.$$

If $N_1 = N$, this probability is maximized by setting $p = 1$, and if $N_1 = 0$, by putting $p = 0$. Otherwise, assume $0 < p < 1$, and to find the maximizing value of p, the essential trick is to take logarithms, which conveniently converts a product of terms into a more tractable sum of terms. Define the *log-likelihood function* to be

$$\begin{aligned} L(p) &= \log(p^{N_1}(1-p)^{N-N_1}) \\ &= N_1 \log p + (N - N_1)\log(1-p). \end{aligned}$$

The logarithm is a monotonic transformation, which means that the maximum of the transformed function is at the same point as that of the original function. To find it is a routine application of calculus, of which Appendix C provides the details. The first derivative is

$$\frac{\mathrm{d}L}{\mathrm{d}p} = \frac{N_1}{p} - \frac{N - N_1}{1-p}.$$

Equating this expression to zero to obtain the first-order condition for a stationary point yields the solution

$$\hat{p} = \frac{N_1}{N}.$$

The first-order condition corresponds to a maximum if the second derivative is negative and

$$\frac{\mathrm{d}^2L}{\mathrm{d}p^2} = -\frac{N_1}{p^2} - \frac{N - N_1}{(1-p)^2}$$

is negative for $0 < p < 1$. The maximum likelihood estimator of the probability of heads is the proportion of heads arising in the sample of tosses. Of course, it would be hard to conceive of any other plausible result.

Next consider a binomial(n, p) distribution where n is given but p is unknown. The object is to estimate p given a sample of N independent drawings, $x_1, \dots, x_N$, each being drawn from the set of $n + 1$ possible discrete values, the integers $0, 1, \dots, n$. By (5.21), the probability of the sample is

$$\Pr(x_1, \dots, x_N) = \prod_{j=1}^{N} \binom{n}{x_j} p^{x_j}(1-p)^{(n-x_j)},$$

where the symbol Π ('capital pi') denotes the N-fold product of terms. Unless $x_j = 0$ for every j or $x_j = n$ for every j, in which cases the likelihood maxima are $p = 0$ and $p = 1$, respectively, it is reasonable to impose $0 < p < 1$. The log-likelihood function is then

$$L(p) = \sum_{j=1}^{N} \left[\log \binom{n}{x_j} + x_j \log p + (n - x_j) \log(1-p) \right]$$

and

$$\begin{aligned} \frac{\mathrm{d}L}{\mathrm{d}p} &= \frac{1}{p} \sum_{j=1}^{N} x_j - \frac{1}{1-p} \sum_{j=1}^{N} (n - x_j) \\ &= \frac{1}{p(1-p)} \sum_{j=1}^{N} [(1-p)x_j - p(n - x_j)] \\ &= N \frac{\bar{x} - np}{p(1-p)}. \end{aligned}$$

Equating this expression to zero and solving for p produces

$$\hat{p} = \frac{\bar{x}}{n},$$

which accords with the binomial mean formula (5.22). Using the quotient rule, the second derivative is

$$\frac{\mathrm{d}^2 L}{\mathrm{d}p^2} = -\frac{Nn}{p(1-p)} - N \frac{\bar{x} - np}{p^2(1-p)^2}(1 - 2p),$$

but evaluated at $\hat{p}$, the second term vanishes. The second-order condition that the second derivative is negative at the maximum point therefore holds in this case also.

As a third example, consider a Poisson-distributed sample $x_1, \dots, x_N$ with unknown mean λ. Poisson variates are drawn from the non-negative integers, 0,1,2,3,…, with probabilities

$$\Pr(X = x) = \frac{e^{-\lambda} \lambda^x}{x!}$$

and the N-fold product of these terms evaluated at $x = x_j$ gives the probability of the random sample of size N. Unless $x_j = 0$ for every j, impose $\lambda > 0$. Taking logarithms then yields

$$
\begin{aligned}
L(\lambda) &= \sum_{j=1}^{N} \log\left(\frac{e^{-\lambda}\lambda^{x_j}}{x_j!}\right) \\
&= -N\lambda + \sum_{j=1}^{N} x_j \log \lambda - \sum_{j=1}^{N} \log x_j!
\end{aligned}
$$

and

$$
\frac{\mathrm{d}L}{\mathrm{d}\lambda} = -N + \frac{1}{\lambda}\sum_{j=1}^{N} x_j.
$$

Solving the first-order conditions produces the expected solution in view of (5.26),

$$
\begin{aligned}
\hat{\lambda} &= \frac{1}{N}\sum_{j=1}^{N} x_j \\
&= \bar{x}.
\end{aligned}
$$

Remembering that $x_i \geq 0$ for all i, the second-order condition is again easily verified.

$$
\frac{\mathrm{d}^2L}{\mathrm{d}\lambda^2} = -\frac{1}{\lambda^2}\sum_{j=1}^{N} x_j < 0.
$$

In each of these cases, maximum likelihood produces the expected formula given the distribution in question. The fact that these solutions are the maximum likelihood estimators is of interest chiefly through the intuition it offers about the ML approach.

14.4 Gaussian ML

To apply the maximum likelihood principle to continuous distributions, probability density functions take the place of probability functions. For illustration, consider the random regressor model, and let assumptions GRRM from Section 12.6 hold. Write the model of observation t as

$$
y_t = \boldsymbol{x}_t'\boldsymbol{\beta} + u_t, \quad u_t|\boldsymbol{x}_t \sim \mathrm{N}(0, \sigma^2).
$$

so that applying (5.7), the distribution of $y_t|\boldsymbol{x}_t$ is

$$
\phi(y_t|\boldsymbol{x}_t) = \frac{1}{\sqrt{2\pi}\sigma}\exp\left\{-\frac{(y_t - \boldsymbol{x}_t'\boldsymbol{\beta})^2}{2\sigma^2}\right\}.
$$

Assuming the observations are independently drawn, the joint density of the sample conditional on the regressors can be written out as

$$
\phi(y_1|\boldsymbol{x}_1)\phi(y_2|\boldsymbol{x}_2)\ldots\phi(y_T|\boldsymbol{x}_T) = \left(\frac{1}{\sqrt{2\pi}\sigma}\right)^T \exp\left\{-\frac{\sum_{t=1}^{T}(y_t - \boldsymbol{x}_t'\boldsymbol{\beta})^2}{2\sigma^2}\right\}. \tag{14.13}
$$

In principle the joint distribution of the complete data set ought to be specified, but this is nothing but the product of (14.13) with the marginal density of $\boldsymbol{x}_1, \dots, \boldsymbol{x}_T$, following the pattern of (6.18). Provided the marginal density does not depend on $\boldsymbol{\beta}$ and σ^2, the marginal factor is optional for inclusion in the likelihood function, since it cannot affect the position of the maximum with respect to these parameters. In practice, the distribution of the regressors does not need to be known.

The likelihood function is found as before, by treating (14.13) as a function of $\boldsymbol{\beta}$ and σ^2, given the sample data. Conveniently, the logarithmic transformation simply inverts the product of the exponentials, so the log-likelihood function is

$$L(\boldsymbol{\beta}, \sigma^2) = -\frac{T}{2}\log(2\pi) - \frac{T}{2}\log\sigma^2 - \frac{S(\boldsymbol{\beta})}{2\sigma^2}$$

where

$$S(\boldsymbol{\beta}) = \sum_{t=1}^{T}(y_t - \boldsymbol{x}_t'\boldsymbol{\beta})^2. \tag{14.14}$$

Observe that maximizing L with respect to $\boldsymbol{\beta}$ can *only* be done by minimizing S, regardless of the value taken by σ^2. It follows immediately that the maximum likelihood estimator is identical with the ordinary least squares estimator, $\hat{\boldsymbol{\beta}}$, from (12.9).

It remains to find the ML estimator of σ^2. The first derivative of L with respect to σ^2 is

$$\frac{\mathrm{d}L}{\mathrm{d}\sigma^2} = -\frac{T}{2\sigma^2} + \frac{S(\boldsymbol{\beta})}{2\sigma^4}.$$

Equating to zero, solving for σ^2, and evaluating at $\hat{\boldsymbol{\beta}}$ gives

$$\hat{\sigma}^2 = \frac{1}{T}S(\hat{\boldsymbol{\beta}}). \tag{14.15}$$

This is different from the 'least squares' formula s^2 in (7.18), since there is no degrees of freedom adjustment. Division of the sum of squares by T rather than by $T - k$ is a small difference when T is large, but since s^2 is an unbiased estimator, it follows by the same token that the ML estimator is biased. This is another feature of the ML approach that deserves careful consideration.

Once again, the ML principle produces (or nearly produces) a familiar and expected result. However, there is a catch. Maximum likelihood requires the distribution of the sample to be specified, and specifically the Gaussian distribution yields OLS as the solution. A different distribution must yield a different estimator. By contrast, when motivating least squares as 'best in the class of linear unbiased (or CAN) estimators', nothing needed to be said about the disturbance distribution beyond the existence of the first two moments. These are two quite separate justifications for the same procedure.

14.5 Properties of ML Estimators

Maximum likelihood is a universal estimation method that in principle has myriad applications. However, except in a number of special cases, only asymptotic properties are known for MLEs. Demonstrating these results is an advanced technical exercise and beyond the scope of this book, but the key conclusions are universal, and deserve to be listed. The following properties hold under a mild set of so-called 'regularity conditions' on the distribution and the sampling procedure. The distribution must feature sufficiently smooth functional forms that derivatives and expected values follow the usual rules, and the law of large numbers and central limit theorem must apply where required. However, beyond these requirements there is no necessity for random sampling. The joint probability or probability density of the sample must be specified, whatever form this may take.

Let $\hat{\boldsymbol{\theta}}$ denote the ML estimator of generic parameter vector $\boldsymbol{\theta}$, with true value denoted $\boldsymbol{\theta}_0$. For example, the regression model is the case $\boldsymbol{\theta} = (\boldsymbol{\beta}', \sigma^2)'$ $(k+1 \times 1)$. Under regularity conditions the estimator has the following properties.

1. $\hat{\boldsymbol{\theta}}$ is CAN:

$$\text{plim}\ \hat{\boldsymbol{\theta}} = \boldsymbol{\theta}_0$$

   and

$$\sqrt{T}(\hat{\boldsymbol{\theta}} - \boldsymbol{\theta}_0) \xrightarrow{d} \mathrm{N}(\mathbf{0}, \mathfrak{I}^{-1}) \tag{14.16}$$

   where

$$\mathfrak{I} = \lim_{T\to\infty} \frac{1}{T}\mathfrak{I}_T,$$

   and if the log-likelihood in a sample of size T is $L_T(\boldsymbol{\theta})$,

$$\mathfrak{I}_T = -\mathrm{E}\left(\left. \frac{\partial^2 L_T}{\partial \boldsymbol{\theta} \partial \boldsymbol{\theta}'} \right|_{\boldsymbol{\theta}=\boldsymbol{\theta}_0} \right). \tag{14.17}$$

   $\mathfrak{I}_T$ is called the *information matrix* of the sample.
2. $\hat{\boldsymbol{\theta}}$ is asymptotically efficient in the CAN class: $\boldsymbol{V}_{CAN} - \mathfrak{I}^{-1}$ is positive semidefinite, where $\boldsymbol{V}_{CAN}$ denotes the asymptotic variance matrix of *any* CAN estimator. This result is known as the *Cramér-Rao theorem*.

Note the change of sign in (14.17). The information matrix is positive definite, and the negative definiteness of the expected Hessian matrix of L follows because the true parameter vector $\boldsymbol{\theta}_0$, by definition, is the maximum point of the expected likelihood function. The name reflects the fact that this matrix summarizes the information about the parameters contained in the sample. If $\mathfrak{I}_T$ takes a large value, a small change in $\boldsymbol{\theta}$ at the maximum implies a large change in the likelihood. The sample is correspondingly informative, and the asymptotic variance of the MLE in (14.16) is correspondingly small.

What is remarkable about Property 2 is its universality. The CAN class can include a large range of possible estimators, linear and non-linear, but the maximum likelihood estimator is known to dominate all of them, regardless of the form of the model and the form of the distribution. The very natural rationale for this result is that, by definition, maximum likelihood makes use of *all* information concerning the distribution of the data other than the actual parameter values. This is a very strong claim, which procedures such as the method of moments do not aspire to because they do not require a distribution to be specified beyond the first two moments, means and variances. Comparison with the asymptotic efficiency of least squares under assumptions CANR (see Section 14.1) is instructive. That result applies to the class of estimators having the linear form (14.2) and subject to the stated assumptions. It does not exclude the possibility that an estimator with a different functional form could dominate least squares, if the data are not Gaussian.

However, powerful as these properties of maximum likelihood appear to be, they must be placed in perspective. It is in many (most?) cases difficult or impossible to know the full specification of the sample data. If the likelihood function specified does not in fact match the actual distribution, none of the properties of true ML are guaranteed. A maximum likelihood estimator applied to data whose true distribution is not as specified is called *quasi-maximum likelihood* (QML) and sometimes, less kindly, 'pseudo-maximum likelihood'. There are some circumstances where this works, and linear regression is the best-known case where the Gaussian assumption is innocuous because there are alternative grounds for treating least squares as an optimal procedure. QML estimators may be CAN, but necessarily they are not asymptotically efficient in the CAN class, this being the attribute the true ML estimator by definition. Worse, QML may not even be consistent for the parameters of interest. Correct specification is a critical issue in ML estimation, and extreme caution is desirable in interpreting estimation results. Unfortunately, the applied econometrics literature contains an abundance of studies that blandly state, in effect, "We estimated our model by maximum likelihood…". In practice this means that a distribution has been assumed, but it rarely means that the assumption has been adequately verified. There are often procedures that are less asymptotically efficient than ML but also less fragile. Assuming Gaussianity is often a good strategy, not merely because the assumption is likely to be correct but also because the consequences of it being incorrect may be more tolerable than alternatives.

14.6 Likelihood Inference

A useful trick for various purposes is known as *concentrating* the likelihood function. This is to eliminate nuisance parameters by expressing their ML solution as a function of the other parameters. In the Gaussian regression model the natural object of concentration is the variance parameter σ^2. Consider writing formula (14.15) as a function of unknown $\boldsymbol{\beta}$

$$\hat{\sigma}^2(\boldsymbol{\beta}) = \frac{1}{T}S(\boldsymbol{\beta}),$$

where S is from (14.14). Then define the concentrated log-likelihood, also called by some authors the *profile* log-likelihood, as

$$\begin{aligned}
L^*(\boldsymbol{\beta}) &= L(\boldsymbol{\beta},\ \hat{\sigma}^2(\boldsymbol{\beta})) \\
&= -\frac{T}{2}\log(2\pi) - \frac{T}{2}\log\hat{\sigma}^2(\boldsymbol{\beta}) - \frac{S(\boldsymbol{\beta})}{2\hat{\sigma}^2(\boldsymbol{\beta})} \\
&= K - \frac{T}{2}\log S(\boldsymbol{\beta}),
\end{aligned} \tag{14.18}$$

where $K = -\frac{T}{2}(\log(2\pi) + 1 - \log T)$ is a constant, not depending on any parameters. Maximizing L^* with respect to $\boldsymbol{\beta}$ leads to the same solution as maximizing L with respect to $\boldsymbol{\beta}$ and σ^2, and

$$L^*(\hat{\boldsymbol{\beta}}) = L(\hat{\boldsymbol{\beta}}, \hat{\sigma}^2)$$

where $\hat{\sigma}^2$ is from (14.15). This is a convenient form because it allows the maximized value of the log-likelihood to be calculated as a function of focus parameters alone. Concentrating is a technique that works for any likelihood function and any partition of the parameters, but is obviously most useful when maximization with respect to the nuisance parameters has an analytic solution, as in the present case.

A leading application of this trick is to test restricted versions of the model. Write $L^*(\dot{\boldsymbol{\beta}})$ to denote the maximized likelihood for a model that incorporates some restrictions on parameters. For example, under linear restrictions $\dot{\boldsymbol{\beta}}$ would be given by (10.25). The *likelihood ratio* statistic is

$$\mathrm{LR} = L^*(\hat{\boldsymbol{\beta}}) - L^*(\dot{\boldsymbol{\beta}}). \tag{14.19}$$

Let the restrictions, r in number, be a null hypothesis to be tested. Provided the null model is nested within the maintained model, the difference in (14.19) is assured to be non-negative. The *likelihood ratio test* is commonly cited as a test of the restrictions in large samples. The classic result from maximum likelihood theory is the following:

Proposition: Under the null hypothesis that r restrictions hold, 2LR is asymptotically distributed like $\chi^2(r)$.

This is a technical result that in its general form requires advanced methods to demonstrate, but in the Gaussian regression case it can be related to known procedures. From (14.18),

$$\mathrm{LR} = \frac{T}{2}\log\left(\frac{S(\dot{\boldsymbol{\beta}})}{S(\hat{\boldsymbol{\beta}})}\right).$$

If $x \approx 1$, then $\log(x) \approx x - 1$. When the null hypothesis is true, the two maximized likelihoods should be close to one another and so

$$\begin{aligned}2\mathrm{LR} &\approx T\left(\frac{S(\dot{\boldsymbol{\beta}})}{S(\hat{\boldsymbol{\beta}})} - 1\right)\\ &= T\frac{S(\dot{\boldsymbol{\beta}}) - S(\hat{\boldsymbol{\beta}})}{S(\hat{\boldsymbol{\beta}})}.\end{aligned}$$

The last member of this equality is approximately proportional to the F statistic of (10.28), where T is assumed large compared to k and the factor of proportionality is $1/r$. Thus, $2\mathrm{LR}/r$ is approximately equal to the F statistic for testing this restriction. As T increases, the $F(r, T-k)$ distribution converges in distribution to the $\chi^2(r)/r$ since $S(\hat{\boldsymbol{\beta}})/T$ can be shown to converge to the constant limit σ^2 according to the law of large numbers. For linear restrictions in the regression model, the LR test and the Wald test are asymptotically equivalent.

In principle, the likelihood ratio test is valid for any type of restriction, linear or non-linear, applied to any model for which the likelihood functions can be formulated. However, once again a cautionary note is in order. The F test equivalence provides an independent verification of the large sample result in the present case, but outside the linear regression framework the imperative of a correct specification of the maintained model is critical.

14.7 Exercises

1 Are the following statements true or false?

(a) Least squares is asymptotically efficient in the class of linear unbiased estimators.

(b) Identification of relationships by instrumental variables depends on the existence of correlations between the instruments and the explanatory variables. At least as many of the former as the latter are necessary.

(c) The likelihood function of a sample of observations is formally identical with the joint probability or probability density function of the sample. The difference is in the interpretation.

(d) CAN estimators are biased except in special cases.

(e) Quasi-maximum likelihood is the estimator obtained by concentrating the likelihood function, also called the profile likelihood.

(f) The asymptotic efficiency of maximum likelihood is a consequence of the investigator's complete knowledge of the distribution of the sample apart from parameter values.

(g) In linear models subject to linear restrictions, the likelihood ratio test is identical with the Wald test.

2 Consider the pair of equations

$$y_t = \beta x_t + u_t$$
$$x_t = \gamma z_t + v_t$$

for $t = 1, \dots, T$, where u_t and v_t are independent normally distributed disturbances with means of zero, variances σ_{uu}, σ_{vv}, and covariance σ_{uv}. z_t is an observed variable, also normally distributed, with mean zero and variance σ_{zz} and zero covariance with the disturbances u_t and v_t.

(a) Obtain the probability limit of $\hat{\beta}$, the OLS estimator of β in the first equation. Specify restrictions under which OLS is a consistent estimator for β.

(b) Specify a restriction, or restrictions, under which the instrumental variables estimator $\tilde{\beta}$ of β using z_t as the instrument is consistent.

(c) If the estimators specified in parts (a) and (b) are both consistent, which of them is preferred, and why?

3 Consider the linear model

$$\boldsymbol{y} = \boldsymbol{X}\boldsymbol{\beta} + \boldsymbol{u} \quad (T \times 1),$$

where $\boldsymbol{X}$ is $T \times k$ and $\boldsymbol{\beta}$ is $k \times 1$, plim $T^{-1}\boldsymbol{X}'\boldsymbol{X} = \boldsymbol{M}_{XX} < \infty$ having full rank, but plim $T^{-1}\boldsymbol{X}'\boldsymbol{u} \neq \boldsymbol{0}$.

(a) Show that the ordinary least squares estimator is inconsistent.

(b) Suppose there exists a matrix $\boldsymbol{W}$ $(T \times k)$ such that plim $T^{-1}\boldsymbol{W}'\boldsymbol{u} = \boldsymbol{0}$, while $\boldsymbol{M}_{WX} =$ plim $T^{-1}\boldsymbol{W}'\boldsymbol{X}$ is a matrix with full rank k. Show how this matrix can be used to derive a consistent estimator of $\boldsymbol{\beta}$.

(c) Further suppose that

$$T^{-1/2}\boldsymbol{W}'\boldsymbol{u} \xrightarrow{d} \mathrm{N}(0, \sigma^2 \boldsymbol{M}_{WW}),$$

where $\xrightarrow{d}$ denotes convergence in distribution and $\boldsymbol{M}_{WW} = \text{plim}\ T^{-1}\boldsymbol{W}'\boldsymbol{W}$, which by assumption is a finite matrix of full rank. Use this information to derive the asymptotic distribution of the estimator you obtained in part (b).

(d) Comment on any generalizations and applications of this procedure that you know of.

4 Consider the regression model with heteroscedastic disturbances:

$$y_t = \beta x_t + u_t \quad u_t \sim \mathrm{N}(0, \gamma z_t^2), \quad t = 1, \ldots, T,$$

where x_t and z_t are both conditionally fixed in repeated samples, and $\mathrm{E}(u_t u_s) = 0$ for $t \neq s$.

(a) Write down the log-likelihood function for this model.
(b) Obtain the first-order conditions for maximization of the log-likelihood with respect to β and γ.
(c) Solve the relations in part (b) to obtain the maximum likelihood estimators of the parameters.
(d) What is the variance of the ML estimator of β? Compare this with the variance of the OLS estimator, and comment.

5 In a random trial, the odds in favour of success are $\dfrac{p_i}{1-p_i}$, where p_i is the probability of success depending on an explanatory variable x_i through the relation

$$\log \frac{p_i}{1-p_i} = \alpha + \beta x_i.$$

(a) Show that the probability of success is

$$p_i = \frac{e^{\alpha+\beta x_i}}{1 + e^{\alpha+\beta x_i}}.$$

(b) Suppose there are N_1 successes in a sample of N random trials. Show that the log-likelihood of the sample is written

$$L(\alpha, \beta) = \alpha N_1 + \beta \sum_{i=1}^{N_1} x_i - \sum_{i=1}^{N} \log(1 + e^{\alpha+\beta x_i}).$$

(c) Find the first-order conditions for a maximum with respect to α and β.
(d) Show that the second-order conditions for a maximum are satisfied, with the Hessian matrix negative definite.
(e) Suppose $\beta = 0$ is known. What, in this case, is the maximum likelihood estimator of α?

6 In a regression model for count data, with a dependent variable y_i taking non-negative integer values, suppose that

$$y_i = \beta x_i + u_i,$$

where $x_i \geq 0$ is a non-stochastic explanatory variable and $\mathrm{E}(u_i) = 0$. Assume that y_i is Poisson-distributed, so that

$$p(y_i|x_i) = \frac{\lambda_i^{y_i} \mathrm{e}^{-\lambda_i}}{y_i!}$$

where $\lambda_i = \mathrm{E}(y_i) = \beta x_i$.

(a) Given a random sample of n pairs (y_i, x_i), what is the maximum likelihood estimator of β?

(b) Compare the ML estimator of β with the OLS regression of y_i on x_i. Show that both estimators are unbiased, but that the MLE has smaller variance.

Part V

Appendices

A

The Binomial Coefficients

Given a positive whole number n, the product of all the whole numbers from 1 up to n is called *n factorial*, denoted by the symbol $n!$. In other words,

$$n! = n \times (n-1) \times (n-2) \times \cdots \times 2 \times 1.$$

Also, by convention $0! = 1$, so $n!$ is defined for $n \geq 0$. The sequence goes 1, 1, 2, 6, 24, 120, 720, 5040, 40320, …, and thereafter gets large very rapidly.

One may think of $n!$ as the number of different ways of picking objects one at a time from a basket containing n objects without replacing them. There are n ways to pick the first one, $n - 1$ ways to pick the next one, and so forth.

The number of ways of picking just k objects from a basket of n objects, for $0 \leq k \leq n$, is then

$$\frac{n!}{(n-k)!}.$$

However, some of these different selections include the same set of objects being picked, just in a different order. To find out the number of ways of picking k distinct objects out of n, regardless of the order, divide by $k!$. Thus, if k is two, the same pair of objects can be picked in two different orders, and if k is 3, there are 6 different ways to pick the same set, and so on. The functions

$$\binom{n}{k} = \frac{n!}{k!(n-k)!}$$

are called the *binomial coefficients*, also referred to as "n choose k". A notation used in some texts as an alternative to $\binom{n}{k}$ is ${}^nC_k$.

The famous *binomial theorem* states that for a pair of numbers x and y and a positive whole number n,

$$(x+y)^n = \sum_{k=0}^{n} \binom{n}{k} x^k y^{n-k}.$$

The n-fold power of the sum, when multiplied out, contains the sum of the powers of x multiplied by powers of y, of all orders from 0 to n, and the numbers of ways for these products to be formed is precisely the number of ways of picking k objects from n objects.

An Introduction to Econometric Theory, First Edition. James Davidson.

Companion website: www.wiley.com/go/davidson/introecmettheory

The binomial coefficients obey the rule

$$\binom{n}{k} = \binom{n-1}{k-1} + \binom{n-1}{k}$$

for $1 \leq k \leq n-1$, while

$$\binom{n}{0} = \binom{n}{n} = 1.$$

The coefficients can be written out as the so-called "Pascal's Triangle". The first 6 rows are as follows, with rows corresponding to n and columns corresponding to k, and for $n > 1$ the entries in row n are the sums of the two adjacent entries from the preceding row.

$$\begin{array}{ccccccccccccc}
n & & & & & & 1 & & & & & & \\
\downarrow & & & & & 1 & & 1 & & & & & \\
 & & & & 1 & & 2 & & 1 & & & & \\
 & & & 1 & & 3 & & 3 & & 1 & & & \\
 & & 1 & & 4 & & 6 & & 4 & & 1 & & \\
k \rightarrow & 1 & & 5 & & 10 & & 10 & & 5 & & 1 &
\end{array}$$

B

The Exponential Function

The letter e stands for the famous mathematical constant

2.718281828459...

where the ellipsis $\cdots$ indicates that there are more digits to add. In fact this is a so-called 'irrational number', and the string of digits does not terminate, nor does it repeat. It is impossible to write e down with perfect accuracy, only as a sequence of approximations. The formal definition is

$$\mathrm{e} = \lim_{n\to\infty}\left(1+\frac{1}{n}\right)^n.$$

Raising e to a power x gives

$$\begin{aligned}\mathrm{e}^x &= \lim_{n\to\infty}\left(1+\frac{1}{n}\right)^{nx}\\ &= \lim_{n\to\infty}\left(1+\frac{x}{n}\right)^n,\end{aligned} \tag{B.1}$$

where the second equality comes about on replacing nx by n, which means replacing $1/n = x/(nx)$ by x/n.

For finite n, the expression in (B.1) can be expanded using the binomial theorem, as

$$\left(1+\frac{x}{n}\right)^n = \sum_{k=0}^{n}\frac{n!}{(n-k)!k!}\left(\frac{x}{n}\right)^k.$$

Consider the first few terms of this expansion when n is very large relative to k. Then

$$\frac{n!}{(n-k)!}\frac{1}{n^k} \approx 1,$$

so the first few terms are very close to

$$\frac{x^k}{k!}.$$

Letting $n \to \infty$ produces the power series representation of the exponential function:

$$\begin{aligned}\mathrm{e}^x &= \lim_{n\to\infty}\left(1+\frac{x}{n}\right)^n\\ &= 1 + x + \frac{x^2}{2} + \frac{x^3}{6} + \frac{x^4}{24} + \cdots + \frac{x^k}{k!} + \cdots\end{aligned} \tag{B.2}$$

An Introduction to Econometric Theory, First Edition. James Davidson.

Companion website: www.wiley.com/go/davidson/introecmettheory

One of the many reasons why the function e^x is useful is the product rule,

$$e^x e^y = e^{x+y}. \tag{B.3}$$

Since $e^0 = 1$, putting $y = -x$ in (B.3) yields

$$e^{-x} = \frac{1}{e^x}.$$

e is the base of the natural logarithms, meaning that for any real x,

$$\log e^x = x$$

and also for $x > 0$,

$$e^{\log x} = x. \tag{B.4}$$

Equation (B.4) allows useful substitutions such as

$$x^a = e^{a \log x}$$

and for $x, y > 0$,

$$\log(xy) = \log x + \log y$$

and

$$\log\left(\frac{x}{y}\right) = \log x - \log y.$$

C

Essential Calculus

The derivative of a function f at a point x, when defined, is the tangent to the function at x. Formally

$$\frac{df}{dx} = \lim_{h \to 0} \frac{f(x+h) - f(x)}{h}.$$

The function is said to be 'differentiable at x' if the limit exists and takes the same value for $h \downarrow 0$ and $h \uparrow 0$. The derivative at x is also written for brevity as $f'(x)$.

Rules for differentiation include the following:

1. Function rules:
   i) If $f(x) = x^a$, $\dfrac{df}{dx} = ax^{a-1}$.
   ii) If $f(x) = e^x$, $\dfrac{df}{dx} = e^x$.
   iii) If $f(x) = \log x$, $\dfrac{df}{dx} = \dfrac{1}{x}$.
2. Linear rule: $\dfrac{d(af + bg)}{dx} = a\dfrac{df}{dx} + b\dfrac{dg}{dx}$, a and b constants.
3. Product rule: $\dfrac{d(fg)}{dx} = g\dfrac{df}{dx} + f\dfrac{dg}{dx}$.
4. Quotient rule: $\dfrac{d(f/g)}{dx} = \dfrac{1}{g}\dfrac{df}{dx} - \dfrac{f}{g^2}\dfrac{dg}{dx}$.
5. Chain rule: $\dfrac{df(g(x))}{dx} = \dfrac{df}{dg}\dfrac{dg}{dx}$.

The *second derivative* of f is

$$\frac{d^2f}{dx^2} = \frac{d}{dx}\left(\frac{df}{dx}\right),$$

also written f''.

A *stationary point* of a differentiable function is a point x^* at which

$$\frac{df}{dx}(x^*) = 0.$$

An Introduction to Econometric Theory, First Edition. James Davidson.

Companion website: www.wiley.com/go/davidson/introecmettheory

A stationary point is a local *minimum* (*maximum*) of the function if

$$\frac{\mathrm{d}^2 f}{\mathrm{d}x^2}(x^*) > 0 \quad (< 0).$$

In a function $f(x_1, \ldots, x_n)$ with two or more arguments, the partial derivatives are

$$\frac{\partial f}{\partial x_i}, \qquad i = 1, \ldots, n.$$

Partial derivatives behave like simple derivatives with the other arguments treated as fixed. The *gradient* of f is the n-vector of partial derivatives, written $\frac{\partial f}{\partial \boldsymbol{x}}$ where $\boldsymbol{x} = (x_1, \ldots, x_n)'$.

The second cross partials obey the rule

$$\frac{\partial^2 f}{\partial x_i \partial x_j} = \frac{\partial^2 f}{\partial x_j \partial x_i}.$$

The *Hessian matrix* of f is the symmetric $n \times n$ matrix of second cross partials, written

$$\frac{\partial^2 f}{\partial \boldsymbol{x} \partial \boldsymbol{x}'}.$$

The *mean value theorem* states that for values x_0 and $x_1 > x_0$, there exists x^* with $x_0 \leq x^* \leq x_1$, such that

$$\frac{f(x_1) - f(x_0)}{x_1 - x_0} = \frac{\mathrm{d}f}{\mathrm{d}x}(x^*). \tag{A4}$$

In words: given two points of the domain, there exists an intermediate point at which the tangent lies parallel to the chord joining the two points of the function.

Integrals are related to derivatives by the rule

$$\int_a^b f'(x)\mathrm{d}x = f(b) - f(a). \tag{C.1}$$

In many cases the form of f can be determined, given f', by inverting differentiation rules. The product rule for differentiation leads to the rule for *integration by parts.*

$$\int_a^b f(x)g'(x)\mathrm{d}x = f(b)g(b) - f(a)g(a) - \int_a^b f'(x)g(x)\mathrm{d}x.$$

D

The Generalized Inverse

It is sometimes helpful to know that a concept of matrix inversion exists for matrices that are either singular or non-square. Where it exists, the *Moore-Penrose inverse* of a matrix $\boldsymbol{A}$ $(m \times n)$ is the unique matrix $\boldsymbol{A}^+$ that satisfies the identities

$$\boldsymbol{A}\boldsymbol{A}^+\boldsymbol{A} = \boldsymbol{A}$$
$$\boldsymbol{A}^+\boldsymbol{A}\boldsymbol{A}^+ = \boldsymbol{A}^+,$$

where $\boldsymbol{A}^+\boldsymbol{A}$ $(n \times n)$ and $\boldsymbol{A}\boldsymbol{A}^+$ $(m \times m)$ are both symmetric. If $\boldsymbol{A}$ is a square nonsingular matrix, $\boldsymbol{A}^{-1}$ fulfils the definition.

The generalized inverse approach complements a number of the ideas in the main text. It is worth taking note of the neat unification of various problems, including singular distributions and generalized solutions to equation systems, that the definition provides.

Examples:

1. Let $\boldsymbol{\Sigma}$ be symmetric $n \times n$, and singular with rank r and diagonalization

$$\boldsymbol{\Sigma} = \boldsymbol{C}\boldsymbol{\Lambda}\boldsymbol{C}'$$

where $\boldsymbol{C}\boldsymbol{C}' = \boldsymbol{C}'\boldsymbol{C} = \boldsymbol{I}$, and

$$\boldsymbol{\Lambda} = \begin{bmatrix} \boldsymbol{\Lambda}_r & \boldsymbol{0} \\ \boldsymbol{0} & \boldsymbol{0} \end{bmatrix} \tag{D.1}$$

where $\boldsymbol{\Lambda}_r$ is $r \times r$ nonsingular. Then define

$$\boldsymbol{\Sigma}^+ = \boldsymbol{C}\boldsymbol{\Lambda}^+\boldsymbol{C}'$$

where

$$\boldsymbol{\Lambda}^+ = \begin{bmatrix} \boldsymbol{\Lambda}_r^{-1} & \boldsymbol{0} \\ \boldsymbol{0} & \boldsymbol{0} \end{bmatrix}.$$

Note that $\boldsymbol{\Lambda}^+$ is the generalized inverse of $\boldsymbol{\Lambda}$, and hence the definition is satisfied. An application is to a unified treatment of the distribution of quadratic forms, already studied in Section 10.2. Consider (6.13) where the variance matrix $\boldsymbol{\Sigma}$ was assumed nonsingular. Let this be replaced by the assumption that $\boldsymbol{\Sigma}$ $(n \times n)$ may be either nonsingular or singular with rank $r < n$. The decomposition $\boldsymbol{\Sigma} = \boldsymbol{K}\boldsymbol{K}'$ exists where

$$\boldsymbol{K} = \boldsymbol{C}\boldsymbol{\Lambda}^{1/2}$$

An Introduction to Econometric Theory, First Edition. James Davidson.

Companion website: www.wiley.com/go/davidson/introecmettheory

where

$$\Lambda^{1/2} = \begin{bmatrix} \Lambda_r^{1/2} & \mathbf{0} \\ \mathbf{0} & \mathbf{0} \end{bmatrix},$$

and K has rank r with generalized inverse

$$K^+ = (\Lambda^{1/2})^+ C'.$$

Then note that

$$\Sigma^+ = (K^+)'K^+$$

and that

$$K^+\Sigma(K^+)' = \begin{bmatrix} I_r & \mathbf{0} \\ \mathbf{0} & \mathbf{0} \end{bmatrix}.$$

Now, writing

$$x \sim \mathrm{N}(b, \Sigma)$$

where in this case the distribution of x is singular with rank r, the generalization of (6.13) is

$$\begin{aligned}(x - b)'\Sigma^+(x - b) &= z'z \\ &\sim \chi^2(r),\end{aligned}$$

where

$$z = (\Lambda^{1/2})^+ C'(x - b)$$

has its first r elements independent standard normal, and its last $n - r$ elements equal to zero.

2. Let A be $m \times n$ with $m > n$ and rank n. Then the matrix

$$A^+ = (A'A)^{-1}A' \quad (n \times m) \tag{D.2}$$

satisfies the definition of a Moore-Penrose inverse. This provides a least squares solution to the system of overdetermined linear equations

$$Ax = b \quad (m \times 1),$$

where x is $n \times 1$. The solution

$$x = A^+b \tag{D.3}$$

has the property that

$$\|Ax - b\| \leq \|Az - b\| \tag{D.4}$$

for all n-vectors z, where $\|\cdot\|$ represents the Euclidean norm. This is the standard least squares derivation from Section 4.2. Notice that AA^+ is the symmetric idempotent matrix that projects b into the space spanned by the columns of A, whereas $A^+A = I_n$. If $m = n$ then A has the regular inverse A^{-1} and $AA^+ = I$, so the left-hand side of (D.4) is zero.

3. Let A be $m \times n$ with $n > m$ and rank m. Then, the Moore-Penrose definition is satisfied by the matrix

$$A^{+} = A'(AA')^{-1} \quad (n \times m).$$

In this case $AA^{+} = I_m$, while $A^{+}A$ is the $n \times n$ idempotent projection matrix. The indeterminate system

$$Ax = b \quad (m \times 1)$$

has multiple solutions for n-vector x. These solutions can be represented by

$$x = A^{+}b + (I_n - A^{+}A)w \tag{D.5}$$

where w is an arbitrary n-vector. Formulation (D.5) in fact covers all the cases. If $m \geq n$ and A^{+} is defined by (D.2), (D.5) reduces to (D.3), and in particular to $x = A^{-1}b$ in the case $m = n$.

Recommended Reading

This is a personal selection of books from distinguished authors that I have found useful for reading, teaching, and reference at one time or another. The categories are rough and to a fair extent overlapping, so don't interpret them too rigorously. Econometrics is now such a large field that there are bound to be significant omissions, but these are for interested readers to discover for themselves. Successful textbooks tend become more obese with each succeeding edition but in the respects that matter, older editions are often just as useful as the latest ones.

Preliminary Reading

Readers should be a bit familiar with either one of these fine texts or a close substitute, of which there are many both in and out of print. Some background in the subject matter of econometrics is assumed.

Introductory Econometrics: A Modern Approach by Jeffrey M. Wooldridge, 5th Ed. (Mason, OH: South-Western, 2014).
Introduction to Econometrics by James H. Stock and Mark W. Watson, 3rd Ed. (Boston: Pearson Education, 2015).
Introduction to Econometrics by G. S. Maddala and Kajal Lahiri, 4th Ed. (Chichester, UK: John Wiley & Sons, 2009).
Basic Econometrics by Damodar N. Gujarati, 5th Ed. (Boston: McGraw Hill, 2011).
Learning and Practicing Econometrics by William E. Griffiths, R. Carter Hill, and George G. Judge (New York: John Wiley & Sons, 1993).

Additional Reading

All by distinguished authors, these are books at roughly the same level as the present one and with the same general motivation. Recommended for an alternative take on the same and related material.

An Introduction to Classical Econometric Theory by Paul A. Ruud (Oxford: Oxford University Press, 2000).

An Introduction to Econometric Theory, First Edition. James Davidson.

Companion website: www.wiley.com/go/davidson/introecmettheory

Introduction to Statistics and Econometrics by Takeshi Amemiya (Cambridge,MA: Harvard University Press, 1994).
Introduction to the Theory of Econometrics by Jan R. Magnus (Amsterdam: VU University Press, 2017)

For Reference

Proofs and additional results for the enthusiast.

Matrix Algebra (*Econometric Exercises*) by Karim Abadir and Jan R. Magnus (Cambridge: Cambridge University Press, 2010). A comprehensive set of matrix results, presented in problem-solution format.
Matrix Differential Calculus with Applications in Statistics and Econometrics by Jan R. Magnus and Heinz Neudecker 2nd Ed. (Chichester, UK: John Wiley and Sons, 1999).
Ignore the scary title! The first part is just an account of matrix algebra covering much of the same ground as Abadir-Magnus. Not for purchase, but possibly useful as an alternative reference.
Linear Algebra by G. Hadley (Reading, MA: Addison-Wesley, 1969).
Long out of print, but I first learned about matrices from Hadley as a student, and I still find it useful.

Further Reading

Just a small selection of fine books with coverage of advanced topics, including time series, panel data, count data and more.

Econometric Theory by James Davidson (Oxford: Blackwell Publishers, 2000).
A Guide to Modern Econometrics by Marno Verbeek, 4th Ed. (Chichester, UK: John Wiley & Sons, 2012).
Econometric Theory and Methods by Russell Davidson and James MacKinnon (Oxford: Oxford University Press, 2004).
Estimation and Inference in Econometrics by Russell Davidson and James MacKinnon (Oxford: Oxford University Press, 1993).
Econometrics by Fumio Hayashi (Princeton, NJ: Princeton University Press, 2000).
Econometric Analysis by William H. Greene, 7th Ed. (Pearson Education, 2012.)
Principles of Econometrics by Henri Theil (New York: John Wiley & Sons, 1971.)
This book is now over 40 years old, but still one of the best.
Econometric Analysis of Cross Section and Panel Data by Jeffrey M. Wooldridge, 2nd Ed. (Cambridge, MA: MIT Press, 2002).
Time Series Analysis by James D. Hamilton (Princeton, NJ: Princeton University Press, 1994).
The Analysis of Panel Data by Cheng Hsiao, 3rd Ed. (New York: Cambridge University Press, 2014).
Regression Analysis of Count Data by A. Colin Cameron and Pravin K. Trivedi, 2nd Ed. (New York: Cambridge University Press, 2014).
Econometrics by Bruce E. Hansen, University of Wisconsin (Published online at https://www.ssc.wisc.edu/~bhansen/econometrics/)

Index

An Introduction to Econometric Theory, First Edition. James Davidson.

Companion website: www.wiley.com/go/davidson/introecmettheory

Printed and bound by CPI Group (UK) Ltd, Croydon, CR0 4YY

23/04/2025

14660952-0002